The end of Liberation?
Liberation in the End!
Feminist Theory, Feminist Theology and their political implications

Befreiung am Ende?
Am Ende Befreiung!
Feministische Theorie, feministische Theologie und die politischen Implikationen

Le libération, est-elle à sa fin?
Enfin la libération!
Théorie féministe, théologie féministe, et les implications politiques

Yearbook of the European Society of Women in Theological Research

Jahrbuch der Europäischen Gesellschaft für theologische Forschung von Frauen

Annuaire de l'Association Européenne des femmes pour la recherche théologique

Volume 10

Bibliographical information and books for review in the Yearbook should be sent to:

Dr. Angela Berlis, A. van Nieuwenaarlaan 3A, NL - 6824 AM Arnhem, The Netherlands

Articles for consideration for the Yearbook should be sent to:

Dr. Charlotte Methuen, Lotharstr. 8, 45131 Essen, Germany

The end of Liberation?
Liberation in the End!
Feminist Theory, Feminist Theology and their political implications

Befreiung am Ende?
Am Ende Befreiung!
Feministische Theorie, feministische Theologie und die politischen Implikationen

Le libération, est-elle à sa fin?
Enfin la libération!
Théorie féministe, théologie féministe, et les implications politiques

Editors:
Charlotte Methuen & Angela Berlis

PEETERS - LEUVEN - DUDLEY, MA

Library of Congress Cataloging-in-Publication Data

Europäische Gesellschaft für die Theologische Forschung von Frauen, Internationale Konferenz (9th : 2001 : Austria)
The end of liberation? Liberation in the end! : feminist theory, feminist theology, and their political implications = Befreiung am Ende? Am Ende Befreiung! : feministische Theorie, feministische Theologie und die politischen Implikationen / editors, Charlotte Methuen & Angla Berlis.
p. cm. -- (Yearboek of the European Society of Women in Theological Research ; v. 10 = Jahrbuch der Europäischen Gesellschaft für Theologische Forschung von Frauen) English, French and German.
Includes bibliographical references (p.).
ISBN 9042912251
1. Feminist theology--Congresses. I. Title: Befreiung am Ende? Am Ende Befreiung!. II. Methuen, Charlotte. III. Berlis, Angela, 1962. IV. Title. V. Jahrbuch der Europäischen Gesellschaft für die Theologische Forschung von Frauen ; 10/02.

BT83.55 .E97 2002
291.2'082--dc21 2002030812

Yearbook of the European Society of Women
in Theological Research, 10

ISBN Peeters 90-429-1225-1
D.2002/0602/143
Cover design by Margret Omlin-Küchler

INHALT – CONTENTS – TABLE DES MATIÈRES

Editorial

This volume brings together the keynote lectures given at the ninth International Conference of the European Society for Women in Theological Research (ESWTR). The theme of the conference was the theme of this volume: "The end of Liberation? Liberation in the End! Feminist Theory, Feminist Theology and their political implications." Some insights into the process of planning the conference, and especially the choice of speakers and their themes are offered by Maria Katharina Moser, Michaela Moser, and Veronika Prüller-Jagenteufel as members of the planning group in their introduction to the theme essays.[1] From the editorial point of view it is necessary only to add a note about language: unusually for ESWTR's conferences, all the key-note lectures were given in English. It was decided to translate Eske Wollrad's interesting paper on defining whiteness into French to make her ideas available to a different language readership. Those who wish to read Eske Wollrad's reflections in English should refer to her article "Beyond the Pale: Towards a Critical White Feminist Theology" in Angela Berlis and Charlotte Methuen (eds), *Feminist Perspectives on History and Religion* (ESWTR Yearbook 8), pp. 169-183. The planned translation of Marcella Althaus-Reid's paper into German unfortunately did not prove possible.

The remaining articles offer a cross-section of responses to the situation of feminist theologians. In her paper, based on the mini-lecture she presented in Salzburg, Monika Walus considers the status of feminist theologians who are also wives and mothers, asking whether it is not in its way "queer". In a discussion paper written for the French section of ESWTR, Huguette Charrier discusses feminine aspects of hope. Regula Strobel critiques the prevalent theological understanding of sacrifice and shows how it pervades not only the church but society. Andrea Günter considers the implications of the way in which the world has been codified as feminine. Finally, members of the North American section of ESWTR reflect upon their cross-cultural experience as theologians who live and work – or who have lived and have worked – in a country other than their own.

The book concludes with a bibliography of new works of interest to feminist theologians and a comprehensive section of reviews, both compiled by Angela Berlis. I would like to express my appreciation of Angela's sterling work in

[1] See pp. 5-9 below.

compiling the bibliography section. Thanks are due also to Maria Katharina Moser, Michaela Moser, and Veronika Prüller-Jagenteufel for their support and for their introduction and to Annick Yaiche for her translations and for her help in proof-reading the French articles.

Charlotte Methuen

Maria Katharina Moser, Michaela Moser,
Veronika Prüller-Jagenteufel

Einleitung

Als "wir"[1] uns im Winter 1999 zum ersten Mal trafen zur Vorbereitung der 9. Internationalen Konferenz der ESWTR, die im August 2001 in Österreich stattfinden sollte, da lagen gut 30 Jahre – säkulare und religiöse – Frauenbewegung und feministisch-theoretische wie feministisch-theologische Wissensbildung mit vielfachen und vielfältigen Prozessen der Ausdifferenzierung und Kontextualisierung in Theorie und Praxis hinter uns und vor uns die von der Vollversammlung der *Society* übertragene Aufgabe, vor dem Hintergrund dieser Geschichte eine Konferenz zum Themenkomplex "feministische Theorie, feministische Theologie und ihre politischen Implikationen" zu planen. Mit diesem Themenkomplex verbanden wir Vorbereitungsfrauen die Frage nach theoretischen wie politischen Bezügen feministischer Theologie, die sich gleichermaßen als akademische Disziplin und als Befreiungsbewegung versteht, die Frage nach Leitkonzepten und Leitbegriffen feministischer Theorie- und Theologie-Bildung, nach Brüchen und Differenzierungen in selbigen und nach den aus diesen Brüchen erwachsenden Denk-Bewegungen, die sich als Neu- oder Weiter-Denken, aber auch als Wieder- oder Trotzdem-Denken gestalten.

Diese Fragestellungen und viele Treffen und Diskussionen mündeten in folgendes Konferenzdesign: Ein Einleitungsreferat am ersten Abend sollte die Fäden aktueller feministischer Theoriebildung und ihrer politischen Implikationen entwirren und einen Überblick über den Status Quo der Debatten bieten.

[1] "Wir" sind Silvia Arzt, Elisabeth Gierlinger-Cerny, Gertraud Ladner, Andrea Lehner-Hartmann, Veronika Prüller-Jagenteufel, Maria Katharina Moser, Michaela Moser, Ursula Rapp und Christa Schnabl – kein vorfindliches Wir, sondern eines, das sich zur Vorbereitung der 9. Internationalen Konferenz der ESWTR konstituiert hat, ein Wir aus neun Frauen, Theologinnen, die sich unterscheiden hinsichtlich ihrer Verortungen in der feministisch-theologischen und akademischen Landschaft Österreichs und denen die Zugehörigkeit zur weißen, österreichischen Mehrheitsbevölkerung gemeinsam ist, ein Vorbereitungsgruppen-Wir, das tatkräftig durch Lucia Goebesberger als Projektkoordinatorin unterstützt wurde.

Der folgende Vormittag sollte Raum bieten, über die anhaltende Relevanz des Begriffs "Befreiung" nachzudenken. Den Denkstoff dafür sollten zwei Referate liefern – eines, das die Bedeutung des befreiungstheologischen Moments in der feministischen Theologie aufzeigen sollte, und eines, das angesichts postmoderner Infragestellungen von Kategorien wie Subjekt, Identität oder Erfahrung Brüchen in befreiungstheologischen und Befreiungsansätzen nachspüren sollte. Diese Brüche und Infragestellungen sollten in Arbeitsgruppen zu den Themen "Differenzen", "Erfahrung", "Weiblichkeitskonzepte", "Universalität – Partikularität", "Subjekt", "Patriarchatsdiskurs", "Identität/Nicht-Identität", "Theorie-Praxis", "politische Strategien", "Solidarität", "Opfer", "Herrschaft und Unterdrückung" weiterdiskutiert werden. Diese auf einer ESWTR-Konferenz erstmals erprobte Form des Arbeitens in Kleingruppen zu Teilaspekten des Konferenzthemas erschien uns Vorbereitungsfrauen geeignet, zum einen das Wissen und die thematische Betroffenheit aller Anwesenden fruchtbar zu machen und dort, wo es um Grundlagenfragen geht, das Gespräch unter Frauen aus unterschiedlichen theologischen Disziplinen zu fördern; zum anderen die Breite des Konferenzthemas sichtbar zu machen und doch einen Weg zu finden, das Thema nicht nur oberflächlich zu diskutieren. Breite wie Tiefe der Auseinandersetzungen wurden an den Thesen zu den jeweiligen Aspekten deutlich, welche die Arbeitsgruppen tags darauf im Plenum präsentierten. Nach diesem Blick auf diese Breite, zu dem auch Mini-Lectures zum Konferenzthema gehörten, sollte wieder eine inhaltliche Konzentration erfolgen in Form von vier Kurzreferaten, die verschiedene kontextuelle Ansätze bzw. Auseinandersetzungen re-präsentieren sollten. Ein Schlussreferat sollte schließlich die Beschäftigung mit dem Konferenzthema bündeln.

Mit diesen inhaltlichen Vorstellungen im Kopf begaben wir uns auf die Suche nach Referentinnen.[2] Mit der Übergabe der Themenstellung an die Referentinnen haben wir in gewisser Weise unsere Konzeption aus der Hand gegeben; letztlich lag das, was aus ihr geworden ist, nun in den Händen der Konferenzteilnehmerinnen selbst. Das, was davon nachlesbar ist, findet sich in diesem Jahrbuch.

Die schwedische Theologin Anne-Louise Eriksson erklärte sich bereit, das Einleitungsreferat zum aktuellen Stand feministisch-theoretischer Diskurse zu

[2] Diese Herangehensweise führte letztlich dazu, dass alle Referate auf Englisch gehalten wurden. Da uns eine Orientierung an Inhalten wichtiger erschien als eine Orientierung an Sprachen, nahmen wir diese Einseitigkeit in Kauf.

halten. Angesichts der Weite der ihr aufgegebenen Themenstellung konzentriert sich Eriksson auf die Frage, wer oder was Frauen in der Theologie sind, die sie anhand der "sex-gender-Debatte" bearbeitet. Sie zeichnet zunächst die Linien der Auseinandersetzung um den Gender-Begriff nach, um eine politische Einschätzung zur Unterscheidung zwischen "sex" als biologischem und "gender" als sozialem Geschlecht zu geben: Politisch notwendig seien Theorien, welche einerseits die Machtungleichheiten zwischen Frauen und Männern sichtbar machen und kritisieren und andererseits Frauen und Männern die Möglichkeit geben, sich selbst als Frauen und Männer zu präsentieren, sich selbst zu vergeschlechtlichen ("to gender one's self"). Das setzt ein analytisches Werkzeug voraus, mittels dessen Frauen als Gruppe identifiziert werden können. Der Gender-Begriff sei hierfür ungeeignet, weil er mittlerweile zu kompliziert und theoriebeladen sei und auch die Verbindung zu reellen Frauen weitgehend verloren habe, meint Eriksson. Sie versucht den Begriff neu zu fassen als nicht-essentialistische Praxis. Ein Ergebnis dieser Sicht ist die überraschende Parallele zwischen der Suche nach einem pragmatischen Zugang zu geschlechtlicher sowie zu "christlicher" Identität.

Marcella Althaus-Reid – eingeladen über die Relevanz befreiungstheologischer Denkbewegungen in der bzw. für die feministische Theologie zu sprechen – entwickelt in ihrem Beitrag eine feministische Theologie jenseits der Grenzen kolonialer Anständigkeit. Sie betont die Notwendigkeit einer "queeren" theologischen Wissensbildung, welche "die geheime Affäre zwischen Theologie und sexueller Ideologie sichtbar macht" und "diese alte Allianz zwischen Theologie und Heterosexualität aus der Sphäre der häuslichen Gewalt herauslöst und öffentlich macht". Theologie war, wie Althaus-Reid anhand von Kolonialisierung und Christianisierung zeigt, immer schon eine sexuelle Praxis. "queere" Theologie als sexueller Akt müsse die Ordnung der Anständigkeit, in der politische, soziale und sexuelle Momente ineinander verwoben sind, destabilisieren und dualistische Denksysteme aufbrechen. So setzt Althaus-Reid einer "vergeistigten", "ent-materialisierten" Theologie, die den Körper von Frauen durch abstrakte Vorstellungen von Transzendenz ersetzt, ein Theologietreiben mit "den Händen unter dem Rock Gottes" entgegen und kreiert damit eine Metapher, die den Rahmen "geordneter" und "anständiger" Heterosexualität sprengt, eine Metapher, die wie "jede Metapher der Intimität mit Gott eine Metapher der Gegenseitigkeit und des lustvollen Tuns in Freiheit" ist.

Lucy Tatman verweigert ein lautes Nachdenken über Brüche im befreiungstheologischen Paradigma und konfrontiert das Wir der Konferenzteilnehmerinnen – und uns als Leserinnen – statt dessen mit der Frage, ob wir – mit diesem "wir" meint sie "in erster Linie feministisch christliche Theologinnen der weißen, bildungsprivilegierten, ökonomisch-reich-im-Vergleich-zum-Weltstandard, westeuropäischen und nordamerikanischen Sorte" – ob wir denn keine theoretische Befriedigung mehr finden in der Befreiungstheologie und daher unser Heil erneut in den Texten anderer, nämlich säkularer feministischer Theoretikerinnen suchen. Am Ende plädiert sie dafür, uns selbst als feministische Theoretikerinnen und als Theologinnen ernster nehmen und den eigenen Arbeiten mit der gleichen Aufmerksamkeit zu begegnen, wie jenen großer TheoretikerInnen anderer Disziplinen. Uns als Theoretikerinnen ernst zu nehmen, bedeute dabei immer auch, uns als Denkerinnen mit Körper, als "embodied thinkers", zu sehen, unsere Körper radikal in unser Denken und Arbeiten einzubeziehen, die Erfahrungen unserer Körper, unsere Schmerzen und Sehnsüchte und Genusserlebnisse, kurz, unser gesamtes "Körperwissen" in Worte zu übersetzen, die mit anderen geteilt werden können. Einander als "embodied thinkers" zu begegnen, bedeute auch, bei der wechselseitigen Lektüre unserer Texte die reale Frau hinter dem Text zu sehen samt ihrer (imaginierten) Alltagsfreuden und -sorgen und in dem Wissen, dass es Stärke braucht, um als feministische Theologin zu schreiben, zu sprechen, zu leben.

So geriet denn die geplante Auseinandersetzung mit der Bedeutung befreiungstheologischer Ansätze zur Auseinandersetzung mit Praxen feministisch-theologischer Wissensbildung und der Bedeutung, die Körperlichkeit und Sexualität für diese haben.

Vier kurze Beiträge sind danach kontextuellen Ausprägungen und Fragestellungen gewidmet. Die deutsche Theologin Eske Wollrad führt die Diskussion zum Frauen-Körper mit ihrer These vom immer schon von Rassenkonstruktionen bestimmten Körper weiter. Sie beschreibt Weiß-Sein als Ideologie, als Zuschreibung und als Praxis, die von feministischen Theologinnen noch nicht genügend untersucht wurde, vor allem nicht im Hinblick auf mögliche Strategien einer Dekonstruktion und Verfremdung von Weiß-Sein im Dienst einer anti-rassistischen Politik.

Die weiteren Referentinnen, die nicht mehr der von Lucy Tatman angesprochenen weißen westeuropäisch-nordamerikanischen Sorte zuzurechnen waren, konfrontierten die Mehrheit der Kongressteilnehmerinnen mit eher fremden Kontexten. Mirka Holubova, Prager Linguistin und Mitinitiatorin eines breit angelegten Oral-History-Projekts zur Frage der Identität von Frauen unter dem Sozialismus, führt in Anlage und Anliegen dieses Projektes ein, in dem sich wissenschaftliches Interesse in den Dienst praktischer Prozesse der (Wieder-)Aneignung von Frauenrealität stellt.

Die muslimische Theologin Sa'diyya Shaik skizziert die komplexe Realität der Gender-Dynamik im Islam und den feministischen Diskurs islamischer Frauen. Kwok Pui-Lan, asiatische Theologin mit Lehrstelle in den USA, thematisiert die Entwicklung ihres theologischen Ansatzes in multikulturellen Kontexten mit den Begriffen historischer, dialogischer und diasporischer Imagination. Es ist gut, dass diese Referate, die auf der Konferenz selbst nicht genügend Raum und Beachtung fanden (aufgrund der Zeitplanung nicht finden konnten), nun in aller Ausführlichkeit nachgelesen werden können. Ein wirklicher interkontextueller Dialog ist (leider) auch in feministisch-theologischen Zirkeln noch ein Seltenheit.

Das Abschlussreferat der Konferenz übernahm die englische Theologin Mary Grey. Ihr leidenschaftliches Plädoyer für ein Überschreiten der Grenzen von Herrschaftsdenken, Rassismus, falschen Vorannahmen etc., in denen westeuropäische feministische Theologinnen noch weitgehend gefangen sind, stellt neuerlich eine explizite Verbindung her zwischen Denken und Politik, zwischen redlichem Anstrengen der Begriffe und konkretem Engagement für Arme und Ausgegrenzte. Grey's "Dream on, sisters!" lässt sich verstehen als Wieder-Aufgreifen der Unverzichtbarkeit einer politischen Utopie für feministische Theologien, die Denken als Praxis verstehen wollen.

Ob unsere Konzeption der Konferenz aufgegangen ist? Es ist hier nicht der Ort für weitere Reflexionen – das Nachlesen der Referate zeigt jedenfalls die Lebendigkeit und vieldimensionale Relevanz feministischer Theologie als befreiende Denk-Bewegung.

Maria Katharina Moser / Michaela Moser / Veronika Prüller-Jagenteufel

Anne-Louise Eriksson

Who and what are "Women" in Theology? Some reflections on gender theory and its implications for feminist politics

To a high degree, feminist theoretical debate over the years has been entangled in disputes between a number of conceptual pairs that tend to be viewed as opposites; or if not exactly as opposites, at least as mutually exclusive. I am thinking first and foremost of the sex-gender divide. But we also have the notion of 'essentialism' *versus* 'constructionism'. And we talk about 'gynocentric' *versus* 'humanist' feminism, a split that corresponds approximately to what we in Swedish speak of as 'same-nature' feminism as opposed to 'specific-nature' feminism. That is, one stresses either that women and men are of the "same" nature, or that they are each of a "specific" nature that differs from the other.

The sex-gender distinction came into use before the feminist discourse had constructed the essentialist – constructionist divide. And when we in Sweden started to talk, and therefore to think, in terms of 'same' or 'specific' nature, Iris M. Young had not yet coined the terminology of 'gynocentric' and 'humanist' feminism.[1] Today all these concepts are part of the feminist discourse and form a common context. When, for example, I try to understand 'gender' as something different from 'sex', I do so in the light of how I understand 'essentialism' or the idea of 'same nature'. In other words, each concept taps into all the others, and the influences between them work in all directions. Still, these four conceptual pairs I have mentioned do tend to be organised in a certain way, so that 'sex' "has to do with" 'essentialism', which "has to do with" 'gynocentrism' which "has to do with" the idea of women being of a 'specific nature' compared to men. At the same time, however, each of these concepts is also constructed in relation to what is considered to be its opposite or what

[1] Iris M. Young, "Humanism, Gynocentrism and Feminist Politics," in: *Women's Studies International Forum*, 8/3 (1985), 173-83.

it differs from. In other words, 'sex' draws meaning not only from essentialism, gynocentrism and 'specific nature' notions, but also from 'gender', and thereby indirectly also from constructionism, humanist feminism and 'same nature' vocabulary.

While it may be self-evident, I find it important to stress that whenever we come across terms in each other's vocabularies, we need to be aware that they may be being used with a different purpose from our own. So their meaning may not be the same as when we use them. Sheila Benhabib is of course right to point out that

> [t]he art of making distinctions is always a difficult and risky undertaking. Distinctions can enlighten as well as cloud an issue. One is always also vulnerable to objections concerning the correct classification of the thought of certain thinkers.[2]

I am aware of running this risk but communication is hardly feasible without some distinctions. What I can offer here is my reading of the history of 'gender' in the feminist discourse. Of course there are other readings.

What I want to do in this paper is to elaborate on the very idea of 'gender'. I will argue that the concept of 'gender' has developed in feminist discourse in such a way that 'gender' has become highly problematic for feminist politics. I will suggest the necessity of yet another rethinking of 'gender' when it comes to identifying women as a group, something we still need to do in order to criticise male dominance. And finally, I will present to you the idea of 'gender' as a practice ruled by pragmatic criteria, and I will therefore speak of 'gender practice' and 'gender pragmatism'.

The sex – gender divide

To my knowledge, it was in psychiatry that 'gender' was first distinguished from 'sex'. The terminology was introduced in the context of transsexuality and the need to talk about a person's sense of male or female identity; this was termed 'gender identity', as opposed to a person's sex as a physical fact or feature.[3] The American psychoanalyst Robert Stoller used the four categories

[2] Seyla Benhabib, *Situating the Self. Gender, Community and Post-modernism in Contemporary Ethics* (Routledge: New York 1992), 89.

[3] See Toril Moi, "Vad är en kvinna? Kön och genus i feministisk teori," in: *Res Publica 35/36* (1997), 71-158.

'sex', 'gender', 'gender identity' and 'gender role' in a work in 1968.[4] Some years later Gayle Rubin, in her famous essay "The Traffic in Women", established the concept of 'gender' as something different from 'sex' in the feminist discourse once and for all.[5]

However the everyday experience of "mismatching" between sex and its "expected" gender raised doubts about the relation between sex and gender. What was questioned was not the distinction as such, but the nature of the relation between the two categories. The distinction in itself seemed, and still seems, justified, and is in many ways fairly easy to understand. It is enough to realise that we can make sense of expressions such as "a feminine man" or "a masculine woman" in order to understand that sex is something other than, and not necessarily linked to, what we perceive to be feminine or masculine. By feminine and masculine I am here referring to traits, behaviours and looks that in a given culture are attributed to women and men, respectively, as opposed to sex, which refers to physical and biological characteristics. In other words, the distinction between sex and gender catches and conceptualises a phenomenon experienced in our lives.

However, this distinction, in one way so simple and clear-cut, does entail problems when used as an analytical tool. Analytically, making the distinction between the physical and bodily "fact"[6] of female or male genitals on one hand, and mind, psychology and behaviour on the other, meant understanding sex as a stable, static category as opposed to gender, which was – and still tends to be – seen as constructed and changing. Sex was considered to be natural and therefore universal, while gender was cultural and therefore varying over time. Feminist theoreticians bent on changing the gendered order therefore came to focus on 'gender' and to a high degree on 'gender' alone.

This makes sense. But: if we focus on gender alone, and gender changes over time and culture, who and what are these women whose lives feminist theory theorises? Gender unrelated to sex cannot function as an identity category.

4 Robert Stoller, *Sex and Gender: On the Development of Masculinity and Femininity* (Science House: New York 1968).

5 Gayle Rubin, "The Traffic in Women: Notes on the 'Political Economy' of Sex," in: Rayna R. Reiter (ed.) *Toward an Anthropology of Women* (Monthly Review Press: New York 1975).

6 Referring to 'sex' as a bodily *fact* is of course highly problematic but the presence or absents of a penis or vagina, or the Y-chromosome, is in my view a "fact". The *meaning* of this fact is however, always a cultural construction. When referring to sex in what follows, I am only pointing out that some people are persons with a vagina while others are persons with a penis.

As already mentioned, femininity and masculinity characterise both men and women, for instance, when we talk about a feminine man. Consequently, gender unrelated to sex cannot identify us as women and men, which means that 'gender' is no good if, for example, we want to analyse power relations between men and women. As I see it, a free-floating, disembodied 'gender' concept cannot serve to divide humanity into two groups, of which one can be seen as oppressed while the other oppresses. This undermines the feminist critique of male superiority and female subordination. 'Gender' is accordingly problematic from the point of view of feminist politics.

Gender essentialism

During the 1980s, the 'gender' concept in feminist discourse therefore underwent a change. 'Gender' increasingly came to be used *as if* it conceptualised a relatively stable category. More and more, it became a category that was viewed as capturing an essence. Women were supposed to be in a certain way as compared to men, who were different from us. The explanation of how we became what we are varied. Few, if any, feminist theoreticians explained this in terms of sex, but in the mid-1980s many followed, for example, Nancy Chodorow, who saw gender as being established during the development of identity in early childhood. According to Chodorow, girls form their identities in relation to their mothers, whom they are supposed to resemble, while boys, who also have mothers as their primary caretakers, form their identities out of difference, seeing that they are supposed to be different from their mothers. Girls and women were therefore supposed to be relational, while boys and men were independent and self-governing. Other theoreticians offered other explanations but it all boiled down to a culturally and/or psychologically, or perhaps better, a socially constructed difference that went so deep into a person's personality that it tended to be viewed as an ontological and universal difference tied to gender. In a work of 1993, the Norwegian professor in sociology, Eva Lundgren, talks about this as 'social essentialism'.[7]

Summarising this far, one could say that the idea of 'gender' as opposed to 'sex' was introduced in feminist discourse in order to stress that differences between men and women are not innate, but a result of cultural construction.

[7] Eva Lundgren, *Det får da vaere grenser for kjønn. Voldelig empiri og feministisk teori* (Universitetsforlaget: Oslo 1993). (English translation: *Feminist Theory and Violent Empiricism* [Avebury: Aldershot 1995])

The differences are therefore not universal, and not something that can justify the marginalisation and exploitation of women. However, the need to identify women as separate from men, in order to analyse women as an oppressed group, led to an essentialism that trapped the concept of 'gender' in a way that undermined its potential for taking women's diversity seriously. The question of diversity therefore became the next issue to explore, and during the nineties the 'many ways', or 'diversity within', has been top priority in feminist theory.

Gender and diversity and a post-modern gender

From a feminist point of view, the fact that women construct gender in diverse ways creates a political dilemma. How can we do theoretical justice to diversity among women without losing the political power that a group identity confers? One way of posing this problem has been formulated by the American feminist philosopher Iris M. Young:

> On the one hand, without some sense in which 'woman' is the name of a social collective, there is nothing specific to feminist politics. On the other hand, any effort to identify the attributes of that collective appears to undermine feminist politics by leaving out some women whom feminists ought to include.[8]

Theories establishing and identifying 'a group of women' as apart from men, at the cost of neglecting diversity, soon attracted criticism from women who were supposed to belong to the group. Non-white, non-middle class, non-North American or non-Western European women pointed out that the group of women which most feminist theories described in the nineteen-eighties left them feeling to a high degree invisible or even non-existent.[9]

The solution seemed to be a notion of a "multi-layered identity". More and more labels were added to identity. This was when the laborious self-presentations in all feminist work surfaced: I am a white, middle-class, middle-aged lesbian or non-lesbian scholar in such and such a field from … and so on and so forth. In the end, a woman could represent only herself. And perhaps not even that.

[8] Iris M. Young, "Gender and Seriality: Thinking about Women as a Social Collective," in: *Signs: A Journal of Women in Culture and Society* 19/3 (1994), 714.

[9] For an early elaboration of this problem see Elizabeth V. Spelman, *Inessential Woman. The Problem with Exclusion in Feminist Thought* (Beacon Press: Boston 1988).

The critique and the need to elaborate diversity were part and parcel of an overall post-modern critique of identity projects, such as the idea of 'women as a group'. During the nineteen-nineties, feminist theory has benefited from, and contributed to, the post-modern and post-structural critique of all claims to universal and essentialist categories. Theoretically, I have found this an exciting and fruitful path to travel. In this period post-modern feminist theory has developed highly complex notions of what gender "is" and how gender is constructed. A good example is Judith Butler's understanding of 'gender' as performance and 'sex' as a cultural construction of a heterosexual matrix.[10] There is of course a lot to be questioned in her work, and many have done so, but as I see it Butler's way of thinking 'gender' is an imaginative challenge to gender theory.

While there are similarities between Butler's notion of 'gender performances' and the notion of 'gender aesthetics' as developed below, I shall not be following Butler's route. Although theoretically challenging, post-modern gender theory poses too many problems when it comes to feminist *politics*. I know it is often said that the lack of possible identity and subjectivity in post-modern theory makes both politics and ethics impossible but that is not my point, nor am I even sure I share such a criticism. My problem with post-modern feminist theory is that 'gender' has become a category so far removed from ordinary life that it runs the risk of being counter-productive in feminist politics. The purpose of feminist politics and, I might add feminist theology, is always to establish a world where women and men have the same possibilities of creating a good life for themselves. We try to achieve this by making visible and changing the ways in which power relationships between men and women are constructed. The concept of 'gender', however, has become so theory-laden and complicated that it tends to lose all connections with not just sex but also actual women and men.[11] Gender inequality is discussed more and more as an academic and theoretical problem, not as a problem that destroys women's actual lives, thereby obscuring the fact that women are suffering from various kinds of oppression for no other reason than that we are women. Feminist politics cannot afford to lose sight of that.

[10] See Judith Butler, *Gender Trouble: Feminism and the Subversion of Identity* (Routledge: New York 1990).

[11] Talking about "actual" women and men poses the same problem as talking about "the fact" of one or the other sex. However, the construction of sexism and gender inequality has to do with people on an empirical level: people with a female sex are systematically disadvantaged in relation to people with a male sex.

Gender as aesthetics, not as identity

What I want to propose first of all is that we relinquish the quest for a collective gender identity. Gender diversity among women is so vast that 'gender' has become a category that cannot serve as a marker of identity. Who and what are women if we look at gender only? What makes us a "we" is not our gender, but rather our sex. Women are people whose sex is female. Gender is something else. Gender is the way we construct and present our sex to each other and the world. For me, gender is aesthetics, and differs not only over time and culture but also between individuals and over a person's lifetime and contexts. Gender cannot identify us as a group, and perhaps not even as individuals. However, our 'sex' still makes us a group apart from people of the male sex.

While reflecting on this issue during the summer, I have also been thinking about the notion of 'church'. I am, after all, a theologian. If it is politically correct to talk about gender and diversity today, it is equally politically correct and necessary to talk about church and diversity. It seems to me that whether we talk about diversity and gender or diversity and church, the problem that needs to be elaborated is the same. I have, therefore, been trying to draw on my "church thinking" in my "gender thinking".

To be recognised as a *Christian* community it seems that we need to be something different, something apart from "the rest". The problem is that "the rest" is not a simple this or that, not atheists or Muslims or Buddhists, but atheists *and* Muslims *and* Buddhists *and* more. And diversity is not only out there. It is also within the Christian community. Christians cannot be likened to either this or that. We are like both this *and* that, for instance both like the pope and like me. Here I should add that I am well aware that when I say "we" about the church, it is a "we" that many of "us" do not share. I am using "we" as an expression of my own sense of identity. I view myself as part of the Christian church.

Being 'church' includes certain cognitive elements as well as a practice. This does not imply that we, the church, hold cognitive beliefs that cannot be found out there, or that "the rest" out there think about life in ways that no one in the church can or wants to share. Nor is it the case that we in the church embody a practice that unites us and sets us apart from "the rest". There is no Christian ethic by which we can be identified. People's opinions about abortion, homosexuality, capital punishment, capitalism, gender equality, war and so on transcend such boundaries and cannot be seen as something that identifies Christians as apart from "others". So how can we be a *Christian* church, when we as a group are so vastly diverse, and when what is outside of us is equally diverse? How can we be recognised as 'church'? And how can we identify ourselves as 'church' if whatever cognition or practice we find inside our Christian community can also be found outside?

These questions are very similar to those surrounding gender and diversity. As a group of women, we likewise need to handle two kinds of diversity. There is the gender diversity within our group: i.e. all the ways in which we are taught to, or forced to, or choose to, present ourselves as women. But there is also diversity in the sense that we are something else, something apart from everything that is not a woman, i.e. male-sexed persons and whatever way they are forced to, taught to or choose to present themselves. Applying my "church language" to gender, I could say that we women gender ourselves in diverse ways that also exist outside our group. So women can no longer be recognised by gender. Gender-bending, or the "stretching" of gender, has erased the line between female and male genders in much the same way as the line between Christians and non-Christians is becoming increasingly tenuous. This is so, not everywhere and not all the time, but in many situations, and, I believe, more and more. The faith police of the world, as well as the gender police, prescribe a single solution: back to difference! But the logic of "difference" from something that is not "us" will inevitably be the death of internal diversity. That is a lesson we learned in the nineteen-eighties as pointed out earlier.

Negotiating gender

What makes a community a Christian community is not a given set of ideas, but rather a cluster of thoughts concerning Jesus Christ. As an individual I share *some* of these ideas: more or less, but always some. One could say that what makes me a Christian is that I, in one way or another, relate my life to Jesus Christ. A Christian community can be recognised by its shared interest in Jesus Christ and by an ongoing discussion within the community about how to relate to Jesus Christ and the practice that best enables us to express the consequences of our relation to him.

In the same way, I suggest that what "makes" me a woman in the sense of constructing my identity as a woman, is the fact that I relate myself to my female sex. What I want to propose is that we see gender as the "practice" of sex. Thus, what makes women a group apart from the group of men is that we all construct our identity in relation to the fact of our female sex and also that we are engaged in an ongoing discussion in our group, and an ongoing negotiation with the world, about how to express our female sex.

Some people enter this conversation, whether on 'church' or on 'gender', with the preconception that there is a right and a wrong way of "practising" our faith and our sex. Others, and I am one of them, would suggest that there is no right or wrong way, but rather various ways that function more or less successfully for one or the other purpose. If my topic today had been church and theology, I would have said that the definition is about ways which function more or less successfully for the purpose of embodying "a province of God". I would then have had to expand and argue a reasonable understanding of "a province of God". On the topic of sex, and from a feminist perspective, I would say: these are ways which function more or less successfully for the political purpose of challenging patriarchal constructions of what it is to be a man or a women. And these are ways which function more or less appropriately to promote gender diversity so that each one of us is encouraged to explore the full potential of our lives.

In theological discourse it is easy to see how, in an endeavour to maintain the boundary between inside the church and outside, patriarchal power spells "death to diversity" within. Theological discourse seems to me to be obsessed with the notion of a "lowest common denominator": the required minimum that Christians have to believe in and do in order to be entitled to call themselves Christian. The obsession with drawing the line has left theologians pre-occupied with theological reductionism instead of theological construction. We would gain in strength and creativity if, instead of thinking about *the least* that people have to believe in or do, we were to think in terms of "all of this". Not: Christian community is at least this, but rather: Christian community is all of this. In the same way, I am convinced that women would benefit from focusing on how to encourage gender diversity among ourselves and how to invest our culture with diversity instead of dwelling on what we are apart from "the rest", i.e. apart from men.

What I want to propose, therefore, is a form of gender pragmatism. How should I present myself as a woman in order to challenge male power over us? How should I practise my sex in order to contribute to women's liberation from all the different kinds of oppression we face? And in talking about "us" and "we" here, I do not intend an "us" and "we" that presuppose a similarity between us, or that necessarily identify women as opposed to men. It is a "we" constituted by a shared practice and a shared pragmatism. A shared practice in that we, as already pointed out, gender ourselves in relation to the fact of our female sex. A shared pragmatism in that the practising of our sex is governed by how well or badly it works. How well or badly it functions for the purpose of making it possible to live any way I want to as a woman, without running the risk of any kind of oppression based on the fact that I practise my sex in whatever way I choose.

Gender pragmatism

I am using the term 'pragmatism' for two reasons. First and foremost I do so because it points away from ontology and essence and steers our thinking in the direction of purpose, work and function. The question to ask about 'gender' is not what it *is*, but how it *works and functions*. If we view 'gender' as a question of aesthetics and practice – of how we express our sex – then what needs to be analysed is not its beginning or foundation, but how it works and functions and what it does to a certain context.

Secondly, I use the term 'pragmatism' because I want to place my way of thinking about gender in the context of 'pragmatic historicism' as developed by theologians such as Delwin Brown, Gordon Kaufman and Sallie McFague and systematised and theorised by Sheila Greeve Davaney in her book *Pragmatic Historicism.*[12] I want to explore and think of 'gender' the way Davaney explores theology, taking seriously the historicist assumptions of human situatedness, particularity and plurality.

In this paper I have tried to give a brief account of how the concept of 'gender' has developed during the last three decades up to a point where it has become so theoretically complicated that it tends to lose contact with the empirical level where women and men are entangled in oppressive structures. I have argued that the diversity of gender rules out its use as a category by which we can be identified, either as a group or as individuals. The history of 'gender' is, however, as long as the history of humanity itself. Throughout history women and men have expressed themselves as sexual beings, using different strategies in order to survive and prosper. Feminist analyses of that history make not only oppression and subordination visible, but also what different kinds of gender practice achieve and make possible in any given context. Thinking in terms of gender pragmatism facilitates such analyses not only when looking in the rear mirror but also with regard to the present. The question to ask will be: which gender strategies work well if, for example, we want to accomplish a theology that "promotes the full humanity of women", to borrow Rosemary Radford Ruether's well-known expression?[13]

Reading 'gender' as non-essential practice, for example in the so called holy scriptures of Christian tradition – in other words, as examples of doing rather

[12] Sheila Greeve Davaney, *Pragmatic Historicism. A Theology for the Twenty-first Century* (State University of New York Press: New York 2000).

[13] Rosemary Radford Ruether, *Sexism and God-talk. Toward a Feminist Theology* (Beacon Press: Boston 1983), 18.

than being – makes it possible for us to expose what men have done to women and how women have tried to survive through submission or resistance. But it also allows us to practise our sex differently, thereby trying out other ways of undermining sexism wherever it confronts us. Gender pragmatism allows us to be in charge. 'Gender' is not destiny. It is possible, at least to some degree, to choose how I express my sex. And just to make sure, I stress once again: I am not talking of gender as a result of sex, but gender as the way I express and practise my sex.

We will probably not always agree on what constitutes the best practice in a specific situation with a view to eliminating all kinds of oppression based on sex. The gender that works best is not something that can be established once and for all. What works will always depend on what we are up against in the given situation. There is no universal essence in gender, which is precisely why we need feminist analyses and an ongoing discussion about what 'gender' achieves. With the help of feminist analyses we can uncover and identify the gender aesthetics that locks women and men into power relations where men have power over women. Such analyses need to criticise male gender practice or male aesthetics that embody violence and dominance. But there is also a need to make women aware of how some female gender practices do not work well as a means of resisting male dominance. And we will probably become painfully aware of how, to a very high degree, female gender aesthetics is quite often re-active instead of independent and self-governed.

The question of how to change all sexist gender practice lies at the heart of feminist politics. For that we need theories of gender that allow for the diversity among us and which do not view gender as determined either by sex or solely by discourse. While the former ignores diversity, the latter ignores human agency. Gender as a practice ruled by pragmatism avoids the trap of determinism, and allows actual women and men to express their sex in diverse ways while at the same time making each one of us an accountable subject in our own life.

La principale thèse de cette contribution est que le concept de genre (*gender*) a évolué de telle manière au sein du discours féministe que le genre paraît extrêmement problématique et peu constructif pour le discours féministe d'aujourd'hui. C'est à partir du sexe biologique, non pas de leur ordre (*gender*) social que les femmes constituent un groupe. La politique féministe a besoin de nos jours de théories qui mettent en plein jour le déséquilibre des rapports de force entre hommes et femmes et en dégagent la problématique. Ces théories doivent aussi laisser toute latitude pour les diverses manières qu'ont hommes et femmes de se présenter et de se situer par rapport à leur sexe (*gender*). C'est pourquoi l'auteur propose de considérer le sexe (*gender*) comme esthétique, pour que le genre soit compris comme pratique du sexe biologique, qui est, lui, déterminé par le pragmatisme. Analyse-t-on le *gender* dans ce sens, comme pragmatisme, que la pensée s'oriente vers l'intention et la fonction, non vers l'ontologie et l'essence. La question analytique n'est donc pas de savoir ce qu'est le *gender* mais comment il fonctionne.

Das Hauptargument dieses Beitrags ist, dass das Genderkonzept sich innerhalb des feministischen Diskurses in einer Weise entwickelt hat, die gender ("Geschlecht") als höchst problematisch, vielleicht sogar als kontraproduktiv für den heutigen feministischen Diskurs erscheinen lässt. Was Frauen zu einer Gruppe macht, ist das biologische Geschlecht ("sex"), nicht das soziale ("gender"). Was heutige feministische Politk braucht, sind Theorien, die die unausgewogenen Machtverhältnisse zwischen Frauen und Männern sichtbar machen und problematisieren. Zugleich müssen solche Theorien Raum für unterschiedliche Weisen schaffen, in denen Frauen und Männer sich selbst präsentieren bzw. geschlechtlich verorten (gender). Deshalb schlägt die Autorin vor, Geschlecht (gender) als Ästhetik zu verstehen; Geschlecht wird so als Praxis des biologischen Geschlechts aufgefasst, das von Pragmatismus bestimmt ist. Wird gender im Sinne eines solchen Pragmatismus analysiert, richtet sich das Denken auf die Absicht und die Funktion und nicht auf Ontologie und Essenz. Deshalb muss die analytische Frage nicht lauten, was gender ist, sondern wie gender funktioniert.

Anne Louise Eriksson (*1952) was ordained in the Church of Sweden in 1975. A Resident Graduate at Harvard Divinity School 1990/91, she was awarded her PhD by Uppsala University in 1995. She was Professor of Theology at the Stockholm School of Theology from 1995 until 2000 and is now a researcher at the Church of Sweden Research Department. Her publications include: *Kvinnor talar om Jesus. En feministisk kristologisk praxis* (Women talk about Jesus. A Feminist Christological Praxis; Nya Doxa: Nora 1999). *The Meaning of Gender in Theology. Problems and Possibilities* (Almquist & Wiksell International: Stockholm 1995). Her main research interests are the connection between feminist theory and feminist theology and the question of how a church with a multi-voiced canon in a plural world can address issues of authority and of norms.

Marcella María Althaus-Reid

Queer I Stand: Doing Feminist Theology outside the borders of Colonial Decency

Queer politics...requires a resistance to regimes of the normal
Jeffrey Escoffier[1]

But if one lifts one's skirt, it is to show one's self –
not to show oneself naked like the truth
(who can believe that the truth remains the truth when one lifts its veil?)
Jean Baudrillard[2]

First Indecencies. Lifting the Skirts of God and Strangers

Is theology the art of putting your hands under the skirts of God? If feminist theology is a revelatory theology, concerned with the liberative presence of God in history, and in the history of women, can we then redefine theology as, for instance, a reflection on God closely related to loving arts of intimacy with the Beloved? Can we express in this metaphor an affectionate and historically grounded reflection on God and women, at the margins of heterosexuality? How does Sophia-Wisdom fit into this loving metaphor? Can we lift her skirts?

Using sexual metaphors for theology is not a novelty; the Bible is full of them. However, the novelty (and the indecency) seems to come, whenever we dis-centre the assumed man-woman sexual identities of the dyadic system of Christianity. The point is that in dis-centring the subject of theology, we end by dis-centring God too. I have no intention of producing any theological shock by saying that doing theology may be related to touching God under her skirts,

[1] Cited by Alderson and Anderson in their introduction to: David Alderson / Linda Anderson (eds), *Territories of Desire in Queer Culture* (Manchester University Press: Manchester 2000), 3.

[2] Jean Baudrillard, cited in Stuart Jeffries, "Body of Evidence" (report of response to *La Vie Sexuelle de Catherine M*) in: *The Guardian Weekend* 30 June 2001, Review, 2.

but simply of making public the closeted affairs between theology and sexual ideology – in other words, of taking this old alliance of theology and heterosexuality out of the sphere of domestic violence and making it public. And this is what we are confronted with in the loving image of putting our hands under the skirts of Sophia-God, by denouncing the immateriality of theology and even feminist theology when they displace the site of women's bodies by transcendental configurations. Unfortunately for us in theology, when transcendence enters the scene, the body leaves. The body may remain of course at a symbolic level of exchange, but the real body, that is the body which speaks of the concreteness of hunger and pleasure, gets displaced. In Feminist Theology, it sometimes gets displaced by desire, if desire is not properly incarnated. The point is that desire may function as an abstraction, and as such, continues rehearsing the revelatory presence of what Butler would call the presence of the ubiquitous Phallus.[3] It is precisely that Phallus which represents the transcendental in theology – a Phallus which depends on a Messianic Prototype, that is the prototype of the mystical penis of Christ. However, subversion is a hermeneutical space present in every interpretation. The mystical penis of Jesus can be subverted not by desire, but by pleasure. It is pleasure which, by the heaviness of its concrete allocation, offers feminist theology antidotes to the unnecessary transcendence of the Father's Phallus in Jesus and in God.

These antidotes in theology do not work following dyadic oppositional systems such as God-Father and God-Mother; or as in a discourse about "the feminine side of God" (which by the way assumes that the core of God's identity is heterosexually male, and femininity is just a side or an extra point of view). The metaphor of theology as the act of putting our hands under God's skirts belongs to another frame of thought, more diverse and irreducible. God's skirts are a suitable divine metaphor for material girls in theology which help us to reflect on God in our lives beyond biological, parental metaphors or even dismantle – perhaps – the ghostly look of Sophia Wisdom, and make of her an unreasonable, illogical God, with the kind of wisdom that patriarchal theology does not recognise.

Moreover, the image of touching God in an intimate way is not completely strange for us. As some discourses in Feminist Theologies have identified one of the persons of the Trinity as a lover, touching that lover under her skirt brings

[3] See Judith Butler, *Gender Trouble. Feminism and the Subversion of Identity* (Routledge: London 1990), 13.

to the realm of theological imagination the reassurance, intimacy, fun and loving dialogue of women and God. In the same way, any metaphor of intimacy with God is a metaphor of mutuality, pleasurable activity and freedom after which neither we nor God are meant to remain the same. God is going to be enriched in the process.

Dislocations: What to Preach? Sex or God?

The first indecent act of the theologian is that recognition that no matter the metaphor you use, theology has been and will remain a sexual praxis. To do theology as an act of defiance, the first rebellions usually come with the awareness that theological reflections are in struggle with heterosexual canonical law. That law is based on a sexual covenant of uniqueness, based on mono-loving activities. Theological Mono-loving is carried through political and economical frames of thought, and it may be necessary to remember here the association between monotheism, monarchism and the subjection of women in marriage contracts. To that theology belongs a practice concerned with reaffirming a particular sexual understanding of the sacred, done by a systematisation of theology and also by liturgical and structural repetitive traditions which have inbuilt sexual, political and economical standpoints. It may be useful to highlight here the concurrency of heterosexual ideological thinking which pervades current theological practices, and can be found from Liberation theologies to Vatican theology, or even some Feminist Theology.

As I am interested in a reflection that may lead us to a praxis of sexual dislocation of theology and ideology, I have called this type of material sexual theology indecent, and its praxis, indecent acts.[4] I called it indecent because this is a theology the main function of which is to destabilise the decent order, that is a constructed political, social and sexual order which has been ideologically sacralised, and whose moralising objective is based on the dyadic reflection on a dyadic God. I am using here the metaphor of "indecency" as it comes from my own Latin American context, in order to start a reflection on Queer theology as a sexual and political theology with an option for the poor. Indecency is part of the dialectic of the "decent/indecent" which regulates the individual and community lives of women in my continent by a strict codification of sexual and gender understandings. It circumscribes and carefully supervises the delimited areas of public and private lives by delimiting

4 For further discussions on this point see my book, *Indecent Theology. Theological Perversions in Sex, Gender and Politics* (Routledge: London 2000)

the territory of the proper and the improper, which by default unveils the Christian sexual construction of society and politics in my continent. The fact is that Christianity has, more than a theology, a sexual programme. The story of colonisation shows this quite distinctively. For instance, Christianity came to Latin America with a sexual intention behind the catechisms intended to produce a conversion not so much to Christ but to the then prevalent European affective patterns of relationships. Although I must concede that little is known of the sexual lives of people in my continent before the arrival of Christianity, it is undeniable that it was different to the Christian European sexual project. The preaching was done on sex, not on God (unless we admit the conceptual interdependency here). This can be seen in history through the struggle for the imposition of European monogamous marriage rituals against the then existent polyamorous unions, homosexual affections and cherished cross-dressing practices which were later de-legalised by becoming non-Christian, and therefore indecent. Yes, Christianity is a sexual project (and not just a gender project, concerned with the subjection of women). However, as we have said before, with every interpretation comes a subversion, and a popular counter-theology of heterosexuality arose in my continent.

For Bigamy and God: Popular Theological Rebellions

I find this point important, because there is a lesson from history here. Is Feminist theology popular? Are Queer theologies rooted in common people's experiences? I must say, yes. Queer theologians find tradition through discontinuation. Indigenous revolts, for instance against the Jesuit missions, were sexual revolts, and as such I consider them part of the church traditions of sexual ideological disruptions. The *Chamames* (religious and political leaders of the Guaraní Nation) called people not to disbelieve in the Virgin Mary and the Trinity, but actively to defend bigamy and concubinage as part of a social, political and religious rebellion against the imposed colonial order. That act was also part of a theological struggle for a different understanding of God and sexuality which has much to do with the way people organise themselves as society. Idolatry was homologised to dissident sexual behaviours.[5] Therefore, what we can now call a sexual discontent was in reality a discontent with

[5] I am indebted for these comments to Merry E. Wiesner-Hanks, *Christianity and Sexuality in the Early Modern World. Regulating Desire, Reforming Practice* (London: Routledge 2000) particularly the chapter on Latin America, 141-79.

Christianity, and a legal discontent against the state. In many countries the Jesuits had the power to hold civil and criminal courts, and their missions (called *reducciones*, literally "reductions") had their own jails and system of punishment for sexual offences such as marrying a first cousin or having two wives. For people who have learned their ecclesiastical history through films such as *The Mission*, it may be disappointing to know how the missions separated couples (or triads) and banned otherwise happy and harmonious relations as part of a political and religious hegemonic project. As a document from a group of elders at the time says, the Christians came to destroy the indigenous nations by destroying their happiness in love.

It is important to reflect on this gesture of sexual defiance of the colonies as a challenge to Christian theology, because through it we can see how people perceived that Christian dogmas were to be destabilised by rebelling against the imposition of monogamy or heterosexual affective contracts. There is a methodological issue there, because that was the people's theology at the time, dismantling oppressive structures of the church not by arguing about the Trinity, but by de-legitimising the Christian sexual project. However, if theology is a sexual act, to stand up for bigamy or polyamorous relationships is to stand also for a queering attitude to Christology, Mariology or the Trinity. Queering theology does not leave theology intact in its systematic structures, traditional positions or ecclesiologies, but uses its own sexual ways of knowing to question the sacred as a heterosexual assumption. That is of course, high sexual revolt in theology. If the theologian puts her hands under the skirts of God, she is establishing a different pattern of dialogue with the sacred and with herself and her community of resistance. This heralds the end of unnecessary transcendence and the beginning of sensual concretisation in theology.

On Queerings: Queering the Theologian

Feminist theology is never neutral, and theologians are not neutral practitioners either. Feminist theologians have ideological and geopolitical investments in their praxis. Christian theology interpelates theologians by making them supposedly "free" to respond to God's appeal, which is a sexual theological appeal. Freedom, in reality, is what is lacking. The heterosexual appeal of God comes with the understanding of a given. One does not need to be a feminist theologian to participate actively in approving or disapproving the heterosexual ideology of theological methods, in the same way that one does not need to be a liberation theologian to do politics in their theological praxis because sometimes, in/difference does it. In/differentiating habits in theology do not work for neutrality but for the identity of the stronger ideology. This is the equivalent of the law of the jungle in Christianity. However, a theologian should stand in full consciousness for what she supports, or at least, any theologian working from a liberationist background as myself would do so. Therefore, when I say that I "stand queer", I want to make clear that I stand in a tension: alone, with full responsibility for my discourse but also with my particular community of struggle. That community is made up of networks of aliens, or the community of strangers who cast a highly suspicious hermeneutic circle in the attempt to unveil the complexity of the sexual base lying below the construction of both the church's dogmatics and its politics. By doing so, Queer theologies also try to find the presence of the stranger God, who stands outside the classroom definitions of heterosexual thinking, and is amongst us.

Why is it important to take a stance – and more precisely a sexual stance – in doing theology? Is it not, for instance, enough to stand for gender equality in a neo-liberal feminist agenda? If we think that we need to take a sexual stance in theology because lesbians, bisexuals or transvestites are trying to make their own contribution to the so-called theologies of story, and thus reclaiming a space of sharing the presence of God amongst us, that may not be the whole truth. If we think that for instance, bisexuals are – and rightly so – looking for a Christology which may convince the church that they too are children of God, that still may be a partial aspect of a queer theology. I agree that even if the pursuit of sexual equality in the church was the only objective of queer theologies, it should be encouraged as a worthy initiative, for, following a contextual methodology, we know that first we engage with critical reality and then we do theology from it as a second act. Moreover, we may also argue that as we have been using social sciences as mediatory sciences in the liberation hermeneutic circle, we have never considered heterosexuality seriously as ideology, so a different sexual theory should be welcome too.

However, there is always much more to come in the work of queer theologies. For sexual theologies are concerned with structures such as the structures of love and knowledge which regulate affective and political decisions in our lives, run economic thought and may even have exiled God from churches and theology long ago. And that is why for me, a queering theology is an encounter between strangers and a pursuit of God the stranger. God is also queer, perhaps the first queer of all.

Doing feminist theology, then, is an act defined in relation to that sexual act of standing critically in relation to heterosexual ideology. They may be post-Christian or reformist responses; it does not matter. The important point is that our identity as theologians is shaped somehow in relation to a certain sexual response. Therefore, post-Christians may have a point in trying to break out of that circle of subjection to a condition which limits exchanges and ways to do theology through the given authorised medium of expression. But so do Queer theologians who have extended an alliance of different, plural sexual understanding to issues of church tradition, ecclesiastical history and dogmatics. Moreover, the post-Christian discourse is still a strongly gendered position, while in Queer theologies there is a deeper problematisation of sexual and gender categories. As we all stand for something while doing theology, I like to make clear my geopolitical decisions. I stand as queer amongst queers, as I stand for the circle of hermeneutic suspicion to be taken towards new limits, and for the presence of the strangers of theology to share stories from which a new, different face of God may appear. This is a call for a body theology, but one which embodies the unknown at our gates, the strangers in theology. By encountering those strangers a different body theology occurs; a theology made with the different shapes that come from the encounter. Queering confronts the theologian's own voice and responsibility too, for as Kosofsky Sedgwick has said, the Queer discourse can become so only when the 'I' is present in it.[6] It is a theology which does not essentialise. In that sense, it is the perfect example of a theology done from someone's story, and the reflection where a theologian stands up in community, in solidarity and in uniqueness. Queer we may stand, with a sense of pride and resistance which comes from the sharing of our own stories and own sufferings, and the silence of a theology which has assumed too many things about sexuality and God. This has been the theology of sexual idealisation, an idealist-based theology now challenged by the materiality of our own strange communities, and the strange God who walks with them.

Queering Gender-Theology

It may be obvious at this point that it is not in reflection on gender, that considerably new sociological category, but in reflection on the sexuality of God that the possibilities of a radical theology exist. By "sexuality of God" I am not simply saying for instance, that God is a gender-fucker, that is, a God for whom gender and sexuality are fluid categories. Neither I am saying that Jesus

[6] Eve Kosofsky Sedgwick quoted by Linda Anderson, "Autobiographical Travesties: The Nostalgic Self in Queer Writing," in: Alderson / Anderson (eds), *Territories of Desire in Queer Culture*, 68-84, here 69.

should be seen exchanging clothes with the Magdalene. What we are pointing at here is the sexual epistemology of salvation.

It is also clear in this context that I am saying that the sexuality of God is not given or disclosed; that it is (to use a metaphor dear to many) closeted, hidden and waiting. The old theological inquiries done long ago, about Jesus' supposed femininity or God's female metaphors (curiously linked to re/production) are such a limited exercise because they never encounter strangers. If gender performances could make a difference, I for one could have started carving a statue of a transvestite, leather-clad and stockinged Christ in the hope of liberating God from dyadic representations as some of my sisters have done "Christas" hanging from their crosses. I say that with the understanding that Christas have been more important than many theological books. Christas made theologians become the voyeurs of a strange God by looking at her exposed nudity transgressing the cross. The presence of the woman on the cross, and the richness of all sort of theological reflections produced by that image have been extensive, but we have still not reached under her skirts. Displaying the symbolics of gender, useful as that is in destabilising theological high truths which are mere gender illusions, will not liberate. If this were not so, I would consider myself to have fulfilled my duties as a believer and as a theologian by simply and only cross-dressing Christ as the Virgin Mary and wondering about the nature of the Messiah's relationships with married men such as Peter. The situation is more complex than that because gender performances actively repeat sexual performances (using Butler's theory) but unless we reach that core of sexual production in gender representations, our analysis will be superficial, or, worse, may even reinforce the idea of sexuality as a given, that dual thinking is a given, that love-knowledge and theological knowledge are different things, that affective relations and economical ones have nothing in common, or that God can be on one side of the political struggle but on the other in sexuality, and that *that* God is straight.

Queer theologians thus are facilitators of the sexual traffic of the church's praxis. They facilitate an encounter amongst strangers which is much more radical than gender-talk. The theological method of sharing sexual stories requires for everybody to engage with honesty in a theology which takes distance from sexual ideologies. It requires for heterosexuals to come out of their own closets too, in order to discuss issues such as monogamy, fidelity and family structures, because they are crucial for Christian theology and practice. Having said that, I for one recognise that when our sisters started with the gender-based inquiry into theology, the path for the improper, for indecency, to come into theology was opened. As feminist theologians opened the gates to encounter the margins, strangers and Queers started to arrive, and amongst them the Stranger-God came in. Elizabeth Grosz has commented that the sex of the author usually leaves traces in the text, and assumes the reader's sexuality too.[7] We may say that language and the materiality of bodies constitute the matrix of theology which leaves traces so that to find a Queer, strange God in Christian theology means that we can read a different and even unlawful theology in reverse. It is us, the strangers in Christianity, who now can write the traces of a strange God amongst us. Why would we like to pursue a theological reflection on a strange God? Amongst other things, for political reasons.

Queering Colonial Theology

I remember Althusser's writings on ideology, and an interesting remark made by him concerning "fragments." He sees fragments as carrying with them the full ideological mechanisms that the centre-totality attributes to itself. The theological fragments or "theologies at the margins" to which we are referring here, share a colonial identity in dependency with their own colonial (or neo-colonial) masters. I have argued elsewhere that a God at the margins is not a marginal God.[8] The latter would be a real God within the margins, and a God with a substantial difference from the charity models which present us with a God coming to our margins, to our borders. It is precisely that movement of coming towards the marginalised which betrays that God. Where does this God belong? Which cartography of salvation has been traced by this movement towards the margins?

The theology at the margins that I would like to pursue as part of a Queer trajectory in theology is not a neo-colonial theology where an economic and affective model of relationships needs to be either expelled from the system or incorporated by providing an understanding alien to what real margins are. Margins are not margins except for within the colonial mentality. The cultural, political and sexual relationship of gods at the margins usually end up ratifying colonial pacts on the materiality of theological practices instead of unsettling them. Theirs are theological projects instead of trajectories and God is a

7 See Elizabeth Grosz Space, *Time and Perversion. Essays on the Politics of Bodies* (Routledge: London / New York 1995), 18.

8 For further comments on this point see my article, "The Divine Exodus of God," in: Werner G. Jeanrod / Christoph Theobald (eds), *God: Experience and Mystery*, *Concilium* 289 (2001), 27-33.

modification of power; there is no sense of transgression here, but of normality, with perhaps the exceptions which constitute normality. Those are margins of gender. Those margins are not queer.

If every theology is always a sexual theology the question is how to disrupt this. A gender-based theology does not have a chance, but neither would a sexually-based one (heterosexual or gay) unless the instability of sex is recognised. The problem with heterosexuality, which I consider a respectable sexual option, is heterosexual ideology, in the Marxist sense of a dominant worldview which acts as an un-discussed method of understanding reality. To say that theology is and always has been a reflection rooted in sexual practices means that there is an epistemology which sacralises sexual exchanges and regulations by a circle of a permanent re-configuration of the sacred, based on heterosexuality's symbolic structures and value system. When it is said that theological practices do not come from heaven, I agree. In fact, I think they come from the theologians' own bedrooms, which also mean from the theologians' own closets. What I am saying is that not only is there an important theological contribution to the formation of heterosexual ideologies in the history of the churches, but that that sexual ideological formation is constitutive of the theological praxis itself. However, heterosexual ideologies come with economic, political, racial and specific cultural understandings and interpretation circles.

Queer theology is a theology of loose alliances amongst sexual dissidents which reconfigures different spaces of thinking and relating to each other. Theologically, there are many implications in this.

The Perv's Handbook of Feminist Theological Ethics

Our question now is: what regulatory, decent order has organised the systematic theological sexual discourse in Christianity? Which sort of classroom ideology is behind a theological ethics which reproduces and encourages an attitude of theological submission to one specific epistemological model such as idealised heterosexuality in the making of systematic theology? Judith Butler confronts us with the issue not of the constitution of gender (which in her opinion leaves sex un-theorised), but of the regulatory norms which act in the materialisation of sex; that is, how sexuality is socially constructed.[9] Following from that, we may like to use hermeneutic suspicion to enquire how sex has been materialised through theological mechanisms. That would be to ask

9 See Judith Butler, *Bodies That Matter: On the Discursive Limits of "Sex"* (Routledge: London 1993), 10.

what sort of regulatory doctrines of grace and salvation, or what Christologies are responsible for the theological construction of sex?

Moreover, we may like to enquire about the connections between a colonial or neo-colonialist theological framework of thought and those constructions of sexuality which not only gave God a penis, but also regulated what that penis was supposed to do. Here we are in the area of classroom ideology which closes its frontiers with precision but also rules which categories of the indecent should remain hidden in the closets of theology and the theologians. As I have said elsewhere, if Paul Tillich was a fetishist with a penchant for S/M religious symbols, I would not join Mary Daly in condemning him for that, but I would like to highlight the fact that in his theology he never addressed his own sexuality, which remained hidden at the core of his theological identity.[10] If Karl Barth had just paid more attention to the fact that he found marriage somehow a dull experience, we could have had a much needed theology of mistresses long ago. The lack of engagement of theologians with their own sexual context at the moment of their reflections has kept the heterosexual roots of theology as an ideology without alternatives. But heterosexuality also has its own closets and fears, and it has its own ethical irresponsibility too.

I call this a *Perv's* Theological Ethics, because per/version is a concept that can be theologically related to alternative versions or options which it is our duty to imagine. Per/version (as a different version, or understanding) is the methodological path to take against projects of sameness.[11] Queer theologies may offer some ethical perversities to consider, as for instance:

1) Consensuality: Queer theology is a theology of alliances in agreement with their own diversity, in a consensual loving dynamic. Consensuality here also means dialogic, even if at times that is about code-breaking. A consensual relationship with the church and with God belongs to a different order than the old hierarchical, autocratic style of organising people and theologies to which we are accustomed.
2) We start our reflections from our own sexual stories. We lift God's skirts only after having lifted our own. In lifting our skirts we remind ourselves of our own identity at the moment of doing theology while we remain committed to theological honesty. It is from an alliance of sexual epistemologies in disagreement with heterosexual ideology that we reflect on grace, redemption and salvation, and not vice-versa.

[10] Althaus-Reid, *Indecent Theology*, 146.

[11] For an extended commentary on the concept of theological perversions see Althaus-Reid, *Indecent Theology*, 87.

3) From different sexual epistemologies, we may find different ways of understanding not only the salvific project but alternative church structures too. For instance, the role of permutations has a pedagogical function in understanding the complexity of the dynamics of change within the church.[12] The scenes of exchanges between femmes and butches, or men in high heels and women in drag have much to teach the churches about change, the importance of performances and the joy of allowing plurality to be embodied in us. From Leather groups or the community organisation of poor transvestites in Buenos Aires come many lessons about the beauty of the economic and affective alliances of the excluded in the world. Feminist theologies have already discovered that pleasure (the materialisation of desire) is a place to start a theology of the body which dismantles dualisms.

Volver a Nuestras Almas *(To Go Back to our Souls)*

We may be doing a theology of encountering strangers, including a stranger God and a Queer Messiah, but in the end, Queering theology brings us back to ourselves, to our own lost soul. This queering trajectory is not only about destabilising, for instance, Jesus' sexuality by finding, for instance, bisexual patterns in the Messiah's own understanding of his messianic project (which I have done as part of my Indecent theological reflections), but about doing a theology for all the strangers who are entombed in us. Queering theology may have an indecent redemptive role, by inviting people to come back to themselves.

Volver a nuestras almas (to go back to our souls) is the expression Peruvian indigenous people use when they feel alienated living in the big cities of the white people and in need of a re-encounter with their true identities. They go back to the mountains, and they say "I'm back in the mountains; I have come back to my soul." Strangely, Queer theology also has a praxis of going back to our souls. This is a path made of ruptures and recoveries in order to find our true selves again. People may need to stand queer against Global Capitalism and to understand the importance of the production of new identities at one and the same time in order to do a theology after Seattle, or after Porto Alegre: a theology which reflects the queerness of the revolution in Chiapas under Subcomandante Marcos, where sexual understandings are changing fast as part of a new and different way of thinking politics, economics and the meaning of

[12] For the use of permutation as a hermeneutical choice, see my article, "Sexual Salvation: The Theological Grammar of Voyeurism and Permutation," in: *Literature and Theology* 15/3 (2001), 241-9.

being human, or a healing theology which dismantles false coherences and ideological scripts in theology to allow people to stand up as human beings for a perverse ethics and a perverse theology which dares to take a departure from monolithic controls concerned with law and not with justice. This is the end of unnecessary transcendence and of tradition as industrial re-production.

As theologians, paraphrasing Elspeth Probyn's analysis of Jeanette Winterson's *Oranges are not the only Fruit*,[13] we may find that the role of theological tradition is to disarrange what we have become as Christian women, that is, that the past shows a discontinuity with our identity as queer theologians. Church traditions may sometimes through their closures and limitations show us our souls by contrast. We are what we were not supposed to be.

This means that a sort of colonial mobilisation is needed when confronting traditions and the history of the church and the theological community. It may be that as in the colonial experience, our Christian past negates us, but by doing so, it also affirms the production of new and multiple identities assumed in our communities. It is precisely that sense of preoccupation with the production of new identities and the role of theological imagination, more than of continuity, which is at the root of a queering theology. What we need is to remake our past, challenging the notion of established links between past and present, or between origins and identity.[14] For Queer, indecent theologies are theologies of disruption which neither look for legitimisation in the past nor for a memory of a harmonious trajectory. It is curious, and *queer*, to discover that, paradoxically, coming back to our souls should not be done through a path of harmony, but in diversity, dis-order and justice. We may say, using words inspired by Pat Califia,[15] that in a theological system which has done its best to wipe out many people, even interfering with their relationship with God, our main duty is to exist. And even if Queer theology is just another utopia kicking against the dogmatics of heterosexual ideology, proving that in the end not even by challenging heterosexual ideology can we transform this world, our duty is still to exist. Doing theology as if touching God under her skirts is a duty of love

[13] See Elspeth Probyn, *Outside Belongings* (Routledge: London 1996), 112. Compare also Linda Anderson's comments in "Autobiographical Travesties," 72-3.

[14] See Anderson, "Autobiographical Travesties," 72.

[15] Pat Califia writes that "if you live in a society that wishes you didn't exist, anything you do to make yourself happy disrupts its attempt to wipe you out, or at the very least, to make you invisible." See Califia, *Macho Sluts. Erotic Fictions* (Alyson: Boston 1988), 15. I take Califia's "to be happy" as equivalent to the right to have integrity and to write theology with sexual honesty.

and justice and an encounter with God amongst us. May we together, by the grace of God, stand always *queer* with love, courage and a passion for justice.

Dans cet article, je soulève sérieusement la question des débats sur la sexualité dans les théologies féministes, et je le fais en *inversant* les choses. Je me demande ce qui se produirait si nous parlions de Dieu en usant de métaphores sexuelles autres que celles qui proviennent des idéologies hétérosexuelles imprégnant nos discours théologiques. J'emploie la métaphore «faire de la théologie comme si nous soulevions la jupe de Dieu», et j'entends par là démontrer deux choses. D'une part l'autorité qu'a l'idéologie hétérosexuelle aussi parmi les théologiennes féministes (à tel point qu'une métaphore sur une relation d'amour entre Dieu/femme et une femme puisse être perçue comme sacrilège, comme on me le fit remarquer à l'issue de la conférence de l'ESWTR de 2001). D'autre part la nécessité de regrouper en théologie diverses épistémologies sexuelles (ou formes de savoir sexuel). La déstabilisation des idéologies hétérosexuelles est devenue, pour la théologie, une nécessité absolue, si nous voulons radicaliser notre vision de la sexualité, de la politique et de l'économie, étant donné la déshumanisation croissante qu'entraînent le néo-libéralisme et la globalisation.

In diesem Artikel möchte ich die Aufmerksamkeit darauf lenken, was es bedeutet, Themen der Sexualität in feministischen Theologien ernst zu nehmen. Dies tue ich anhand der Frage, was geschieht, wenn wir sexuelle Metaphern für Gott benutzen, die nicht von heterosexuellen Ideologien, die unsere theologischen Diskurse durchziehen, herrühren. Indem ich das Betreiben der Theologie mit der Metapher "den Rocksaum Gottes lüften" beschreibe, möchte ich zwei Dinge demonstrieren. Erstens, dass die heterosexuelle Ideologie sogar unter feministischen TheologInnen Autorität besitzt (dies geht so weit, dass die Metapher einer Liebesbeziehung zwischen Gott/Frau und einer Frau als sakrilegisch erfahren werden kann, wie mir nach der ESWTR-Konferenz 2001 bedeutet wurde). Zweitens geht es um die Notwendigkeit, unterschiedliche sexuelle Epistemologien (oder Formen des sexuellen Wissens) in die Theologie einzugliedern. Die Destabilisierung heterosexueller Ideologien in der Theologie ist ein Projekt, das uns zu dem radikalen sexuellen, politischen und ökonomischen Denken führt, das die Theologie im Kontext entmenschlichender Prozesse des Neoliberalismus und der Globalisierung dringend braucht.

Dr ***Marcella Althaus-Reid*** is an Argentinian Materialist theologian who works at the intersection of Liberation Theology and Queer Theory. Amongst numerous articles and chapters in books, she is the author of *Indecent Theology. Theological Perceptions on Politics, Gender and Sexuality* (Routledge: London 2000). She is Senior Lecturer in Christian Ethics and Systematic Theology in the Faculty of Divinity of the University of Edinburgh, Scotland. Together with Prof Lisa Isherwood, she is executive director of the new Routledge series *Queering Theology*.

Lucy Tatman

Western European-American Feminist Christian Theologians: What Might It Mean to Take Ourselves Seriously?

In early 2000 I was asked to write a paper for ESWTR's conference in Salzburg in August 2001 in which I provided answers to the question, "What about liberation theology is or may be theoretically problematic for feminist theologians?" For months I thought about this question, re-read some admittedly dusty texts, and became deeply frustrated. At the same time I was thinking about the theme of this conference, thinking about the possible relationships between feminist theology/ies and feminist theory/ies and their political implications. As I thought, questions flooded my mind. Why, I began to wonder, do 'we' (and by 'we' I mean primarily feminist christian theologians of the white, educationally-privileged, economically-rich-by-world-standards, Western European and North American variety), why do 'we' feel a need to criticise liberation theology now? Why do we feel a need to turn to feminist theory now? The very question 'what about liberation theology is problematic for feminist theologians?' revealed to me that we now feel as though liberation theology is not theoretically satisfactory for 'us', that it somehow does not address our needs. Scratch the question a bit deeper, and it reveals, moreover, that we had been searching for *answers* there, over there, in (primarily) Latin American theological texts. I had to ask myself, why? Why were we seeking our theoretical salvation in the words of others?

Once I had asked myself this question, I had to ask another. Is it a coincidence that now, at the very moment we feel as though we have not found salvation, theoretical or political, in liberation theology, we are turning our gaze upon secular feminist theory? Are we perhaps seeking our salvation there now? Again in the texts, the words of others? Why do we think, or is it simply, hope, that we will find responses to our needs, our concerns, in the work of these others? Finally finding my way to the heart of the question, I had to ask myself, why in the name of God can we not take *ourselves* seriously as theorists? I understand *this* question to be simultaneously political, and ethical, and deeply epistemological. *Do* such feminist christian theologians comprise one or more epistemic communities? *Do* we create knowledge both symbolic and concrete? Simultaneously political and ethical? Do we create knowledge that can change lives? *Do we?* I think we do.

And so in this paper, I about to commit a grave sin. I am *not* going to list or describe what is problematic about liberation theology from a feminist christian theological perspective. Nor am I going to talk much about secular feminist theories. I am going instead to talk about feminist christian theology and feminist christian theologians of that bland, white, Western Euro-American sort, and about what obstacles might make it difficult to take ourselves seriously as theorists, as theologians, as makers of life-changing knowledge.

I want to begin taking us seriously by telling you a story, a true story. I am here today because once upon a time one of those bland, white, Euro-American feminist theologians, one of us, was gang raped. For years she tried to put it behind her. Then one day she had a breakdown. Her body, her psyche, everything about her, pretty much ground to a halt. At the time she had some writing commitments, which she was unable to fulfill. She gave my name to someone, suggested that they ask me to step in. They did; I did. One thing led to another, led to another, led to my presence, via Australia, at the first European Women's Synod. Five years later, and here I am. She should be here, but she is not.

The story I am telling you right now is about a woman, a privileged, white Western feminist christian theologian, who was gang raped. It has to do with the way she tried to deny her body, and her body's insistence that her pain be acknowledged, that her pain be taken seriously. It has to do with the way she tried to deny her psyche, and her psyche's insistence that both her brokenness and her yearning for wholeness mattered, that her health needed to be taken seriously. If we are to take ourselves seriously as theorists, as theologians, we must start with our bodies and our psyches. It is as simple, and as difficult, as that. If we do not care for ourselves, one day we will be unable to think a coherent thought, unable to write a word. The Euro-American feminist christian theological world is missing at least two important texts: books that will forever remain unwritten, books that may have shattered, or at least cracked, some aspect of that symbolic universe that holds us imprisoned. Books erased by a gang of male rapists. I don't know how many times I have heard some version of this question from Womanist theologians and ethicists: "White woman, where is your anger?" Scratch that query a bit deeper, and the question becomes, I believe, "Woman, why don't you, why can't you take yourself seriously? Until you do, until you can take yourself seriously, we can't even talk to each other." My point is that it is not enough for us to be like a sponge, willing, eager to absorb the words, the knowledge of others. We must also cultivate something within us that we can offer in return, some life-giving liquid to share.

Accordingly, we must take our bodies, our experiences and interpretations of our bodies, our pains and pleasures and longings and joys, with utmost seriousness. Our bodies *know* the meanings of crucifixion, the meanings of redemption, the meanings of sin and the meanings of grace. It is up to us to translate this deeply embodied knowledge into words, into words that can be shared with others. But we, even though we have at our fingertips better theoretical tools for writing the body than any secular feminist theorist – and here I am thinking of terms and phrases such as incarnation, body and blood, earth creatures, bone of my bone, flesh of my flesh, with my body I thee worship, resurrection – even though we have these incredibly rich metaphors and models in our hands, we are pathetically bad at writing our bodies.

I say we, but that is not entirely correct. Some queer and some lesbian theologians *are* writing bodies, but most heterosexual feminist christian theologians are not. I honestly don't know why you aren't, but I do know this. It is both unjust and dangerous to place the burden of embodying feminist christian theologies on the shoulders and laptops of queer and lesbian theologians. To do so perpetuates the theological marginalisation of the body – all bodies, not simply bodies interpreted as queer or lesbian. It perpetuates that deathly boring mind/body dichotomy, or, if you prefer, binary opposition in which all that is bodily is associated with evil, with the sensual and sexual; and it puts some of you in the awkward/impossible position of Jerome's beloved virgins – those women whom he exhorted to deny their bodies so completely that they would become like a 'man'. Just because we are all too familiar with (and perhaps sick of) this dichotomy, this impossible virginal position, I am afraid we are still being screwed by it.

As I understand it, we are feminist christian theologians precisely because we do not want to reproduce, re-enact the sins of the Church Fathers against women, against the goodness of bodies, against the material stuff of creation. If this is so, then we literally have no choice but to write our bodies 'good', to write *all* bodies 'holy'. No one else is going to do it for us. To paraphrase Adrienne Rich, there come times, and this may be one of them, when we have to take ourselves seriously, or give up, and consent to Adam's naming of reality.[1]

[1] See Adrienne Rich, "Transcendental Etude," in: *The Dream of a Common Language* (WW Norton & Co: New York / London 1993), 74.

To take ourselves seriously as theorists involves, I believe, first of all taking our bodies, and our words about our bodies, seriously. But this is not all. To take ourselves seriously as theorists means taking our theoretical discipline seriously. Whatever else it may be, theology is theory. One problem is that we do not live in a time or culture that values christian theology as a body of knowledge. In fact, theology as such seems to be an embarrassment to many. As far as the study of religion goes, christianity is the least trendy religion imaginable. Further, secular theorists all know that God is merely a (dead) projection or wish fulfillment and we should be over it by now. Even though many of us here today name ourselves christian theologians, I don't see how it is possible for us to escape unscathed from the stigma that comes from being associated with an embarrassing discipline, a non-trendy religion, and that elephant in the living-room known as God. Nonetheless, here we are, and theology is what we do. God, or the sacred, or the holy, is one of our three main topics, the other two being humanity and the world. These three topics and their inter-relations constitute our subject-matter, which gives us rather a lot to theorise about. In fact, our subject-matter requires us to imagine and to theorise an entire symbolic universe in which the sacred, and the world (more broadly, creation), and human beings all a) exist, and b) fit together somehow. In theoretical terms, I am talking metaphysics. In other words, we cannot avoid having, and writing from, certain fundamental assumptions about the nature of reality, about Being. Although I perceive no way around this fact, by which I mean "no way around the fact that every single person has and thinks and acts upon the basis of certain fundamental assumptions about the nature of reality," there are currently at least three intensely political/theoretical issues associated with it, all of which need to be addressed.

1) As 'theory', metaphysics is a deeply western concept which has been declared 'dead' – although the 'death' in question refers, importantly, only to one particular set of assumptions concerning the nature and structure of reality, specifically that symbolic universe in which God is on top, with everything else arranged in chains below Him. (Some being more enchained than others.)
2) Following on from the above, I don't know about you, but I have seen no proof of this particular corpse. Rather, in almost every newspaper, and certainly in every one of George W. Bush's utterances, I find evidence that some version of this symbolic universe is still shaping knowledge claims, government policies, indeed all our lives today. While I wish it were dead, I am afraid it is alive and kicking.

3) The distance between 'metaphysics' and 'meta-narrative' is short indeed. If, these days, there is one criticism guaranteed to shut up a thoughtful theorist, it is the accusation that she is proposing a meta-narrative: making universal claims, defining reality for all, silencing those who would speak 'in a different voice'. She is exercising her power over the powerless; it's an example of western imperialist colonising discourse, etc. A thoughtful theorist, it is implied, should focus on particulars, limit her work to specifics, perhaps even tell stories *only* from her own experience.

As is probably clear, I am quite fond of particulars, specifics, and stories. But I am also aware that every story implicitly presupposes a universe in which that story makes sense or fits, a universe which that story somehow embodies. To put it bluntly, I do not believe there is any way that a theologian can ever avoid making metaphysical assertions. We all make them, either explicitly or implicitly, whenever we say or write anything at all. Should then we bland, Western Euro-American feminist christian theologians stay silent? I think not. I think we would do well to remember and extend the wisdom of Audre Lorde, who knew there is no way our silence will protect us, perhaps especially from a symbolic universe ruled over by God the Father, in which the only proper place for a privileged white woman (who is always lawfully wed, of course) is in her husband's home, picking out the new wallpaper.[2] No. Our words, our work is needed now more than ever. Now more than ever because so few secular theorists comprehend the strength, tenacity, and on-going danger to all our lives posed by the western christian symbolic universe.

During 2000 and 2001 Judith Butler was presenting to various audiences in the US and England, and perhaps elsewhere, a paper in which she discussed the notion of gay and lesbian marriages. I was told (by friends who heard her in November 2000 and May 2001) that she highlights the danger of handing over to the state the power to recognise and make 'real', make 'legitimate' these intimate relationships, while also noting the very real problems that same sex couples experience when they are from different countries but neither state recognises their relationship as 'real'. My friends tell me that it's a powerful, insightful paper. And when I asked one of them what she said (in England) about religion, or about the church recognising or performing same-sex marriages, I was told, I'm quoting, "Nothing." Nothing.

[2] Audre Lorde, 'The Transformation of Silence into Language and Action', in *Sister Outsider*, The Crossing Press, Freedom, CA: 1984. p. 41.

Which brings me back to the fear that feminist christian theologians will produce nothing but meta-narratives, perhaps even a grand narrative according to which the western world will come to comprehend itself. Can we stop and ponder this carefully for a moment? ... *Wouldn't that be a miracle*? Wouldn't that be cause for celebration? Imagine it. As imperfect and partial and inevitably flawed as such an understanding of reality would be, wouldn't it be a whole lot more healthy for all bodies, for all of creation, than the symbolic universe in which we currently live, move, and have our being?

As I understand it, at this time the Western christian symbolic universe looks something like this. A vague idea of the cosmos has replaced the earth as the centre of the universe. God, still very much God the Father, although now He is of course not to be understood as being in any way gendered, has been relocated slightly from His abode in heaven (formerly above the Northern Hemisphere) to His abode in heaven (now out beyond the reaches of the furthest stars). In practical terms, He is still up there and we are still down here. Although He is slightly less omnipotent than He used to be, he is nevertheless still omnipotent; we just can't fathom how. Here on earth heterosexual, nuclear, middle-class families are what God wants. As for individual humans, there are three subject-roles available for each sex to choose from. Men can be a son, a husband/breadwinner, or a sinner/pervert. Women can be a virgin, a wife, or a whore. Of course, virgins are useless as far as men are concerned, and whores are dangerous (they know too much), so all women should want to be a wife. The truth, and there is still only one truth, although now there are also a lot more lies floating around, is located in heaven above with God and the Hubble telescope. When we die, if we have loved God, our souls, though probably not our bodies, will ascend to heaven, and we will enjoy eternal life. Should things get too bad on earth there is every chance that God will destroy it (or allow the whole thing to be destroyed), and make a new and improved one.

Yes, it's a caricature, but there is too much truth in it. Unbelievably, the theoretical earthquake that was the Enlightenment has not drastically altered the classical western christian paradigm. However, the symbolic universe I just described is not exactly an Augustinian universe. I am going to suggest that at this time the shaking we feel beneath our feet is actually the after-shock from the Protestant Reformation. Where I am from, people are only now living, embodying the belief that their personal relationship to God or the sacred does not need to be mediated through the Church, by a priest or minister, in the words of a creed or through any communal ritual. Only now, I believe, are large numbers of us actually living lives shaped by a post-Reformation western christian symbolic universe. Today marriage is, both symbolically and in practice, the most valued relationship possible. In the West, it is more important for a woman to be married than to be a mother. Marriage is so highly valued that same-sex couples are, increasingly, demanding the rite from the Church and the right from the state. And we are beginning to get it. I'm fairly positive that this is not what Martin Luther had in mind when he suggested that marriage was a good thing, but I'm also increasingly convinced that it is symptomatic of a post-Reformation symbolic universe, a symbolic universe we really haven't even begun to theorise, a symbolic universe ignored, for the most part, by secular feminist theorists.

If my suspicion is correct, then I perceive no way at all that anything any of us writes could achieve the status of a grand, post-Enlightenment narrative. Our meta-narratives will at best be minor-narratives, read by few and disregarded entirely by many. Our minor-narratives are not often read even by other feminist theorists. Nevertheless, it is still our job, our calling and vocation as theologians to produce knowledge about the sacred, creation, and human beings that could, potentially, change lives. To envision and put into words a 'different heaven and earth', to use Sheila Collins's gorgeous expression. However, I think it is safe to assume that as theorists we will not experience instant gratification. We will not bear witness, in our lifetimes, to the incarnation of our different heavens and earths. At best, I think, we can and are making little differences, here and there. Specific, localised, and usually temporary little differences.

Long before secular feminist theorists started celebrating split and heterogeneous subjects, notions of fragmentation and multiplicity, feminist theologians were writing of, and piecing together, patchwork quilts, finding use for, making beauty and warmth, from bits and pieces, multiple scraps, split and frayed rags. Such familiar, homey metaphors don't often appear in 'High Theory'. But I am loath to give them up, finding much hard-earned wisdom within them. To affirm consciously that my own theology is constructed on the basis of a patchwork epistemology is to acknowledge what I, and I believe many of us here, are in fact, doing: combining old ideas in new ways, new patterns. Threads from Schleiermacher, from Whitehead, a needle borrowed from Heidegger, the whole thing stretched in a frame from Beauvoir.... But to affirm a patchwork epistemology is also, implicitly, to acknowledge the curiously intractable truth that no matter how many different 'points' one 'stands' in during the day, no matter how contradictory those points, no matter how split and multiple one's life may be lived during the day, at night every one of us is in just one place, under just one blanket. There are a lot of people in the world, and not enough blankets to go around. Many more quilts are needed.

A patchwork epistemology therefore carries with it a strong political and ethical claim. All bodies deserve a place to sleep at night in peace, and no bodies ought to freeze to death for want of a blanket, or of basic shelter. Quite often things really are this simple. While I think that as theologians we *must* find ways to honour and celebrate multiple differences and complexity, I fear that some of the more dazzling theoretical complications we produce (or are seduced by) may distract us from some painfully basic truths. However, trying to communicate basic truths, such as, for instance, that bodies require blankets, can be as fraught with difficulty and misunderstanding as the communication of more complex theoretical concepts.

This leads me to yet another issue making it difficult to take ourselves seriously as theorists. In order to be recognised and acknowledged as theologians by each other as well as by non-feminist theologians, it would seem that we must write in a recognisably "theological" language, address recognisably "theological" topics, and adhere to a recognisably "theological" methodology. In other words, both our individual and communal epistemic credibility depends to a certain extent upon our own acceptance and reiteration of the disciplinary practices of our field. Yet many of us are familiar with these words from Luce Irigaray, words filled with a trembling, terrible truth. "If we keep on speaking the same language together, we're going to reproduce the same history. ... If we keep on speaking sameness, if we speak to each other as men have been doing for centuries, as we have been taught to speak, we'll miss each other, fail ourselves. Again... Words will pass through our bodies, above our heads. They'll vanish, and we'll be lost."[3] What has been happening? How, as an epistemic community, have we been trying to speak a new language to one another, while, simultaneously, speaking recognisably theological utterances? I've thought about this question for about ten years now, which is to say, the answer I will offer to it is only one possible answer, but it also influences everything I have or will say today.

Back in the early 1970s Rosemary Radford Ruether wrote about the need for humans to cultivate the Garden, about the need for reconciliation, the reconciliation of spirit and matter, mind and body, technology and environment: reconciliations upon which she believed and believes the salvation of life on earth

[3] Luce Irigaray, *This Sex Which Is Not One*, trans. by Catherine Porter with Carolyn Burke (Cornell University Press: Ithaca, NY 1985), 205.

depends.[4] Mary Daly was writing about the Second Coming, daring to suggest it was being made incarnate in the women's liberation movement.[5] The Garden, reconciliation, salvation, the second coming are all recognisably theological metaphors. And all are recognisably NOT referring to a symbolic universe in which humans were once evicted from the Garden, in which only a transcendent god has the power to effect the reconciliation of humanity with Himself, in which God alone is responsible for the salvation of human beings and the world, in which it can only be Jesus Christ who comes again. It was obvious, back in the old days, that a new theological paradigm was taking shape, that the meanings of these familiar metaphors were being changed, drastically. It was so obvious that it didn't need to be said, then. Today, I think it does need to be said.

A new theological paradigm is a tricky thing, composed of several inter-related elements. First of all it presents a new world view, or a new understanding of the nature of reality. To be precise, it is a new set of metaphysical presuppositions, both cosmological and anthropological. Second, this new understanding of heaven, earth, and human beings is conveyed through discipline-specific metaphors, which are further layered into models. Crucially, the meanings of the metaphors and models are inextricably tied to those underlying assumptions about the nature of reality. Third, the metaphysical presuppositions, metaphors and models are all suffused with value judgements. In other words, to understand what someone means when they say 'sin' it is necessary to know within which theological paradigm they are speaking. Less obvious, but just as true, to understand what someone means when they say 'woman' it is necessary to know within which theological paradigm they are speaking. Put differently, in two or more theological paradigms the signifier might be the 'same', but what is signified is not.

To me, one of the most lovely things about the feminist christian theological paradigm that began to be created throughout the late nineteen-sixties and -seventies, and which was, yes, created primarily but not exclusively by privileged white western women, is that it posits and affirms a process metaphysics. Or, all of reality is understood as being in the process of constant, ceaseless change. All of it, human and non-human alike. Nothing is or could be fixed or static. Becoming, and not being, is at the heart of this feminist theological

4 See Rosemary Radford Ruether, "Motherearth and the Megamachine," in: Carol P. Christ / Judith Plaskow (eds), *Womanspirit Rising: A Feminist Reader in Religion* (Harper & Row: New York 1979), 43-52.

5 See Mary Daly, "After the Death of God the Father," in Christ / Plaskow, *Womanspirit Rising*, 53-62.

ontology. What any particular object or person might become, how they will change, how they will affect the becoming/changing of others, is deeply unpredictable. One of the most perplexing things for me about some recent theoretical analyses and criticisms of early (and later) feminist christian theological texts is the charge that some authors (like Ruether, Daly, Carter Heyward, Sallie McFague, etc) are positing essentialist understandings of "woman". "Essentialist." The word is even more damning than "meta-narrative". It conveys an understanding of human beings as having a fixed, static, unchanging, core essence. Either all humans have the same core essence, it is implied, or all women have the same core essence, which is different from the core essence shared by all men. As a concept, essentialism quite literally has no place in the feminist christian theological paradigm I am talking about. It makes sense, has intelligibility, only in a symbolic universe in which there is a place for the eternally immutable, or the changeless forms that material, corruptible stuff reflects only imperfectly. But the point is that to interpret these feminist christian theologians as essentialists is to miss the fact that they are writing in and from a set of ontological assumptions that presupposes no fixed, static, or unchanging essence of *anything*. It is as though an apple were being used as an interpretive lens through which to criticise a bunch of grapes for not being an apple.

If we want to be taken seriously by each other, let alone by non-feminist theologians or non-theological feminists, then I think we need to read each others' texts with the same care and attention we give to Butler or Foucault or Derrida (or name your favourite theorist). I think it would be helpful to name the theological paradigm within which we each, as individuals, write, as well as the theological paradigm we, some of us, are collectively continuing to create. Only when we understand each others' most fundamental assumptions can we engage in meaningful discussion, or meaningful disagreement, with each other.

I have the feeling that we, those of us who are relatively privileged North American or Western European feminist christian theologians, do not collectively realise what we have done and/or are now doing. We have created, are continuing to create, a new theological paradigm. New theological paradigms are about as rare as new scientific paradigms, yet, unbelievably, it has happened, it is happening now, and we are the epistemic community that is doing it. I find it so exciting to be a feminist theologian that sometimes I have to jump up and down. How did I, how did we, get to be so blessed? But a blessing is also a burden. If I choose to accept the blessing of my vocation, I also must accept responsibility for it. To me, this means that I must take seriously indeed the theoretical implications that I perceive in this new theological paradigm.

For instance, if creation, all of it, on a cosmic scale, is understood to be composed of a limited amount of stuff that continuously cycles between being energy and/or matter, then there is no way to affirm any notion of an individual, self-consciously aware sort of afterlife. The particular, unique combination of matter and energy that I am (which is constantly changing in any case), will one day dissolve completely, and 'I' will then spread out and recombine in who knows how many different forms. 'I' will cease to be. I find this thought quite freeing, but I suspect that we have some work to do to make it more pastorally palatable. Another example. If 'god' or the holy is understood in terms such as divine matrix, source, resource, power in mutual relation – and if all of us come from this divine matrix of possibilities, if it is the source of all, if we are all empowered by it through our interactions with others – then there is no consistent way (or reason) to elevate Jesus as man or god over the rest of us. Theologically, it is now possible to do without christology, full-stop. Let me be clear. I am not denying the historical importance of this individual to christianity, but I am insisting that theologically he is no longer necessary. In fact, he may be a huge stumbling block for many. Accordingly, we are in urgent need of a feminist christian theological non-christology.

I am trying to suggest that the blessing of a new theological paradigm lies, at least in part, in the fact that it frees us to choose whatever topics we like, to choose whatever methodology we like, but our responsibility is to make them theological through our use of theological metaphors and models, that is of metaphors and models which convey a particular metaphysics. It is our responsibility, I believe, to be explicit about which metaphysical assumptions we presuppose. It is our responsibility to figure out which metaphysical assumptions another presupposes – before we criticise her work. Again, before we can engage meaningfully with one another, we first need to understand each other.

There is a great deal of theory out there that can assist us. I would be terribly hampered in my own work if I could not draw upon Irigaray, Kristeva, Wittig, Lorde, Rich, Arendt, Wittgenstein, Foucault, Haraway, Butler. But I can't bring myself to be faithful to any of them. Nor, I must admit, can I take them as seriously as I take other feminist christian theologians.

I have suggested that to take *ourselves* seriously as theologians, as theorists, requires that we begin with our bodies. Likewise, I believe that to take *each other* seriously as theorists requires that we affirm one another as embodied thinkers. When I read another's words I try to remember that a living creature wrote them – a woman who laughs and cries and loves and whose shoulders probably ache after a long day in front of the computer. A woman who needs friends and touch and the occasional quiet cup of tea just as much as I do. A woman who worries about when she will have time to clean the bathroom, and who sometimes has bad-hair days. It helps me to remember that any woman who is a feminist theologian in this day and age is, has to be, a strong, strong woman. Let us then trust in each others' strength and dare to wrestle, hard, with each other, with each others' words, texts. Straining, sweating, let us meet one another as nakedly, as honestly as we can bear. Let us name our wants, our needs, our desires – to each other. Let us be passionate in our disagreements, loud in our cries. Let us be as lovers, refusing to let each others' longings go unmet. Let us neither pull back, nor interrupt the other when she is voicing unfamiliar demands. Let us open ourselves as fully as we can as we attend to one another. Let us celebrate the heat and wet and pressing, insistent, untamed yearning in each others' texts. Above all else, let us take pleasure in each others' work, in each others' words: those incarnations of the flesh that can be shared with many. As theorists, let us vow never to be monogamous; as theologians, I don't know about you, but, theologically, I long to make indecent love with Marcella, and Mary, and Michaela, and with you.... With word and flesh let us take each other seriously as lovers of theology.

Dieser Text, der mit der Absicht verfasst wurde, eher gehört als gelesen zu werden, ist eine lockere Sammlung von Gedanken und Reflexionen über die Schwierigkeit, westliche europäisch-amerikanische feministische christliche Theologie als bedeutungsvolle Theorie aufzufassen. Der Beitrag behandelt zudem die Schwierigkeit, diejenigen, die eine solche Theologie betreiben, als würdige epistemische Handelnde zu betrachten. Implizit wird davon ausgegangen, dass eine solche Theologie und solche TheologInnen nur dann und erst dann ernst genommen werden, wenn wir sie und einander voll Leidenschaft lieben lernen.

Écrit pour être écouté plutôt que lu, ce texte est un recueil de pensées et de réflexions sur la difficulté de croire à la théologie chrétienne féministe occidentale, – européenne et américaine, – et de se convaincre de ses fondements théoriques. Il aborde aussi la difficulté de percevoir ceux et celles qui se livrent à la théologie féministe comme des acteurs épistémiques dignes de ce nom. Il est sous-entendu que la théologie féministe, de même que ses adeptes, ne seront pris au sérieux qu'à condition que nous l'aimions et que nous fassions découvrir les liens d'amour existant entre nous.

Lucy Tatman (1965) is a feminist theologian (Quaker) and philosopher currently thinking about the relationship between the sacred and the epistemic, moral and political agency of various female subjects in western culture. She also teaches academic writing at the University of California, San Diego, while continuing her search for that elusive tenure-track position.

Mirka Holubová

Women's Memory: Searching for Identity within Socialism International oral history project co-ordinated by the Gender Studies Centre, Prague

Women's Memory is the first international long-term oral history project to take as its aim the identification of specificity of gender-based experience during various periods of the totalitarian regime in the region of East and Central Europe. The research team, coordinated from the Gender Studies Centre (GSC) in Prague and directed by Pavla Frýdlová, seeks to move beyond historical facts in order to understand their meaning and significance for women's everyday lives. That is, big historical events are seen, articulated, and evaluated in the context of individual life stories, and historical upheavals, such as those of 1948, 1968 or 1989, are given importance only in so far as they are embedded in the personal concrete experience of women of various generations and social origins.

1. History of the Project

The idea of the project originated in the early 1990s when the countries of East and Central Europe became a focus of interest of many Western feminist scholars and activists who came to the region eager to learn more about the emancipation of women in socialist societies. Some of them admired the achievements of local women which they themselves had to fight for in the course of the 1970s (social status, equal access to education economical independence, maternity benefits, pre-school facilities for children, etc.). Others were astonished by what they saw as a lack of self-esteem among women and the persistence of a deeply rooted patriarchal society regardless of the officially claimed equality.

In a relatively short time, a number of essays and even monographs were published on these topics, particularly in the Anglo-American academic context. Most of this work was not only based on a completely different cultural and social experience from that of the women who were the object of study, but it also applied to the region quite inappropriate discourses and analytical paradigms. Most of these early studies only served to create misunderstandings in the West about women from East and Central Europe and vice-versa;

Eastern European women could not recognize themselves in their "Western" portraits.

It became clear during our many discussions with women of the numerous women's regional organizations that it was highly important to evaluate our own history according to our own criteria rather than importing these from quite different contexts, and to embrace our own "otherness". The idea of women's identities during the socialist area became the centre of our attention.

The idea of a large-scale international comparative project entitled *Women's Memory* was first formulated by a prominent Czech human rights activist, Jiřina Šiklová, professor of sociology at Charles University. Over fifty women's organizations expressed interest in joining the project, but it soon became obvious that an ambitious project of this size would require resources comparable to Spielberg's Holocaust project. The enthusiastic members of the GSC, however, decided to take off without any funding and conducted the first pilot interviews as early as the autumn of 1997.

Aims and Objectives

The socialist model of the emancipation of women was a unique systematic and complex concept of the liberation of a woman, or rather, an experiment in both theory and practice. Our aim was to record the life experience of women of three generations: those born before 1920, those born during the 1930s, and those born between 1950 and 1960. Our main interest is to document how women who spent most of their active lives in the area of socialism, reflect today upon their lives. The aim is to dismantle many myths related to the notion of a "socialist woman" and in the light of individual testimonies to see how their own experience differed from those of their mothers and grandmothers.

Methodology

Feminist sociology challenged the traditional male dominated interpretation of the world by introducing new themes. At the same time it developed new methods of interpretation while emphasizing the importance of personal experience, as well as the self-reflection of both the interviewer and the respondent. Feminist social scientists give preference to narrative and biographical methods. History, in their understanding, does not represent a set of events, but is a result of interaction between individuals, who give meaning to what is going on. It is the meaning and significance attributed to events by individuals which retroactively shapes historical "reality". Our interpretation of events does not depend purely on facts of what happened, but on our evaluation of them. These evaluation patterns do not depend on our school education but are passed down from generation to generation. Parents, and particularly mothers, play an important role in deciding the selection of the values to be transmitted, which are those considered essential to the formation of the attitudes of future generations. It is primarily women who influence this selection of the memory of a nation, that is, of the memory of humankind.

The choice of biographical method and the method of oral history for this project seems to us quite logical, since these methods are rooted in the oral transmission of information and particularly of family narratives. We are interested in lived experience rather than so-called objective truth.

Autobiographical narration proves the capacity of women to describe and reflect upon their experience, to verify and re-examine the experience, to keep coming back in circles, no matter whether they are talking about their crises, the important decisions they have taken in their lives, or their memories of childhood. As the Montenegro writer Ljiljana Habjanovic-Djurovic[1] puts it in the motto to her novel *Women's Genealogy*, women always spin the web of their experience, "threading it like pearls on the string of the eternal genealogy of women". Women's genealogy is not only a process of discovering women's codes by following the female line in the family history. It is also a process of developing feminist epistemology, which is always focusing on women's identification and self-awareness.

This project is understood to be an *open model* of testing feminist methodology as well as our own roles within it. Feminist methodology is a challenge as well as a process. This process is a dynamic one, and by no means can it be measured by any quantitative method, or compared to other related processes. This, of course, does not mean that it cannot be subject to criticism. On the contrary, a critical re-examination of the methodology as well as of the participants themselves is an integral part of this process. We understand this process to be emancipatory, anti-ideological, feminist, and most of all open. The feminist character of the project lies primarily in our attitude to the respondents: they are by no means the *objects* of the project; rather, they are its *raison d'être*.

Following the assumption that the "personal is political", the aims of the project are not theoretical, but practical. They could be seen as serving "public enlightenment"; they target a wide public audience, civic society. The major characteristics of the project are the inseparable connection between two leading criteria: on the one hand its political orientation towards the practical needs

1 Ljiljana Habjanovic-Djurovic, *Ženski rodoslov* (Narodna knjiga Alpha: Belgrade 1997).

of civil society, and on the other the need to meet academic standards. The project is oriented not towards the "product" or a "result" but the process itself.

The methodology has been thrashed out at five international workshops that took place in the space of one year. From the very beginning it has been clear to all of us that this was a process of mutual learning through an ongoing re-reading of each interview and through an ongoing international communication.

Interview: This is understood as a process of interaction between the interviewer and the respondent, based on a mutual trust, which is seen as an irreplaceable condition of the communication. The absolutely equal position between those involved in the interview is a key ethical question of the project. The purpose is not just to collect "data", but also to bring women to a reflection on their own identity. A basic scheme of the interview was elaborated. There is an outline which we keep in the back of our minds and which serves to each of us as a supportive tool of communication with the interviewed woman. Some of the interviews may last for several hours; often it takes several meetings to complete the testimony. Without a deep commitment of each of us such a demanding task would be impossible.

Selection of the women interviewed: This is one of the main conditions of the quality of the interview. Each life story is important to us, but not every woman is able or willing to present it. Needless to say, a full anonymity is guaranteed; only the initial of the family name is included in the records of the interview, and women are free to change their first name or the names of places they talk about. There is a variety of ways of searching for the women to be interviewed. We started with women in our social circles, and followed contacts of friends. A personal recommendation is often crucial for the success of the interview as it would otherwise be nearly impossible to ask about intimate issues such as sexual relations, child birth, abortion, family planning, etc. We also use the snowball method, asking the interviewed women for to suggest women they know as candidates, but we never went through the way of media advertisements. The process of getting to know the woman before the actual interview takes place is equally important. The interviewees often call several times, write letters or even visit the GSC. Some of them participated in a recent congress on the project in Berlin.

Transcription of the Interview: This is never a literal transcript. We have reached a compromise between accuracy, readability and comprehension. Even though we leave out all interjections or uncompleted words, the specific character of the oral communication must remain in the text.

The research teams are interdisciplinary groups of philosophers, linguists, historians, ethnologists, psychologists, sociologists, politicians, journalists and fiction writers. The themes of interpretation (identity, self-development, women's politics, values and attitudes) can be developed only through the repeated re-reading of the interview material from a variety of points of view.

2. Outcomes: two categories

I. Permanent, concrete outcomes

A. International Archive
This includes all the original records and transcriptions. Each interview includes supplementary materials (protocol, biogramme, key word index for archival purposes, and résumé in English or German). Access to the Archive is defined according to the general law on archives of the Czech Republic. Particular national archives are either based in the respective women's organizations or affiliated with universities (Bratislava, Belgrade). In the future, all the materials collected as a result of the project will be available to experts of different fields and to future generations.

B. Lectures, seminars, conferences and publications
At both national and international levels, related to particular themes, or inter-regional (Czech-German, Czech-Polish, Czech-Slovak).

II. Longer-term outcomes

These can be defined as the permanent impact on the participating women both in the role of interviewers and of interviewee.

This consciousness-raising process begins already in the actual process of interviewing. Many of the women we interviewed were genuinely surprised that we were interested in their lives at all. Others were trying for the first time to recapitulate about their own lives; the interview enabled them to see themselves from a new perspective. The very fact that somebody else is interested in their life boosts many women's self-confidence.

The impact of the project on the participants in the processes which take place outside of the actual dialogue, such as transcription, completion of the text, often accompanied by further discussions with the respondent, mutual reading of the interviews and their evaluations in the workshops, mutual enrichment and self-education at both national and international levels. Throughout the project we are learning what *multiculturalism* really means, while all the clichés about the grey uniformity of life in East Central Europe are rapidly being eroded. Despite some similarities, each of these countries is, indeed, very unique and different.

3. What has been accomplished

The first pilot set of interviews was conducted in the Czech Republic in 1996-1997. The experience was shared with teams in the former GDR and the Polish group in Krakow. These teams were working together on methodology, evaluations and techniques of conducting and transcribing the interviews. Regular working contacts with teams from Yugoslavia, Croatia and Slovakia resulted into a joint workshop on the island of Brac in the Spring of 1999. The six national teams who took part in this first workshop (Czech republic, Slovakia, Germany, Yugoslavia, Croatia, Poland) still represent the core of the project today.

The project is co-ordinated at GSC in Prague, an institution which is also building up the project's archives. Each national team has autonomous status and does individual fund-raising (grants from H. Boell Foundation, OSF, Phare programme EU, etc.). Only the German project is fully funded by the government (Ministry for the Family, Seniors, Women and Youth).

All the participating teams have agreed to conduct 30 interviews with women of each generation before the end of 2002, including supplementary material if their financial resources allow. All teams work very closely together. Their highest co-ordinating body is the meeting of national directors. Any new national team wishing to join the project must adopt our methodological consensus and the rules of cooperation. (Teams from Monte Negro, Bulgaria, Macedonia, Bosnia and Herzegovina, Ukraine have joined the project.)

The working languages for the international project coordination and communication are German and English.

Brief account of the outcomes

At the present time (July 2002), the international team have conducted approximately 350 interviews which have generated around 13 000 pages of transcription. Depending on finances, the whole project should be completed by the end of 2004.

There have been eight books published in national languages, namely in Czech and Serbian. Three interviews have been published by the journal *One Eye Open* in the GSC and two volumes of interviews have appeared: *Vsechny nase vcerejsky. Pamet zen I., II.* [All our Tomorrows. Women's Memory I & II] (Nadace Gender Studies: Prague 1998). Two booklets have been published in German and English.

The members of the Czech team serve as multiplicators and trainees in a number of similar projects; the most recent include *Memory of the Roma Women* in co-operation with the Museum of Roma Culture in Brno.

The interviews are gradually being complemented by supporting materials and studies which are meant to explain the historical context. Other supporting materials include those relating to legislation regarding women, available statistical and demographic data, historical discourse on the question of women, the history of the most widely read local journal for women, *Vlasta*, including its representation of women, etc.

The first outcomes of the project were presented to an international expert audience in Berlin in May 2001 at the congress *Women's Memory – the Future Needs Memories*. The congress included an exhibition of historical documents and materials. Among the Congress guests was Margarita Doer, a German historian whose three-volume study of National Socialism *Wer die Zeit nicht miterlebt hat* was based on a similar methodology.[2] Her support of our project as well as the interested of both the academic and wider audience provided a great deal of support to our work.

After the period of collecting materials – which will differ in the individual countries – is finished, the period of evaluation of the material on both the national and international levels will begin.

Women's Memory ist das erste internationale Langzeitprojekt für *oral history*, das die Besonderheiten der je nach Geschlecht unterschiedlichen Erfahrung während verschiedener Zeiträume totalitärer Regimes im Gebiet Ost- und Zentraleuropas beschreibt. Das Forschungsteam, das vom Zentrum für Gender-Studies in Prag koordiniert wird und unter der Leitung von Pavla Frýdlová steht, beabsichtigt, über die historischen Fakten hinaus zu gehen, um deren Bedeutung für das Alltagsleben von Frauen zu verstehen. Das heißt, große historische Ereignisse werden verstanden, artikuliert und evaluiert im Kontext individueller Lebensgeschichten; historischen Aufbrüchen, wie denen der Jahre 1948, 1968 oder 1989 hingegen wird nur insoweit Wichtigkeit beigemessen, als sie in die persönliche, konkrete Erfahrung von Frauen verschiedener Generationen und sozialer Schichten eingebettet sind. Dieser Beitrag stellt die Methodologie und einige Forschungsresultate des Projekts vor.

Mémoires de femmes est le premier projet international à long terme de tradition orale ayant pour but d'identifier la spécificité des expériences faites par chacun des deux sexes durant diverses périodes du régime totalitaire dans la région d'Europe de l'Est et Centrale. L'équipe de recherche, coordonnée par le Centre d'Études du Genre de Prague et dirigée par Pavla Frýdlová, cherche à comprendre, au-delà des faits historiques, la portée de ces expériences dans la vie quotidienne des femmes.

[2] Margarete Doer, *Wer die Zeit nicht miterlebt hat* (Campus: Frankfurt am Main 1998).

Certains grands événements historiques sont consciemment vus, articulés et évalués uniquement sous l'éclairage de destins individuels, et ce sont les expériences personnelles de femmes de diverses générations et origines sociales qui donne leur poids aux bouleversements historiques de 1948, 1968 ou 1989. L'article présente la méthodologie de ce projet et quelques uns des résultats déjà obtenus.

Miroslava Holubová is a philologist, translator, and lecturer in the history of the women's rights movement. She is an associate member of the Gender Studies Centre Prague, a member of the Women's Commission of the Ecumenical Council of Churches in the Czech Republic, a member of the Association for Equal Rights. She was involved in the organisation of the first Eastern European Regional Conference of the ESWTR in Prague in 1998 and is coordinator of EWC Antenna in Prague. Since December 2001 she has been working with the Ministry of Interior of the Czech Republic in the field of public administration reform.

Kwok Pui-Lan

Historical, Dialogical, and Diasporic Imagination in Feminist Studies of Religion

I have been reflecting on my long intellectual journey to "struggle to know." Why is knowing a struggle? It is a struggle because you have to spend years learning what others tell you is important to know, before you acquire the credentials and qualifications to say something about yourself. It is a struggle because you have to affirm first that you have something important to say and that your experience counts. As Leila Ahmed, a professor in women's studies in religion, reminiscences about her graduate training at Cambridge University:

> Many of us from the Third World arrived having lived through political upheavals that traumatically affected our lives – for this quite simply has been the legacy of imperialism for most of our countries. But it was not those histories that we had lived that were at the center of our studies, nor was it the perspectives arising from those histories that defined the intellectual agenda and preoccupations of our academic environment.[1]

Women's articulation of their experiences of colonisation is so new; these women have been much represented, but until fairly recently have not been allowed the opportunities to represent themselves. Even if they have "spoken," their speech acts are expressed not only in words but also in forms (story-telling, songs, poems, dances, and quilting, etc.) that the academic and cultural establishments either could not understand or deemed as insignificant. These knowledges have been ruled out as non-data: too fragmented, or insufficiently documented for serious inquiry.

How do we come to know what we know? How do postcolonial intellectuals begin the process of decolonisation of the mind and the soul? What are the steps we need to take and what kind of mindset will steer us away from

[1] Leila Ahmed, *A Border Passage: from Cairo to America – a Woman's Journey* (Farrar, Straus and Giroux: New York 1999), 211.

eurocentrism, on the one hand, and a nostalgic romanticism of one's heritage or tradition, on the other? In this essay, I attempt to trace the itinerary of how the mind "imagines," for without the power of imagination, we cannot envision a different past, present, and future. Without interrogating the mind's "I/eye," we are left without alternative perspectives to see reality and to chart where we may be going. For what we cannot imagine, we cannot live into and struggle for.

What is imagination? How does the postcolonial's mind work? In an earlier essay, I followed the notion that to imagine means to discern that something is not fitting, to search for new images, and to arrive at new patterns of meaning and interpretation.[2] Since then, I have begun to see that the process of imagining is more complex, especially when we do not want to construe the imagining subject as the "transcendental I" within the liberal project who has the power to shape the world and to conjure meanings. In other words, I have attached more importance to the cracks, the fissures, and the openings, which refuse to be shaped into any framework, and which are often consigned to the periphery. These disparate elements that staunchly refuse to follow the set pattern, the established episteme, the overall design that the mind so powerfully wants to shape, interest me because they have the potential to point to another path, to signal radical new possibilities.

As I reflect on my own thinking process as an Asian feminist theologian, I discern three critical movements, which are not linear but overlapped and interwoven in intricate ways. They are more like motifs in a sonata, sometimes recurrent, sometimes disjointed, with one motif dominating at one moment, and another resurfacing at another point. I would like to reflect on these three movements – historical, dialogical, and diasporic imagination – to indicate how my mind has changed or remained the same.

[2] Kwok Pui-Lan, "Discovering the Bible in the Non-Biblical World," *Semeia* 47 (1989), 25-42, reprinted in *Discovering the Bible in the Non-Biblical World* (Orbis Books: Maryknoll 1995), 8-19, here 13.

Historical Imagination

History is best figured not as an accurate record or transcript of the past but as a perspectival discourse that seeks to articulate a living memory for the present and the future.
Elisabeth Schüssler Fiorenza[3]

How do you trace where you have come from? How do women create a heritage of our own? When women's history emerged in the scene, feminist scholars argued that one could not simply add women and stir, but had to question the so-called historical data, periodisation, historiography, and in fact, the whole writing of history, as if women counted. The project is to accord or restore to women the status of a "historical subject." But how do we track the scent of women who were multiply marginalised, shuttled between tradition and modernity, and mostly illiterate and who therefore left no trail that could be easily detected? Hispanic journalist Richard Rodriguez uses the metaphor "hunger of memory" to describe this passionate and relentless quest for one's own historical and cultural past.[4]

In the past two decades, there has emerged a significant body of work reconstructing the history and lived experiences of Third World women and racial minority women in the United States. The accomplishments of the womanist scholars are especially impressive. For example, Delores Williams has used the figure of Hagar as a heuristic key to recover the struggle for survival and quality of life of African American women.[5] The works of Zora Neale Hurston, Anna Julia Cooper, and Ada B. Wells-Barnett have been given their due attention by Katie Geneva Cannon, Karen Baker-Fletcher, and Emilie Townes, respectively.[6] More recently, Joan Martin has deployed slave narratives as

[3] Elisabeth Schüssler Fiorenza, *In Memory of Her: A Feminist Theological Reconstruction of Christian Origins*, Tenth Anniversary edition (Crossroad: New York 1994), xxii.

[4] Richard Rodriguez, *Hunger of Memory: The Education of Richard Rodriguez* (David E. Godine: Boston 1981).

[5] Delores S. Williams, *Sisters in the Wilderness: The Challenge of Womanist God-Talk* (Orbis Books: Maryknoll 1993).

[6] Katie Geneva Cannon, *Black Womanist Ethics* (Scholars Press: Atlanta 1988); Karen Baker-Fletcher, *A Singing Something: Womanist Reflections on Anna Julia Cooper* (Crossroad: New York 1994); and Emilie M. Townes, *Womanist Justice: Womanist Hope* (Scholars Press: Atlanta 1993).

resources to uncover the work ethic of enslaved women.[7] Evelyn Brooks Higginbotham and Cheryl Townsend Gilkes have recovered the roles and leadership of black women in the black churches from historical and sociological points of view.[8]

In my first book, *Chinese Women and Christianity 1860-1927*, I painstakingly reconstructed Chinese women as actors, writers, and social reformers in the unfolding drama of the Christian movement at the turn of the twentieth century.[9] The research brought me to many mission archives and major libraries both in China and the USA and required a different historical imagination, akin to what Foucault has termed "insurrection of subjugated knowledge." As I look back at my work, I wish I had had more exchanges with non-western scholars who were probing the houses of memory of their foremothers, for I have learned much from Higginbotham's work on the women's movement in the Black Baptist Church and Leila Ahmed's book on women and gender in Islam.[10] I would also have benefited from the scholarship done by historians and anthropologists who investigated the relationship between race, gender, and imperial power.[11] While I focused on the Chinese archives, Chung Hyun Kyung documented the emergence of Asian feminist theology as a grassroots movement and provided information on the historical context and social organisations that formed the backbone for the movement.[12] Similarly, women scholars from other Third World contexts have also recounted the histories and struggles of Christian women against patriarchy and other forms of oppression in their societies.

7 Joan M. Martin, *More than Chains and Toils: A Christian Work Ethic of Enslaved Women* (Westminster John Knox: Louisville 2000).

8 Evelyn Brooks Higginbotham, *Righteous Discontent: The Women's Movement in the Black Baptist Church, 1880-1920* (Harvard University Press: Cambridge, MA 1993); Cheryl Townsend Gilkes, *"If It Wasn't for the Women...": Black Women's Experience and Womanist Culture in Church and Community* (Orbis Books: Maryknoll 2001).

9 Kwok Pui-lan, *Chinese Women and Christianity, 1860-1927* (Scholars Press: Atlanta 1992).

10 Leila Ahmed, *Women and Gender in Islam: Historical Roots of a Modern Debate* (Yale University Press: New Haven 1992).

11 For example, Ann Laura Stoler, "Carnal Knowledge and Imperial Power: Gender, Race, and Morality in Colonial Asia," in: Micaela di Leornardo (ed.), *Gender at the Crossroads of Knowledge: Feminist Anthropology in a Postmodern Era* (University of California Press: Berkeley 1991), 55-101; Ann McClintock, *Imperial Leather: Race, Gender and Sexuality in the Colonial Contest* (Routledge: London / New York 1995).

12 Chung Hyun Kyung, *Struggle to Be the Sun Again: Introducing Asian Women's Theology* (Orbis Books: Maryknoll 1990).

With such a body of knowledge before us, it is time to look back and to clarify some of the issues that have arisen in the ensuing discussions of our works. The first issue concerns what kind of subjectivity we have accorded those women who have historically not been granted subject status. For example, black ethicist Victor Anderson has charged that womanist scholars have essentialised blackness as if it consisted only of suffering, endurance, and survival of life. He further argues that they have followed the masculine construction of the black heroic genius, and stress black women's capacities for survival even against all unprecedented oppression.[13] But as Stephanie Y. Mitchem has retorted, the womanists have presented much more multiple and variegated descriptions of suffering, without collapsing all forms of oppression together as equal and homogeneous.[14] Furthermore, as Elisabeth Schüssler Fiorenza has persistently argued, historical writings are rhetorical, serving particular political functions, and are not to be construed of as "objective" or "value-neutral."[15] The emphasis on the historical and moral agency of black women is necessary, as Katie Geneva Cannon argues, because the white racist culture reinforces the stereotypes of the inferiority of the black race and promulgates negative images of black women.[16] Like the black women writers they have studied, womanist theologians and ethicists keep in mind the need for self-affirmation and assertion by the black community, to which their works are accountable. To recover black foremothers as strong, resourceful, and enduring is to re-write a tradition to live by, and to celebrate black women's audacity of creating a way out of no way. Perhaps, when the womanist tradition is more nuanced and developed, and when the social conditions inflicted by white racism improve, we will be able to see black women assuming more varied subject positions in religious discourse.

In the postcolonial Asian context, Wong Wai Ching has argued that Asian women theologians have a tendency to present Asian women either as victims of multiple oppression or as national heroines fighting courageously for freedom and emancipation. Based on an analysis of the deployment of gender in the

[13] Victor Anderson, *Beyond Ontological Blackness: An Essay on African Religious and Cultural Criticism* (Continuum: New York 1995), 104-17.

[14] Stephanie Y. Mitchem, "Womanist and (Unfinished) Constructions of Salvation," in: *Journal of Feminist Studies in Religion* 17/1 (2001), 85-100, here 93-94.

[15] Elisabeth Schüssler Fiorenza, *Rhetoric and Ethic: The Politics of Biblical Studies* (Fortress: Minneapolis 1999).

[16] Cannon, *Black Womanist Ethics*, 6.

nationalist discourse in nineteenth-century India, Wong generalises that Asian theologians have constructed Asian women as schizophrenic subjects – poor and oppressed, yet heroic and courageous. She contends that Asian feminist theologians have uncritically appropriated such an antithetical image of women as framed by nationalist ideology. Since Asian women have been constructed as "the poor woman," Asian feminist theology tends to follow the similar plot of revolving around the themes of suffering and liberation. She writes: "'the poor woman' and its parallel, 'the heroine,' in the national discourse freeze women as a sign representing cultural essentials and cultural difference for both nationalists and feminists in Asia."[17] As such, Asian feminist theologians have oversimplified women's multiple experiences, diverse interests, and social locations. They have also inadvertently supported the nationalist politics and agendas of Asian male theologians, and as a result, their feminist theology shares the assumptions and rhetoric of their male counterparts, such as the recovery of Asian identities, the commitment to socio-political transformation, and the prioritising of practice over Western academic theory.

I find that Wong tends to oversimplify the ideas of the individual Asian feminist theologians and the development of Asian feminist theology in general. The works of Chung Hyun Kyung, Mary John Mananzan, and myself have presented a much more multiple and diverse portrayal of Asian women than the binary constructs of "victim" and "heroine." The social analysis of Korean feminists, who survived through Japanese colonialism and who currently live in a divided country in the most highly militarised zone of the world, is very different from that of Indian feminists struggling against abject poverty, the caste system, dowry, and the mobilisation of Hinduism as a national ideology. While these feminists are concerned about the multiple oppression of women, their interpretations of why women suffer are culturally and historically specific. Wong herself might have inadvertently created the binary construct while trying to fit the ideas of Asian theologians into her mould. Furthermore, Wong surprisingly fails to distinguish between male and female theologians' relationship to national struggles and nationalist discourse. While the struggle for independence provided the historical backdrop for Asian women to enter the public arena, Asian feminist theologians are keenly aware of the patriarchal biases of the national male elite both during independence struggles and in the subsequent fight for democracy. Asian feminist theologians do not blindly

[17] Wong Wai Ching, "Negotiating for a Postcolonial Identity: Theology of 'the Poor Woman' in Asia," in: *Journal of Feminist Studies in Religion* 16/2 (Fall 2000), 5-23, here 20.

follow the lead of the male theologians, nor do they willingly participate in and support their epistemological framework. Very often, it was these theologians' chauvinism that drove the women theologians to become feminists in the first place – as in the cases of Sun Ai Lee Park and Aruna Gnanadason.

Since both Anderson and Wong rely on elements of postmodern thought to critique the construction of an "essentialised" subject in womanist and Asian feminist discourse, it may be worthwhile to re-examine whether the postmodern critique of subjectivity is appropriate and helpful in these contexts. While postmodern thought may be instrumental in deconstructing the notion of modern "man" as the transcendental unified subject, its application to other contexts where the enslaved and the colonised have never been allowed to assume subject status must be carefully interrogated. Furthermore, it is necessary to distinguish between a Western habit of "essentialising" and "homogenising" human experience and the self (as most clearly seen in the colonial enterprise) and the womanist and Asian cultural constructions of the self, which are rooted in and understood through the communal experience. When Williams uses the literary figure of Hagar, she is not interested in the individualist protagonist of the narrative, nor does she try to "essentialise" Hagar's experience to speak for all black women. Rather, she explores how the ancient story may serve as an historical prototype to lift up salient aspects of black women's collective experience and as a model to write black women's history.

Similarly, Chung Hyun Kyung has used the stories of comfort women, who were conscripted and lured to serve as sexual slaves for Japanese soldiers during World War II, as a root story for Korean feminist theology.[18] Again, she does not intend to "universalise" the experiences of these 200,000 comfort women to speak for all Korean women who belong to different social classes and backgrounds. Nevertheless, she finds these stories to be powerful heuristic models to expose the interlocking oppression of sexism, militarism, colonialism, and sexual violence.

One may wonder why these theologians dwell on the memories of Hagar and the comfort women and do not move on. But as Thomas Laqueur has eloquently written, "It is precisely by remembering in public that the past can become past – and that memory becomes survivable by entering into history."[19]

[18] Chung Hyun Kyung, "Your Comfort vs. My Death," in: Mary John Mananzan et al. (eds), *Women Resisting Violence: Spirituality for Life* (Orbis Books: Maryknoll 1996), 129-40.

[19] Thomas Laqueur, "The Naming of the Dead," in: *London Review of Books* 19/11 (5 June 1997), 3-8, here 8.

The historical imagination aims not only to reconstitute the past, but also to release the past so that the present is livable. The fact that Hagar and the comfort women are not erased from historical memory is a powerful testimony to the fact that an alternative vision of "social temporality"[20] is possible. Hagar, the Egyptian slave woman, was erased for the most part from the Hebrew scriptures, while the comfort women were covered up as a national shame by Korean politicians and historians. But these women complicate history, for they insist that slave girls and prostitutes exist in the same temporality with the master, the mistress, the military, and the powerful. These figures disrupt national history, mock the identity formation of a people, challenge sexual normativity, and resist any forms of erasure. Like the haunted ghost in Toni Morrison's *Beloved*,[21] they come back again and again to demand that their stories be remembered. They stubbornly refuse to submit that history is written only by the winners.

Memory is a powerful tool in resisting institutionally sanctioned forgetfulness. Too often, the memory of multiply oppressed women is inscribed on the body, on one's most private self, on one's sexuality. We have yet to find a language to speak in public about how the body in such circumstances remembers and passes the knowledge on from generation to generation. While French feminist theorists have debunked the law of the father, explored the possibility of women's writing, and urged women to seek their own *jouissance*, many Third World women regard such high-level theory as an excess and a luxury. The body, in an enslaved and colonial context, speaks a language of hunger, beating, and rape, as well as resistance, survival, and healing. It is not that the female subject is so marked with pain that she cannot enjoy pleasure, but rather that the pleasure she seeks lies not so much in asserting her own individualist sexuality or sexual freedom as found in white bourgeois culture, but in the commitment to communal survival and in creating social networks and organisations so that she and her community can be healed and flourish.

From reading the texts of these women theologians, I do not find that they rest their hope on the final *eschaton*, on an unpredictable utopia, or on historical progress. History for them is too full of ambiguities and unpredictable twists and turns to be constructed as linear, progressive, sprinkled with unchecked optimism. The hope for some of the disfranchised women may be

[20] See Homi K. Bhabha, *The Location of Culture* (Routledge: London 1994), 171.
[21] Toni Morrison, *Beloved: A Novel* (Knopf: New York 1987).

a place to dry their fish on the beach, enough seeds for next spring, or money enough to send their children to school. The future is not a grand finale, a classless society, or even a kingdom of God, but more immediate, concrete, and touchable. It may be the pooling of communal resources, of living better than last year, or of seeing grandchildren grow up healthy and strong. It is an historical imagination of the concrete and not the abstract, a hope that is more practical and therefore not so easily disillusioned, and a trust that is born out of necessity and well-worn wisdom.

Dialogical Imagination

> *The term* dialogical imagination describes *the process of creative hermeneutics in Asia. It attempts to convey the complexities, the multidimensional linkages, and the different levels of meaning that underlie our present task of relating the Bible to Asia. This task is dialogical, for it involves ongoing conversation among different religious and cultural traditions.... Dialogical imagination attempts to bridge the gaps of time and space, to create new horizons, and to connect the disparate elements of our lives into a meaningful whole.*
>
> Kwok Pui-Lan[22]

When I wrote the article "Discovering the Bible in the Non-Biblical World" (1989), I was interested in how an Asian Christian woman can enter into dialogue with the cultures and religions of the first-century biblical world. I said:

> The Chinese characters commonly translated as dialogue mean talking with each other. Such talking implies mutuality, active listening, and openness to what one's partner has to say. Asian Christians are heirs to both the biblical story and to our story as Asian people, and we are concerned to bring the two into dialogue with one another.[23]

In a certain sense, my articulation of dialogical imagination was an attempt to work through some of the dilemmas and contradictions of being "Asian" and "Christian." I want to revisit several of my assumptions again to see how my mind has changed in the intervening years.

[22] Kwok, *Discovering the Bible*, 13.
[23] Ibid., 12.

The primary issue concerns the subject who is doing the "dialogical imagining." The subject I had in mind then was very influenced by the construction of the Western liberal subject, unrestrained by social and historical location, free to create, to think, to mould consciousness, such that he or she can shape disparate parts into the "whole." As a doctoral student at Harvard, I was influenced by Gordon Kaufman's understanding of theology as an imaginative human construction and his Kantian notion of human consciousness.[24] The power of human imagination also undergirds Gadamer's "fusion of horizons" in which two different historical worlds or horizons can be fruitfully brought together.

As a postcolonial subject who has been thrown into situations not of her choosing and who has to negotiate different cultural worlds constantly, I have to admit that the drive to "imagine the whole" – a unified country, an undefiled nation, an intact cultural tradition – is strong and often irresistible. It is a longing for what one has never possessed and a mourning of a loss one cannot easily name. It may also be a quest for certainty that one knows is not there! While I do not wish to undermine anyone's desire for a meaningful whole, I want to caution against the enormous power of that desire – the lure of shaping things into one, unified, seemingly seamless whole. While such a desire may have the positive effect of resisting the fragmented and disjointed experience imposed by colonialism, it may also lead to the danger of reification of the past and the collapse of differences from within.

Although I still think that human creativity can often transcend social and historical circumstances, I did not pay enough attention in that essay to the analysis of the fragmented subjectivity or the multiple fractures of the colonised subject's mind and psyche in the imaginative process. In his response to my work, the late George Soares-Prabhu, a distinguished Indian biblical scholar, has written:

> Unlike a Hindu reading of the Vedas, or a Buddhist reading of the Pali Canon, an Asian reading of the Bible is never a "natural" reading, taking place spontaneously within a living tradition. It always has to be a deliberate strategy, a forced and somewhat artificial exercise, a reading against the grain, a challenge to church orthodoxy or academic parochialism.[25]

[24] See, for instance, Gordon Kaufman, *The Theological Construction: Constructing the Concept of God* (Westminster: Philadelphia 1981).

[25] George M. Soares-Prabhu, "Two Mission Commands: An Interpretation of Matthew 28: 16-20 in the Light of a Buddhist Text," in: *Biblical Interpretation* 2/3 (1994), 264-82, here 270.

My hope to bring the biblical and Asian traditions together through dialogical imagination may have underestimated the fact that an Asian reads the Bible from a situation of great alienation. And I did not sufficiently problematise how the "Asian story," which is so diverse and complex, could be brought into a mutually illuminating relationship with the equally multifaceted "biblical story." Throughout the 1990s, mostly due to my readings in postcolonial theories, I have rethought some of my own assumptions about the relation between "Asia" and "the West" – a process necessitated by the fact that I now live and teach as a member of a racial minority in the United States.

I do not believe that most Asian male and female theologians consciously or unconsciously construct an "essentialised" notion of "Asia" and proceed to write and articulate an "Asian" theology. Most of these theologians have travelled widely in Asia and any ecumenical Asian gathering, with its diversity of languages and national costumes, would show how any easy generalisation of "Asia" is doomed. The naming of theology as "Asian" must therefore be seen as a discursive and political construct, arising out of the particular historical moment of the recovery of political and cultural autonomy in the 1960s. Though Asian theologians might have vastly diverse understandings of what constituted "Asian," the deployment of the term signified a collective consciousness against the theological hegemony of the West and a concomitant affirmation that God's revelation and actions could be discerned through the histories and cultures of Asian peoples. The self-affirmation of Asian peoples as part of the people the God was crucial at that time and a dominant theme in Asian theology.

It is also important to remember that soon after independence, most Asian countries had to fight simultaneously against the legacy of imperialism and the centralisation of power by the national bourgeois or the military junta. In denouncing authoritarian governments and military dictatorships, progressive Asian theologians recognised clearly that the culture in any Asian country was not monolithic, but multifaceted and stratified. Thus, C. S. Song urged the use of popular myths, stories, and legends of the common people, and *minjung* theologians in Korea rediscovered shamanism, the mask dance, and political satire as resources for doing theology.[26] Such an approach differed markedly from

[26] See C. S. Song's many books: for example, *Tell Us Our Names: Story Theology from an Asian Perspective* (Orbis Books: Maryknoll 1984); Commission on Theological Concerns of the Christian Conference of Asia, *Minjung Theology: People as the Subjects of History* (Orbis Books: Maryknoll 1981).

earlier attempts of indigenisation, in which Christianity was brought into dialogue mostly with the elite or high cultures of Asia. When Asian feminist theologian entered the scene, they, too, paid special attention to women's popular cultures, for they were wary of the patriarchal biases in the elitist traditions.

The emphasis on the use of Asian resources, by, for instance, the Ecumenical Association of Third World Theologians and the Programme for Theology and Cultures in Asia, was timely and necessary because of the colonial legacy of theological education. Asian students were busy digesting the Tillichs, Bultmans, and Barths, while their compatriots were demonstrating on the streets or taking turns going to prison for democracy. For, sadly, theological training in Asia at the time continued the process of colonising Asian minds, even long after the colonisers had packed up and gone home. For Asian theologians who were trying to gain their own voices, Asian theology should have emerged from and responded to Asian realities, rather than reflect someone else's theological puzzles conceived in the far-away Western academy. These Asian theologians were not interested in creating a distinctive "Asia," the essence of which can only be found in the pristine past, undefiled by colonisation (as in Orientalism or nativism). Instead, they wanted to establish a dialogue with the living traditions of Asia, especially with people's religiosity, and with emergent issues in Asian politics and history. They did not construct "Asia" and the "West" or "Asia" and "Christianity" as binary opposites. The fact that one can construct "Christianity" – often understood to be a Western religion – by Asian stories and idioms subverts the binarism of what is "Asian" and what is "Western." Asian liberation theology assumes the posture of a "fighting literature" because it challenges and undermines the power of setting up rigid boundaries in the attempt to safeguard the cultural purity of Western Christianity.

Having said that, I would argue that in emphasising the use of Asian myths, stories, and religious resources (as opposed to Western influences), Asian theologians have not sufficiently theorised how Asian cultures have been transformed by the colonial regimes – be they French, British, Japanese, Spanish, Portuguese, Dutch, or American. The question of how colonisation has reconstituted or reconfigured Asian cultures has not been discussed with the intellectual rigor it clearly warrants. Since many Asian countries have gone through a lengthy period of colonisation, how can we conceptualise the complicated process of cultural encounter between the colonisers and the colonised? The many modes of such cultural interaction – parody, mimicry, hybridity, syncretism, double inscription, contact zone, translation, and transculturation –

discussed with profound insights in postcolonial literature,[27] have unfortunately seldom entered into theological discourse.

Moreover, the impact of global capitalism on cultural formation in general and on theology in particular has not been clearly articulated, because the analysis of the religio-cultural dimensions is often separated from the rapid changing socio-economic conditions, especially in the Asia-Pacific region. For example, some of the grassroots theological movements, such as *minjung* theology, lost their appeal and efficacy both in their own contexts and abroad during the period of economic expansion in the 1980s, when the so-called "Asian miracle" began to take place. Today, Taiwan, South Korea, Hong Kong and Singapore, for instance, can hardly be called "developing" countries. Indeed, some of the Asian cultural traditions have been revived to serve the interests of global capitalism (the Chinese silk changsam comes in vogue in Hollywood), and various religious fundamentalisms have been resuscitated to serve nationalist interests. In East Asia, the unholy alliance of capitalism, patriarchy, and Neo-Confucianism sustains the booming economy by supporting oligarchies of old men and by providing a flexible supply of cheap female labour.

The above analysis does not imply that dialogical imagination as an interpretive strategy is no longer useful in some respects, particularly in its emphasis on interreligious dialogue and interpretation as a creative process,[28] but it does call for a more explicit discussion of its theoretical grounding and a deepened engagement with postcolonial theories and cultural studies. In the face of cultural and religious pluralism, many liberal theologians have also used the model of dialogue or conversation as a mode to engage the "other."[29] In fact, the terms "pluriphonic," "multivocal," "symphony" or "assembly of voices" have popped up frequently in religious and theological discourses as ways to imagine inviting "others" to the table. But it should be pointed out that in our postcolonial world, all the voices are not equal and some cultures dominate

[27] See for example, Stuart Hall, "When Was 'The Post-Colonial'? Thinking at the Limit," in: Iain Chambers and Lidia Curti, (eds), *The Post-Colonial Question: Common Skies, Divided Horizons* (Routledge: London 1996), 242-60, here 251.

[28] I am grateful for Dr. Mrinalini Sebastian's comments at the "Post-Colonial Hermeneutics" seminar of the Bossey Ecumenical Institute, 2001. She affirms my emphasis on interreligious dialogue and as a literary critic, she stresses that the term "imagination" allows for creativity.

[29] David Tracy, *Plurality and Ambiguity: Hermeneutics, Religion, Hope* (Harper and Row: San Francisco 1987), 92-94; Paul G. Knitter, "Toward a Liberation Theology of Religions," in: John Hick / Paul F. Knitter (eds), *The Myth of Christian Uniqueness: Toward a Pluralistic Theology of Religions* (Orbis Books: Maryknoll 1987), 178-200, here 181-90.

centre-stage, with the power to push the rest to the periphery. The debate on multiculturalism in the USA has pointed to the inadequacy of its attempts to deal with diversity because it fails to confront the dominant white culture's power to define, appropriate, and assimilate minority cultures, in other words, its power to set the rules of the game. Following Homi Bhabha, I have come to see the limitations of *cultural diversity* when articulated within a liberal paradigm, which treats different cultures as mutually interacting and competing on the same footing in the public arena. Such an approach often assumes the stance of cultural relativity, which calls for cultural exchange, the tolerance of diversity, and the management of conflicts through democratic means. Instead, Bhabha uses the term *cultural difference* to underscore that the interaction of cultures in the postcolonial world is always imbued with power and authority. Difference arises not because there are many pre-constituted cultures existing side by side, but is manufactured through particular discourses at critical moments when the status quo is questioned:

> Cultural difference is not difficult, if you like, because there are many diverse cultures; it is because there is some particular issue about the redistribution of goods between cultures, or the funding of cultures, or the emergence of minorities or immigrants in a situation of...resource allocation.[30]

Furthermore, the tensions and anxieties elicited by cultural difference are always overlaid and heightened by the issues of race, class, gender, and sexuality.

Dialogical imagination will need to consider the theoretical challenge coming from the studies of the contact zone, which foreground the modes and zones of contact between dominant and subordinate groups, between people with different and multiple identities.[31] The interaction between two cultures with asymmetry of power is often not voluntary and one-dimensional, but is full of tensions, fractures, and resistance. The imposition of the colonisers' language, the institution of the Queen's birthday as a public holiday, and the naming of street and school as Prince Edward Road and King's College are but a few conspicuous examples. Many Asian people remain hostile to the Christian church, because it continues to signify the pain and suffering of the

[30] Gary A. Olson and Lynn Worsham, "Staging the Politics of Difference: Homi Bhabha's Critical Literacy," in: Gary A. Olson / Lynn Worsham (eds.), *Race, Rhetoric, and the Postcolonial* (State University of New York Press: Albany, NY 1999), 3-39, here 16.

[31] Mary Louise Pratt, *Imperial Eyes: Travel Writing and Transculturation* (Routledge: New York 1992).

colonial contact. While the creation of a new narrative discourse of Christianity through the use of Asian idioms and stories may be a sincere attempt on the part of Asian theologians, it can be seen as yet another reinscription of colonial power to further the tendrils of eurocentrism, if it does not self-consciously challenge imperialistic impulses. As such, it would be an ironic example of colonisation of the mind – this time, not by the colonisers, but with the full consent and complicity of the formerly colonised.

Dialogical imagination also has to capture the fluidity and contingent character of Asian cultures, which are undergoing rapid and multidimensional changes. We can no longer conceive culture as static, offering a secure group boundary and an unambiguous sense of belonging. Many postcolonial theorists and cultural critics have deployed travelling metaphors to denote the transient and unsettling nature and displacement which characterised late twentieth-century culture. Instead of speaking of the home or the roots, James Clifford proposes the *route* to capture the sense of "travelling-in-dwelling" and "dwelling-in-travelling."[32] Closely related to this is the notion of *transition*, which destabilises a fixed time and space, and resists pinning down by preconceived identities or satisfaction with ready-made answers. Provisional and going in different directions, the notion of transition is radically open to new spaces and questions. In a more religious vein, there is the time-honoured notion of *pilgrimage*, conceived either as an outward or upward journey, wherein one leaves the local and the familiar to search for the sacred, the global, or the divine. Whether or not one finds it is not the ultimate question, for in going, one leaves traces for others to follow and to critique. This brings me to the diasporic imagination, which occupies much of my current thinking.

[32] James Clifford, *Routes: Travel and Translation in the Late Twentieth Century* (Harvard University Press: Cambridge, MA 1997), 36.

Diasporic Imagination

> *It made the colonies themselves, and even more, large tracts of the "post-colonial" world, always-already "diasporic" in relation to what might be thought of their cultures of origin. The notion that only the multi-cultural cities of the First World are "diasporia-ised" is a fantasy which can only be sustained by those who have never lived in the hybridized spaces of a Third World, so called "colonial", city.*
>
> Stuart Hall[33]

Diaspora has increasingly become a global phenomenon because of cultural and economic regrouping after decolonisation, forced or voluntary migration, and transnational linkages in an age of global capitalism, communications, and transport. The term "diaspora," with its root in the Jewish experience, has become a travelling concept, appropriated by and extended to a wide range of cultural and geographical contexts: Jewish, Muslim, African, Latin American, Caribbean, Chinese, Japanese, Indian, Russian, Iranian, and so forth. In doing research for this essay, I was surprised to find that there were almost 950 entries with the keyword "diaspora" in the titles within the Harvard University library system. On the Chinese diaspora alone, publications can be found issuing from the United States, Australia, France, Hong Kong, and Southeast Asia in several languages. How can we capture and theorise the diasporic moment, which has become such a far-reaching global experience at our historical juncture?

William Safran suggests that there are several characteristics of the Jewish diaspora, which include: (1) a collective forced dispersion of a religious and ethnic group from the "centre" to two or more "peripheral" places; (2) retaining a collective memory or myth about the original homeland; (3) the belief that they are not fully accepted by the host land; (4) regarding their ancestral homeland as their ideal home to be returned to when conditions are appropriate; (5) the belief that they should be committed to the maintenance or restoration of the safety or prosperity of their homeland; and (6) continuing identification with that homeland, personally or vicariously.[34] Although Safran wants to create something like an "ideal type" based on the Jewish experience of Babylonian captivity and the Roman exile and their contemporary history after the establishment of the Jewish nation-state, when the return to the homeland

33 Hall, "When Was 'The Post-Colonial'?" 250.

34 William Safran, "Diasporas in Modern Societies: Myths of Homeland and Return," in: *Diaspora* 1 (1991), 83-99, here 83-84.

becomes a historical possibility, his description does not fit the experiences of all Jewish people at all times.[35] In particular, Jewish people scattered throughout the world may have constructed their "homeland" differently (and not just in Palestine), and secularised Jews may have an understanding about their communal myth/history quite different from orthodox religious narratives.

Since the 1960s, the term "diaspora" has been more generalised to apply to many contexts, besides the classic cases of Jewish, Greek, and Armenian diasporas. Such a development is the result of the migration of formerly colonised peoples to the metropolitan West, the weakening of the nation-state, and the displacement of people because of the massive transnational flows of capital and labour in late capitalism. Today, the term "diaspora" shares a broader semantic domain that includes words like immigrant, expatriate, refugee, migrant worker, exile community, and ethnic and racial minorities.[36] Diasporic discourse is currently appropriated by peoples who may not have experienced forced dispersion, who do not share the longing a return to the homeland, or who may shuttle between the homeland and the host land in continuous commute. It connotes at once the experience of de-centred and yet multiple-centred, displaced and yet constantly relocated peoples who criss-cross many borders. Diasporic discourse has become a fluid and challenging site to raise questions about the construction of the centre and the periphery, the negotiation of multiple loyalties and identities, the relationship between the "home" and the "world," the political and theoretical implications of border-crossing, and the identity of the dislocated diasporised female subject. James Clifford describes the situation of those living in diaspora in this way:

> Diaspora communities, constituted by displacement, are sustained in hybrid historical conjunctures. With varying degrees of urgency, they negotiate and resist the social realities of poverty, violence, policing, racism, and political and economic inequality. They articulate alternate public spheres, interpretive communities where critical alternatives (both traditional and emergent) can be expressed.[37]

In his important book *The Black Atlantic: Modernity and Double Consciousness*, Paul Gilroy attempts to write the diasporic history of black people in Britain,

[35] Jon Stratton, "(Dis)Placing the Jews: Historicizing the Idea of Diaspora," in: *Diaspora* 6 (1997), 301-29, here 307.

[36] Khachig Tölölian, "The Nation State and Its Others: In Lieu of a Preface," in: *Diaspora* 1 (1991), 3-7, here 4.

[37] Clifford, *Routes*, 261.

Europe and the Caribbean back into a history over-determined by African American narratives. He argues that black culture is multiply centred, diasporic in the Atlantic space, and cannot be narrowly inscribed in an ethnically or racially defined tradition. He opines, "The history of the black Atlantic yields a course of lessons as to the instability and mutability of identities which are always unfinished, always being remade."[38] He is fond of using the images of the ships and sea voyages to imagine the map/history of crossing, migration, exploration, and travel. As his images of travel and movement from place to place may reflect a more masculinist script, I want to propose another trope to signify diasporic imagination. It is the image of the weaving shuttle going from one end to another end, having to stop at each warp to decide whether to go on top or to go under, having to negotiate new ways of crossing and to come back from the opposite direction after it has crossed once. Each of these warps may have a different colour and texture, reflecting the multiple axes of gender, sexuality, class, ethnicity, age, religion, and so on. The challenging part is that once the weaver seems to have finished the weaving, she has to unravel again, to begin anew, or to re-invent herself.

I want to conjure a female diasporic subject as multiply located, always doubly displaced, and having to negotiate an ambivalent past, while holding onto fragments of memories, cultures, and histories in order to dream of a different future. Such a female subject may not easily find a language with which to speak, as the heroine of Maxine Hong Kingston's classic Chinese American novel *The Woman Warrior* has her tongue clipped. And when she speaks, she has to constantly spin and weave the Chinese stories, legends, and myths into the new fabric of American culture and history.[39] In *Joy Luck Club*, Amy Tan weaves a complex tapestry of women's memories across generations, with both continuities and ruptures and elements from here and there – the United States and China.[40] The texture of the tapestry is rich and thick because there are two weavers at the same time – the mother and the daughter. The intergenerational difference of the weavers is clearly shown, as the same story may be knotted and tied differently to the whole piece, one showing the front, the other the reverse side in a quite contrasting manner.

[38] Paul Gilroy, *The Black Atlantic: Modernity and Double Consciousness* (Harvard University Press: Cambridge, MA 1993), xi.

[39] Maxine Hong Kingston, *The Woman Warrior: Memoirs of a Girlhood among Ghosts* (Knopf: New York 1976).

[40] Amy Tan, *The Joy Luck Club* (Putnam: New York 1989).

Since the diasporic female subject is multiply located, it would require multiple tactics of intervention to unravel the dominant discourses and to negotiate a different cultural politics. In considering how to apply current theories in the emergent field of Chinese cultural and literary studies, Rey Chow demonstrates how the diasporic mind of "here" and "there" is constantly negotiating, shifting, and changing contexts. While she is skilfully trained in postmodern and poststructuralist theories, she is mindful that the postmodern moment may not have arrived in Third World countries, where myths of modernity are still running strong. While adept in French and Euro-American feminist scholarship, she is keenly aware that much of this work is done in a relatively secure and safe environment, which may not be able to provide tools to weave the complex tales of women crossing borders, constantly shuttled between tradition and modernity.[41] At the same time, she does not let the postcolonial intellectuals in the West off the hook, repeatedly challenging their assumed positions as "authentic" spokespersons or informants of the Third World, when they are less vigilant about their own privileges of class, education, and sometimes gender.[42]

The works of Rey Chow and other theorists in diasporic and borderland discourses have helped me raise new questions and make fresh connections in the feminist study of religion. If religion has been deployed to provide powerful narratives of "home" and "roots", feminists need to interrogate how such narratives of communal identities have been constructed leaving out women and others whose identities have been policed or negated. Judith Plaskow's classic text *Standing Again at Sinai: Judaism from a Feminist Perspective* is important not only as the first book-length work of Jewish feminist theology, but also as a heart-wrenching reminder of how women's participation has been disallowed or discredited at critical moments of the shaping of communal story and memory.[43] Plaskow's work points to the need for women to examine, however painful the process may be, the myth/history that a diasporic people have created and retold for survival and continuity. Bringing questions and ruptures to the "continuous" memory, Plaskow opens new possibilities for renegotiating identity and forms of community. At the same time, one has also to be

[41] Rey Chow, *Writing Diaspora: Tactics of Intervention in Contemporary Cultural Studies* (Indiana University Press: Bloomington 1993), 55-72.

[42] Ibid., 17.

[43] Judith Plaskow, *Standing Again at Sinai: Judaism from a Feminist Perspective* (Harper Collins: San Francisco 1990).

mindful of the complicit roles women have played in spawning the myths of origin and upholding the rituals and celebrations that put them in a subordinate position, while simultaneously giving shape and meaning to "home" in a less than friendly environment. Laura Levitt writes about her ambivalent search for "home" as a Jew in the feminist discourse and as a female subject in rabbinic discourse. She writes:

> This home was the site of a great many conflicting desires. It was a place of both comfort and terror. The knowledge that home could be both de/and re/constructed was visceral.... From the beginning I was engaged in a process of reconfiguring home on many fronts.[44]

Levitt's experience of finding herself simultaneously situated on the boundaries of different discourses, shifting in and out, is shared by Islamic feminists who must resist multiple axes of patriarchal marginalisation at the same time: globalisation, Islamisation, and local nationalisms. With Islam as a transnational religion and Mecca as the "home" of Muslims, Islamic feminists have to find their way through the dense web of significations of their national/transnational, religious, and familial narratives. Miriam Cooke observes that they have to reject the Islamic groups' using women as passive cultural emblems, resist the patronising "compassion" of Western feminists, and sustain their struggle through imaging an alternative vision of women in Islam. Since these Islamic feminists have to balance "their collective and individual identities while interacting with multiple others," Cooke argues that they have developed a multiple critique: "a multilayered discourse that allows them to engage with and criticize the various individuals, institutions, and systems that limit and oppress them while making sure that they are not caught in their own rhetoric."[45]

The image of having to negotiate with multiple others to develop an oppositional discourse and praxis can also be aptly used to describe a postcolonial feminist interpretation of Christianity. Diasporic imagination has to de-centre and de-compose the ubiquitous logic and "common sense" that says that the cultural form and norm of Christianity is defined by the West. It resists a

[44] Laura Levitt, *Jews and Feminism: The Ambivalent Search for Home* (Routledge: New York 1997), 2. Home as a place of terror is made more poignant by her being raped by a stranger in her home, as she discusses in her book.

[45] Miriam Cooke, "Multiple Critique: Islamic Feminist Rhetorical Strategies," in: *Nepantia: Views from the South* 1/1 (2000), 91-110, here 100.

predetermined and prescribed universalism and a colonial mode of thinking by insisting on re-territorisation of the West and by tracing how the so-called "centre" and "periphery" of Christianity has always been doubly inscribed and mutually constituted. I have argued that Christian feminist theology is an intercultural discourse. For example, the feminist consciousness of nineteenth-century white feminists was much related to their constructions of the identities and subject status of enslaved women and colonised women. They developed their sense of superiority by deploying racial rhetoric and by portraying women in the colonies as waiting for their benevolence and their "gospel of gentility."[46] Reading history cross-culturally, we can see the policing of European and American women's sexuality in the Victorian period occurred at a time when colonial and missionary discourse condemned promiscuity, polygamy, foot-binding and veiling in what has been called "colonialist feminism." A diasporic consciousness, which is located here and there, reads back metropolitan history and regimes of knowledge from multiple vantage points because people in diaspora are "outsiders" from within.

Diasporic imagination recognises the diversity of diasporas and honours the different histories and memories. The diasporic experiences of being a Chinese in the United States is different from those of a Chinese in Indonesia or in Peru. The Jewish, Armenian, Chinese, Japanese, and Asian Indian diasporic communities in the United States are different not only because of history and religion, but also because of class, race, and ethnicity. As different "outsiders" within, the diasporic communities can learn from others to forge new cultural, religious, and political coalitions. I have been interested in Jewish feminist discourse for some time because I want to learn how Jewish women have re-imagined their tradition, which is so much intertwined with Christianity. At the same time, as a Christian theologian, I have to pay attention to the charge of anti-Jewish and anti-Semitic tendencies that surface not only in white feminist theological reconstruction, but also in the work of Third World feminists.[47] But I have begun to see that apart from the "Jewish-Christian" axis, there are other axes that I can relate to Jewish women's experiences. In my postcolonial

[46] See my essay, "Feminist Theology as Intercultural Discourse," in: Susan Frank Parsons (ed.), *The Cambridge Companion to Feminist Theology* (Cambridge University Press: Cambridge 2002), 23-29.

[47] Amy-Jill Levine, "Lilies of the Field and Wandering Jews: Biblical Scholarship, Women's Roles, and Social Location," in: Ingrid Rosa Kitzberger (ed.), *Transformative Encounters: Jesus and Women Re-viewed* (Brill: Leiden 2000), 329-52.

study of Christianity, I have found anti-Semitism, women's subordination, and colonialism to be operating in the same episteme of nineteenth-century European religious discourse. The critique of liberalism and colonialism as two sides of the same coin by Laura Levitt has shed further light on the intersection of postcolonial critique, feminism, and religious discourse.[48] The imperial impulse of cleansing the Jews as the Others within Europe had much to do with the universalising of Western culture and homogenising the Others from without. The evolutionary understanding of religion in the late nineteenth century, for instance, was premised on Christianity's displacement of Judaism on the one hand and the falsification and misrepresentation of "other" religions on the other.

As a Chinese in diaspora, I also detect a "Chinese-Jewish" axis that features prominently in my own consciousness. Quite a significant number of leading scholars in Chinese studies in the United States are Jewish. My professor at Harvard, who guided me in the study of Chinese culture and listened patiently to my feminist critique, was the late Professor Benjamin Schwartz. A Jewish scholar of great learning, he had once spoken about the Dao of the Chinese in a Jewish synagogue. Some Jewish scholars, such as Vera Schwarcz, have found study of Chinese history to be a fruitful comparison with Jewish cultural memory in trying to construct what she calls a "bridge across broken time."[49] From the other side, the Jewish diasporic discourse and the critique of the narratives of "homeland" offer an invaluable mirror for my critical interrogation of Chinese identity, whether it is founded on the land, a "shared" tradition, or an "imagined community." The Jewish diasporic discourse, in its radical critique of the Zionist ideology and the questioning of the power of the state of Israel, offers profound testimony to the richness and strength of the Jewish tradition, which provides comfort and consolation in times of weakness and prophetic witness in times of power.

A diasporic consciousness finds similarities and differences in both familiar territories and unexpected corners; one catches glimpses of oneself in a fleeting moment or in a fragment in someone else's story. André Aciman, a Jewish writer originally from Alexandria who writes about exile, diaspora, and dispossession and who calls himself "a literary pilgrim" may well be right when he says:

[48] Levitt, *Jews and Feminism*, 51-62.

[49] Vera Schwarcz, *Bridge across Broken Time: Chinese and Jewish Cultural Memory* (Yale University Press: New Haven 1998).

We write about our life, not to see it as it was, but to see as we wish others might see it, so we may borrow their gaze and begin to see our life through their eyes, not ours. Only then, would we begin to understand our life story, or to tolerate it and ultimately, perhaps, to find it beautiful...[50]

Dieser Beitrag ist ein Beispiel dafür, wie eine asiatische postkoloniale feministische Theologin über Wissensprozesse, Wissensbildung und die Implikationen für feministische Religionswissenschaften reflektiert. Drei überlappende und miteinander verwobene Prozesse historischer, dialogischer und "diasporanischer" Vorstellungskraft werden untersucht. Historische Vorstellungskraft beschäftigt sich mit der Politik eines "historischen Subjekts", der Rolle der Erinnerung, der Ethik historischer Rekonstruktionen und widerständischer, sanktionierter Vergesslichkeit. Dialogische Vorstellungskraft beleuchtet sowohl das Problem, wie "Asien" und "der Westen" zu definieren sind, als auch die Möglichkeit einer interkulturellen Hermeneutik sowie die Frage kultureller Differenz. "Diasporanische" Vorstellungskraft behandelt die Erfahrungen von Exil, Migration, Immigration und Transnationalismus im Spätkapitalismus. Es untersucht die vielfache Verortung eines diasporanischen weiblichen Subjekts und zeigt auf, wie die jüdische Diasporaerfahrung zur Erhellung der Ausbildung einer modernen diasporanischen Identität beitragen kann.

Cet article illustre la réflexion d'une théologienne féministe de l'Asie post-coloniale sur le savoir, l'acquisition des connaissances et leurs implications pour les sciences religieuses féministes. Il examine trois sortes d'imagination connexes et chevauchant: l'imagination historique, dialogique et diasporique. L'imagination historique s'intéresse à la politique du «sujet historique», au rôle de la mémoire, à l'éthique des reconstructions historiques et des défaillances de mémoire résistantes et sanctionnées. L'imagination dialogique élucide les problèmes de définition de «l'Asie» et de «l'Occident», la possibilité d'une herméneutique interculturelle et la question de la différence culturelle. L'imagination diasporique prend en compte les expériences d'exil, de migration, d'immigration et de trans-nationalisme dans le capitalisme tardif. Elle explore l'ubiquité d'un sujet féminin diasporique et montre comment l'expérience diasporique juive peut contribuer à éclairer l'élaboration d'une identité diasporique moderne.

Kwok Pui-lan is William F. Cole Professor of ChristianTheology and Spirituality at Episcopal Divinity School, Cambridge, Massachusetts, USA. Her recent books include *Discovering the Bible in the Non-Biblical World* and *Introducing Asian*

[50] André Aciman, "A Literary Pilgrim Progresses to the Past," in: *Writers on Writing: Collected Essays from The New York Times* (Henry Holt and Co: New York 2001), 1-7, here 6-7.

Feminist Theology. She has co-edited *Women's Sacred Scriptures* and *Postcolonialism, Feminism, and Religious Discourse* and is co-editor of the *Journal of Feminist Studies in Religion*.

Eske Wollrad

Plus qu'à fleur de peau – Défier les constructions de la blancheur

"[...] de la parole tu bâtis le village mais du silence ho!
c'est le monde que tu construis."
Patrick Chamoiseau[1]

Le silence est un non-dit, qu'il serait trop embarrassant ou menaçant d'exprimer, peut-être même les deux à la fois. Le silence duquel nous construisons le monde nourrit le pouvoir, favorise l'opacité des structures violentes, et maintient l'écart entre "nous" et "eux". Créer une théologie féministe de la libération dans un contexte postmoderne signifie localiser les domaines du silence, briser leur pouvoir par des interventions critiques, et rendre étranger ce qui est admis comme normal, standard, universel.

La blancheur est un de ces domaines du silence. Actuellement au centre de notre regard sur l'appartenance raciale, elle est la condition normale, standard, universelle, celle qui fut forgée comme simplement "humaine".

Je vais examiner, ici, des interprétations de la blancheur sur trois niveaux, tous trois étroitement liés: la blancheur idéologie (la suprématie du blanc), la blancheur signalement (l'identité blanche) et la blancheur se matérialisant dans une expérience (la réalité du blanc). Je m'interrogerai ensuite sur le pouvoir qu'a le postmodernisme de modifier ces aspects, et s'il en a un, sur ce qu'il modifie, et ce qui, par ailleurs, demeure incontesté. Mais je vais, au préalable, esquisser les principales hypothèses sous-jacentes à mon approche de la blancheur.

1) La blancheur n'a rien à voir avec la couleur de peau ou une série de phénotypes. C'est un terme politique, une énorme force politique mobilisant l'action et l'interaction des hommes, ainsi que l'idée qu'ils se font d'eux et des

[1] Patrick Chamoiseau, *Solibo Magnifique* (Gallimard: Paris 1988), 137.

autres. Elle doit être, par conséquent, analysée comme telle. La blancheur fut dès le début utilisée pour légitimer le pouvoir et les privilèges d'un certain groupe au préjudice des autres, et l'est toujours.

2) La blancheur est un terme relationnel qui n'a pas de vie en propre et ne prend de sens qu'en relation avec la non-blancheur, notamment la "noirceur", le noir étant l'Autre, diamétralement opposé au blanc. La blancheur ne prend, en outre, une signification qu'en relation avec d'autres axes de pouvoir, tels que le sexe, la classe, le mode de vie. Il n'y a pas de "véritable essence" de la blancheur.
3) Il serait extrêmement dangereux d'amalgamer la blancheur et la totalité des blancs. Un tel amalgame ferait des positions des blancs des positions essentielles, et paralyserait le potentiel qu'ils ont d'actions réellement antiracistes, nourrirait des sentiments de culpabilité et finalement de refus.
4) Analyser le racisme en général, et la blancheur en particulier, sont deux choses différentes. Cette dernière implique un profond changement de sens par glissement de l'objet au sujet racial. Ou, comme le dit Toni Morrison, auteure africaine américaine: "Mon projet est l'effort de détourner le regard critique de l'objet racial vers le sujet racial; de ce qui est décrit et imaginé à qui décrit, qui imagine; de celui qui sert à celui qui est servi."[2]

À la différence des théories antiracistes qui concentrent leurs efforts sur ceux que l'on appelle les non-blancs, l'analyse critique de la blancheur ouvre une nouvelle voie d'assignation à tous, non seulement aux noirs ou aux gens de couleur, en général, des positions différenciées sur l'échelle des relations complexes et toujours changeantes entre les races, les sexes et les classes.

1. Idéologie: la suprématie blanche, le silence et ce que le postmodernisme ne changea pas

Au début de mon dernier cours sur "La blancheur et la théologie féministe", je distribuai aux étudiants un questionnaire comportant des questions telles que: "Vivez-vous dans un voisinage à dominance blanche?" ou: "Avez-vous déjà eu des relations intimes avec un blanc ou une blanche?" Aussitôt après avoir regardé la feuille de papier, une étudiante blanche s'écria: "Mais c'est un questionnaire pour gens de couleur!" Elle avait raison. Du point de vue d'une blanche, une personne vivant dans un entourage blanc, ayant intériorisé la suprématie des blancs, ne qualifie pas son voisinage. Un blanc ou une

[2] Toni Morrison, *Jouer dans le noir. Blancheur et imagination littéraire* (Christian Bourgois Éditeur: Paris 1993), 113.

blanche ne précise pas aimer un être blanc, en parlant de son amant ou de son amante. Un blanc ne parle pas de sa blancheur. Il n'a pas à en parler. Lorsque j'évoque un confrère ou une consœur, si je ne le précise pas, il est clair qu'ils sont blancs.

Du point de vue du sujet dominant, la blancheur n'est pas un fait notable. C'est un vide[3] ne pouvant se définir que par la négative, par ce qu'il n'est pas: exotique, sexuel, de couleur. Le chercheur blanc Ross Chambers parle de la blancheur comme d'un phénomène "aparadigmatique"[4], situé hors du paradigme de "race", puisque les études raciales ne se réfèrent explicitement qu'au concept de la *non blancheur*.

Des théoriciens racistes inventèrent, toutefois, notamment au XIXe siècle, d'innombrables "races de couleur", et s'inventèrent, du même coup, eux-mêmes (soit explicitement, soit implicitement) comme "blancs", reliant la blancheur à la pureté des origines, à la civilisation, à la beauté, à l'ordre, à la rationalité et à la maîtrise de soi, la définissant ainsi à la fois comme vide et plénitude, comme norme universelle. Toute autre chose et tout le monde devait se mesurer à son aune.

La puissance de la blancheur repose sur son statut aparadigmatique: elle est en dehors de tout cadre de référence, dissimulée derrière les mots. Le monde blanc puise son pouvoir dans le silence. Vous objecterez que ce n'est plus vrai dès lors que le système référentiel postmoderne ne présuppose plus d'identité cohérente de l'Occident blanc, que ce concept, en tout cas, fut fortement ébranlé. La question est, dorénavant, de savoir si le postmodernisme va pouvoir miner le silence pesant sur la blancheur.

Premièrement, la blancheur est un sujet public, produit et reproduit par l'extrême droite et les groupes néofascistes. Mais ce n'est pas à présent mon propos. Ce qui m'intéresse sont les représentations *quotidiennes* et l'établissement de la blancheur par opposition aux représentations et à l'établissement manifestement racistes de la blancheur.

Deuxièmement, la dernière décade assista à l'émergence d'études critiques blanches et à la multiplication des publications sur la blancheur raciale, notamment aux États-Unis. Ce que l'on ne peut hélas pas affirmer des théologies féministes blanches, tant aux États-Unis qu'en Europe (je serais heureuse que

[3] Voir Ruth Frankenberg, *White Women, Race Matters: The Social Construction of Whiteness* (University of Minnesota Press: Minneapolis 1993), 204.

[4] Ross Chambers, "The Unexamined" dans: Mike Hill (ed.), *Whiteness: A Critical Reader* (New York University Press: New York / London 1997), 189.

vous puissiez me prouver que j'ai tort). À quelques insignes exceptions près, je pense au livre de Mary Elizabeth Hobgoods *Dismantling Privilege*[5], les théologiennes blanches n'ont pas produit de substantielles recherches sur la blancheur et ses implications théologiques. Pourquoi?

Le nombre croissant de publications sur la blancheur incita quelques chercheurs à parler d'une "crise de la blancheur"[6]. Je ne suis pas d'accord. Je ne vois aucune crise de la blancheur, mais des retours aux discours raciaux perpétuant le silence sur la blancheur, à un niveau toutefois plus subtil.

De nombreuses théories sur le racisme se détournent de la "race" à proprement parler, pour porter leur attention sur la "culture". Il est intéressant qu'elles le fassent, en l'occurrence, précisément à l'instant où la blancheur commence à faire l'objet d'études pertinentes. Elles prétendent que nous n'avons pas à faire aujourd'hui à un racisme "classique" préconisant différentes races "humaines" établies, mais à un nouveau racisme fondé sur l'idée de cultures différentes, homogènes en soi. Ce nouveau racisme – souvent qualifié de "racisme différencié" ou de "racisme culturaliste"[7] – aurait supplanté le racisme classique, fondé sur la fiction de la "race" biologique. Il est vrai que le concept de culture comme unité ontologique mérite attention, mais une insistance excessive sur le racisme culturaliste peut contribuer à marginaliser un grand nombre de groupes d'humains, en faire des groupes sur lesquels s'exerce le racisme, et reproduire, par-là, un schéma indissolublement lié à la suprématie blanche, celui du silence pesant sur la blancheur.

[5] Mary Elizabeth Hobgood, *Dismantling Privilege. An Ethics of Accountability* (The Pilgrim Press: Cleveland 2000), 36-62.

[6] Voir Joe L. Kincheloe, Shirley R. Steinberg, "Addressing the Crisis of Whiteness" dans: Joe L. Kincheloe, Shirley R. Steinberg, Nelson M. Rodriguez, Ronald E. Chennault (eds), *White Reign: Deploying Whiteness in America* (St. Martin's Press: New York 1998), 3-29.

[7] Voir Etienne Balibar, Immanuel Wallerstein, *Rasse, Klasse, Nation. Ambivalente Identitäten* (Argument: Hamburg 1998).

2. Nous ne sommes blancs que lorsque quelqu'un ne l'est pas – Le concept d'identité blanche

*"Sujet d'examen: D'aucuns sont nés blancs
d'autres parviennent à la blancheu
et à certains la blancheur s'impose. Traitez ce sujet."*
Phil Cohen[8]

La blancheur fut, dès ses origines, toujours en mouvement, se réinscrivant sans cesse dans les changements d'acception du mot "race" des sociétés. Or, en conceptualisant la blancheur de certains groupes et en les déclarant *blancs*, la suprématie blanche ne s'est-elle pas elle-même inscrite en faux contre leur blancheur, à certains moments de l'histoire, selon les circonstances politiques, historiques et socio-économiques spécifiques survenues? L'identité blanche n'est jamais *acquise*, on ne saurait la *conserver*. L'identité blanche peut se perdre et s'acquérir. La blancheur est toujours un *devenir*.

Devenir blanc est un processus qui dure toute la vie. On apprend à voir la blancheur, un apprentissage qui requiert une énorme capacité d'abstraction, afin de mettre en relation une feuille de papier blanc et certains êtres humains. Les enfants font très tôt cet apprentissage, mais une fois la blancheur établie comme "pièce d'identité", ses implications sombrent dans l'obscurité. Le moyen le plus sûr de construire l'identité blanche devient alors le silence. Ne rien dire, c'est tout dire. Aux États-Unis comme en Europe, la blancheur est parfois mentionnée dans les théologies féministes blanches, comme une des identités de la femme blanche, mais à peine reconnue comme un problème. La blancheur ne frappe généralement que lorsque *d'autres* femmes, des femmes de couleur, notamment des noires, paraissent sur la scène discursive. C'est comme si elles "apportaient" avec elles la *cause raciale*, comme si elles la possédaient. Ce sont des femmes ayant à défendre une *cause*. Les théologiennes féministes blanches traitent d'ordinaire sans autre forme d'explication, de LA femme. Il va de soi qu'il s'agit de la femme blanche. La blancheur n'apparaît que par contraste, lorsqu'une théologienne noire est mentionnée. Les femmes se présentent alors sous le label *femme blanche*, bien qu'apparemment cette

8 "Exam question: Some people are born white; others achieve Whiteness; and some have Whiteness thrust upon them. Discuss." Phil Cohen, "Laboring under Whiteness" dans: Ruth Frankenberg (ed.), *Displacing Whiteness: Essays in Social and Cultural Criticism* (Duke University Press: Durham / London 1997), 244.

facette identitaire ne transmette aucune information nécessaire aux lectrices pour comprendre la position de ces femmes. Leur blancheur disparaît d'ailleurs dès que la femme noire a quitté la scène discursive. Nous ne sommes blanches que lorsque quelqu'un ne l'est pas.

Mais qu'est-ce que "l'identité blanche"? Poser la question, signifie déjà se situer dans le postmodernisme, et défier la cohérence des blancs, cohérence imaginée, construite par eux. Comment les théories post-structuralistes et post-coloniales abordent-elles la question de l'identité blanche?

Une véritable prouesse des théories post-structuralistes fut d'avoir libéré le sujet des notions de fixité et de pureté des origines. Les féministes post-structuralistes dépouillèrent, elles, le sujet des premières théories féministes, à savoir la "femme", de son essence, et le déconstruisirent. Les études post-coloniales et culturelles furent de même centrées sur la construction de l'identité raciale des noirs et des gens de couleur. À mesure, donc, que le genre et la race de "l'autre" (des femmes et des gens de couleur) étaient analysés comme des constructions discursives, la blancheur, construction socio-politique, demeura largement floue. Du silence nous construisons un monde dans lequel le moteur des projets raciaux demeure omniprésent *et* lointain. La plupart des féministes blanches et des théories post-coloniales laissent la blancheur indifférenciée, la situent parfois même d'un point de vue essentialiste. Tandis que le postmodernisme décrit les identités comme fragmentées, instables et fluides, l'identité blanche, elle, demeure le plus souvent homogène, cohérente et entièrement incontestée par les opérations de déconstruction postmodernes.

La théologienne womaniste Emily Townes soulève un autre aspect du problème. Elle critique le discours postmoderne comme étant souvent exclusif, et dit que les "catégories d'altérité et de différence peuvent dévier, dans le meilleur des cas, vers l'abstraction, au pire, devenir des instruments d'hégémonie."[9] Selon Townes, l'existence matérielle concrète et l'abstraction peuvent et doivent se rencontrer dans le postmodernisme.[10]

La blancheur est liée à l'existence matérielle concrète, à l'argent, à l'éducation, et a accès aux espaces publics.

[9] Emily Townes, *In a Blaze of Glory: Womanist Spirituality as Social Witness* (Abingdon Press: Nashville 1995), 49.

[10] Ibid., 50.

3. Représenter la blancheur – Le silence et le regard blanc

Je revient à quelques implications concrètes et quotidiennes de la blancheur. La blancheur n'est ni juste une idéologie ni un mode particulier de construire l'identité. La blancheur est aussi une réalité. Une personne étiquetée blanche peut compter sur tout un éventail de privilèges. La satisfaction concrète de ces privilèges dépend de sa classe, de son sexe, de sa nationalité, de sa culture etc. La blancheur est donc le lieu de privilèges relatifs[11]. L'un de ces privilèges est que cette personne n'est pas renvoyée à sa blancheur. Elle peut se soustraire à cette référence. Et pouvoir se soustraire, c'est déjà *œuvrer en faveur des races*. Faire le silence sur la blancheur est refuser une puissante réalité, et c'est en soi une conséquence du privilège blanc. Certaines représentations de la blancheur, ainsi, quand quelqu'un dit, par exemple: "Je ne me considère pas comme blanc. Je n'aime pas les étiquettes", sont des faux-fuyants.

Ce qui m'intéresse à présent ne sont, toutefois, pas les représentations verbales de la blancheur, mais davantage les représentations tacites, notamment le regard blanc. La critique culturelle indienne Raka Shome écrit: "L'un des moyens les plus opprimants qu'a la blancheur de marquer le corps de "l'autre" est le regard."[12] Elle continue: "Opérant dans une culture politiquement correcte de multiculturalisme de société, la blancheur apprit à camoufler son langage dans un vocabulaire politiquement correct. Son langage non-verbal trahit, cependant, encore un racisme insidieux dissimulé dans ses interactions avec 'l'autre'». Shome parle de cette "chose dans leur regard", les blancs, dit-elle, "vous réservent bon accueil, mais leur regard vous donne la sensation qu'ils scrutent les profondeurs de votre corps et vous font subir un examen. [...] J'ai toujours l'impression qu'ils recherchent dans mon corps la différence."[13]

Le regard scrutateur objectivant le corps des femmes noires et d'autre couleur, peut comporter une nuance de gentillesse en apparence. La critique culturelle arabo-allemande Nicola Lauré- al Samarai appelle sarcastiquement ce genre de regard blanc le "regard de solidarité."[14] Elle entend par-là cette

[11] Voir Ruth Frankenberg, "Weiße Frauen, Feminismus und die Herausforderung des Antirassismus" dans: Brigitte Fuchs, Gabriele Habinger (eds), *Rassismen & Feminismen. Differenzen, Machtverhältnisse und Solidarität zwischen Frauen* (Promedia: Vienna 1996), 56.

[12] Raka Shome, "Whiteness and the Politics of Location: Postcolonial Reflections" dans: Thomas K. Nakayama, Judith N. Martin (eds.), *Whiteness. The Communication of Social Identity* (Sage: Thousand Oaks / London / New Delhi 1999), 120.

[13] Ibid., 121.

[14] Entretien personnel, printemps 2001.

familiarité crue, qu'elle ressent chez des inconnus blancs, dont le regard condescendant semble dire "qu'il est bon que nous soyons sœurs" en lui donnant une tape amicale sur l'épaule.

Le regard blanc objectivant présume qu'il ne peut y avoir, par définition, de regard en retour. L'objet est regardé, le sujet regarde. L'un des mythes de la suprématie blanche consiste à croire que les noirs et les gens de couleur n'ont pas leur propre regard sur la blancheur et les blancs comme peuples *blancs*. Selon le critique culturel africain américain Bell Hooks, "les noirs ont partagé, depuis l'esclavage, dans leurs échanges, une connaissance *particulière* de la blancheur, glanée au cours d'un examen très minutieux des blancs. [...] Leur but était d'aider les noirs à faire face à leurs situations et à survivre dans une société à dominance blanche."[15] Hooks associe la blancheur à une chose "terrible, terrifiante, terrorisante"[16] et souligne qu'"aucune consolation ne fera disparaître le terrorisme."[17]

C'est à *l'âge* du postmodernisme, l'une des plus grandes gageures de ne pas élaborer de théories sur la construction artificielle du physique et de l'identité, mais d'intervenir pour remettre en question la suprématie blanche *comme pratique*. La pratique est la véritable sauvegarde de la suprématie blanche car, pour demeurer vivante, la blancheur doit être représentée. Il n'est guère étonnant que la critique de la pratique provoquât les réactions les plus violentes de la part des blancs. Selon Raka Shome, "les blancs [...] sont souvent surpris et irrités en constatant que le fonctionnement 'normatif' de la blancheur au quotidien soit souvent observé dans les moindres détails par d'autres."[18] L'étonnement, la perplexité et la colère pourraient être le point de départ productif d'affrontements sincères avec des regards à l'opposite pour lesquels la blancheur ne fut jamais la condition standard, normale, universelle. Se préoccuper sérieusement de ce regard est commencer à défier la blancheur par le biais de l'étrangeté, de la singularité, de la spécificité.

4. Conclusion et dernières questions quant au développement d'une théologie féministe de la libération

Nous avons à l'avenir besoin d'une approche de la blancheur passant par les grands axes du pouvoir, de l'espace et de l'histoire, et ces axes doivent se

[15] bell hooks, *Black Looks: Race and Representation* (South End Press: New York 1992), 165.
[16] Ibid., 170.
[17] Ibid., 175.
[18] Shome, "Whiteness and the Politics of Location," 123.

croiser. Nous avons besoin d'une compréhension non essentialiste et historiquement précise de la blancheur, ainsi que d'une optique théologique féministe distinguant les genres, car le racisme s'exerce *avant tout* sur eux. Le christianisme dominant inscrivit de tous temps la blancheur sur les représentations humaines du divin. Il nous faut donc d'autres représentations du divin et nous devons analyser comment la blancheur imprègne nos images de Dieu. Nous devons en outre étudier les traductions bibliques afin de voir dans quelle mesure elles introduisent les concepts dominants de la blancheur dans les textes et comment les commentateurs inventent un univers biblique stratifié, dont les couches sont des races. Il faut repérer dans l'histoire des Églises les traditions chrétiennes qui en idolâtrant la blancheur, fécondèrent les premiers projets raciaux. Révisons le langage de nos cultes et de notre vie quotidienne, et je suis sûre que le terme de "langage inclusif" revêtira une nouvelle dimension. Et enfin, je pense, non en dernier lieu, que nous devons impérativement nous interroger sur les sources que nous considérons comme cruciales pour la théologie, et les examiner d'un œil critique. Quelles voix font autorité dans nos approches?

Nous avons encore du travail sur la planche, et devons tenir compte de certains "mais". Car il y a de sérieuses questions à soulever.

1) Énoncer clairement ce qu'est la blancheur et en faire une étude critique est, sans aucun doute, une tâche majeure de la théologie féministe de la libération. Or, si nous, les blanches, engageons l'examen critique de la blancheur, ne perpétuons-nous pas ce que nous n'avons eu de cesse de faire jusque là, à savoir parler de nous-mêmes? Un examen critique de la question n'implique-t-il pas de recentrer le débat sur la blancheur au lieu de le décentrer?
2) Il faut proscrire la croyance en l'essence de la blancheur. Concentrer l'attention uniquement sur la blancheur comme fiction peut annihiler sa réelle conséquence, à savoir la terreur exercée par la blancheur au quotidien. Il serait extrêmement problématique que les travaux de recherche sur la blancheur deviennent une entreprise intellectuelle réservée à une petite élite universitaire, détachée de l'action politique concrète contre le racisme.
3) Que signifie l'action politique concrète contre le racisme? Avec qui acceptons-nous de nous coaliser? Où cherchons-nous les coalitions? Sur quoi sont fondés nos projets politiques? Sur la politique identitaire ou sur une colère partagée et la détermination de changer quelque chose?

En tant qu'antiraciste militante, je crois que l'action politique et le travail de coalition sont la clé du développement de la théologie féministe de la libération. La situation des femmes blanches est étroitement liée à la direction qu'elles sont déterminées à prendre. Les positions ne sont pas figées et nous pouvons, par notre comportement, obtenir autre chose. Dans une interview, Alice Walker, écrivain américain africain, critiqua la position soi-disant figée des blancs sous l'étiquette "blanc". S'adressant aux blancs, elle dit:

"À présent, votre comportement vous aidera à devenir quelque chose de complètement différent. Car vous portez un nouveau nom. Quel est-il? Que sera-t-il?"[19]

Traduction d'anglais par Annick Yaiche

Multidimensional analyses, the heightened awareness of difference, and the instability of subject positions intrinsic to a postmodern frame do not necessarily include the analysis of Whiteness as the power which organizes instabilities and re/produces "difference", "Otherness", and "diversity". Likewise, "feminist theology" is still the code expression for White feminist theology and – surrounded by "other" theologies marked as "colored" – it may or may not mention the term "White" without scrutinizing it. In this article I explore constructions of Whiteness on three interconnected levels: Whiteness as an ideology (White supremacy), as a description (White identity), and as materialized in experience (White practice). I further show how these constructions of Whiteness intersect with gender, class, religion, and lifestyle. That is, against an essentialist notion of "the White woman" Whiteness is examined in a differentiated way by taking into account the variety of subject positions White women assume within the matrix of domination. Finally, I call for a feminist theology of accountability, which engages in decentering Whiteness as part of a liberating agency.

Multidimensionale Analysen, ein gesteigertes Bewusstsein von Differenz und die Instabilität von Subjektpositionen, die einem postmodernen Kontext zu eigen sind, schließen die Analyse von Weiß-sein als jene Macht, die Instabilität organisiert und "Differenz", "Anderssein" und "Diversität" re/produziert nicht notwendig ein. Auf die gleiche Weise "steht" "feministische Theologie" noch stets für Weiße feministische Theologie und – umgeben von "anderen" Theologien, die als "farbige" bezeichnet werden – hinterfragt sie den Begriff "Weiß-sein" oder nicht. Dieser Beitrag untersucht Konstruktionen des Weiß-seins auf drei zusammenhängenden Ebenen: Weiß-sein als Ideologie (Weiße Vorherrschaft), als Zuschreibung (Weiße Identität) und in Bezug auf ihrem Niederschlag in Erfahrungen (Weiße Praxis). Er zeigt auf, wie sich diese Konstruktionen des Weiß-seins mit Geschlecht, Klasse, Religion und Lebensstil überschneiden. Das heißt, im Gegensatz zu einem essentialistischen Verständnis von "der Weißen Frau" wird Weiß-sein auf differenzierte

[19] Alice Walker, to Larry Bensky, en "Telling Secrets: An Interview with Alice Walker", *San Francisco Focus*, September 1992, 75.

Weise untersucht, indem der Vielfalt von Subjektpositionen, die Weiße Frauen innerhalb der Matrix von Dominanz einnehmen, Rechnung getragen wird. Schließlich fordere ich eine Feministische Theologie der Rechenschaftspflicht, die das Engagement für eine Dezentrierung des Weiß-seins zu einem Teil ihres befreienden Handelns macht.

Eske Wollrad fit des études de théologie protestante à Göttingen, Berlin et New York. Elle fit une maîtrise en Théologie sacrée à l'*Union Theological Seminary* (New York City) et passa son doctorat à l'université de Kassel. Son livre sur la théologie womaniste et sa réponse du point de vue d'une féministe blanche furent publiés en 1999. Eske Wollrad travaille au Centre d'Études interdisciplinaire sur les femmes et le genre à l'université de Oldenburg, en Allemagne. Elle a établi le "European Research Forum on Whiteness and Gender".

Sa'diyya Shaikh

Islam, Feminisms and the Politics of Representation

Introduction, Positioning and Context

I will begin by making my positioning explicit. My name is Sa'diyya Shaikh, an Arabic name. I am South African, born and raised solely on the continent of Africa, and my ancestry is Indian. I have to date, never visited India although the first language I learned to speak was Gujerati, an Indian language, and the staple diet of my family is still curry. I am most fluent and comfortable speaking English. I am a Muslim woman, whose existential, spiritual and ethical universe is based on an Islamic worldview, a religion whose roots are to be found in 7th century Arabia. The first time I ever visited the Middle East was on pilgrimage at the age of nineteen.

My coming of age was formulated within the socio-political context of apartheid South Africa. The aspect of my religious tradition that resonated most strongly in confronting this reality was the fact that Islam spoke to a humanity that transcended boundaries of race and that demanded human agency in the quest for social justice. In my confrontation with patriarchy in my social and cultural milieu sometimes paraded under the guise of religion and tradition, it was this same social justice imperative that urged me to struggle with what exactly constituted Islam and the Islamic legacy – and what it means to be a gendered human being as well as a believer. My academic pursuit of Islamic studies is premised on a view of the integrity of the relationship between intellectual pursuits, social responsibility and spiritual commitments.

By this extended introduction I am not only intending to situate my own ideological and personal positioning but also to make salient the notion of plurality and diversity encapsulated within the world of Islam which encompasses realities of people from varying socio-cultural and political realities. Therefore, my positioning is also an explicit rejection of those intellectual, political and popular idioms that argue for a homogenous religious civilization, a reductionist assumption that is most pervasively prevalent in depictions of Islam.

Within the diverse worlds of Islam gender issues have been indigenously engaged with, argued about, harmonized, problematized, synthesized, negotiated and re-negotiated in varying ways throughout history. In this era there are Muslim women and men who find Islam to be a source of human well-being and profound social egalitarianism. There are also however, Muslim women in many parts of the world who experience oppression and marginalization in the name of Islam. Currently one can find Muslim leaders who hold forth endlessly about the fact that Islam accords women high status and liberation while simultaneously promoting hierarchical and discriminatory power relationships between men and women. There are, however, also Muslim leaders who contest sexism and resist the masculinist bias of inherited traditions, many of whom relentlessly strive on the path of gender justice in Islam.[1]

Similarly, there are some Muslim women who have internalized the patriarchal dimension of their heritage and become its proponents, while, at the other end of the continuum, there are those who have exited the religious tradition as a response to experiences of patriarchal realities. Moreover, different groups of Muslim women come from varying cultural and geographical backgrounds so that a Jordanian Muslim women is often grappling with very different realities from an Indonesian or Senegalese Muslim women.[2] The realities of gender dynamics in Islam are as complex and polymorphous as the realities of women in other religious, social and political contexts.

Among those unwilling to compromise on the Islamic imperative to gender justice, there are some who define themselves as feminists, while there are others who do not sit comfortably with such an identification. Let me define at the outset what I understand by the term feminism: It includes a critical awareness of the structural marginalization of women in society and engaging in activities directed at transforming gender power relations in order to strive for a society which facilitates human wholeness for all based on principles of gender justice, human equality and freedom from structures of oppression.[3]

However, the current debates on feminism, gender, and women's rights in Islam are ideologically charged since they are embedded in a history of larger

1 In South Africa, the resistance of Muslim activists to patriarchy and sexism in their religious communities has been embraced as the "gender jihad".

2 For a discussion on the varying realities of Muslim women from different parts of the world see Azizah Al-Hibri, "Islamic Law," in: Alison M. Jaggar / Iris M. Young (eds), *A Companion to Feminist Philosophy* (Blackwell: Cambridge, MA / Oxford 1998), 541-549.

3 Qur'anic scholar Amina Wadud describes feminism as the "radical notion that women are human beings": see the preface to the second edition of *Qur'an and Women: Rereading the Sacred Text from a Woman's Perspective* (Oxford University Press: New York / Oxford 1999), xviii.

civilizational polemics between the Islamic world and the West.[4] Gender discourses in contemporary Islam are prefigured by the history of a political conflict between Islam and Christianity, the European colonial encounters in different parts of the Muslim world and the nationalist responses by colonized peoples. The processes of globalization in tandem, with neo-colonial configurations of power, currently pervade not only the concrete economic and socio-political spheres of most parts of the world but also the areas of knowledge production.[5]

From the perspective of many Muslims, Euro-American cultural hegemony remains coupled with a xenophobia directed at Islam and Muslims. This is reflected in the enduring legacy of problematic types of Orientalist scholarship on Islam, and on the popular level, the continuing stereotyping of Islam as a violent, medieval and especially misogynist religion. In many Muslim societies, gender issues have acquired a symbolic field which extends beyond simply redressing prevailing injustices to the politics of cultural loyalty.[6]

American scholar Gisela Webb points out that one of the unfortunate consequences of misrepresentations of Muslims in the West is the creation of a siege mentality among many Muslims.[7] This mindset reinforces a reactive and defensive posturing towards the West. Alternatively, in some parts of the Muslim world the overall ascendancy of Euro-American powers in an increasingly shrinking globe, together with a sense of economic and political frustration with local despotic governments which are sometimes financed by western powers, also contributes to strongly anti-western sentiment.

Akbar Ahmed suggests that Muslim religious leaders who adopt a blanket opposition to the West are "in danger of rejecting the essential features of Islam such as love of knowledge, egalitarianism and tolerance because these

[4] Clearly neither "the Muslim world" nor "the West" exist as homogenous or discrete entities. I am simply using them as descriptive categories to the extent that they reflect perceptions of shared identity among respective communities.

[5] For an incisive analysis of Islam and postcolonial relations of power see Majid Anouar, *Unveiling Tradition, Postcolonial Islam in a Polycentric World* (Duke University Press: Durham NC 2000).

[6] For a discussion of the politics of gender and identity see Lila Abu-Lughod (ed.), *Remaking Women: Feminism and Modernity in the Middle East* (Princeton University Press: Princeton NJ 1998).

[7] Gisela Webb, "Teaching Islam as a World Religion to Undergraduates: Challenges and Opportunities in the Age of Globalization and Multiculturalism," in *Religion and Education*, 25/1&2 (Winter 1998), 31.

are visibly associated with the West."[8] Moreover part of this siege mentality ironically contributes to an occidentalist view that perpetuates similar "othering" constructs relating to western immorality, greed and brute force. This type of dichotomous categorization of "Islam vs. the West" *à la* Samuel Huntington results in monolithic constructions which efface the complex nature of realities and multiple ethical discourses prevalent in both Muslim and western societies.[9] It also eclipses the reality that there are growing communities of Muslims in the West, many of whom are culturally western as well as religiously Muslim. These contemporary socio-political dynamics have especially strong ramifications for discourses of gender and feminism in Islam.

Legacies of Imperial Feminism

Contemporary Euro-American feminist approaches which reinforce reductionist views of Islam as a peculiarly sexist religion are seen as part of the broader western enterprise to discredit and misrepresent Islam. Ironically many Muslims also misrepresent feminism by stereotyping it with all that is considered negative and problematic in western culture. Azza Karam, a contemporary Muslim scholar, summarizes these tensions in describing some of the difficulties in using feminist discourse in the Muslim world:

> The term "feminism"... in post-colonial Arab Muslim societies is tainted, impure and heavily impregnated with stereotypes. Some of these stereotypes are that feminism basically stands for the enmity between men and women, as well as a call for immorality in the form of sexual promiscuity for women. ...some religious personalities ...have associated feminism with colonialist strategies to undermine the indigenous social and religious culture.[10]

Some Muslim scholars have reacted with blind defensiveness to this perceived western feminist attack on Islam. In legitimately attempting to repudiate the unpalatable and inaccurate stereotypes of certain Orientalist discourses, these

[8] Akbar S. Ahmed, *Postmodernism and Islam: Predicament and Promise* (Routledge: London / New York 1992).

[9] Huntington's argument regarding the inherently conflictual relations between Islamic and Western civilizations was first articulated in his article "The Clash of Civilizations," *Foreign Affairs* 72 (Summer 1993), 22-49.

[10] Azza M. Karam, *Women, Islamisms and the State* (St Martin's Press: New York / MacMillan: Basingstoke 1998), 5-6.

Muslim scholars have unwittingly become equally reductionist by romanticizing the Muslim legacy as one that has unequivocally empowered Muslim women.[11] This stance makes it increasingly difficult to approach the questions of gender relation in an honest manner, seeking to identify and redress realities of injustice.

Moreover, those Muslims who have invested in the maintenance of a patriarchy use the civilizational polemic with which western feminism has been associated in order to discredit and malign Muslim women who are involved in feminist activity as agents of western colonialism.[12] These accusations are particular charged due to the legacy of imperial feminism where missionaries and other emissaries of the Empires justified their political attacks on Islam and Muslim cultures by suggesting that their colonial "civilizing mission" was also intended to free the poor oppressed women in Islam. The ideological hypocrisy of this colonial narrative is exemplified by the case of the British Consul General in Egypt, Lord Cromer, who in the late 19th century was the champion of Egyptian women's unveiling while in his homeland, England, he was the president of the men's league for opposing women's suffrage.[13] While this reflects European men's manipulation of western feminist discourse in furthering the project of imperialism, many western feminist women were also enmeshed in the colonial mindset as reflected in their interactions with women from colonized nations.

A particularly illustrative case is the nature of relationships between the Euro-American and Arab feminists in the International Alliance of Women (IAW), an international feminist organization.[14] This group began as a western suffragist alliance; in 1923 expanded its focus to broader questions of women's empowerment and invited "eastern" feminists to participate. The ideological tensions between eastern and western feminists came to a head in 1939 when western members of the organization registered protests and appeals for the release of a Czech Jewish member incarcerated by the Nazis, but

[11] For a discussion of this type of apologia see Barbara Stowasser's examination of Shaykh Sha'rawi's work in Barbara Stowasser, *The Islamic Impulse* (Croom Helm: London 1987).

[12] Margot Badran, *Feminists, Islam and the Nation* (Princeton University Press: Princeton 1995), 24.

[13] Laila Ahmed, *Women and Gender in Islam: Historical Roots of a Modern Debate* (Yale University Press: New Haven 1992), 153.

[14] A detailed account and rich analysis of the relationship between the IAW and Arab feminists is offered by Margot Badran, *Feminists, Islam and the Nation* (Princeton University Press: Princeton 1995).

refused to do so when a Palestinian member was imprisoned by the British.[15] Arab women saw this as symptomatic of the double standards and ideological biases of western feminists. For Arab women the limits of international feminism became apparent due to the "failure of western feminists to confront imperialism and its negative implications for democracy and feminist ideals."[16]

Dominant strands of western feminism were subject to extensive and continuing critique into the latter part of the twentieth century, not only by Arab women but also from a spectrum of other women outside of the centers of white, Euro-American, privilege.[17] This body of criticism by various women, including African American, and Chicana women as well as women from the many parts of the third world, sparked extensive debates that articulated some of the central problems with second wave feminism well into the 1980s.

Third World Feminist Critique and Islam[18]

Many Third World women have argued that while the genesis and historical development of western feminism primarily reflected Eurocentric realities, Euro-American feminists regularly assumed that they could speak for the experiences of all women.[19] Feminists from the Third World and African American womanists argued that this presumption of a universal womanhood represented only the realities of a particular group of women, namely, First World, White, middle class women.[20] Such discourses marginalized and eclipsed the

[15] Ibid., 33.

[16] Ibid., 246.

[17] For such critiques see following collections: Cherríe Moraga / Gloria Anzaldúa (eds), *This Bridge Called My Back: Writings by Radical Women of Color* (Persephone Press: Watertown, MA 1981); Chandra Mohanty (ed.), *Third World Women and the Politics of Feminism* (Indiana University Press: Bloomington 1991).

[18] There is clearly no singular third world woman or third world situation. The term is used to describe the relationships of structural domination between First and Third World peoples while fully recognizing the diversity of experiences and realities among different groups of Third World people. It has also been used interchangeably with the description "women of color" For a more extensive discussion of defining "third world feminism " see Chandra Mohanty, "Cartographies of Struggle: Third World Women and the Politics of Feminism" in: idem (ed.), *Third World Women*, 1-47.

[19] See Valerie Amos and Pratibha Parmar, "Challenging Imperial Feminism," in: *Feminist Review* 17 (1984), 3-19; Chandra Mohanty, "Under Western Eyes: Feminist Scholarship and Colonial Discourse," in: idem (ed.), *Third World Women*, 51-80.

[20] A classic example of this approach in second wave feminism is reflected in Betty Friedan's *The Feminine Mystique* (New York: Dell 1975), in which the plight of women was described as the boredom and non-fulfilment of being only housewives who were put on a false pedestal

realities of women with different experiences and who came from diverse contexts. Subsequently many western feminists, particularly from the 1980s onwards, have acknowledged their own positioning and have significantly responded to issues of pluralism, representation and hegemony.[21] However I would argue that when it comes to issues of Islam and Muslim women, feminists more easily discard judicious analysis and reiterate negative stereotypes. Thus some western feminists, who would otherwise be sensitized to questions of diversity, persist in making sweeping claims about Muslim women or Islam without engaging the necessary levels of complexity and specificity. Moreover, as I will illustrate, such western discourses on Muslim women are predicated on unquestioned cultural and social assumptions which do not allow for the engagement of specific Muslim societies in their own terms. Thus I believe that some of the key critiques offered by feminists from the Third World continue to reflect the conceptual difficulties and ideological biases experienced by many groups of Muslims with regard to certain developments in western feminism. I will explore two specific dimensions of a third world feminist critique that apply to certain western feminist discussions on Muslim women, particularly relating to questions of cultural hierarchy and representation.[22]

and not integrated into the public sphere of work. African American scholar bell hooks points out that the "generic" woman described by Friedan does not remotely represent women of color or poor and working-class women who often had to work "as maids, as babysitters, as factory workers, as clerks, or as prostitutes and did not belong to the leisure class of housewife" [bell hooks, *Feminist Theory: From Margin to Center* (South End Press: Boston 1984), 2]. Similarly, Black South African women were often political activists, breadwinners and heads of households in Black townships where men were absent because of the politico-economic apartheid structures of the migrant labor system in South Africa which causes many Black men to leave their household in the search for employment. The effects of migrant labor include disintegrated Black families, urban prostitution, and a gender imbalance between rural and urban areas. Black women often become the heads of single-parent families and are left alone to face the rigors of earning an income, raising children and maintaining a home, often under economically and socially debilitating circumstances.

21 Much of the critical and vigilant work amongst Western feminists addressing issues of representation, difference and authority emerged in the latter part of the eighties and nineties. This includes works such as Elizabeth Spelman, *Inessential Women, Problems of Exclusion in Feminist Thought* (The Women's Press: London 1990); Nancie Caraway, *Segregated Sisterhood* (University of Tennessee Press: Knoxville, KY 1991) and Anne Russo, "We Cannot Live Without our Lives: White Women, Antiracism and Feminism," in: Mohanty (ed.), *Third World Women*, 297-313. This type of non-hierarchical scholarship was limited and marginal during the formative period of second-wave western feminism.

22 For a broader discussion of such critiques in relation to other Third World women see Mohanty, "Under Western Eyes," 51-69.

Cultural Hierarchy and Representation: The Example of Veiling

Firstly, within many western feminist discourses about Third World women, the standards of First World women have often been used as the superior norms against which third world and non-western women are measured. Often western cultural ideals are imposed on women coming from very different religious and cultural traditions.

Secondly, the homogenization of women within dominant western feminist paradigms relates to the construction of women as *a priori* victims and as "powerless".[23] This approach does not examine particular material conditions and ideological frameworks which generate a certain context of disempowerment for a specific group of women. Instead, various examples of disempowered women are used to prove the general thesis that women as a group are "powerless".[24] Women become identified as an oppressed group prior to the process of analysis. The crucial fact that groups of women are constituted through the processes and structures of social relations is obscured.

In exemplifying the way in which these two critiques of western feminist analyses apply to discourses on Muslim women, I will examine some of the popular Western understandings of Muslim women's veiling, head covering or *hijab*. While the term *hijab* literally means barrier or curtain, in this context it has come to signify the notion of concealing garments that women wear outside their homes in keeping with an Islamic ethics of modesty.[25] Conceptually it encompasses a range of different forms of covering that Muslim women adopt which are contingent on socio-historical factors and range from a headscarf to loose clothing to a veil.

It is certainly true that some discourses of the *hijab* are based on the coercion, the "othering" and the subjugation of women. This is most apparent in cases where women are forced to veil and are punished if they resist, as was the case for example, for Afghani women under the Taliban rule. However, this type of coercive discourse is by no means universal. Those western feminist discourses that represent the *hijab* as simply symbolic of Muslim women's subjugation misses both the particularity of such a phenomenon as well as the multiple level of meanings that it may have for different Muslim women.

[23] Ibid., 56.

[24] Ibid., 57

[25] See Barbara Stowasser's comprehensive discussion on the term and concept of hijab in her article "The *Hijab*: How a curtain became an Institution and a Cultural Symbol," in: Asma Afsaruddin (ed.), *Humanism, Culture and Language in the Near East: Studies in honor of Georg Krotkoff* (Eisenbrauns: Winona Lake 1997), 87-104.

For example, during the British colonial occupation of Egypt many Muslim women adopted the *hijab* as a symbol of their resistance to colonial definitions.[26] During the 1979 Iranian revolution many middle class Iranian women donned the *hijab* as a symbol of their resistance to the Shah and western cultural encroachment. The latter represents a very different meaning of the *hijab* from the post-revolutionary Iranian enforcement of the *hijab* on women. In a contemporary study of Islamist movements, anthropologist Fedwa el Guindi found that educated and professional Islamist women have deliberately donned the veil as an assertion of their identity which reflects a syntheses of modernity and tradition.[27]

Hijab within Muslim societies thus does not constitute a singular symbolic field. It has come to represent varying meanings within multivalent realities. On the one hand there are large numbers of women who believe it is a religious requirement exemplifying the Islamic requirement of modesty and they choose to wear it since they seek to be obedient to God. Other women have stated explicitly feminist and anti-capitalist motivations for their veiling. They argue that the veiling detracts from patriarchal prioritization of women's physical and sexual attractiveness. Moreover it provides resistance to a perceived western consumerism where money and energy are constantly spent in keeping up with changing fashions which in reality keep women hostage to their appearances and to the market.[28] Finally, it is necessary to remember that norms for dressing are socially and culturally specific and there is no reason that Muslim women's clothing need to be measured against specific western norms of dressing.

Moreover numerous sociological and anthropological studies have illustrated the ways in which veiling has increased female mobility in different parts of the Muslim world. In Iran and Egypt for example, the wearing of the *hijab* has neutralized public space for many traditional families, thus making it more acceptable for women to occupy such space.[29] This has lead to a greater female presence in various aspects of public life including the crucial areas of

[26] Laila Ahmed, *Women and Gender in Islam*, 164.

[27] Fedwa El Guindi, "Veiling Intifah with Muslim Ethic," in: *Social Problems* 28 (1981), 465.

[28] Even this is not universal since there is evidence that the Egyptian fashion industry has responded to women who are interested in a more fashion conscious mode of *hijab*. Accordingly, they have marketed all kinds of headcoverings which include berets and pillbox hats to be worn over the scarf. See Stowasser, "The *Hijab*," 87-104.

[29] See Ziba Mir-Hosseini, *Islam and Gender: The Religious Debate in Contemporary Iran* (Princeton University Press: Princeton 1999), 7.

education and skills training and has for the most part facilitated increasing participation of women in the public sphere.

The position that veiling reinforces the patriarchal assumption that public space is a sexualized, male space, so that women who enter it need to erase the femaleness of their bodies if they are to be legitimately present, is worth considering. However, it should also be noted that the reality of a sexualized male public space is not unique to the Muslim world: in many parts of the western world, one's visual space is constantly assaulted by pictures of scantily clad women advertising commercial products.

Ultimately in any study of dressing and *hijab* among Muslim women, it is necessary to look at the complexity of the varying narratives and to treat Muslim women as subjects instead of objects of research. Such an approach will prioritize Muslim women's self-understandings, it will look at the varying ways in which veiling operates in relation to women's agency, it will recognize sites of resistance as well as contradictions and ambivalence within the discourses, instead of treating it as evidence of the monolithic victimization of women.

Furthermore, to the extent that Muslim women engage this debate, there is much diversity in the ways in which we discourse the question, meaning and necessity of the particular forms of religiously appropriate dressing, a diversity which has often remained unrepresented in many western feminist discussions of veiling. One-dimensional western feminist depictions of Muslim women as always oppressed by the phenomenon of veiling are thus both misrepresentative and reductionist. An example of contemporary feminist scholarship on Islam that most aptly encapsulates both misrepresentation as well as victim constructions of Muslim women is the 1997 edition of a sociology textbook by feminist sociologist Linda Lindsey called *Gender Roles: A Sociological Approach*.[30] Whereas the titles for the sections on Judaism, Christianity, and Hinduism merely give the name of the respective traditions without any adjectives, the section examining Islam is titled "Islam and Purdah: Sexual Apartheid". This immediately reduces all the complexity of Muslim gendered practice to the issue of the veil which is a misrepresentative caricature of the complexity of Muslim societies and Islam. Moreover, it forecloses any serious engagement with aspects of this religious tradition which are potentially or actually liberating for Muslim women. These types of homogenization, generalization and objectification of Muslim women result in the perpetuation

[30] Linda L. Lindsey, *Gender Roles: A Sociological Approach* (Prentice Hall: Upper Saddle River [3]1997).

of dominant patriarchal and colonial discourses which freezes women and the colonized into rigid categories. Such approaches suppress the ways in which particular groups of women challenge, subvert and resist patriarchy at various points. They thereby undermine a politics of resistance and the construction of women as subjects capable of agency and transformation.

Alternative Paradigms

In reviewing some of the alternative conceptualizations of women, third world feminism offers a broader paradigm through which some of the concerns of Muslim may be articulated. Indian feminist Chandra Mohanty asserts that there are no monolithic "third world women" or "third world situations" for that matter. Rather the term "third world" is utilized as "an analytical and political category" which makes connections in terms of the struggles of women in the third world against racism, sexism, colonialism and neocolonialism in the context of particular balances of power in the world.[31] This definition thus refers to "a common context of struggle" which facilitates the formation of politically oppositional alliances and coalitions in the face of specific exploitative structures.[32] The alternatives posed by many third world feminists are premised on the understanding that the gendered social subject has a number of simultaneous social identities which overlap, interlink and position particular women at the nexus of different social hierarchies.[33] The recognition and representation of such heterogeneity is an initial and fundamental premise from which any study of third world women may proceed.

Similarly feminists working in the area of postmodern and post-structuralist theory have also contributed to the debunking of essentialist notions of "women" and "feminism". The postmodern approach undercuts singular feminist narratives through embracing cultural diversity, recognizing multiple feminist epistemologies and focusing on the specificities and particularities of the women's different contexts.[34]

[31] Chandra Mohanty, "Cartographies of Struggle," 4.

[32] Ibid., 7.

[33] See Desiree Lewis, "Feminisms in South Africa," in: *Women's Studies International Forum* 16 (1993), 538.

[34] Azza Karam warns, however, that even within this approach there are researchers who duplicate the older ideological biases of focussing on investigating the specificities of Muslim women's oppression rather than looking at newer ways to study the specificities of women's empowerment strategies: "Feminisms and Islamisms in Egypt: Between Globalization and Postmodernism," in: Marianne March / Anne S. Runyan (eds), *Gender and Global Restructuring* (Routledge: London / New York 2000), 207.

Postmodernism, third world feminism and critiques from other women on the margins has resulted in the development of varying understandings and different articulations of feminism over the last two decades. There is thus a reconfiguring of the contours of feminism that is more attuned to specificities of different groups of women and acknowledges the varying forms of feminist praxis. Within this type of fluid and dynamic understanding of feminisms, it is possible to detect a range of Muslim women's gender activism or Islamic feminisms.

Islamic Feminisms

While some Muslims eschew the term feminist, increasing numbers have begun to utilize the term to describe themselves. The value of retaining the term feminism is that it enables Muslim women to situate their praxis in a global political landscape. This in turn creates greater possibilities for alliances, exchanges and mutually enriching interaction between different groups of women. These connections enable varying groups of women to share and learn from each others experiences, whether this is an exchange of feminist tools of analysis, of varying ways of implementing activist initiatives or simply an exposure to other forms of justice-oriented gender praxis. Furthermore the usage of feminist language is helpful in that creates a finely tuned vocabulary for a constellation of ideas which are linked to a critical consciousness surrounding gender politics. To accept feminism as a western concept is in the last analysis to concede the most visible discourses around women's rights and gender justice as the property of the west and to marginalise the indigenous histories of protest and resistance to patriarchy by non-western women. Therefore I use the term "feminist" to refer to Muslim women's activities that are aimed at transforming masculinist social structures.

Muslim women with feminist commitments need to navigate the terrain between being critical of sexist interpretations of Islam and patriarchy in their religious communities while simultaneously criticizing neo-colonial feminist discourses on Islam. The fact that Muslim women resist both narratives, sometimes moving between their critiques, is a consequence of the way in which they are situated within this larger minefield. Miriam Cooke describes this adoption of different speaking positions as a "multiple critique."[35] I find her notion compelling in that it allows one to conceptualize the notion of dynamic and multi-layered subjectivities of Muslim women in varying contexts as well as the reality that one's speaking position is influenced by one's audience.

[35] Miriam Cooke, *Women Claim Islam* (Routledge: London / New York 2000).

However, Cooke's position and theorization of this concept also reflect some fundamental problems. She suggests that "the term Islamic feminism invites us to consider what it means to have a difficult double commitment, on the one hand to a faith position, and on the other hand to women's rights both inside the home and outside."[36] I would contend that implicit in this statement of a "difficult double commitment" is an acceptance of the assumption that Islam and women's rights belong to essentially different domains so that Muslim women bring them together strategically as "an act of radical subversion" as part of the "postcolonial women's jockeying for space and power" (as she puts it). This account runs contrary to the self-definitions of many Muslim feminists who see their feminism as emerging organically out of their faith commitment and whose contestation of gender injustice is more than simply the result of a postcolonial power struggle

Nonetheless the notion of multiple critique is useful in capturing the complexity of Muslim women's positioning. Most Muslim women reject those feminist discourses that have been implicated and continue to be implicated in attacking Islam and Muslim culture. However in relationship to our own faith communities, we are positioned simultaneously as critics of the assumptions of male normativity, and as female believers who present an alternative way of understanding and approaching gender relations in Islam.

Among the most revolutionary elements in the works of Islamic feminism is the view that feminist commitment are integral to their Islam and responsive to the core Qur'anic call to justice. The primary incentives for some feminist Muslim scholarship is the reality that there is dissonance between the ideals of Islam which are premised on an ontology of radical human equality and the fact of that in varying social contexts Muslim women experience injustice in the name of religion.[37] Some look at the way in which Islamic teachings are subject to social contexts and argue that patriarchal interpretations are the result of the exclusively male constitution of much of institutional Islam.[38] Others acknowledge the tension between patriarchy and egalitarianism in the Islamic legacy

[36] Ibid., 59.

[37] See the collection edited by Azizah Al-Hibri: "Women in Islam," volume 5/2 of *Women's Studies International Forum* (1982).

[38] See, for instance, Riffat Hassan, "Equal before Allah? Woman–Man Equality in the Islamic Tradition," in: *Harvard Divinity Bulletin* 17/2 (1987), 2-14, and Amina Wadud, *Quran and Women: Rereading the Sacred Text from a Woman's Perspective* (Oxford University Press: New York 1999).

but argue for the primacy of egalitarianism as representative of the spiritual and ethical ideals of Islam, ideals that need to be constantly worked towards.[39]

There is a significant group of Muslim scholars whose feminist work appears to be permeated with strong spiritual and religious bases. American feminist scholar Elizabeth Fernea has demonstrated this point on the basis of interviewing Muslim women in various parts of the world:

> Islamic belief is also the stated basis of most behavior I felt to be feminist. ... In Egypt, Kuwait, Turkey and the US, Islamic women begin with the assumption that the possibility for equality already exists in the Qur'an itself. The problem as they see it is malpractice, or misunderstanding of the sacred text. For these Muslim women, the first goal of a feminist movement is to re-understand and evaluate the sacred text and for women to be involved in the process, which historically has been reserved for men.[40]

Some Muslim women scholars have argued that while women indeed have multiple identities which are contingent on specific contextual realities, among many Muslim women there is an overarching sense that a belief in Islam provides a core existential ground for one's way of understanding the world, one's self and the ultimate purpose of human life.[41] This suggests that for some Muslim feminists, Islam is not one among many equally weighted identities but rather a primary source of understanding one's very being in the world. This does not, however, imply that all Muslim women's understandings of Islam are the same or that there is a monolithic Islamic identity that stands unaffected by other social, political and cultural factors. Indeed the manner in which Islam is understood and experienced in diverse contexts is mediated by numerous factors including national, ethnic, economic and cultural forces, although the essential components of belief and one's existential relationship to God and the

[39] See, for instance, Laila Ahmed, *Women and Gender in Islam* (Yale University Press: New Haven 1992) and Fatima Mernissi, *The Veil and the Male Elite* (Addison Wesley: New York 1991).

[40] Elizabeth Fernea, *In Search of Islamic Feminism: One woman's global journey* (Doubleday: New York 1998), 416.

[41] For discussions by Muslim women scholars on the centrality of Islam in their advocacy of gender justice and the rejection of secularist biases in some contemporary forms of feminism, see interviews with Azizah al Hibri, Amina Wadud, and Heba Rauf Ezzat in Fernea, *In Search of Islamic Feminism*, and compare also Maysum al Faruqi, " Women's Self-Identity in the Qur'an and Islamic Law," in: Gisela Webb (ed.), *Windows of Faith: Muslim Women Scholar-Activists in North America* (Syracuse University Press: Syracuse 2000), 72-101. Webb's volume is one of the best contemporary collections of essays by Muslim women scholars.

world, the five pillars of Islam, are significantly shared dimensions of how Muslims experience their existence, cosmology and eschatology.

Islamic scholar Maysam Faruqi points out that while many other dimensions of identity like race or gender are not necessarily subject to one's own choice, being Muslim in the world is a choice that implies a particular constellations of theological, spiritual and religious beliefs.[42] In analyzing this paradigmatic assertion one may argue this Muslim woman sees her religious identity as a primary identity which is then mediated by a number of secondary identities including gender, nationality, ethnicity, class, etc.

Whether Muslim women see their religious identities as core to their self-definition or not, I believe that it is accurate to suggest that Muslim feminists are committed to

> questioning Islamic epistemology as an expansion of their faith position and not a rejection of it...and offer[ing] a critique of some aspect of Islamic history or hermenutics, and [that] they do so with and or on behalf of all Muslim women and their right to enjoy with men full participation in a just community.[43]

Scholarship and Activism

There is currently a vibrant presence of Muslim women scholars and activists in various Muslim communities around the world. In reviewing varying types of Muslim women's gender activism in different parts of the world, feminist scholar Margot Badran has identified different modes of feminist expression among Muslim women. These are firstly, various types of *feminist writing* from scholarship to fiction; secondly, *everyday activism* including initiatives in social services, education and professions; and thirdly, organized *movement activism* including political and even confrontational movements for women's emancipation.[44]

Particularly within the last few decades, Muslim women are engaging some of the primary sources of the religious legacy, namely the Qur'an and *sunnah*, not only individually but also as a political initiative. Many of these scholars are deeply committed to their faith and religion and are invested in redressing

[42] Maysam Faruqi, "Women's Self-Identity in the Qur'an and Islamic Law," in Webb (ed.), *Windows of Faith*, 74.

[43] Cooke, *Women Claim Islam*, 61.

[44] Margot Badran, art. "Feminism," in: The *Oxford Encyclopedia of the Modern Islamic World* (Oxford University Press: New York 1995).

the male bias of the inherited legacy. Here one finds radical and illuminating understandings of Qur'an, Islamic law, theology, and mysticism from the perspective of women. For example, in contemporary Iran, there is plethora of emerging women's discourse on Islamic law and Qur'anic exegesis which contest women's marginalization in society. This has occurred most explicitly in the popular women's journal, *Zanaan*, where feminist scholars have explicitly contested and decentered the male clerics from the domain of interpretation and have advocated the reading of the Qur'an as a woman.[45]

Similarly, African American scholar Amina Wadud has authored a book which has gained international popularity: *Qur'an and Women: Rereading the sacred text from a Woman's Perspective*. This was first published in Malaysia and has since been translated into Indonesian, Turkish and Arabic and used as a formative text in approaching gender justice in Islam. Fatima Mernissi, a Morrocan sociologist, has not only provided a feminist detective work on retrieving the history of powerful women in Islamic history in her work *The Forgotten Queens of Islam*, but in her work *The Veil and the Male Elite* has also revisited authoritative *hadith* traditions regarding the Prophet and the early companions. Using traditional Islamic *hadith* methodology she illustrates that some of the misogynist traditions are inauthentic and have been fabricated to serve the interests of a particular narrator and respond to the historical exigencies. In the book *Women and Gender in Islam*, Egyptian historian Laila Ahmed focuses on the ways in which gender discourses evolved historically within the formative Muslim communities and examines how both patriarchal and egalitarian gender discourses have since developed within some Muslim societies.

On the ground, organizations like *Sisters in Islam*, which is based in Malaysia, have provided a critique of wife-battering from an Islamic perspective and have lobbied for stronger penalties for male offenders; they have also been actively involved in educational and consciousness raising activities among Malaysian women. In South Africa, the *Muslim Youth Movement* and the *Call of Islam* have promoted women's leadership including, *inter alia*, questions of sermon giving, mosque attendance campaigns, and gender egalitarian reformulation of Muslim personal law. In the United States, *Karamah*, Muslim Women Lawyers for Human Rights, whose members have varying levels of expertise in both

[45] For a detailed discussion of the politics surrounding the feminist exegesis that takes place in *Zanaan* see Ziba Mir-Hosseini, *Islam and Gender: The Religious Debate in Contemporary Iran* (Princeton University Press: Princeton 1999).

Islamic and American law, have worked to protect Muslim women from sexist applications of Islamic law while simultaneously working to protect the civil rights of Muslim Americans. These are but a few examples of the gender activism and feminist work of different groups of Muslim women.

I maintain that activities emerging from a commitment to the imperative of gender justice in Islam are crucial to the articulation of genuinely engaged and transformative Islamic feminisms. Rejecting colonial feminist representations of Muslim women as the "victimised" and voiceless "other", Muslim women are contributing to the redefinition of feminist discourse that includes the authentic self-representations of heterogenous groups of women. This approach is one which embraces the particularity of context and the multiple identities of women. By definition it makes salient the question of religious identity in the experience of Muslim women. It allows for the collusion of feminist discourse with Muslim women's articulation of their engagement with gender issues. It also creates the space for meaningful dialogue and "horizontal comradeship" between groups of Muslim women and women from other religio-cultural contexts.

Dieser Beitrag untersucht die ideologischen und politischen Komplexitäten, die mit Debatten über Frauen und Geschlecht im Islam einher gehen. Die Autorin skizziert Spannungen, die den westlichen feministischen Diskurs über den Islam historisch bestimmt haben, und deren Auswirkungen auf heutige Diskussionen über muslimische Frauenfragen. Aus der Perspektive einer Feministin aus der Drittwelt kritisiert sie die dominanten westlichen feministischen Erzählungen über "andere" Frauen und analysiert so die Art und Weise, wie Repräsentationen von Moslemfrauen oft implizit aufbauen auf dem Vorverständnis der Normativität westlicher Kulturprämissen sowie auf der Sichtweise, islamische Frauen seien weitgehend Opfer und besäßen keinerlei Macht. Die Autorin verdeutlicht ihre Kritik, indem sie populäre westliche Auffassungen über den Schleier, die Kopfbedeckung oder den *hijab* islamischer Frauen untersucht. Sie illustriert die vielfältigen Arten, wie islamische Frauen selbst das Verschleiern verstehen und es einsetzen. Die Autorin zeigt so, dass monolithische Konstruktionen, die das Selbstverständnis spezifischer Gruppen nicht ernst nehmen, das Handeln, die Subjektivität und den Aktivismus islamischer Frauen in einer Art verschweigen, die an das traditionelle Patriarchat erinnert. Am Ende skizziert die Autorin Alternativen, die eine egalitärere und fruchtbarere Interaktion zwischen westlichen und islamischen Feministinnen gewährleisten werden.

Cet article explore la complexité idéologique et politique qu'entraînent les débats sur les femmes et le genre (gender) dans l'Islam. L'auteur souligne les tensions qui ont historiquement marqué le discours féministe occidental sur l'Islam et les conséquences des débats actuels sur le thème de la femme musulmane. Elle critique, de son point de vue de féministe du Tiers-Monde, le discours dominant des féministes occidentales sur les «autres» femmes, et analyse les représentations des femmes musulmanes, qu'elle trouve souvent implicitement édifiées par conjecture sur les prémisses culturelles occidentales et leur caractère normatif, ainsi que sur l'opinion que les musulmanes sont en majorité d'impuissantes victimes. Elle illustre sa critique en examinant les convictions populaires occidentales sur le port du voile, du foulard ou *hidjab* par les musulmanes, et y oppose à l'aide d'exemples, les multiples façons qu'ont les musulmanes, elles-mêmes, de comprendre et d'utiliser le voile islamique. Elle démontre que l'abus de constructions monolithiques ignorant l'image qu'ont d'eux-mêmes certains groupes, en l'occurrence un groupe de femmes, concourt, à l'image du patriarcat traditionnel, à étouffer leur action, leur subjectivité et leur activisme. L'auteur esquisse enfin des solutions qui permettraient une interaction plus égalitaire et fructueuse entre féministes occidentales et islamiques.

Sa'diyya Shaikh is a South African Muslim woman. She is a doctoral candidate in the Department of Religion at Temple University. Her research interests in Islamic studies include areas of feminism, Quranic Studies, Sufism and interfaith dialogue. From 1999-2001, she was involved in directing and facilitating interfaith programs focusing on social justice issues for emerging religious leaders under the auspices of the National Conference for Community and Justice based in New York City. She is a long-standing member of the Circle of Concerned African Women Theologians and the Gender Desk of the Muslim Youth Movement in South Africa. She is currently teaching at the University of Cape Town.

Mary Grey

Must We Live without our Dreams? Believing in a Future from within the Ashes of the Second Millennium

1. Introduction

The title of our Conference – *At the end of Liberation – Liberation at the end?* – presented me immediately with my title. For, dreaming and envisioning an alternative world has been an integral part of Feminist Theology as I have known it since the immense surge of energy following its arising – *womenspirit rising* – in the late nineteen-sixties.[1] And what a challenge I have been presented with in dealing with the rich mix of ideas and theories of this conference.

Feminist Theology – at least as most us began to encounter its challenges – was born of this optimism. As we began to understand the struggles of our foremothers of past centuries the utopianism, the conviction that the forgotten and excluded contributions of women would fashion a better and transformed world has fuelled our energies and our hopes. Yet, as my colleagues have been telling us in the last few days, despite nearly forty years of analysis, of struggle in academy, faith community and in our own networks, the new heaven and earth continue to elude us. If world poverty is our gauge, then statistics indicate worsening poverty, with women's well-being firmly at the bottom of the scale. If equality of leadership and authority in the churches is our yardstick, while there is considerable progress in some churches, and some faith communities, the Catholic Church is in the midst of a seemingly unshakeable, intransigent opposition to women's leadership as the recent international conference over the ordination of women in Dublin, Ireland, has shown.[2] While there is much

[1] *Womenspirit Rising* is the title of the reader edited by Carol Christ and Judith Plaskow (Harper and Row: San Francisco 1978). It remains an important resource to this day.

[2] The Vatican prevented the ecumenical speaker Aruna Gnanadason of the WCC from presenting a paper, on the grounds that this would be seen as interference in the internal affairs of other churches. Both the main speaker, Sister Joan Chittester, and Sister Myra Poole were threatened with expulsion from their respective congregations should they take part in the conference.

progress to be celebrated in terms of access to education, to government posts and to many professions in some countries, progress is far from even and in some countries women's situation has regressed.

But does this mean the death of dreams? Here are two examples of the fragility of women's contexts: in 1990, at the *European Ecumenical Forum for Christian Women's Conference* in York a group of women from the former East Germany surprised many of us participants by performing a mime for the Assembly. We had imagined them euphoric at the fall of communism and alleged liberation of the country. Instead of this, we watched them walking in a circle, symbolising the loss of dreams. Now they were once more in the wilderness like the children of Israel. But one key difference – without a vision of the Promised Land. The socialist dream was dead – only the alluring and inescapable embrace of advanced western capitalism beckoned.

Ten years later, at a gathering at the Boldern Academy on the mountains outside Zurich, Switzerland, the consequences of not only political change but the war in the former Jugoslavia, Bosnia and Kosovo, and consequent re-mapping of the Balkan countries emerged clearly, as groups of young women testified as to what this loss of dreaming meant for them.[3] A young woman from the Ukraine laughed at me. "You ask about dreaming?" she scoffed: "Mere survival is all that we can even dare to work for." Deepening spirals of poverty, complete vanishing of hope and lives defined by the struggle to survive from day to day – all this sums up what they were saying.

But, as my colleagues have suggested, the sense that we have lost our way has come also from within the academic world itself. As feminist theologians *we* cite feminist *theorists*, but it is mostly a one-way traffic. As the British feminist theologian Tina Beattie put it recently, in her article "Global Sisterhood or Wicked Stepsisters: Why Don't Girls with God-Mothers Get Invited to the Ball?"[4] She criticises secular feminists for their "patriarchal blind spot" in not acknowledging the significance of Christianity (and the role of faith itself) in many women's lives. This point was made also by Elina Vuola in her

But, as Joan Chittester courageously said: "We will not let a little letter from Rome prevent us from coming and speaking!" (Martin Browne, "Women Raise their voices," in *The Tablet*, 7 July 2001, 1001).

3 Summer Academy, Boldern, Switzerland 1999: The Conference theme was: "A Cow for Martha – A Computer for Hilary: Women's Visions of Economics and Spirituality."

4 Tina Beattie, "Global sisterhood or Wicked Stepsisters: Why Don't Girls with God-Mothers Get Invited to the Ball?" in: Deborah F. Sawyer and Diane M. Collier (eds), *Is there a Future for Feminist Theology?* (Sheffield Academic Press: Sheffield 1999), 115-125.

lecture as part of this Conference.[5] But feminist theologians too are at fault for not acknowledging just how effectively the secular sisterhood silences women's theological voices:

> It is as if [*writes Tina Beattie*] Cinderella is pretending that of course she has been invited to the ball, and steadfastly refuses to acknowledge that she has been confined to the entrance hall while the ugly sisters are having a ball without her in the banqueting halls of the ivory tower.[6]

To enter the world of so-called mainstream theology, and male-dominated institutions, then, is to confront the painful absences of our work from recent key works of prominent male theologians (again with some notable exceptions). We are frequently criticised for remaining in a backwater and for not engaging more with the key theologians and theological movements of the day. David Ford, the Regius Professor of Divinity at Cambridge University, in a recent survey of British Theology, includes Feminist Theology as one of the "network theologies", which implies that this is the key identifying feature of what we are about.[7] Professor Ursula King (a former President of this Society, and personal friend and colleague of many of us here), wrote in the same collection of essays cited above of the need for feminist theologians to get out of their own isolation

> – whether institutionally imposed or intellectually adopted – and develop a more fully dialogical approach not only among themselves in different parts of the world or with women of many different faith traditions, but also from reflecting on their own experiences of solidarity and sisterhood on some of the burning questions of our time.[8]

I could continue in this vein. Has Feminist Theology become another orthodoxy with its own inflexible canons? Have what were originally meant as sharp critical positions with regard to the traditions now become obstacles to further development? Is Feminist Theology so tainted with European colonial superiority, with layers of racist myopia and false assumptions that it has lost

5 For the work of Elina Vuola, see her *Limits of Liberation: Praxis as Method in Latin American Liberation Theology and Feminist Theology* (Suomalainen Tiedeakatemia: Helsinki 1997; repr. Sheffield Academic Press: Sheffield 2001.

6 Beattie, "Global Sisterhood," 116.

7 David Ford, in a series of articles in *Church Times* (UK), 4 May–8 June, 2001. The issue referring to Feminist Theology is 1 June, 14-15.

8 Ursula King, "Feminist Theologies in Contemporary Contexts: A Provisional Assessment," in: Sawyer / Collier (eds), *Is there a Future for Feminist Theology?* 100-114.

all credibility? Have we – as another collection of essays, admittedly conservative in character, accuses – so completely lost touch with the transcendent, the Holy, that we do not deserve the word theology?[9] Or even the word "feminist"? Small wonder that, as my title suggests, that it could seem that we have lost our way – the plot, the dream, the transforming vision – and that we now seek a way to arise from the ashes of this confusion.

2. ESWTR: Focus on Context

One of the strengths of Feminist Theology/Women's Studies Theology has always been to take context seriously: the political, social, economic, ecological and cultural scene is not just the backdrop to our theology but has furnished a dialogical method. Over the last thirty years the tool "women's experience" has never been understood merely as limited to the world of the individual, but increasingly related to her culture, race, sexuality, historical background and economic position. Whatever the limitations, the criticisms and sense of failure with which we are confronted, since the founding of this society in Magliaso, Switzerland, 1986, this has been an unswerving commitment. In the first *Jahrbuch* of the Society in 1993 Catherine Halkes charted the long struggle that led to its founding.[10] It is important to recall what we owe to the efforts of the founding members and to the support given from various institutions for the birth of the society.

Since its founding, although the focus of the Society has been on the position of women in theology in the academy – however widely and loosely this has been defined – and the need to address the specific exclusionary policies, the economic or racial barriers keeping women out, there has always been a genuine attempt to enter into a dialogue with women's life-situations in a global context. Within Europe itself, there has never been a moment when our analysis and perspectives have reduced the continent to a monolith, or seen Europe as a seamless garment. The Society has always attempted to address diversity, change and conflict, sensitive to divisions south/north and east/west within and outside Europe. Over the last 15 years we have addressed the so-called "new Europe" from within and without its barriers and asked what

[9] Susan Frank Parsons (ed.), *Challenging Women's Orthodoxies in the Context of Faith* (Ashgate: Aldershot 2000).

[10] Catherina Halkes, "Towards a History of Feminist Theology in Europe," in: Annette Esser / Luise Schottroff (eds), *Feminist Theology in a European Context* (ESWTR Yearbook 1; Grünewald: Mainz / Kok Pharos: Kampen 1993), 11-37.

Liberation Theology has meant from this distinct perspective. We have confronted the challenges of postmodernism and noted ambiguities as regards the position of women. We have investigated Utopianism as we approached the new millennium. And now, as my introduction indicated, there is a sense not only that this Society has not achieved what it hoped for, but that also the entire enterprise of Feminist Theology is foundering.

My approach here is now threefold. I address the specific opportunities and threats of the contemporary context. I try to assess the critiques aimed at us – and our self-critique – from this light, and then will attempt to sketch the theological tasks ahead.

3. Globalisation: The New Context

Even though the word *globalisation* refers primarily to the financial and economic spheres, it impacts on the lives of women in many ways, with many serious, even life-threatening, implications. The ambiguity of globalisation – what aspects we want to encourage, or which we need to reject as disastrous for women and all poor communities – must be at the heart of our theological agenda. If you take a walk around the centre of any of the great European western cities at night, looking for somewhere to have a meal, you are confronted by a bewildering choice of Indian, Bangladeshi, Chinese, Thai, Italian, Greek, French, Mexican restaurants. You will equally be confronted with the omnipresent Macdonalds, Burger King, Kentucky Fried Chicken and so on. In American cities the choices are probably multiplied by hundreds. What are the issues – economic, social moral – behind what looks like simply a delectable free choice? Let's pursue this global picture of cultural mix a little further:

> A traveller across the desert wastes of Sahara arrives at last at Timbuktu, where the first denizen he meets is wearing a Texan baseball cap. Pilgrims in the Himalayas in search of the ultimate wilderness in the furthest kingdom find Everest strewn with rubbish, in tins, plastic bags, Coca-Cola bottles and all the remnants of the modern global picnicker. Explorers of the Arctic complain that empty plastic bottles of washing up liquid are embedded in the ice. Tony Giddens opened his Reith lectures with the tale of an anthropologist trekking to a remote corner of Cambodia for a field study, only to find her first night's entertainment was not traditional local pastimes, but a viewing of *Basic Instinct* on video. The film, at this point, had not even reached the cinemas in London.[11]

[11] Polly Toynbee, "Who's Afraid of Global Culture?" in: Anthony Giddens / Will Hutton (eds), *On the Edge: Living with Global Capitalism* (Jonathan Cape: London 2000), 191-212, here 191.

There we have it: globalisation in all its ambiguity. Globalisation has thousands of expressions; as Canadian eco-feminist Heather Eaton writes,

> Ideologically, it appeals to a sense of adventure, entrepreneurship and superiority; with inviting expressions about global prospects for business, such as "gateways to the world, go global, track global competition, spread global wings, crossing international borders, and becoming master of one's domain."[12]

Anthony Giddens identifies several key meanings of globalisation: the worldwide communication revolution, the "weightless economy" or "the new knowledge economy" with financial markets at its leading edge.[13] We might want to argue that it is this factor which is the crucial and all-encompassing one, with financial markets open 24 hours a day, with the trend in the north and west for 24 hours a day open supermarkets. Thirdly, it refers to a post-1989 world, that is, a world after the fall of communism, at least in Europe. And, fourthly, transformations happening on the level of everyday life. One of the characteristics of this they consider to be the improved situation of women and the growing equality between women and men. (We might want to challenge what this means in different contexts.) The striking uniting fact for all these four points is that these changes are global and all-encompassing:

> All borders are coming down-economic, political and social. There is a new conception of time, risk and opportunity.[14]

> Globalisation is so powerful an idea because of the sense of there being no escape. Its coming down the tracks straight at you...The food and chemical industries are coalescing; so are banking and insurance; so are information technology and television.[15]

and then, a sinister note:

> But don't forget globalisation also means the globalisation of crimes, drugs and the like. The Mafia now operates globally. Laundering drugs money is a global business.

[12] Heather Eaton, "Ecofeminism and Globalisation," in: *Feminist Theology* 24 (May 2000), 21-43, here 43.

[13] Giddens, "Anthony Giddens and Will Hutton in Conversation," in: Giddens / Hutton (eds), *On the Edge*, 1-51; here 1-2.

[14] Ibid., 3.

[15] Ibid., 4.

> There are real fears that the laundering of Russian Mafia cash could pollute the entire Western banking system. And any police response has to be global too.

Arguing critically and more historically, globalisation is nothing new.[16] The present scene has certainly been prepared for by five centuries of social, economic and political domination.[17] For example, before the 16th century, there were of course great powers in the world, there were conquering powers (the Roman empire, the Mogul empire, the Chinese), although they were not global powers, in the way the US is now. The system we are dealing with began with the expansion of western economic interests, western political domination. Most of the great corporations that now rule the world began to mushroom from the middle to the end of the 19th century. This marked the transition from a more organic economy to an extractive economy of mining.[18]

Key features of this global capitalism are:

- its dominating aim: it aims to subordinate every other interest. This domination is deliberate, systemic, hierarchical and patriarchal.
- it has an instrumental character. It controls the development of science and technology, aiming to manage nature (space) – think of the GM food controversy – and history (time). The results of this are an accumulation of things, artefacts, machines, gadgets without which, so we are persuaded, it is impossible to live, and without which it is impossible for our children to live. Even though one of the myths it relies on is that of endless growth, progress, change, optimistic spin on culture, in its male-dominated character it is no different – despite the earlier rhetoric of gender equality – from the patriarchal orientation of pre-modern, pre-capitalist societies.
- It is ambiguous. Iulio de Santa Ana writes:
  It aims at freedom, but imposes oppression. It aims at happiness, but creates pain and suffering. It says that it affirms life, but it brings death. ... It deals more with having than with being, but it is a having that influences the being.[19]
- Finally, even if it is a process where different projects co-exist, one project has always dominated, and still continues to dominate. This project has a

[16] For this section I am indebted to Julio de Santa Ana's analysis of globalisation, presented at the *Kairos 2000* colloquium, Hofgeismar, June 2000. (Available on Internet: www/econ-theo.org/).

[17] See especially the paper by Kwok Pui-Lan in this volume.

[18] See Thomas Berry, *The Great Work* (Bell Tower: New York 1999).

[19] See Iulio De Santa Ana, www.econ-theo.org.

fascinating almost bewitching effect on us. Capitalism is the new religion in its idolatry of money. It has hijacked our imaginations and desires. And it is global. There is no space where you can stand outside it. (Or at least, that is what we are made to think.)

The net result is, as eco-feminist Vandana Shiva has pointed out, that

> With globalisation, life itself has emerged as the ultimate commodity. Planet Earth is being replaced by Life Inc. in the world of free trade and deregulated commerce. Through patents and genetic engineering, new colonies are being carved out.[20]

If the 20th century was the petroleum century, she argues, the 21st will be the century of biology. This has a direct impact on the theological enterprise since there has been a loss of diversity in the meaning of "life", which has shrunk to the business model of life:

> Implicit is that business is the greatest possible model of life; far superior to governments, nationalities, cultures etc. There is no talk of differentiated and diverse cultures of people, of ethnicity or gender, of animals and land, of national or international regulations or indeed that there is any genuine limitation to this frontier of capital exchange. This "globe" of which they speak is an utter abstraction with no accountability to anything but economics.[21]

Even then, it is a drastically shrunken notion of what economics is. Women's contribution is certainly not factored in. Alongside all this what we are facing – and the thousands of demonstrators, women and men of all ages in Genoa, in Seattle, in Davos, in Cologne are risking lives to make this point, as the recent violence in Genoa makes all too clear – is the threat to democracy by the power being given to the global corporations. Corporations are the new colonisers everywhere, controlling education programmes, television, art, energy, agriculture, even the cultural and religious symbols in which our values are enshrined, promising happiness and redemption in this car, gadget, bathroom, holiday, jewels or clothing. There is no aspect of personal or communal life which is not targeted.

Because of the all-consuming mandate for profit, environmental, health and safety hazards are ignored. There are disastrous consequences for the lives of

[20] Vandana Shiva, "The World on the Edge," in: Gidden / Hutton (eds), *On the Edge*, 112-119, here 118.

[21] Eaton, "Ecofeminism and Globalisation," 43.

poor women. From Saigon to San Francisco, from Calcutta to the former East Germany, the lives of poor women have been reduced to grinding poverty, to slave labour in inhuman conditions.

To summarise, we may have lost our dreams, but "the world of global dreamers" is colonising the dreaming space, in which:

- The world's money, technology, and markets are controlled and managed by gigantic global corporations;
- A common consumer culture unifies all people in a shared quest for material gratification;
- There is perfect global competition among workers and localities to offer their services to investors at the most advantageous terms;
- corporation are free to act solely on the basis of profitability without regard to national or local consequences;
- Relationships, both individual and corporate, are defined entirely by the market;
- There are no loyalties to place or community.[22]

4. What have we achieved?

The overall message of those six points is that it becomes urgent that there is a theological and spiritual response. Global capitalism and the systems I am describing are occupying the ground that religion should occupy. They have assumed the status of a world religion and demand an effective spiritual response, and not a response that ducks the issue. No wonder that we lose the dream: capitalism is dreaming for us with all the seductive power of bad dreams! Any theology in this context must be subversive theology. Feminist theology has to recover its own subversive role in this response and even make new coalitions and alliances in order to do so. Secondly, it is important to distinguish between what we have genuinely achieved – and celebrate this – and what we have failed to do. Within the latter, we need to understand the complexities of the reasons for so-called "failure".

The greatest achievement – as I see it – is that no-one can speak of *feminist theology* any more. Not because it is not important, but because we have truly become a family of global contextual theologies. (In this sense the label of *network theologies* is correct, except that networking is not all that we do). Just to give one illustration: Rosemary Ruether's book *Women and Redemption*

[22] David Korten, *When Corporations Rule the World* (Earthscan: London 1995), 131.

discusses theology of redemption globally and contextually from within real situations of women's communities, letting women's voices speak for themselves.[23] I know of no similar book from a male theologian giving such attention to global context. David Ford's recent and acclaimed book *Self and Salvation* makes almost no reference to works of Feminist theology.[24] What I note as a challenge for the future is the need for better networking within Europe itself, in all its new contours, of the kinds of theologies that women are doing. Some of the discussions in this conference point to the specific problems arising from the very richness of the diversity among us. The Women's Commission of EATWOT and some of the national networks are better at this kind of fluid organisation than we are, and the geographical areas they cover are far larger.

Secondly, the *tools* and *methods* around which we organised are still vital. Experience in its increasingly complex interlocking varieties and related to contextual factors, narrative/story, recovery of lost historical memories, of dangerous memories – these remain well-used and reliable tools. We owe a great debt, for example, to the historians who have recovered so many of the lost traditions of women's leadership in all our countries. It is within the historical memory of our own Society that the Rhineland mystics, the Flemish mystics, the Beguines, the foundresses of religious congregations throughout Europe, the Jewish women who resisted the Holocaust, Celtic women saints, Islamic women leaders in Europe, Islamic and Jewish biblical female traditions have been restored to the public arena, both in the world of scholarship and in more popular domains.

Thirdly, *praxis* remains a contested area. From Latin American theology – especially that of from Gustavo Gutiérrez – we learnt that theology is a second order activity. To cite David Ford again, "feminist theology is a *praxis* theology."[25] He presumably means that Feminist Theology wants to changes things, especially unjust systems, and that it is consequently in dialogue with world order. This includes the positive dimension that Feminist Theology has always considered itself a critical theology of liberation,[26] but also has a

[23] Rosemary Radford Ruether, *Women and Redemption* (SCM: London 1998).

[24] David Ford, *Self and Salvation* (Cambridge University Press: Cambridge 1999). The exception is the use made of Constance Fitzgerald's study of Thérèse of Lisieux.

[25] David Ford, "A Long Rumour of Wisdom," Inaugural Lecture, Cambridge, 1992.

[26] See Elizabeth Schüssler Fiorenza, "Feminist Theology as a Critical Theology of Liberation," in: *Theological Studies* (1975), 606-626; Mary Grey, "Feminist Theology: a Critical Theology of Liberation," in: Christopher Rowland (ed.), *The Cambridge Companion to Liberation Theology* (Cambridge University Press: Cambridge 1999), 89-106.

negative implication, one that includes all liberation theologies. If their intent is political justice, then they are reductionist, empty of theological content – so the criticism goes – and what they are doing is not real theology, which must be about God. This I will return to as a contemporary challenge. But as regards achievement, *praxis* must still be a key category which redeems theology itself from the dusts of abstraction and irrelevance. In their papers in this volume, Eske Wolrad calls for a praxis to eliminate the practice of white superiority. Sa'diyya Shaikh wants to situate the term "Third World Feminism" in praxis in a global context. Where *praxis* works as conceptual tool, it offers beacons of hope in the new desolations that women are confronting.

Fourthly, we need to remember and celebrate that we have been listened to and do make a difference, even if this is more modest than we might have hoped. In 1995 the Superior General of the Jesuit Order promulgated 26 Decrees of the Congregation of the Society. The 14th Decree was titled "Jesuits and the Position of Women in the Church and the Civil society".[27] It calls for a process of conversion, the first step of which is an attentive listening to women:

> Many women feel that men do not listen to them. There is no substitute for this listening. More than anything else it will bring about change. Unless we listen, any action we may take in this area, no matter how well-intentioned, is likely to bypass the real concerns of women and to confirm male condescension and to reinforce male dominance.[28]

Nor is this mere verbiage. The decree then outlines eight steps following from this process of listening.[29] Commitment in such a key document is indeed a major step: but there are many other signs that our work is taken seriously even if there is no explicit attribution to Feminist Theology. Words like compassion, empathy, vulnerability, mutuality begin to be commonly used; inclusive language in *some* circles at least is welcomed; the "discipleship of equals" of Schüssler Fiorenza is often cited as calling for a new ecclesiology; the feminist discourse on embodiment has inspired the gendered approach to sexuality as well as kick-starting the re-thinking of masculinity. There may be no explicit

[27] See James Hanvey SJ, "Healing the Wound: Discourses of Redemption," in: Parsons (ed.), *Challenging Women's Orthodoxies*, 205-222.

[28] Ibid., 205.

[29] These include explicitly teaching the equality of women in Jesuit ministries, supporting movements that oppose the exploitation of women, respectful co-operation with female colleagues in shared projects, and the use of inclusive language. Cited in Hanvey, 206.

attribution to the work of Feminist Theologians – but, what is it we seek? Compliments or genuine change?

If I were to choose two themes from feminist theological activity that now occupy centre stage they would be particularly the discourse on embodiment and that of power. "Embodiment" is a cluster word embracing the debates both about sex/gender theory and about sexuality in their entirety,[30] but it also highlights the real life situation of bodies, poor, suffering, ageing, and vulnerable, female and male. It brings forgotten categories of disability into the spotlight. It focuses on the agency of persons rather than on victimhood. The real theological challenge in a context of globalisation is to recover the holiness of the sacramental body, in the sacredness of ordinary living and relations, to enable imaginative alternatives to the commercialised representations of the commodified body, which is the creation of the media.

The second theme would be "power", which has always been at the centre of our endeavours. We have worked, struggled, and resisted power as dominance and control as an integral part of the patriarchal system and in its unjust, oppressive political manifestations. That we have not toppled the system is part of this sense of loss of dreams. The economist Amartya Sen speaks of the tragedy of the "missing women" across the world which he ascribes to the "terrible phenomenon of excess mortality and artificially lower survival rates."[31] Sen argues that if life expectancy and fertility rates are calculated to estimate what the expected number of women there would be, and the result is compared with the actual number, then the numbers of "missing women" is something like twenty-nine million in China, twenty-three million in India, and a total of around sixty million.[32] The systemic patriarchal oppression of women, rigidly controlling whether women live or die, is not shifted by policies based on "well-being" or rights-based approaches. Sen argue for agency and empowerment-based programmes. In all the development programmes I am involved with in Rajasthan, in north-west India, *empowerment* is the key word, and empowerment of the most vulnerable people. In one incident I experienced, a group of mothers with their children lived by the side of the road in great poverty and a complete lack of self-esteem. They just did not believe their situation could change. One day a huge truck raced along and ran over one their

[30] See the papers of Anne-Louise Eriksson, Marcella Althaus-Reid and Lucy Tatman in this volume.

[31] Amartya Sen, *Development as Freedom* (Oxford University Press: Oxford 1999), 104-107. He refers to his own article "Missing Women," in: *British Medical Journal* 304 (1992).

[32] Sen, *Development as Freedom*, 104. Other estimates make it around 100 million.

children, a little girl. The stricken mothers tried to make a cordon across the road and stop the lorry. Of course they were not strong enough, the lorry raced off, but not before they had taken down the number and were able to contact the police. The police caught the driver and the next day the pictures of the women were in the newspapers. The women could hardly believe it: "We did that!" they cried. It was a key moment in their sense of empowerment.

In a globalised context it is difficult to see how the Davids of this world can topple the Goliaths – the global corporations – as we are witnessing in the current dramas. As before, I ask: what is the specifically theological task here? Is it here that we can build on what has already been achieved in working on alternative meanings of power? Enabling power can be another word for grace, the spiritual energy of community. I observe in India that it is the power of faith that gives women strength to keep going, even if the particular faith might not stand up to a feminist critique.[33] As women from diverse faith communities, Islamic, Hindu, Buddhist, Jewish and Christian, our shared power of resistance is deep-rooted in faith convictions. Can this show a way forward?

5. Acknowledging Tensions

Celebrating achievements is important, but acknowledging failures and engaging with criticism is even more vital. How do we face the challenge of confronting endemic racism, of heterosexism, neo-colonialisms and the many blindnesses of which we – at least in western feminism – may be accused? I think the first step is always to acknowledge the truth – in the context of the place where we do our theology, in all the complexities and configurations of power. And never to underestimate both the seriousness of this, the deeply embedded nature of many of our prejudices, the mistakes we have made in handling power.

The next step is then to engage with the content, ever mindful of the globalised context. Here I bring into play three contested areas: connection/difference; dependence/autonomy; ethics of care/nurture/sacrifice over against justice. First, I want to uncouple the polarity between connection and difference. There has been a long debate about these concepts, the point being that the stress on "making connections", a "spirituality of connectedness" would blot out our differences and otherness and would lead to policies of assimilation.

[33] The philosopher Martha Nussbaum criticises Amartya Sen for ignoring the power of religion in this respect: Martha Nussbaum, *Women and Development* (Oxford University Press: Oxford 1999), 178-190.

The problem is that by focusing on these as polarities we lose the force of both. As Rosi Braidotti wrote in 1994:

> In the European history of philosophy, "difference" is a central concept insofar as Western thought has always functioned by dualistic oppositions, which create subcategories of otherness, or "difference from". Because in this history, "difference" has been predicated on relations of domination and exclusion, to be "different from" came to mean "less than", to be worth less than.[34]

Politically, otherness and difference have come to be the crucial issue for Europe, emerging as the politics of exclusion. Anne-Louise Eriksson has appealed for contextually specific theories of gender performance that allow diversity.[35] Theologically, for us the task is to engage with global theologies of diversity within ESWTR, learning from their richness, responding to their ethical challenges, naming exclusion for what it is, and exposing the ever-new policies of greed and imperialism. But "connectedness" is not the reverse side of the coin: rather, it emerges from the discourse of ecology, naming the connectedness between all forms of life. As such, it has constructive and destructive possibilities. Its usefulness in political theology is in building effective groupings of solidarity, to be worked for and not assumed. For example, if womanist theologian Dolores Williams writes that

> Womanists not only concern ourselves about the liberation of women, we also struggle long with Black men, and children for the liberation, survival and positive quality of life for our entire oppressed black community[36]

where does this lead white European feminist theologians? Not simply to regard this as an example of "difference" but, surely, to engage honestly with the implications, to work in solidarity for justice for the black community and maybe to seek to understand some of the limitations of European white feminist theology. Exploring sacred connections can also function as the basis of a spirituality that values the bodily realities of daily living, where this is experienced as gifted, graced, and not threatened by multiple deprivations.

[34] Rosi Braidotti, *Nomadic Subjects: Embodiment and Sexual Difference in Contemporary Philosophy* (Columbia University Press: New York 1994), 147.

[35] See her paper in this volume.

[36] Dolores Williams, "Straight talk, Plain Talk," in: Emilie M.Townes (ed.), *Embracing the Spirit* (Orbis: Maryknoll 1997), 97-121.

Secondly, the whole area of care/sacrifice/nurture is fraught with even more tensions in a globalised world. As Feminist Theologians we have been strong in our condemnation of theologies of sacrifice, expiation and suffering which nail women to the Cross of the world.[37] But that has never meant that all meanings of sacrifice have been abolished. There are thousands of women who have willingly embraced lives of hardship for loved ones, for community, for the sake of peace and justice, and many have paid the price of doing so with their lives. We are conscious of the names of many of our sister theologians in extreme situations of poverty and danger in many parts of the world, working for justice with secular sisters, with women of faith like Aung San Suu Kyi in Burma. That is where authentic spiritualities of sacrifice arise, hand in hand with spiritualities of resistance and protest against injustice.

Sacrifice is often linked with the existential situation of many mothers: and the ethics of care and nurture have tried to tease out essentialist notions of motherhood from the commitment to build right relationships of justice in the care of infants and children. Globalisation brings new dilemmas for women here. I begin with the story of Vicky Diaz, a 34-year-old mother of five:

> A college-educated former schoolteacher and travel agent in the Philippines, she migrated to the United states to work as a house-keeper and nanny to the two-year old son of a wealthy family in Beverly Hills, Los Angeles.[38]

This is a story of the globalisation of mothering. Vicky is paid $400 a week, from which she pays her own family's domestic live-in worker in the Philippines, who is also paying for her own children to be cared for. Living in this global care chain is not easy. Vicky says:

> Even though it's paid well, you are sinking in the amount of your work. Even while you are ironing the clothes, they still call you to the kitchen to wash the plates. It was also very depressing. The only thing you can do is to give all your love to the child (the 2 year old American child). In my absence from my children, the most I could do with my situation is to give all my love to that child.[39]

[37] See Mary Grey, *Redeeming the Dream* (SPCK: London 1989; Sahitya Prakash: Gujurat 2000).
[38] Arlie Russell Hochschild, "Global Care Chains and Emotional Surplus Value," in: Giddens / Hutton (eds), *On the Edge*, 130-146, here 130.
[39] Ibid.

The point is that global capitalism spawns global care chains like this, chains usually from a poor country to a rich one, or a poorer to a less poor, expressing an invisible ecology of care, one kind of care depending on another one. Increasingly, even excluding forced migration for the sake of prostitution, which is happening increasingly from the former communist countries as well as from Asia and Africa, the people migrating from one country to another will be women. Rhacel Parrenas's research shows how women such as Vicky talk unceasingly about going home, about their families, children and the birthdays, but it is not they but their wages that go home.[40] The solutions to this global care chain are complex. They include the political re-valuing of care and the recognition that the low value given to care goes hand in hand with the declining value paid to basic food crops, relative to manufactured goods. The low market value of care keeps the status of women who do it low. Production, not reproduction, is the focus of globalisation.

A second example of the politics of mothering under globalisation is even more chilling. The anthropologist Nancy Scheper-Hughes researched the communities associated with the impoverished sugar plantations of the Alto de Cruzeiro in north-east Brazil, where child death through chains of poverty was the norm. Initially she was shocked and resistant to the way the mothers coped with the death of what they called their "angel babies":

> I resisted for a long time accepting at face value what impoverished Northeast Brazilian women told me about their lack of grief, regret or remorse accompanying the frequent deaths of their young infants – deaths they sometimes aided and abetted by reducing or withdrawing foods and liquids to babies seen as "doomed" in any case. "Infants are like birds" women of Alto do Cruzeiro said. "Here today, gone tomorrow. It is all the same to them." "They die," other mothers explained, "because they themselves wanted to die, because they had no 'taste', no 'knack' for life. We feel no remorse, only pity for the little creatures who die so young, before they have let us know what kind of person they are."[41]

Nancy Scheper-Hughes interprets this lack of grief and of maternal remorse for the over-production of these angel-babies in terms of a political economy of

[40] Rhacel Parrenas' research is cited in Hochschild, "Global Care Chains," in Giddens / Hutton (eds), *On the Edge*, 130-136. It will be published as Rhacel Parrenas, *The Global Servant: Migrant Filipina Domestic Workers in Rome and Los Angeles* (Stanford University Press: Palo Alto, CA).

[41] Nancy Scheper-Hughes, *Death Without Weeping: The Violence of Everyday Life in Brazil* (University of California Press: Berkeley / Los Angeles 1992), 146.

emotion within a culture of scarcity where there is constant anticipation of loss and premature death.

These two examples – out of possibly thousands – manifest the consequences of globalisation, where the market's lack of commitment to community and place even shapes how mothers interpret the (inevitable) death of their babies, where money controls where maternal love should be directed. There is nothing glorious here about vulnerability and dependency, however much theology stresses this is the human situation before God. But rather than polarising autonomy versus economic and social dependency, its agency that is the key. The question is, how can we theologise agency in this new situation?

The way forward must lie in making visible the backbreaking labour undertaken by women which sustains life, and by re-connecting the economy to the foundations of society which promote a culture of peace and non-violence, a global society devoted to the flourishing of all interdependent life-forms. Again, the theological dimensions of this task need exploration.

6. Conclusion

In drawing these many strands together, our achievements, our failures and the challenges of the new context of globalisation, I want to assert the absolute primacy of our right to dream – and to dream our dreams! If global capitalism has tried successfully to be manipulative and hi-jack our dream, replacing it with fantasies of unattainable consumer goods, unattainable not only to the budgets of ordinary people, but also ecologically from the earth's resources, we have to call a halt. We need to see that neo-liberalism is actually anti-Utopian.

We need to reclaim this lost power of dreaming. We need to dream the impossible dream and to believe again in the dream's power. We need to ask each other, "What do we really want?" "What is our heart's desire?" This is the question behind all the great myths of the world, the great religions of the world. If our heart's desire is not what the global corporations tell us it is, then what is it? Name it and tell alternative stories of longing.

This is a deeply spiritual question. But it is one with which Feminist Theology has been engaged from the beginning. *Transformation* has always been our goal: transformation of ourselves, our communities, our societies; transformation from the killing systems of death to cultures of life for all. We have engaged in the project of transformation with a passion for justice which is far profounder a passion than merely a zeal for reform. It is a passion that embraces passionate knowing, desiring, believing as well as commitment to action emerging from the compassionate heart. The global crisis is a spiritual crisis at heart. If there is one task for us, it is not to be better theorists than feminist theorists, sociologists, scientists, and anthropologists. It is to be faithful to our task as theologians and scholars of Religion and Religious Studies, who by our engagement in faith communities, scholarship and society offer a way forward in this brokenheartedness, this society that has lost its heart, soul, spirit, and integrity to the forces of the market.

To say "no" to the killing systems is a deeply subversive act. It is also the mystical stance of resistance to injustice. It means, in the final analysis, to refuse to be reduced to mere activism, but to live a powerful contemplative witness to an alternative reality, one from which we are already living, energising the whole enterprise of theology, energising courage, quest, and visionary powers.

Must we live without our dreams? Dream on, sisters. Redeem the time, redeem the dream – but let us embody the dream too, in the name of the sacredness of life and the preciousness of all living beings, in communion with all who have gone before us, and committed to those who will follow.

Der Traum von einem neuen Himmel und einer neuen Erde ist ein wesentliches Merkmal feministischer Theologie. Bedeutet die Tatsache, dass sie sich uns fortwährend entziehen, dass die Träume tot sind? Eine der Stärken feministischer Theologie war, den Kontext und die Erfahrung ernst zu nehmen: im neuen Kontext der Globalisierung und des unregulierten globalen Kapitalismus müssen spezifische Bedrohungen und Möglichkeiten des veränderten Kontextes angesprochen werden. Globalisierung basiert – trotz vorhandener positiver Aspekte – auf Beherrschung. Durch ihre Vergötzung des Geldes hat sie sogar die Herrschaft über unsere Wünsche übernommen und unsere Träume kolonisiert. Feministische Theologien müssen ihre subversive Rolle wieder entdecken, indem sie erneut ihr Vertrauen in die Methode setzen; sie müssen fortfahren, Spannungen zwischen widersprüchlichen Kategorien anzugehen. "Embodiment" (Verkörperung) und Machtanalyse erweisen sich im heutigen Kontext als ausschlaggebend, und die geteilte Macht des Widerstands eröffnet ein Leuchtfeuer für den Weg vorwärts. Die unsichtbare Arbeit der Frauen, die Leben erhält, sollte als Grundlage einer Ökonomie erkannt werden, die eine Kultur des Friedens fördert.

La théologie féministe a rêvé d'un renouveau du ciel et de la terre, et ce fut là une de ses caractéristiques essentielles. Le rêve va-t-il alors s'évanouir à mesure que ciel et terre nous échappent? Une force de la théologie féministe fut de toujours tenir compte du contexte et de l'expérience. Or, la mondialisation et le capitalisme global incontrôlé forcent à se demander, dans ce nouveau contexte, quelles menaces et quelles voies renferme la nouvelle situation. La mondialisation a, certes, des aspects positifs, mais s'étaye aussi sur la domination. Elle est même parvenue, à travers l'idolâtrie de l'argent, à dominer nos désirs et à coloniser nos rêves. Les théologies féministes doivent redevenir subversives, en reprenant confiance dans la méthode, et continuer à supporter les tensions entre des catégories qui soulèvent la controverse. *Embodiment* (l'incarnation) et l'analyse du pouvoir restent cruciaux dans le contexte contemporain et la résistance, qui est un pouvoir partagé, doit être un phare guidant nos pas. L'action invisible des femmes, visant à protéger la vie, devrait être reconnue comme le fondement d'une économie favorisant une culture pacifique.

Mary Grey is D J James Professor of Pastoral Theology at the University of Wales, Lampeter; she was formerly Profesor of Feminism and Christendom at the Catholic University of Nijmegen. She regularly visits the desert of Rajasthan, India, as part of the NGO "Wells for India" and is currently working on Sacred Longings, a book on spirituality and globalisation.

Monika Walus

Die Frau als *locus theologicus*?

Für Narcyza und viele andere

Ich möchte gerne die mitteleuropäische ESWTR-Konferenz, die im Jahr 2000 Jahr in Polen stattfand, zum Anlass nehmen, meine Erfahrungen nun bei der internationalen Konferenz in Salzburg darzustellen.

Wir haben heute[1] die energischen Bekenntnisse der amerikanischen Quäkerin Lucy Tatman und der argentinischen ehemaligen 'queer'-Theologin Marcella Althaus-Reid gehört. Sie waren voller Kraft und Gefühl. Ich zweifle nicht daran, dass sie wirklich dem entspricht, was sie in ihrem Alltag erfahren. Hier aber, bei dieser Konferenz wie auch in meinem eigenen feministischen Milieu in Polen, herrscht eine andere Situation. Deshalb möchte auch ich ein *Coming Out* wagen und mein Bekenntnis ablegen: Ich bin Mitteleuropäerin, genauer gesagt, Polin, verheiratet und deshalb bin ich 'queer'.

Diskussionsthemen der Konferenz in Lublin

Vom 13. – 16. August 2000 fand an der Katholischen Universität Lublin eine regionale mittel- und osteuropäische Konferenz der ESWTR (die erste in Polen) statt. Das Thema lautete: "Mutterschaft als locus theologicus". Es war ein einmaliges feministisches Ereignis in Polen, da es die erste Begegnung dieser Art war. Über 60 Frauen aus 14 Ländern waren zu dieser Konferenz von Frauen für Frauen gekommen. Die anwesenden Frauen repräsentierten verschiedene Religionen, Konfessionen und Traditionen. Wir haben vor allem unsere Verschiedenheit, aber auch unsere Gemeinsamkeiten entdeckt. Obwohl dank des Buches von Elzbieta Adamiak, "Die schweigende Anwesenheit", in Polen feministische Themen öffentlich diskutiert werden, war diese Konferenz das erste öffentliche Treffen von Frauen, die an feministischer Theologie

[1] Der folgende Beitrag ist die Erweiterung eines Kurzvortrags, den ich bei der ESWTR-Konferenz in Salzburg nach den Vorträgen von Lucy Tatman, " Western European-American Feminist Christian Theologians: What Might It Mean to Take Ourselves Seriously?", und von Marcella Althaus Reid, "Queer I stand" gehalten habe.

interessiert sind. Wir haben bei der Konferenz mehr Themen 'eröffnet' als 'abgeschlossen' und mehr Fragen gestellt als beantwortet. Im folgenden will ich auf ein paar davon näher eingehen. Sie gehen weit über den Rahmen der dortigen Diskussion hinaus und erweisen sich im Kontext der Salzburger Konferenz als hochaktuell.[2] Es ist üblich, von Früchten einer Konferenz zu reden. Ich möchte eher von entdeckten Mängeln und Bedürfnissen sprechen.

Eines der heißesten Diskussionsthemen in Lublin war die Frage nach der Erfahrung der Mutterschaft, besonders im religiösen und theologischen Kontext. Nicht nur in der römisch-katholischen Kirche in Polen, der ich angehöre, hören wir oft, Mutterschaft sei eine typisch weibliche Erfahrung. Als sichersten Weg zu Gott, der den Vorzug verdient, stellt man jedoch vor allem das Priesteramt und das Ordensleben in den Vordergrund. Beide werden als besondere Berufung verstanden. Eine Mutter zu sein, ist hingegen etwas *Normales* und *Natürliches*, das ganz einfach die Mehrheit der Frauen betrifft.

Für die Berufung zur Nonne wird ein spezielles Charisma, eine besondere Gnadengabe vorausgesetzt. Um Mutter zu sein, genügt es einfach, Frau zu sein. Oft wird gesagt, eine Nonne verzichte auf ihre natürliche Neigung zur (biologischen) Mutterschaft und werde statt dessen zur geistigen Mutter. Man geht folglich davon aus, dass eine Mutter einfach ihren natürlichen Instinkten, ihrer Natur als Frau folge. Was die Berufung einer Frau zur Nonne angeht, so werden hier oft Ausdrücke verwendet wie: 'sich Gott ganz opfern', 'sich vollkommener Gott hingeben', 'näher bei Gott stehen', 'ein Leben der Vollkommenheit führen'. In offiziellen Dokumenten habe ich noch nie die Aussage gefunden, dass sich eine Frau als Mutter oder als Ehefrau *ganz Gott hingeben* könne, oder dass Ehe oder Mutterschaft besondere, gnadenvolle Wege zu Gott seien. Natürlich ist es die Berufung der Frau. Ist es dies aber, um näher bei Gott zu stehen oder nur deshalb, um Kinder zu gebären und zu erziehen?

Mutter zu sein ist *natürlich*, Ordensfrau – geweihte Jungfrau – zu sein hingegen *übernatürlich*. Dazu habe ich ein paar Fragen. Ist die Mutterschaft (k)eine Berufung? Gibt es für Frauen nur eine einzige Berufung, nämlich die zur Nonne? Wenn dies der Fall ist, weshalb wird Mutterschaft dann derart gepriesen? Diese Frage darf nicht einfach abgewunken werden. Denn: Wozu sollen Frauen Mutter werden, wenn das Ordensleben quasi *ex opere operato* doch höher steht und näher zu Gott bringt? Wir wissen alle, dass Mutterschaft allzu leicht zu anderen Zwecken missbraucht werden kann – ich möchte nur an das Lob der Mutterschaft in Kriegszeiten erinnern, wenn Vater Staat gerade viele Söhne braucht.

[2] Bilder und Texte der Konferenz in Polen waren im Konferenzsaal ausgestellt.

Manchmal beschleicht mich das Gefühl, Mutterschaft sei auch in feministischen Kreisen (nur den polnischen?) nicht besonders populär. Es ist eher feministisch, 'lesbisch' oder 'frei' zu sein oder einer Geschiedenen volles Verständnis entgegenzubringen. Wenn über Mutterschaft diskutiert wird, geschieht dies oft in kritischer Weise und meist nicht ohne politische Akzentsetzungen. Ehe und Familie sind eher 'out', es sind patriarchale Institutionen, die suspekt sind. So jedenfalls ist es in Warschau... . Doch war ich während der Konferenz in Salzburg wirklich überrascht, als ich von drei jungen Frauen auf meine Frage nach ihren Lebensplänen die gleiche Antwort bekam: "Es mag vielleicht nicht feministisch sein, aber ich möchte gerne heiraten und Kinder kriegen." Unsicher, fast schüchtern wurde es gesagt. Ich habe mich gefragt, warum es "vielleicht nicht feministisch" ist? Ist dieser Wunsch in diesen Kreisen *queer*?

Berufung von Frauen?

Es gibt in meiner Kirche zahlreiche Frauen, die sich zum Ordensleben berufen fühlen, angefangen von der Karmelitin bis hin zur Missionarin. Gibt es mehrere Wege, Mutter zu sein? Ist es zum Beispiel eine Berufung, Adoptivmutter zu sein, oder ist es ein ganz natürlicher Lebensweg? Ich kenne ein paar kinderlose Ehepaare, die keine Kinder adoptieren. Und andere, die auf eigene Kinder verzichtet und gleich mehrere Kinder adoptiert haben. Handelt es sich dabei um eine Berufung oder ist dies ganz *natürlich*? Was ist mit den Frauen, die sich (manchmal ohne verheiratet zu sein) entscheiden, kranke Kinder zu adoptieren? Oder solchen Frauen, die den Weg einer älteren Schwester oder einer Tante gehen... . Diese Frauen übernehmen die Rolle der abwesenden oder kranken Mutter, erziehen Geschwister, betreuen später die Kinder der eigenen Geschwister und nicht selten auch deren Kindeskinder. Es sind die alleinstehenden Frauen, die sozusagen Herz und Rettungsdienst der Großfamilie sind. Uns allen sind wahrscheinlich solche Frauenschicksale bekannt. Es waren und sind in jeder Epoche und jedem Land natürliche Wege der Frauen zu Gott. Wenn ich daran denke, sehe ich eine lange Prozession solcher Frauen vor mir, die uns vorangingen. Ich spüre ihre Anwesenheit, aber ich kenne ihre Namen nicht, sehe keine Gesichter und höre keine Ratschläge; ich kenne auch die Zeremonien und Sitten nicht, die ihnen auf ihrem Lebensweg eine Stütze waren. Es ist schwer, in meiner Kirche die Berufungen von Frauen, ihre Geschichten und Erfahrungen zu finden – aber in feministischen Texten ist dies nicht unbedingt leichter. Ich höre oft, dass wir die Spiritualität verschiedener Orden hochschätzen, die sich allmählich entwickelt haben und einer bestimmten Lebensform entsprechen; so sind etwa die Spiritualität der Karmelitin oder

der Charité-Schwester aus dem Alltag heraus entstanden. Können wir analog von verschiedenen Arten der Spiritualität von Müttern sprechen? Gibt es für Frauen verschiedene Wege und spirituelle Traditionen, Mutter zu sein? Etwa eine Spiritualität der Mütter, deren Kind krank auf die Welt kam und die es betreuen, ohne dass die Chance besteht, es je gesund zu sehen. Oder eine Spiritualität der Frauen, die ein Kind erziehen, ohne es ihr eigenes nennen zu dürfen, weil sie für es einfach 'neben' den anwesenden oder manchmal anwesenden Mütter da sind. Oder eine Spiritualität der Mütter, die ihre Kinder aus verschiedenen Gründen nicht selbst erziehen können oder dürfen, die die Erziehung anderen überlassen und mit ansehen müssen, dass eine andere Frau mehr Respekt und Liebe gewinnt… . Wo sind die Traditionen der Frauen, wo werden die Wege der Mütter sichtbar, die es fertig brachten, so viel Schmerz und Freude 'zusammenzunähen' und mit Lob und Freude zu sticken? Wo wird über die Spiritualität der Mütter berichtet, die nicht nur die Geburt, sondern auch den Tod ihres Kindes miterleben mussten? Wir lesen voll Respekt von den Passionsschwestern, die die Qual der Leiden Jesu Christi miterleben. Seit geraumer Zeit wissen wir mehr von zahllosen Müttern, die ihre todkranken Kinder jahrelang betreuen, manchmal ohne Ehepartner, der diese *Berufung* nicht mittragen will. Das Leben einer (manchmal einsamen) berufstätigen Mutter eines todkranken oder unheilbar kranken Kindes sollte vielleicht einmal im Kontext der Lehre vom vollkommenen Leben und von der vollen Hingabe an Gott interpretiert werden, oder vor dem Hintergrund der Worte Jesu, der sich dem Evangelium zufolge mit Kindern identifizieren wollte.

Ein großes Schweigen herrscht auch über den *natürlichen* Austausch von Kraft und Liebe: die kleinen Mädchen, die heranwachsen und später als starke Töchter ihre nunmehr schwachen und kranken Mütter betreuen… .

Diese vielfältigen Erfahrungen von Frauen sind sicher eine Quelle der Erfahrung von Gottes Anwesenheit, ein *locus theologicus*. Dies gilt nicht nur für 'Spezialfälle' der Mutterschaft, sondern für jede Art der Mutterschaft. Die Wege der Mütter, auf denen – sehr evangeliumsgemäß – das Kind immer mehr wächst und die Mutter immer mehr zurücktritt, sind die Grundlage einer, oder besser gesagt, verschiedener Arten von Spiritualität. Wer hat sie aufgehoben, aufgeschrieben, aufgewertet? Wem sind sie Hilfe und Stütze? Sind sie jemals wieder neu zu entdecken?

Manchmal habe ich den Eindruck, dass sehr viel in der Theologie auf der Erfahrung des zölibatären Lebens basiert. Dies ist gewiss ein berechtigter Standpunkt, aber er umfasst nicht das ganze Spektrum des Lebens. In polnischen feministischen Kreisen habe ich oft den gegenteiligen Eindruck: Hier werden alle weiblichen Erfahrungen betont, mit Ausnahme der Erfahrungsquelle der Mütter. Es gibt uns aber, ihr unzufriedenen Töchter... .

Geistliche und natürliche Mutterschaft

In der Kirche redet man oft von geistlichen und natürlichen Müttern. Woher kommt das? Eine Nonne, die ihre Mitschwester erzieht, ist eine geistliche Mutter. Geistliche Mutterschaft ist eine Ehre, eine geistliche Gabe, ein Charisma. Biologische Mutterschaft ist ebenfalls eine Ehre und eine Gabe. Aber – wie ich schon oft gehört habe – dabei handelt es sich um etwas *Biologisches*. Und das bedeutet, es kommt von selbst, da es ja natürlich ist. Folglich wird es weniger als Charisma denn als *Natur* eingeordnet. Nach wie vor bin ich mir nicht sicher, wie Tanten oder Schwestern einzuordnen sind, die zwar nicht ihre eigenen, aber doch mit ihnen verwandte Kinder erziehen: Sind sie biologische, *natürliche* oder geistliche Mütter? Andererseits kann ich mir gut vorstellen, dass meine süße und von mir begeisterte Tochter eines Tages zu mir sagen wird, dass eine andere Frau ihre geistliche Mutter ist. Ich hoffe, dass ich dann auch zur Schwester meiner Tochter werde und mit ihr lernen kann. Ich glaube, dass es möglich ist, aber im Augenblick ist es sehr schwer, Töchter zu finden, die mit ihrer eigenen Mutter befreundet oder auf sie stolz sind und zugeben, dass sie etwas Geistliches von ihrer Mutter gelernt haben. Noch schwerer ist dies in einer feministischen Umgebung... . Eine gute Beziehung zwischen Tochter und Mutter ist sogar in den populärsten Märchen verpönt; wir kennen zur Genüge all die Märchen, die mit Stieftöchtern und Stiefmüttern bevölkert sind. Die gute Fee kommt immer von *außen*, aus der übernatürlichen Welt, während die Mutter entweder abwesend oder machtlos ist. In allen Fällen hat sie keine Möglichkeit, irgendeine Art Spiritualität, Macht oder Atem an die Tochter weiterzugeben. In diesen Geschichten lernen die Töchter nicht von ihren Müttern, zu tanzen oder zu gewinnen. Es ist am Ende der Prinz, der den Ausweg aus der geschlossenen Welt weist.

Eigentlich ist es am leichtesten, positive Worte über Mütter in alten konservativen Texten zu finden. Das gibt zu denken.

Sakramentales oder geweihtes Frauenleben?

Zurück zu den Überlegungen am Rande der Lubliner Konferenz und zu den Vorträgen von Lucy Tatman und Marcella Althaus Reid: Das Leben einer Nonne, zu deren Aufgabe die Erziehung von Kindern gehört, ist ein geweihtes Leben und ein Opfer im Namen Jesu. Das Leben der Frau hingegen, die in ihrer Ehe und ihrem Haus Raum für eigene und möglicherweise auch fremde

Kinder geschaffen hat, ist nicht geweiht – trotz der Gnade des Sakraments. Es sei daran erinnert, dass in der römisch-katholischen Kirche Ehe und Priesterweihe als Sakrament verstanden werden. Gelübde von Nonnen werden als Zeichen vollkommenen Lebens und vollständiger Hingabe gelobt, sind aber kein Sakrament. In welchem Verhältnis stehen Sakrament und Lebensweihe eigentlich zueinander? Meistens wird es so gedeutet, dass die Ordensfrau mit ihrem ganzen Leben auf Gott hin ausgerichtet ist, während die Ehefrau auf ihre Familie, genauer gesagt auf ihren Mann orientiert ist. Es ist leider kinderleicht, dafür entsprechende Zitate von Paulus zu finden. Hat dies möglicherweise etwas mit der untergeordneten Rolle der Frau zu tun? Da sie sich den Entscheidungen des Ehemannes unterwerfen musste, konnte sie ihren eigenen spirituellen Weg weniger selbstständig verfolgen. Aber wäre es in diesem Fall nicht wirklich besser, *nicht* zu heiraten, sich *nicht* zu opfern, sondern *vollkommener* zu leben, ungestört von Mann und Kindern? Die wenigen Ehefrauen, die heilig gesprochen wurden, waren meistens Töchter aus Adelsgeschlechtern. Im Gegensatz zu bürgerlichen Ehefrauen waren sie Partnerinnen ihres Mannes. Die Autorität ihres Vaters spielte dabei im Hintergrund eine große Rolle. Sie konnten es sich leisten (obwohl nicht ohne Schwierigkeiten), ein jungfräuliches Leben zu führen, Gerede am Hof zu ignorieren und in ein von ihnen gegründetes Kloster zu ziehen.

Kehren wir zurück zum Thema "Berufungen" und Frauenrollen. Es ist doch eigentlich paradox: In Israel konnten alle Menschen, egal ob Frau oder Mann, sich als Braut Gottes verstehen. Das Christentum versteht sich als vollkommene Offenbarung Gottes, glaubt vollkommenen Zugang zu Gott zu haben, im Katholizismus aber scheint die Nähe zu Gott nur unverheirateten, zölibatär lebenden Menschen (Frauen) möglich zu sein. Die verheirateten Frauen und Mütter scheinen nicht in den Genuss dieses Privilegs kommen zu dürfen. Ich glaube jedoch nicht, dass es möglich ist, in einer Ehe ohne die besondere Gnade und Anwesenheit Gottes leben zu können. Ein verheirateter christlicher Theologe (Martin Luther) sagte einmal: "die Ehe zwingt zum Glauben". Die Ehe ist also ein Weg zum Glauben. Ähnlich heißt es auch im jüdischen Zohar: Wenn andere Frömmigkeitspraktiken als Wege zu Gott nicht vorhanden sind, bleibt immer noch die Ehe. Es ist aber in der traditionellen christlichen Theologie wie auch in der feministischen Theologie schwer, etwa in der Soteriologie, Texte zu finden, die von der Ehe als Ausgangspunkt der Theologie ausgehen. Entspricht es denn auch feministischer Erfahrung, dass die Ehe ein *locus theologicus* sein kann? Ich frage dies aus Unkenntnis feministischer Theologie, aber auch aufgrund meiner Erfahrungen mit feministischen Kreisen in Polen und bei der Konferenz in Salzburg.

Den bereits angesprochenen Gegensatz zwischen Müttern und Ordensfrauen finden wir auch bei den Selig- und Heiligsprechungen in der römisch-katholischen Kirche. Die Berufung zum Priesteramt oder zum Ordensleben wird als besondere Leistung und jahrelange geistliche Entwicklung der betreffenden Person angesehen. Mutterschaft hingegen gilt nicht als spezielle geistliche Leistung. Vielleicht gibt es deshalb so wenige *heilig gesprochene Mütter, die nicht gleichzeitig auch Ordensfrauen waren?* Ist es vielleicht schwerer, eine heilige Mutter zu sein als eine heilige Ordensfrau? Oder ist es schwieriger, sie zur Kenntnis zu nehmen? Finden wir doch einmal eine heilig gesprochene Frau, die keine Nonne war und womöglich gar verheiratet war, so handelt es sich meistens um eine Königin, eine verwitwete Frau oder eine Rekluse... . Ehefrau zu sein ist *natürlich*, Mutter zu sein ist *natürlich*, sozusagen normal. Nonne zu sein, scheint ein erkennbares, sichtbares Zeichen der Gnade zu sein. Moment mal – ist das nicht *die* Definition der Sakraments? Ist nicht die Ehe das Sakrament? Ist eine Ehefrau ein sichtbares Zeichen der Gnade? Ich möchte gerne mal eine heilig gesprochene Ehefrau sehen... .

Die Gottesmutter und die anderen Mütter

Es ist vielleicht unmodern, Vorbilder zu haben – doch nimmt das Interesse am Leben von Filmstars und Fotomodels nicht gerade ab. An welche Frauen denkt eine Christin, wenn sie eine historische Frau als Vorbild oder Vorläuferin sucht? Wir in Polen denken in der Regel sofort an Maria. Heilige Frauen sind in Polen fast ausschließlich Nonnen. Vielleicht haben diese Mädchen, die eine von Nonnen geleitete Schule besucht haben, einfach einen besseren Zugang zu heiligen Gründerinnen. Im allgemeinen ist man davon überzeugt, dass das Leben einer Nonne sich vom Leben einer Laiin so gravierend unterscheidet, dass sie kaum Gemeinsamkeiten haben. Die Kluft zwischen Ordensfrauen und Laienfrauen ist immer noch riesengroß, und zwar nicht selten von beiden Seiten aus. Es ist einsichtig, die Mutter Gottes ist das beste Vorbild des Glaubens für alle. Das gefeierte Muster der Jungfräulichkeit, die allerheiligste Jungfrau Maria führte ein unauffälliges, bescheidenes Leben ohne Nonnenschleier, ohne Regel, ohne geistlichen Seelenführer, ohne Schwesterngemeinschaft – statt dessen aber hatte sie ein Kind. Es ist schon relativ schwer, verständlich zu machen, warum die allerheiligste Jungfrau das beste Vorbild für Mütter ist. Aber wenigstens kann man es vom Evangelium her plausibel machen. Ist Maria jedoch auch ein Musterbeispiel für Ehefrauen? In Schlesien war die heilige Anna, die Mutter Marias, die Patronin der Ehefrauen. Als apokryphe Figur hat sie es aber heutzutage schwer.

Die Erfahrungen von Ehefrauen, etwa aus der Zeit der Kirchenväter sind leider (trotz der bekannten Ehefrauen berühmter Theologen) nicht überliefert. Denn die heiligen Frauen haben uns keine Texte darüber nachgelassen und ihre Männer zogen es vor, Traktate *de virginitate* zu schreiben. In der feministischen Tradition wiederum sind eher traurige Gleichnisse wie das über die Fische und das Radfahren beliebter. Nachdem Frauen, die solche Gleichnisse erzählen, sich zuerst als Kritikerinnen der Ehe etabliert haben, gehen sie am Ende selbst eine Ehe ein.

Das beste Vorbild für eine Mutter ist die Gottesmutter. Als meine Tochter anfing, mich dies zu lehren, ist mir das noch klarer geworden. Ich fürchte aber, dass in Polen Vorstellungen von einer Familie vorherrschen, in denen Mutter und Kind die Hauptrollen spielen. Väter stehen eher im Abseits, sind vielleicht abwesend. Die Gefühle der Mutter konzentrieren sich auf das Kind, das alle mütterlichen Erwartungen, Sehnsüchte und Lebensziele erfüllen soll. Denn sie hat ja alles für ihr Kind geopfert. Wie lässt sich dieses Schema von Marias Mutterschaft herleiten? Für Maria war Gott, der zu ihrem Sohn wurde, die einzige Hauptperson; bei manchen Frauen hingegen wird das Kind zu Gott. Vielleicht sollte doch deutlicher gesagt werden, dass die ganze Liebe der *Ehe*frauen Gott gehören solle, auch dann, wenn – oder besonders dann, wenn – sie Mutter geworden sind... besonders dann, wenn sie Ehefrauen sind... . Aber vielleicht ist das ja nur ein polnisches Problem?

Auf der Suche nach heiligen Ehefrauen

Gibt es Frauen, die Feministinnen sind *und* Kinder haben und aus dieser Perspektive schreiben? In Polen kenne ich keine. Die bekanntesten Warschauer Feministinnen sind "frei", manchmal lesbisch, oft in einer sogenannten freien Beziehung oder im Konkubinat lebend. Die Ehe erfreut sich bei polnischen Feministinnen keiner großen Beliebtheit. Ich habe bei der Konferenz in Salzburg erwartet, dass es bei zwei Vorträgen aus lesbischer Sicht wenigstens *einen* weiteren aus der Sicht einer verheirateten Frau oder Mutter geben würde. Ich habe unter den Zuhörerinnen viele Frauen gesehen, die ich gerne gebeten hätte, ebenfalls das Wort zu ergreifen. Es ist sicher lehrreich, interessanten, gar exotischen Vorlesungen zuzuhören. Ich habe den Eindruck, dass in meiner Kirche theologische Texte meist aus dem Blickwinkel zölibatärer Männer geschrieben sind, während es in feministischen Kreisen Mode ist, Vorträge aus der Perspektive lesbischer Frauen zu hören. Dies ist verständlich, auch in Polen. Trotzdem bedaure ich, dass ich nicht mehr darauf gepocht habe, zu hören, was mir selbst wichtig ist. Denn in Polen hören wir in den *Gender Studies* recht viel von Lacan, Irigaray, Cixous usw. und über den lesbischen Standpunkt. Ich finde es ja wirklich interessant, aber mit meinem eigenen Leben hat es nun einmal wenig zu tun. In dieser Gesellschaft bin ich 'queer'. Im Kreise der Feministinnen bin ich eine verheiratete Katholikin, im Kreis der römischen Katholiken und Katholikinnen bin ich Feministin.

Wir haben oft gehört, dass frau in der Kirche Jungfrau oder Mutter sein kann. Was ist eine Ehefrau? Was ist eine Frau in der Kirche, wenn sie weder Jungfrau noch Mutter ist? Ist die Ehefrau sozusagen ein Durchgangskorridor zwischen Jungfrau und Mutter? Ehefrauen haben in der Kirche keine Identität, obwohl die Ehe ein Sakrament, das heißt, sichtbares Zeichen der Gnade bleibt. Oft wird gesagt, die Mutterschaft sei Siegel und Ziel der Ehe. Ist eine Ehe ohne Kinder weniger wert? Ist Ehefrau zu sein eine Berufung? Da die Ehe nach katholischer Überzeugung ein Sakrament (und damit ein sicheres Zeichen der Gnade) ist, fragt frau sich, warum heilige Ehefrauen so schwer zu finden sind. Ich möchte eine heilig gesprochene Ehefrau sehen, die nicht als Mutter heilig gesprochen ist.

Gibt es eine eigene/n Spiritualität/en der Ehefrauen? In der Kirche gelte ich manchmal als besonderer Fall, in feministischen Kreisen mache ich ähnliche Erfahrungen. Wenn man sich in Polen mit Frauen- und Geschlechterforschung beschäftigt, bekommt man leicht den Eindruck, dass Feministinnen unverheiratet, lesbisch oder geschieden, aber vor allem atheistisch zu sein haben. Als römisch-katholische, verheiratete Frau und Mutter bin ich 'queer'. Für Ordensangehörige gibt es Gemeinschaften, Rituale, bestimmte Ausprägungen von Spiritualität und eine besondere Theologie, die sie bei ihrer Berufung unterstützen sollen. Man glaubt manchmal, Mütter bräuchten keine besondere Gemeinschaft, Rituale, Spiritualität oder Theologie, da Mutterschaft 'natürlich' sei und deshalb entweder überhaupt nicht oder 'weniger' Gottes Anwesenheit und Gnade spiegele. Im Fall der Berufung wird das 'Extra' oft als Gegenüber des Üblichen, etwa der Mutterschaft, verstanden. Die einen haben das höhere Niveau, das übernatürlich begründet wird, die anderen haben das niedrigere Niveau, das natürlich, angeboren ist. Auf dieser Ebene wird die Frau (besonders als Ehefrau und Mutter) angesiedelt. Es ist wie ein Echo der platonischen Weltsicht, nach der alles Alltägliche praktisch wertlos war. Hier hatten Frauen und Sklaven ihren Platz. Wichtig war die Diskussion auf der Agora, dem Platz der Männer. Spuren solcher Gedanken sind oft noch zu finden in der Bewertung kirchlicher Arbeit. Während Priester meistens als Seelsorger bezeichnet werden, wird die Arbeit von Ordensfrauen – unabhängig von ihrer Ausbildung oder ihrer Leistung – Seelsorgehilfe genannt.

Die Identität einer feministischen Katholikin in Polen

Was würde es bedeuten, wenn wir uns entsinnen würden, dass Mutterschaft eine Berufung ist? Einerseits würden wir wahrscheinlich die Entwicklung und Anstrengung mittragen, eine Spiritualität der Mutterschaft auszuprägen. Würden wir andererseits nicht das Paradigma natürlich – übernatürlich vertreten und damit das Alltägliche, darunter die Mutterschaft, sozusagen veredeln wollen? Die Konferenz in Lublin – Mutterschaft als *locus theologicus*, als Quelle theologischer Erfahrung – wollte diese altgriechisch/patriarchalen Paradigmen nicht übernehmen. Ich würde es lieber umgekehrt sagen: die Erfahrung der Frauen, die Erfahrung des Alltags und der Alltäglichkeit ist die Quelle der Theologie. Hier können wir die Anwesenheit Gottes entdecken.

Ist Mutterschaft auch eine Quelle für feministische Erfahrung und feministische Theologie? Vielleicht ist es eher die Tochterschaft. Es ist unmöglich, *dieses* Wort ins Polnische zu übersetzen, ohne ein gänzlich neues Wort zu bilden, das fremd und suspekt klingt. Von der Sohnschaft hingegen hören wir regelmäßig.

Eines der heißen Eisen der Lubliner Konferenz war die Frage nach der Identität der feministischen Katholikinnen. In Polen geht man davon aus, dass eine Feministin ungläubig und kinderlos ist. Polnische Feministinnen erklären oft, dass Katholikinnen keine echten Feministinnen sein könnten. Ich habe entdeckt, dass konservative Priester und atheistische Feministinnen in Polen eigentlich dasselbe sagen: Eine Frau kann nicht katholisch *und* feministisch zugleich denken. Zu den Früchten der feministischen Bewegung in Polen gehört die neue Redewendung der Katholikinnen: "Ich bin zwar keine Feministin, aber…". Wir sind zu dem Schluss gekommen, dass es echte Feministinnen und weniger echte und sogar unechte Feministinnen gibt. Ich kann diesem Gedankengang durchaus folgen. Denn es gibt ja Fragen, wie etwa Abtreibung, die für die meisten Katholikinnen nicht annehmbar sind, für Nicht-Katholikinnen aber als Zeichen feministischer Identität gelten. Wer aber darf sich Feministin nennen? Wer entscheidet darüber, was eine Feministin ist? Ich sehe dies als Problem beider Seiten an. Es ist deutlich, dass gläubige Frauen nicht überzeugend sind. Andererseits nehmen aber auch die (polnischen) Feministinnen nicht eine vielseitige Kirche wahr, zu der auch Frauen gehören, sondern nur eine patriarchale, frauenfeindliche Institution. Manchmal denke ich, dass atheistische Feministinnen zwar viel über manche Männer in der Kirche wissen, aber kaum etwas über die Frauen in der Kirche. Es ist entmutigend zu sehen, dass viele Feministinnen (nur die polnischen?) gegen jegliche Diskriminierung von Frauen sind – vorausgesetzt, die Frau ist nicht römisch-katholisch.

In feministischen Kreisen bin ich 'queer'. Ich sage dies aber nicht wie Lucy Tatman oder Marcella Althaus Reid mit Stolz und Würde. Mir tut es einfach leid. Habe ich zu viel erwartet? Muss es diese Spannung zwischen Müttern und Töchtern, zwischen Nonnen und Ehefrauen, von Frauen untereinander wirklich geben? Ist es möglich, die Unterschiede als interessante Erweiterung und nicht als trennendes Problem zu sehen? In persönlichen Kontakten geschehen manchmal kleine und große Wunder. Aber meine Freundinnen bekommen manchmal von *Frauen* zu hören: Du bist doch Nonne, worüber redest du mit dieser (Ehe-)Frau? Du bist doch atheistisch, wozu hast du dann Kontakt mit dieser Katholikin? Du bist doch lesbisch, was willst Du denn mit dieser (Ehe-)Frau anfangen?

Ich kündigte eingangs an, von Mängeln und Bedürfnissen zu sprechen, die mir bei den Konferenzen bewusst geworden seien. "Queer I stand", eine Anspielung auf Luthers "Hier stehe ich", ist für Marcella Althaus Reid – und, freilich unter anderem Titel, auch für Lucy Tatman – eine Erfahrung der Macht und Ermächtigung; für mich hingegen ist diese Aussage ein Beweis für das Vorhandensein von Mängeln und Bedürfnissen. Mir scheint, dass das Gefühl, *queer*, anders zu sein, für Lucy Tatman und für polnische Feministinnen sehr wichtig ist. Vielleicht hilft es ihnen bei ihrer Identitatsuche, bei der Bildung ihres (Selbst-)Bewusstseins und gibt es ihnen Kraft. Ähnlich mag dies auch für viele Katholikinnen gelten. Bei mir ist es umgekehrt: Zu meiner Identität gehören auch meine unterschiedlichen Freundinnen und Kolleginnen, und ich möchte gerne, dass sie miteinander ins Gespräch kommen. Manchmal habe ich den Eindruck, dass diese Frauen sich gegenseitig nicht brauchen und am liebsten in voneinander separierten, geschlossenen Frauenwelten leben würden. Ich empfinde diese Spaltung der Frauen als schmerzlich. Es tut mir weh, wenn ich im feministischen Milieu Witze über die "braven, blöden katholischen Mädchen" höre; und genauso weh tut es mir, wenn ich scharfe Worte höre über die "wütenden Feministinnen, die Familie und Kinder hassen." Ich kann und will es nicht vergessen: die Tatsache, dass ich meine Tochter in Krankenhaus bei mir im Zimmer haben und stillen konnte, verdanke ich *diesen Feministinnen*. Und ich kann und will auch sie nicht vergessen: die vielen starken Frauen in der Kirchengeschichte, die keine *blöden braven Mädchen* waren, Schulen für Mädchen gründeten, Häuser für Frauen in Not und vieles mehr taten.

Ich gehöre zwei verschiedenen Welten an und in beiden bin ich *queer*. Auf Marcella Althaus Reids "hier stehe ich", erwidere ich: ich bin weder stolz darauf noch damit einverstanden. Denn wie könnte ich damit zufrieden sein, da einstweilen nicht alle meine Freundinnen gemeinsam an einem Tisch sitzen können. Aber ich habe einen Traum: Ich würde gerne meine Freundinnen und Kolleginnen zu meinem Geburtstag einladen. Alle, so unterschiedlich sie sind, damit wir miteinander sprechen können. Vielleicht werde ich, wenn es soweit ist, noch nicht zu alt zum Tanzen sein – vielleicht werden wir dann alle gemeinsam tanzen.

La maternité est-elle une source d'expérience féministe? Une source où peut puiser la théologie féministe? Faisant jouer la complexité et l'étrangeté contenue dans le fait d'être une théologienne catholique féministe polonaise mariée, cet article traite de la possibilité que renferment la maternité et le mariage, expériences constituant la vie quotidienne de nombreuses femmes, de répondre à une vocation, d'être un lieu de rencontre avec Dieu, un espace où peut se développer un esprit de discernement théologique.

Is motherhood a source of feminist experience and for feminist theology? Drawing upon the complexity and 'queerness' of being a married Polish Catholic Feminist theologian, this article discusses the ways in which motherhood and marriage, the experiences which make up many women's everyday lives, are also callings through which God can be encountered and from which theological insights may spring.

Monika Walus (*1965) ist Theologin und arbeitet an einer Doktorarbeit über Pneumatologie. Sie ist verheiratet und hat Kinder.

Huguette Charrier

L'Espérance au Féminin

Un cœur que peuvent satisfaire lieu et temps ne connaît rien de son immensité.
Rainer Maria Rilke[1]

Au cours de l'Histoire et à travers des figures successives, Dieu se révèle comme libérateur et sauveur de l'humanité. La conscience croyante, elle-même inscrite dans le temps, interroge ce Dieu-là: entre le salut qu'il promet – et qui est donc déjà là – et l'expérience qu'elle fait du mal subi ici et maintenant, elle n'a d'autre issue que d'espérer. Qu'en est-il de cette visée de la conscience espérante qui, depuis sa position souffrante, regarde le salut qui vient? Et plus particulièrement, qu'en est-il de cette conscience quand elle est celle des femmes? Notre perspective sera délibérément phénoménologique; elle intégrera dans la théologie de l'espérance le concept de "genre", devenu classique. Elle pourrait nous conduire jusqu'au seuil de la prière ou même de la célébration d'un temps déjà racheté.

Le temps pour une conscience qui le vit et le pense

Nous avons appris qu'il n'y a pas d'"avant la création" puisque le temps – qui mesure le changement selon l'avant et l'après – ne subsiste pas par lui-même. Il nous arrive pourtant d'imaginer, de plonger le plus loin possible en arrière, vers nos origines, de compter en années-lumière ces temps astronomiques qui enveloppent toutes choses; parfois nous les voyons emportés en une course vertigineuse et parfois comme réceptacle immobile où se déroule aujourd'hui notre existence. Et ces immensités nous effraient. Ephémères nous sommes, serrés dans une vie ridiculement brève, la mort à l'horizon. Sur le passé nous n'avons nulle prise et notre avenir n'est que désir, crainte et attente. Et quand nous disons "maintenant", le futur est déjà passé. Notre temps à nous s'écoule, s'enfuit, est révolu, perdu, jamais ne se rattrape.

[1] *Sonnets à Orphée*, VIII.

Notre raison tente de maîtriser ce vertige: elle découpe le temps cosmique en séquences, marque sur ce long ruban l'origine de la vie, des espèces, le divise en périodes, l'âge d'or, de bronze, de fer, où se répartissent les techniques de l'humanité: ce temps-là, même ainsi domestiqué, surplombe de très haut la vie mortelle des peuples et des individus. Et même si nos calendriers nous sont d'utiles repères, ils ne nous libèrent pas de la course du temps.

Le paradoxe est pourtant qu'il faut une conscience, si infirme soit-elle, pour penser le temps, pour dire "maintenant". Il faut qu'elle soit présente à elle-même et à la réalité concrète, il faut qu'elle sente que l'instant vécu vient d'être traversé par quelque chose qui, l'instant d'avant, n'était pas là. C'est le sourire ou le rictus tout à coup sur le visage de l'autre et rien n'est plus comme avant; c'est la lettre qu'on vient d'ouvrir et une larme a jailli; c'est l'instant de l'accident, et une vie est brisée; c'est une main offerte où le pardon s'installe; c'est l'instant de la tentation, comme sur le Pinacle du Temple et tout peut basculer. On a senti comme le passage du passé vers le futur à travers l'instant présent. On peut dire que notre présence a l'instant vécu nous sauve de la fuite du temps.[2]

Pour dire la temporalité, nous usons de ces termes contrastés: l'instant et la durée. En tout instant qui passe peut s'amorcer une durée; on passe de l'un à l'autre sans percevoir de frontière: l'instant est un point qui se déplace vers l'avenir: ce que Bergson évoque sous l'image de la dune de sable dont la crête, imperceptiblement se déplace sous l'impulsion du vent; ce qu'aussi un chercheur contemporain illustre en faisant glisser une masse de grains de sable, mobiles, fluides à la surface, solidifiés en profondeur: où passe la frontière entre fluide et solide? Ces zones de passage sont particulièrement intéressantes, ce sont des tropismes: celui des plantes, et aussi des états intérieurs, perceptibles seulement à travers la parole.[3]

2 Nul mieux que Vladimir Jankélévitch n'a décrit l'instant fugitif, ce "je ne sais quoi qui advient dans l'espace infinitésimal d'une étincelle", "phosphorescence de l'instant, apparition naissante-mourante": *Le je ne sais quoi et le presque rien*, 1: *La manière et l'occasion* (Seuil: Paris 1980), 113.
Dans son cours de Sorbonne, en 1961 sur "la tentation", il cherchait à surprendre "l'instant du péché avant qu'il soit commis, cet instant comme condensation passionnée et dramatique du Temps."

3 Selon Nathalie Sarraute, le tropisme est "un mouvement si délicat qu'il n'est pas perçu du dehors". A partir d'une parole banale, un bouleversement intérieur se produit et surgit l'inattendu. Le temps n'est plus celui de la vie réelle, mais d'un présent démesurément grandi": *Tropismes* (Denoël: Paris 1938), 10-11.

Or, il n'est pas certain que ces entre-deux soient éprouvés de la même manière, qu'on soit homme ou femme. Ne nous arrêtons pas aux vues simplistes qui attribueraient aux hommes l'instant créateur et aux femmes la durée sécurisante. A eux la décision, l'action guerrière qui fait basculer le destin, à elles la stabilité du foyer, la patience des gestations, la disponibilité sexuelle, la fidélité. Il convient d'introduire ici, au lieu de ces stéréotypes dépassés, la notion de "genre".

Où intervient le concept de "genre"

Autour du sexe biologique, et dans toutes les cultures, se construit et s'élabore un ensemble de repères, d'indices, de modèles, qui se transmettent de génération en génération. Sur ces représentations de l'appartenance des individus à un genre déterminé se structurent les sociétés, se répartissent les rôles, dans les sphères familiale, professionnelle, politique. Des individus on attend qu'ils se conforment à leur genre, c'est là le prix de leur intégration. Le genre est "une façon d'être au monde".

C'est donc aussi une certaine manière de vivre le quotidien, l'instant. "A partir de la question du genre, le quotidien va apparaître important dans l'historiographie des femmes", dit Ivone Gebara. Or le quotidien, pour beaucoup d'entre elles, "c'est le combat pour vivre aujourd'hui, chercher du travail, faire la cuisine, laver les enfants et le linge, échanger des gestes d'amour; le quotidien, c'est le monde des relations courtes... capables souvent de changer les relations plus larges". De tout cela naît une conception particulière du temps.[4]

Une théologie qui se veut en prise sur le vécu, soucieuse d'intégrer la dimension existentielle, attentive aux lieux, temps et cultures, ne peut ignorer la différence sexuelle, si fondamentale. Il ne s'agit pas ici de destin mais de ressources propres à construire une histoire. Et puisqu'il sera ici question d'espérance on peut supposer qu'il y a bien une manière féminine d'habiter l'espérance, comme d'habiter le temps, instant et durée. A condition encore d'éviter les clichés obsolètes, comme ceux qui consistent à dire que l'espérance serait une vertu mixte, masculine et féminine à la fois: masculine à cause de l'accomplissement attendu, féminine par ce lâcher-prise et cette vigilance nécessaires. Nous dirons plutôt qu'il faut, pour que l'humanité puisse espérer, qu'elle s'installe dans ce lieu inconfortable pris entre réalisme et désir. Que

[4] Ivone Gebara, *Le mal au féminin: une approche théologique à partir du féminisme* (Travaux de doctorat Université catholique de Louvain, NS 18; L'Harmattan: Paris 1999).

dans ce lieu-là puissent se faire entendre à la fois et par une critique réciproque, la voix des femmes et celles des hommes, je ne sais si cela est possible dans la durée, mais l'espérance, nous l'avons dit, n'est qu'une vertu de passage, transitoire, tout comme l'humain, d'ailleurs, "et l'herbe des champs".[5]

L'espérance, vertu du temps ou la conscience espérante

Parmi les vertus théologales, l'espérance n'est pas la plus grande, mais bien la charité. Et si, au cours des temps toutes trois demeurent, au-delà, l'espérance sera dépassée, car nous verrons et posséderons ce qu'aujourd'hui nous espérons. Et "voir ce qu'on espère, ce n'est plus l'espérer" (Ro 8,24).[6]

Il y a les biens que nous possédons et ceux que nous attendons. Nous jouissons des premiers et portons notre désir sur les autres. Vertu du manque absolu, s'il est vrai que les biens que nous attendons sont sans commune mesure avec ceux que nous connaissons. Nous ne connaissons pas ce que nous attendons, notre désir ne peut se représenter son objet: la conscience désirante ne se représente pas ce qu'elle désire. Elle aime, mais quoi? elle ne peut le dire.[7] Il y a la promesse, l'espérance se fonde sur une parole qui promet. Certes, mais l'objet de cette promesse est désigné par les mots de notre langue, référence à notre humaine expérience. Peut-être avons-nous expérimenté un "salut": on échappe à noyade, à une arrestation, à l'incendie: on est sauvé; mais quand Dieu promet un salut, on peut supposer que nos expériences humaines ne nous renseignent guère sur la nature de ce salut. Quant au "péché" dont nous serions sauvés, c'est pour nous une notion si obscure et si soumise aux appréciations humaines – justement à ses codifications successives au cours des temps – qu'il est à craindre que cette notion ne nous soit d'aucun secours. On dira: "Pensons plutôt *vers quoi* nous sommes sauvés, l'avenir nous importe plus que le passé". Nous attend un amour infini qui est salut infini. Si cela est, il dépasse tout ce qui se peut concevoir sur la terre et dans les enfers. Où l'on retrouve encore cet incommensurable, dont la meilleure approche est de voir dans les expériences temporelles la figure inversée de l'objet de la promesse.[8]

[5] Ps 103, 15-16.

[6] "Quand viendra ce qui est parfait, ce qui est imparfait disparaîtra" (1 Co 13,10). "La foi, l'espérance et la charité demeurent toutes trois, mais la plus grande d'entre elles, c'est la charité" (1 Co 13,13).

[7] Il s'agit là de cette "vigilance extrême qui mortifie les dénominations", Stanislas Breton, *Unicité et monothéisme* (Ed. du Cerf: Paris 1981), 9.

[8] "Aussi radical que soit le mal, il ne saurait être aussi originaire que la bonté", Paul Ricoeur, *La symbolique du mal* (Aubier: Paris 1960), 150.

La Bible, déjà, nous a enseigné cette lecture du réel: l'impie prospère et le juste est humilié. Job s'en indigne, cite Yahvé au tribunal de sa courte vue, et finit la main sur sa bouche; mais au terme, il ose une certitude: l'espérance de "voir son créateur". Job traverse les temps, il crie encore aujourd'hui. Pas d'espérance sans dénonciation du mal omniprésent et affirmation d'un rétablissement du bien. Cela passe par la conscience, elle-même modelée par une culture, située dans l'espace et l'Histoire, voire affectée du coefficient de "genre". Et nous voici au rouet: une conscience androcentrée pourra dénoncer comme perturbant l'ordre du monde les aspirations des femmes à "se sauver" de leur sujétion. Une conscience "féministe" risquera de croire que les femmes, pour se "sauver" ne doivent compter que sur elles-mêmes. Or s'il y a un salut, il est pour toute l'humanité et il est donné.

L'espérance théologale est donc vertu de transition: entre l'image à peine discernable dans le miroir et le face à face. Et s'il est vrai que la volonté de Dieu – ce que Jésus est venu accomplir – est "qu'ils te connaissent, toi et celui que tu as envoyé"[9] alors l'espérance est sur le chemin de la connaissance de Dieu: vertu pédagogique. Elle tient en même temps une connaissance acquise et une visée vers l'insu. En sa dynamique désirante, elle a un objet qu'elle ne désigne que par le mot "Dieu". Il n'est pas blasphématoire de penser Dieu comme un vocable. Peut-être est-ce même la meilleure façon de dire notre incompétence radicale à le connaître: poser ce vocable comme une enveloppe, un contour, en attendant le temps où, au terme de nos métamorphoses, "nous le verrons tel qu'il est".[10] Le mot "Dieu" pour fixer l'imagination, orienter le désir, sans prétention de savoir.

L'espérance n'est pas de l'ordre du "projet", lequel anticipe sur la réalisation finale de l'objet achevé. Ni non plus de l'ordre de l'utopie fondée sur l'idéalisation. Paradoxalement, l'espérance, comme vertu pédagogique conduit au-delà d'elle-même: elle exige de nous une démaîtrise et un laisser faire, et elle s'alimente dans la prière qui est, comme le dit superbement Simone Weil,

[9] Jn 17,3. La "volonté de Dieu" a été souvent invoquée pour imposer soumission et patience à ceux et celles qu'opprimaient l'ordre établi et les dominations iniques. L'Evangile n'autorise pas ce recours. Au contraire: Jn 6,39: "La volonté de celui qui m'a envoyé, c'est que je ne perde rien de ce qu'il m'a donné, mais que je le ressuscite au dernier jour." Nous voyons là l'objet de l'espérance théologale.

[10] 1 Co 13,12: "Alors je connaîtrai comme je suis connu."

"le sommet de l'attention".[11] Etre attentif, c'est être là, dans l'instant, et durer. La conscience espérante, en ce lieu-là, rachète le temps.[12]

Le temps rédimé

Ce vingtième siècle aura laissé derrière lui, avec les charniers, les caves de torture, les prisons surpeuplées, l'enfance violée, les femmes égorgées, les chars de guerre broyeurs de liberté, un condensé de misère que ne compenseront jamais ni l'exploration de Mars, ni la maîtrise de la génétique ou d'une communication vide de message. Et si, comme on l'a dit, il convient de tenir à la fois et pour une unique prière la Bible et les journaux du matin, il faut affirmer que le temps, le nôtre et tous les temps, ont besoin d'être rachetés. Ira-t-on jusqu'à dire que les situations extrêmes sont les lieux privilégiés de l'espérance? Ces situations sont marquées au coin de l'absurde et de l'horreur. En Tchétchénie, une femme est accusée de complicité de meurtre à l'encontre de son mari. Sans preuve. Interdite de parole, sans défense aucune. Elle est enceinte de ce mari assassiné. Condamnée à mort. Les hommes, gardiens de la Charia, l'exécuteront sitôt l'accouchement. La mettront à mort dès qu'elle aura donné la vie. L'enfant viendra au monde sans père ni mère. Il naîtra en pleine mort, en pleine obscurité. Sera élevé dans le noir. Adulte, il sera, à son tour, gardien de la Charia.

Situation-limite, mais non moins exemplaire: on attend des femmes "en raison de leur infériorité existentielle, qu'elle paient le prix fort du sacrifice: elles doivent faire plus d'effort pour obtenir le salut".[13]

Mais sans doute, les femmes "rachètent" le temps d'une autre manière: elles entreprennent, même quand la cause est perdue d'avance. Quand le futur est incertain, quand le ciel est rouge, les mères de la Place de Mai font leur ronde en-dessous. Elles maintiennent l'avenir dans la sphère du possible. Les femmes afghanes, emmurées et grillagées, se projettent dans le futur incertain, anticipent une réalisation, non plus pour elles-mêmes mais pour leurs propres filles: leur espérance traverse les temps. Les africaines excisées qui refusent de perpétuer la coutume sur leurs filles, non seulement misent sur la survenue d'autres pratiques, mais elles espèrent que va basculer la signification de ce temps-là qu'elles ont vécu. Racheter le temps, c'est déplacer du sens, c'est dire:

[11] Simone Weil, *La pesanteur et la Grâce* (Plon: Paris 1988), 134.

[12] En 1941, lors des vendanges en Ardèche, chez les Thibon, "Je récitais le Pater chaque matin avec une attention absolue: Simone Weil, *Attente de Dieu* (Fayard: Paris 1966), 48.

[13] Ivone Gebara, *Le mal au féminin*.

le temps n'ira pas vers le modèle en cours. Elles mettent d'autres mots sur les rites, les expliquent autrement. Elles disent "mutilation" là où il y avait "intégration"; elles disent "barbarie" là où il y avait "ordre établi". Leur espérance crée du sens. Elles dénoncent, elles gardent mémoire. Elles sont une mémoire en attente d'inscription dans le temps d'après.

Ni musée, ni conservatoire, cette mémoire du cœur est une conscience; comme si elles étaient à l'affût, elles guettent le moment où ce sens nouveau pourra se dire comme révélation et comme projet. Ainsi Eve veillait sur l'Adam endormi pour le révéler à lui-même au moment venu: ensemble ils ont organisé le Jardin. Non pas que l'espérance soit ici ramenée au quotidien, au contraire, elle maintient la tension entre ce quotidien et le temps de la plénitude.

Ou, comme le dit encore Ivone Gebara: "affirmer la quotidienneté du salut ne signifie pas nier toutes les possibilités ouvertes par une perspective d'un au-delà de l'Histoire."[14] Il faut être attentif à ne pas affirmer l'au-delà en dépit de l'Histoire concrète. "Il n'y a pas d'espérance hors de cette inconfortable tension."[15]

"Yahvé rachète à la fosse ta vie Et te couronne d'amour et de tendresse.
Yahvé qui fait oeuvre de justice Et fait droit à tous les opprimés"
(Ps 103, 4-6)

Il faut supposer qu'une conscience soit capable de vivre le malheur absolu et d'affirmer dans le même instant ces deux versets du Psaume. Je ne parle pas ici de prière mais d'affirmation et je m'interroge sur un contenu de conscience. Si l'on concède qu'il convient de qualifier de "conscience espérante" celle qui serait capable de tenir ensemble ces visées antagonistes, il faut dire que cet état de conscience concentre en un même instant, ponctuel – le temps de prononcer ces versets – à la fois l'indignation, le tourment, l'effroi d'une situation vécue hic et nunc, et la sérénité, la paix, la gratitude de l'ordre rétabli; et cela non pas successivement, non comme deux situations distribuées sur la ligne du temps, mais simultanément. Il semble que la conscience humaine n'ait pas ce pouvoir. On dira que, précisément, il est ici question d'espérance théologale et non d'espoir humain. On en appellera à "la grâce" et le problème sera classé. Voire. Une "religion dans les limites de la simple raison" exige autre

[14] Ibidem.
[15] Ibidem.

chose. En ce cas, renonçant à la contemporanéité des contenus de conscience contradictoires, on repoussera dans l'au-delà "la tendresse et la justice". Mais qui ne voit que ces mots n'ont de sens que pour le temps de nos vies et que, justement, cet "au-delà", s'il existe, est hors de nos repères de temps et d'espace: les méchants ne sont nuisibles que le temps que vivent leurs victimes. L'alternative est d'enfermer la visée de l'espérance dans l'aujourd'hui. L'impasse est totale. Mais aussi, seule une quête de l'impossible mérite qu'on s'y attache. Là sans doute est le sens de la "sequela Christi" dont le monopole n'appartient pas aux disciples répertoriés, béatifiés et canonisés, mais où sont convoqués ceux et celles qui ont été dénoncés, torturés, jugés d'avance et finalement anéantis dans la nuit infâme: on l'a dit, "le Golgotha n'est pas la capitale de la douleur" et il y a, toujours et partout dans le monde plus de douleur qu'au Golgotha.

Hoffnung ist die Tugend der Zeit. Ähnlich wie der Glaube wird sie zugunsten dieser Vision vergehen: "Wie kann man auf etwas hoffen, das man sieht?" (Röm 8,24). Das hoffende Subjekt behält in seinem Bewusstsein gleichzeitig die Erfahrung des Unglücks und die Gewissheit, gerettet zu werden. Die "weibliche" Hoffnung – Frauen kennen sie allzu gut – besteht darin, etwas zu tun, obwohl von vorneherein feststeht, dass die Sache verloren ist, und die Zukunft im Bereich des Möglichen zu erhalten. Es ist ihre persönliche Art, "die Zeit zu erlösen". So haben Frauen in den größten Unglückszeiten der Menschheit die Zeit erlöst. Gemeinsam mit den Männern werden sie nun die kommende Zeit konstruieren.

Hope is a virtue of time. Like faith, hope will give way to vision: "For who hopes for what is seen?" (Rom 8.24). Those who hope are simultaneously conscious of the experience of misfortune and of the certainty that they will be saved. "Feminine" hope – which women know only too well – consists of the ability to do something which from the outset is a lost cause and yet to believe that the future lies in the sphere of what is possible. It is their own way of "redeeming time". In this way women have redeemed time even in humankind's most unhappy moments. Together with men, women will construct the times which come.

Huguette Charrier a enseigné la philosophie pendant de nombreuses années. Membre de l'AFERT section française et de "Femmes et hommes en Eglise" elle s'intéresse particulièrement à la notion de "genre" comme outil d'analyse des phénomènes de société. Elle apporte également sa contribution à la revue "Les réseaux des Parvis".

Regula Strobel

Theologische Interpretationen der Kreuzigung Jesu und die gesellschaftliche Normalität des Opferdiskurses[1]

Elisabeth Schüssler Fiorenza hat in ihrem ganzen theologischen Arbeiten die Doppelperspektive vor Augen gehalten: Die Neugestaltung von Himmel und Erde. Beides gehört zusammen: Ohne eine neue Erde wird ein anderer Himmel bedeutungslos, und ein neues theologisches Symbolsystem ist dringend nötig, um Veränderungen auf der Erde zu unterstützen.

Wenn ich die vorherrschende Theologie innerhalb der christlichen Traditionen betrachte, stelle ich fest, dass die Vorstellung eines neuen Himmels und das Neugestalten der Erde vorwiegend, wenn nicht ausschließlich mit einer Person verbunden wird, mit Jesus von Nazaret. Und auch hierbei ist es ein kleiner Teil seiner Existenz, der im Zentrum steht und das zu einem neuen Himmel und einer neuen Erde führende Heil enthält: seine Kreuzigung, interpretiert als heilbringende Erlösung oder als befreiende Konsequenz seines Handelns.

Christliche Identität wird nach innen und nach außen am Kreuz festgemacht. Im praktischen Kirchenalltag wird das Kreuz bei den verschiedensten Gelegenheiten als Segenszeichen verwendet: bei der Taufe und der Firmung eines Kindes, bei der Segnung des Brotes in der Eucharistie, zur Eröffnung oder zum Abschluss eines Gottesdienstes. Das Kreuz hat auch eine zentrale Stellung in der kirchlichen Ikonographie. Die als orthodox deklarierte Deutung des Gekreuzigten, "Gott/Jesus – gestorben für uns", wird einerseits von den Gläubigen und Mitarbeitenden in den Kirchen eingefordert, andererseits ist diese Aussage durchaus auch bei Kirchenfernen präsent. Das Kreuz gilt als Erkennungszeichen von Christen. Rudolf Augstein, Journalist und Herausgeber des deutschen Magazins *Der Spiegel*, hat diese identitätsstiftende Funktion auf den

[1] Dieser Artikel wurde für die Festschrift zum 65. Geburtstag von Elisabeth Schüssler Fiorenza geschrieben.

Punkt gebracht: "Ohne gekreuzigten Christus ist der christliche Glaube nichts."[2]

Der Weg zu einer neuen Erde und einem neuen Himmel führt m.E. über eine Veränderung dieser zentralen Stellung des Kreuzes und vor allem über die Verabschiedung von verschiedenen seiner theologischen Interpretationen, die dazu beitragen, Frauen und andere Unpersonen im herrschenden Kyriarchat[3] in die Opferrolle einzubinden. Deshalb weise ich im ersten Teil dieses Artikels auf Parallelen zwischen dem theologischen und dem säkularen Opferdiskurs hin und zeige, wie auch theologische Interpretationen der Kreuzigung Jesu, die sich von der Opfertheologie distanzieren, noch den säkularen Opferdiskurs stützen. Im zweiten Teil geht es darum, einige Perspektiven für ein neues Reden vom Kreuz zu skizzieren.

1. Kritische Blicke auf vier theologische Interpretationen der Kreuzigung Jesu und deren Parallelstruktur im säkularen Opferdiskurs

Die vier Deutungen der Kreuzigung Jesu, die ich mit den Kurzformeln "Opfer zum Heil der Welt", "Hingabe zur Erlösung der Menschheit", "Konsequenz seines Engagements" und "Zeichen des Widerstands" bezeichne, enthalten gefährliche Züge, die auch im säkularen Bereich die Denkstrukturen prägen und verheerende Wirkungen haben. Sie tragen dazu bei, die gesellschaftliche Normalität des Opferdiskurses unangetastet zu lassen. Die zwei ersten Interpretationsmuster haben ihre theologischen Hintergründe in der traditionellen kirchlichen Lehre, die beiden letzten sind in lateinamerikanischer Befreiungstheologie und bei deren RezipientInnen in der ersten Welt anzutreffen.

1.1 Opfer zum Heil der Welt?

In der westlich-abendländischen Theologie wurde *eine* der Interpretationen der Hinrichtung Jesu, die Opfertheologie, bevorzugt. Sie ist von den christlichen

[2] Vgl. seinen Artikel in der Zeitschrift *Die Woche*, April 1995.

[3] Elisabeth Schüssler Fiorenza hat den m.E. treffenden Begriff Kyriarchat geprägt, um die vielfältige pyramidale Struktur der gegenwärtigen Machtverhältnisse in unseren Gesellschaften zu analysieren, an deren Spitze sich weltverbreitet und mehrheitlich Herren weißer Hautfarbe mit einem guten Bildungs- und Finanzhintergund befinden. Die pyramidalen Machtstrukturen von Klasse, Rasse, Geschlecht, Neokolonialismus, Heterosexismus überlagern sich teilweise und multiplizieren die entsprechenden Unterdrückungserfahrungen der Betroffenen. Vgl. Elisabeth Schüssler Fiorenza, *Jesus – Miriams Kind, Sophias Prophet* (Chr. Kaiser / Gütersloher Verlagshaus: Gütersloh 1997), 31-41.

Kirchen weiterverkündet und über die Mission in alle Regionen der Welt getragen worden. Sie hat die Denkstrukturen der westlichen Kultur mitgeprägt und ist zu einem Stück des kulturellen Unbewussten[4] geworden.

Die Opfertheologie begegnet uns in den verschiedensten Lebensbereichen – in Gesprächen mit Unterdrückten, mit EhepartnerInnen und in der Begleitung von Leidenden ebenso wie im Bereich von Leistungssport, Wirtschaft und Politik als säkulare Opferideologie.

Opfertheologie und ihre betäubende Wirkung

Die Opfertheologie wird in zwei Varianten ausformuliert, deren Ausgangspunkt jedoch in beiden Fällen die Sünde der Menschen ist. Sie macht das Opfer, Jesu Kreuzigung, notwendig, um die Menschen aus den Klauen des Teufels loszukaufen (Variante 1) oder um bei Gott Wiedergutmachung zu erwirken (Variante 2). In beiden Varianten ist es Gott, der die Folgen der menschlichen Sünde tilgen und die Menschen erlösen will. Jesus führt diesen göttlichen Heilsplan aus. Er ist gehorsam und gibt – wie es von Gott gewollt ist – am Kreuz zum Heil und zur Rettung der Menschen sein Leben dahin.

In dieser Opfertheologie lässt sich eine klare Struktur erkennen: Einer hegt ein grosses Ziel und bestimmt einen anderen, der dieses Ziel unter Einsatz seines Lebens realisieren soll. Von diesem wird die gehorsame Ausführung seines Willens erwartet. Jesus bringt das Opfer, und andere, wir alle, profitieren davon.

Feministische Theologinnen kritisieren diese theologischen Interpretationen der Kreuzigung Jesu nicht nur wegen des fürchterlichen Gottesbildes, das sie tradieren.[5] Kritik ist auch nötig wegen des großen, Gewalt stützenden Potenzials, das diesen theologischen Interpretationen inhärent ist. Erstens, weil die Kreuzigung Jesu durch die römische Besatzungsmacht in eine göttliche Heilsgeschichte entrückt und dadurch idealisiert wird. Das Opfer eines totalitären Regimes wird als Opfer für uns, für unsere Erlösung interpretiert. Durch diese

[4] Mit kulturellem Unbewussten meine ich u.a. Denkstrukturen und Werthierarchien, die unser Leben prägen und die wir akzeptieren, ohne sie zu durchschauen.

[5] Zur Kritik am Gottesbild vgl. u.a. Dorothee Sölle, Elga Sorge, Christa Mulack, Carter Heyward. Sölle und Heyward formulieren dabei explizit, dass die Problematik des Gottesbildes dieser Theologie durch die Auferstehung Jesu nicht aufgehoben wird. "Der Gott, der leiden macht, ist auch durch spätere Aufhebung des Leidens nicht zu rechtfertigen. Kein Himmel kann so etwas wie Auschwitz wiedergutmachen": Dorothee Sölle, *Leiden* (Kreuz-Verlag: Stuttgart [6]1984), 183.

Umdeutung wird der Gewalttat der Herrschenden göttlicher Sinn und Zweck zugeschrieben. Damit geht einerseits eine Entschuldung der Herrschenden und andererseits eine Idealisierung des Opfers (*victim*) römischer Herrschaftspolitik einher. Es sei hinzugefügt, dass es im Deutschen für "Opfer von" Verkehrsunfällen, Gewalttaten usw. (engl. *victim)* und "Opfer für" auch in einem religiösen Kontext (engl. *sacrifice)* nur einen Ausdruck gibt. Damit kommt in die deutschsprachige Diskussion dieses Themas eine gewisse Unschärfe, weil nicht immer klar ist, welcher der beiden Aspekte gemeint ist. Aber gerade die Verschmelzung der beiden unterschiedlichen Begriffe in einem Wort macht auch die in der christlichen Opfertheologie vollzogene Identifikation von *victim* und *sacrifice* in all seiner Problematik deutlich.

Zweitens fördert diese Art von Kreuzestheologie die Akzeptanz von Denk- und Handlungsstrukturen, die Menschen immer wieder zu Opfern machen. Die Opfertheologie bereitet den Boden, dass diese Strukturen problemlos aufgebaut werden können und meist kritiklos fortbestehen. Sie wirkt betäubend, weil sie als normal und gut, ja sinnvoll und erlösend erscheinen lässt, dass einer (Gott-Vater) einen andern (Jesus) dazu bestimmt, sich aus Liebe für das Heil der Menschen zu opfern, und sei es zum Preis seines eigenen Lebens. Menschen werden durch diese Opfertheologie daran gewöhnt, dass wichtige Ziele Opfer erfordern. In dieser Gewöhnung und Selbstverständlichkeit liegt das Narkotisierende, weil die Frage gar nicht mehr aufkommt, ob es überhaupt Ziele geben kann, für die Menschen geopfert werden dürfen.

Gewöhnung an Opfer nicht nur bei Kirchentreuen

Die Opfertheologie prägt viele kirchlich sozialisierte Menschen und lässt sie gar nicht wahrnehmen, wie stark dieselbe Grundstruktur in unserem Alltag präsent ist. Denn die Einflüsse dieser Theologie reichen weit über das kirchliche Milieu hinaus in säkulare Bereiche, in denen wir dies nicht unbedingt erwarten würden. Die Grundstruktur der Opfertheologie hat unsere abendländische Kultur und Gesellschaft durchdrungen. Davon sind auch all jene betroffen, die sich von den Kirchen schon längst verabschiedet haben.

Es wird auch im gesellschaftlichen Kontext als selbstverständlich erachtet, dass zum Erreichen gewisser Ziele Opfer erbracht werden müssen. Die Ziele müssen uns nur erstrebenswert erscheinen oder plausibel gemacht werden. Solange es andere sind, die auf dem Weg zum Ziel als Opfer auf der Strecke bleiben, stimmen wir dieser Grundstruktur meist zu. Denn wir sind an sie gewöhnt, sie muss schon längst nicht mehr begründet werden, sondern gilt in der Gesellschaft unhinterfragt: "Es ist einfach so." Die Mobilität hat ihren

Preis und fordert Opfer, ebenso wie Budgetsanierungen, die NATO-Bomben in Ex-Jugoslawien oder die Bestrafungsaktionen gegen Bin Laden in Afghanistan.

Christliche Opfertheologie kann zwar nicht für das Handeln der Herrschenden verantwortlich gemacht werden, denn damit würden die EntscheidungsträgerInnen in Wirtschaft, Politik und Kirche zu schnell entlastet. Aber die lange Tradition und weite Verbreitung der Opfertheologie hat erstens ein Klima der Akzeptanz geschaffen, sowohl bei den Opfern oder potentiellen Opfern, als auch auf Seite der EntscheidungsträgerInnen. Dieses Klima der Akzeptanz verhindert oder erschwert zumindest, zu durchschauen, was geschieht.[6] Zweitens hindert die Gewöhnung an Opfer die meisten Menschen daran, aus dem gesellschaftlichen Opferdiskurs auszubrechen und jene zu entlarven und anzuklagen, die solche Opferstrukturen aufrecht erhalten wollen.

Höhere Aktienrenditen fordern Opfer

Die Denkstruktur, in die wir durch die theologische Idealisierung des Opfers eingeübt werden, ist äußerst problematisch. Mit der Vorstellung, dass Opfer sinnvoll, ja heilbringend seien, wird den Entscheidungen der Wirtschaftselite der Boden bereitet. Und gleichzeitig werden jene, die deren Entscheidungen zum Opfer fallen, dazu gebracht, diese als richtig oder zumindest als unumgänglich zu akzeptieren.

In der Logik des Opferdiskurses, dass Menschen geopfert werden dürfen, entscheiden die Machthaber, für welche Ziele welche Menschen über die Klinge springen müssen. Mit dem Ziel der Profitmaximierung werden die Arbeitenden angehalten, immer mehr zu leisten und sich bis zum Letzten (Herzinfarkt, Magenkrebs, Nervenzusammenbruch) zu verausgaben. Oder sie werden durch noch schneller arbeitende Maschinen ersetzt und infolge von Restrukturierungen entlassen. Denn im Interesse, den Börsenwert der Aktien eines Unternehmens zu steigern, müssen die Betriebe "schlank" gemacht werden, das heißt, weniger Lohnkosten verschlingen.

Die Inhalte kirchlich-christlicher und säkularer Opferideologie sind verschieden, aber die Denkstruktur ist dieselbe. Die kirchlich-christliche Erlösungstheologie formuliert den Glauben an einen Gott, der bereit ist, für das

[6] Elisabeth Schüssler Fiorenza hat mit ihrer feministisch-kritischen Hermeneutik wesentlich dazu beigetragen, Texte, Situationswahrnehmungen und -interpretationen zu entlarven, die versuchen, uns einzulullen in Realitäten, die wir akzeptieren sollen. Dank ihrer Hermeneutik können sowohl Texte jeglicher Art (biblische, literarische, geschichtliche, politische usw.) sowie gesellschaftliche politische Situation neu, befreiend gelesen werden.

Heil der Menschen seinen einzigen Sohn zu opfern. Parallel dazu sind die Kapitalgeber bereit, Menschen für die Steigerung der *shareholder values* bzw. Aktienrenditen zu opfern.[7] Die Ziele, für die Opfer gefordert werden, sind im theologischen und im wirtschaftlichen Opferdiskurs unterschiedlich. Aber es ist gefährlich und zu spät, wenn wir erst bei den Zielen zu diskutieren beginnen, ob es legitim sei, für das Heil der Menschen oder die Steigerung der *shareholder values* Menschen zu opfern. Alle Ziele können durch Indoktrination und / oder Gewalt plausibel gemacht und durchgesetzt werden.

Es gilt deshalb, diese Denkstruktur zu verändern, nach der es Ziele und Werte gibt, für die Menschen geopfert werden dürfen oder sollen. Und vor allem können wir als ChristInnen dieses Verhalten nicht mehr länger als Erlösung ausgeben. Weder soll unser Heilwerden auf einer brutalen Hinrichtung durch das römische Imperium beruhen, noch dürfen die satten Profite einiger weniger *shareholders* weiterhin mit dem Leben anderer bezahlt werden.

Viele halten die Opfertheologie für überholt, obwohl sie in Liturgien, Liedern und Predigten nach wie vor verbreitet wird. Häufig erfährt sie dabei allerdings eine Modifikation, indem Jesus nicht mehr als Opfer dargestellt wird, sondern als einer, der sich für das Heil der Menschen freiwillig hingibt.

1.2 Hingabe für die Erlösung der Menschen

Um dem grässlichen Gottesbild, das mit der Opfertheologie tradiert wird, zu entkommen, interpretieren Theologen wie etwa Jürgen Moltmann die Kreuzigung als Hingabe Jesu an Gott und für uns. Jesus ist in dieser Deutung nicht mehr in der Rolle des Opfers und des gehorsamen, instrumentalisierten Sohnes, sondern er handelt und entscheidet selbst.

Um von einem opferheischenden Gottesbild abzurücken, wird die Freiwilligkeit betont, mit der Jesus in den väterlichen Heilsplan eingewilligt habe. Er habe nicht einfach gehorcht, sondern sich aus freien Stücken hingegeben, in einer tiefen Willenseinheit mit dem Vater. Jesus sei im Geschehen der Hingabe nicht nur Objekt, sondern auch Subjekt. Seine Kreuzigung sei ein bewusst angetretener Leidensweg, bejahtes Sterben auf Grund seiner Leidenschaft für Gott.[8]

[7] Vgl. auch Franz Segbers, "Wider den Götzen Markt. Athen und Jerusalem im Erbe", in: Willibard Jacob / Jakob Moneta / Franz Segbers (Hg.), *Die Religion des Kapitalismus. Die gesellschaftlichen Auswirkungen des totalen Marktes* (Edition Exodus: Luzern 1996), 70-85, hier 83, und Franz J. Hinkelammert, *Der Glaube Abrahams und der Ödipus des Westens. Opfermythen im christlichen Abendland* (Edition Liberación: Münster 1989), 11-119.

[8] Vgl. Jürgen Moltmann, *Der Weg Jesu Christi. Christologie in messianischen Dimensionen* (Chr. Kaiser: München 1989), v.a. 194-196.

Zwei Aspekte dieser Interpretation der Kreuzigung Jesu sind neu und wichtig: Die Befreiung des Gottesbildes von Sadismus und die Erkenntnis, dass Opfer nicht nur willenlose Instrumente in der Hand anderer sind bzw. dass die Identität der Opfer sich nicht in der Opferrolle erschöpft. Problematisch bleibt in diesem Denken allerdings, dass die Hinrichtung Jesu durch das römische Imperium nach wie vor in einem göttlichen Heilsplan angesiedelt wird. Verschärfend kommt hinzu, dass die Kreuzigung zu einem freien Willensentscheid Jesu umgedeutet wird. Es wird suggeriert, Jesus habe seine eigene Kreuzigung für uns gewollt.

Opfer werden zu Subjekten, die sich hingeben
Das in der Opfertheologie fremdbestimmte Opfer, das gehorsam war bis zum Tod am Kreuz, ist in dieser Interpretation zum selbstbestimmten Subjekt geworden. Der Sohn gibt sich freiwillig hin. Er hat den Heilsplan verinnerlicht. Was Gott-Vater von ihm wollte, hat er zu seinem eigenen Willen gemacht. Allerdings ändert sich dadurch an den Fakten nichts. In völliger Willenseinheit mit dem Vater setzt Jesus, der Sohn, sich jetzt freiwillig für das ein, was beide wollen, und gibt sich ganz hin. Das sogenannt selbstbestimmte Subjekt macht nichts anderes als das, wozu es vorher als Opfer bestimmt und im Gehorsam aufgerufen war. Die einzige Veränderung geschieht auf der Ebene des Gottesbildes: Obwohl Gott nach wie vor den Heilsplan entwirft, ist er nicht mehr der Opfersüchtige, der die Kreuzigung seines Sohnes will oder zulässt. Das Image von Gott-Vater ist aufgebessert worden dadurch, dass der Sohn sich freiwillig hingibt.

Eine parallele Struktur dazu erkenne ich in den Veränderungen der Managementdirektiven der letzten Jahre: Nicht mehr harte Verfügungen und Befehle sind "in", sondern Motivationsarbeit. Alle Angestellten sollen sich mit dem Betrieb identifizieren, weil sie dann mehr und bessere Leistungen erbringen. Sie können auch ihre Zielvorgaben selbst formulieren. Faktisch hat sich dadurch jedoch nichts geändert; denn die Angestellten werden sogenannt freiwillig genauso hochgesteckte Leistungsvorgaben formulieren wie die ihnen früher von ihren Vorgesetzten verordneten. Vielleicht werden sie sogar noch höher ausfallen, weil der Leistungswille honoriert wird.

Verinnerlichte Ziele der Herrschenden
So wird auch im wirtschaftlichen Bereich darauf hingearbeitet, dass die "Opfer" die Ziele der Entscheidungsträger, der *shareholders*, verinnerlichen. Gute MitarbeiterInnen sind die, die sich mit dem Betrieb identifizieren und sich hohe Ziele stecken. Da sie die Ziele selbst formuliert haben, sind sie auch bereit,

Überstunden zu machen, ohne sie in Rechnung zu stellen. Denn diese abzurechnen, würde heissen, unrealistische Zielvorgaben formuliert zu haben oder die versprochene Leistung nicht in der normalen Arbeitszeit erbringen zu können. Beides wirkt sich etwa gleich negativ aus für das nächste MitarbeiterInnengespräch, die Beförderungsaussichten und die Lohnverhandlungen.

Mit der Verinnerlichung der Ziele der Herrschenden und der totalen Hingabe an deren Verwirklichung ist den Wirtschaftsmagnaten doppelt gedient: Sie müssen keinen Druck mehr ausüben, damit die Ziele verwirklicht werden, und zugleich wird ihr Image durch den sogenannt partizipativen Führungsstil aufpoliert. Beseitigt ist damit das Bild des leistungsheischenden Molochs, der jene wegrationalisiert, die die erforderlichen Leistungen nicht erbringen, das heißt, den erwarteten Gewinn nicht erwirtschaften.

Die Interpretationen der Kreuzigung Jesu als Opfer und als Hingabe für die Erlösung der Menschen schaffen sowohl bei den Herrschenden als auch bei den Opfern Akzeptanz für das oben beschriebene Verhalten und verhindern oder erschweren zumindest ein Ausbrechen aus diesen Denkstrukturen, auch bei denen, die unter die Räder kommen. Für die Wirtschaftsführer ist es völlig normal, die Werte zu definieren, für die Opfer gebracht werden müssen; es ist in ihren Augen auch normal, dass sie bestimmen, wer im Interesse der Profitmaximierung geopfert werden muss. Und wenn sie die Opfer dazu bringen, dass sie sich freiwillig und in völliger Identifikation mit den Interessen der *shareholders* zu hohen Leistungsvorgaben entscheiden, sind sie ihr Image als profitgierige *shareholders* los.

Diese zwei Interpretationen (Opfer und freiwillige Hingabe) sind in Europa im kirchlichen Alltag nach wie vor weit verbreitet. Einen anderen Akzent setzen lateinamerikanische BefreiungstheologInnen und westliche TheologInnen, die sich von ihnen inspirieren ließen.

1.3 Konsequenz seines Engagements

BefreiungstheologInnen verkündigen keinen Gott, der die Kreuzigung Jesu gewollt hat – auch nicht zur Erlösung der Menschen. Gott steht in ihrer Theologie nicht auf der Seite der Henker und Machthaber, die ohne zu zögern liquidieren, wer sich ihren Plänen nicht fügt oder wer sich für Gerechtigkeit und Leben für alle einsetzt. Sie sprechen auch nicht von einer Hingabe Jesu am Kreuz zu unserer Erlösung.

BefreiungstheologInnen sind sich bewusst, dass die Rede vom erlösenden Charakter der Hinrichtung Jesu lange dazu gedient hat, Leidende, Arme und Entwürdigte in ihren Leidenssituationen festzuhalten, auch wenn die Ursachen für deren Leiden in menschlicher Ungerechtigkeit und Ausbeutung zu suchen waren. Sie machen deutlich, dass nicht unfreiwilliges, aufgezwungenes Leiden erlösende und befreiende Funktion hat, sondern nur freiwillig akzeptiertes Leiden, das aus dem Kampf für eine gerechtere und menschlichere Welt resultiert. Unfreiwilliges Leiden als erlösend zu propagieren, bedeutet für sie, aktiv an der Ausbeutung und Unterdrückung der Armen mitzuwirken.

BefreiungstheologInnen interpretieren Jesu Kreuzigung als unausweichliche Konsequenz seines unerschütterlichen, aber freiwilligen Einsatzes für Gott und seine/ihre Gerechtigkeit.[9] Wer den Willen des Vaters tue, gerate unweigerlich in die Konfrontation, in den Kampf, in das Leiden – ans Kreuz eben.

Jesus hätte unter den Drohungen zusammenbrechen und sich zurückziehen können,[10] aber er hätte dadurch auch seine Glaubwürdigkeit eingebüsst. Jesus habe trotz Drohungen seitens der Mächtigen an seinem Einsatz *für* und an seiner Vision *vom* Leben in Fülle für alle festgehalten. Aber wer konsequent bleibt, muss mit der Kreuzigung, oder heute mit Folter und Repressionen vieler Art rechnen. Auch die, die sich heute für Gerechtigkeit und Leben für alle einsetzen, müssen diesen Konsequenzen ins Auge sehen. Erlösung und Befreiung sind, so ihre Überzeugung, nicht ohne Leiden und Kreuz zu haben.

Wichtig ist allerdings, dass in dieser Interpretation niemand andere dazu bestimmt, sich für dieses oder jenes Ziel zu opfern und hinzugeben, sondern dass jede und jeder selbst und freiwillig entscheidet, für welchen Einsatz und welches Ziel er oder sie welche Konsequenzen in Kauf nehmen will.

Die Kreuzigung Jesu als Konsequenz seines unbeirrbaren Engagements für Gerechtigkeit zu interpretieren, erscheint mir aber als ebenso problematisch wie die zwei vorangegangenen Interpretationen. Auch hier bleiben die Botschaft und die Gewöhnung an Opfer letztlich dieselben: Wer etwas erreichen und

[9] Z.B. Miguel d'Escoto, zitiert nach Dorothee Sölle, in: Dorothee Sölle, *Gott denken. Einführung in die Theologie* (Kreuz-Verlag: Stuttgart 1990), 166.

[10] Ob er sich dadurch der drohenden Kreuzigung hätte entziehen können, ist eine andere Frage: Totalitäre Regimes verzeihen und vergessen nicht so schnell! Aber es gehört zur (All)Machtphantasie / Illusion der Opfer, zu meinen, wenn sie sich anders verhalten hätten, wären sie nicht zum Opfer geworden, hätten sie den Täter umstimmen können. Geschlagene Frauen übernehmen häufig diese Täterperspektive (sie selbst hätten die Schläge provoziert). Damit passiert nicht nur eine Schuldzuschreibung an sich selbst als Opfer; gleichzeitig ist dies vielleicht auch die einzige Möglichkeit, nicht gänzlich in der Ohnmacht zu versinken und zu resignieren. Vielleicht ist dies Ausdruck des Bemühens, auch in der hoffnungslosen Opfersituation doch noch eine minimale Handlungsperspektive zu behalten: zu meinen, die Möglichkeit zu haben, es ein nächstes Mal durch das eigene Verhalten verhindern zu können, erneut geschlagen zu werden.

verändern will, muss damit rechnen, seitens der Mächtigen in Gesellschaft und Kirche Benachteiligungen und Unterdrückung zu erfahren.

Wer sich einsetzt, muss mit Repressionen rechnen

In dieser Interpretation wird ein kausaler, scheinbar unabänderlicher und unvermeidbarer Zusammenhang hergestellt zwischen dem Engagement Jesu für das Reich Gottes und seiner Kreuzigung, die von anderen Menschen verfügt wird. Damit wird jenen, die sich für Gerechtigkeit einsetzen und von den Machthabern in Gesellschaft und Kirche z.T. brutal und verunglimpfend kalt gestellt werden, vermittelt: Wer sich einsetzt, muss mit Nachteilen rechnen. Frauen, die in persönlichen Beziehungen oder auf gesellschaftlicher Ebene für Frauenrechte eintreten, müssen die z.T. gewalttätigen Reaktionen von Männern (und Frauen) in Kauf nehmen und ertragen. Wer sich im Betrieb in Arbeitskämpfen exponiert, kann nicht damit rechnen, im selben Betrieb bis zur Pensionierung angestellt zu bleiben.

Die Struktur dieses Verhaltens, dass Herrschende andere Menschen, die sich ihren Plänen nicht fügen, einfach eliminieren, wird nicht hinterfragt, ihre Gewalttätigkeit nicht als abnormal deklariert, um ihr den Boden der Akzeptanz zu entziehen. Im Gegenteil. Sie wird gestützt und gestärkt durch die Botschaft, die allen Engagierten vermittelt wird: wer sich engagiert, hat als Konsequenz mit Repressionen zu rechnen. Dies wird wie ein eigenmächtiges Gesetz tradiert, wie ein Sachzwang, dem auch die Herrschenden unterworfen sind. Dabei gerät in Vergessenheit, dass es immer freie Entscheidungen der Mächtigen sind, Gewalt auszuüben, Restrukturierungen von Betrieben durchzuführen und dabei einseitig nur die Steigerung der *shareholder values* im Auge zu haben.

Unsichtbar gemachte Gewalttäter

Die Kreuzigung Jesu und anderer Frauen und Männer ist nicht die Konsequenz des Engagements für Gerechtigkeit. Die Kreuzigung ist allein Konsequenz und Resultat der Gewaltanwendung der Herrschenden.

Verschweigen wir dies – ja formulieren wir gar, das Kreuz sei die Konsequenz des Handelns Jesu –, machen wir die Täter unsichtbar und schieben Jesus die Schuld und Verantwortung für die Kreuzigung zu. Wird das Kreuz zur Konsequenz des Engagements Jesu erklärt, kann sich die römische Besatzungsmacht die Hände in Unschuld waschen. Denn mit dieser Interpretation wird das Opfer der Repression zur Person, die das Ganze zu verantworten hat. Wie schon in der Interpretation der Kreuzigung als Opfer und als Hingabe verschwindet auch hier die Gewalt der Herrschenden, die die Opfer produziert, aus dem Blickfeld. In den ersten beiden Deutungen, weil die Kreuzigung in einen metaphysischen Heilsplan integriert wird, dessen Urheber Gott ist, hier weil die Kreuzigung zur Konsequenz des Einsatzes für Gerechtigkeit deklariert wird. Wo aber Gewalt unsichtbar gemacht wird, wird zu ihrer Aufrechterhaltung beigetragen. Die Machthaber / Täter werden dadurch aus ihrer Verantwortung entlassen und für ihre Gewalttätigkeit nicht zur Rechenschaft gezogen. In diesem Klima des Verschweigens und Vertuschens können sie weiterhin ungestört Gewalt ausüben.

Verstärkt wird diese Verschleierung der Gewalt durch die Betonung der Freiwilligkeit, mit der diese "Konsequenz" des Engagements getragen werde. Ich weiß, dass BefreiungstheologInnen sich dadurch abgrenzen von einer grundsätzlichen Idealisierung des Leidens und deutlich machen, dass nur jenes Leiden befreienden und erlösenden Charakter hat, das aus dem Kampf gegen Ungerechtigkeit "resultiert". Aber diese Repressionen werden nicht freiwillig getragen, sondern von den Herrschenden aufgezwungen! Das Engagement für Solidarität und Gerechtigkeit ist freiwillig – ja. Aber die Gewalt wird von den Mächtigen verordnet. Sie als freiwilliges Leiden der Engagierten zu beschreiben, macht diejenigen unsichtbar, die Kreuzigungen und Repressionen befehlen.

Indem die Gewalttäter sprachlich unsichtbar gemacht werden, geraten sie auch in der Realität aus dem Blickfeld und werden nicht mehr als solche wahrgenommen. Damit bleiben wir weiterhin im herrschenden Opferdiskurs stecken. Es bleibt dabei, Opfer sind unumgänglich auf dem Weg zu Erlösung und Befreiung.

1.4 Zeichen des Widerstandes?

Im Anschluss an die befreiungstheologische Interpretation der Kreuzigung Jesu wurde in den letzten zwei Jahrzehnten vor allem in politisch engagierten Kreisen in Europa vom Kreuz als Zeichen des Widerstandes gesprochen. Das Kreuz wurde von Widerständigen auch mitgetragen und hundertfach aufgerichtet, etwa im Hunsrück, um gegen die Stationierung von Mittelstreckenraketen zu protestieren. Aber ist es ein Zeichen des Widerstandes?

Kreuzigung – Machtdemonstration der Herrschenden

Die Kreuzigung Jesu und damit auch das Kreuz sind Zeichen für das Handeln der römischen Besatzungsmacht und anderer Machthaber, die sich entschieden haben, Menschen auf brutale und abschreckende Art und Weise zu beseitigen. Das Kreuz ist ein Zeichen der Machtdemonstration der Herrschenden und ihres

Umganges mit Menschen, ähnlich wie Hinrichtungsinstrumente anderer Zeiten und Orte, wie etwa die Scheiterhaufen der Inquisition, das Fallbeil der französischen Revolution, die Brennöfen und Gaskammern der Konzentrationslager des Naziregimes. Bei all diesen Instrumenten der gewalttätigen Machtdemonstration kommen wir nicht auf die Idee, sie als Zeichen des Widerstandes zu interpretieren.

Warum wird das Kreuz, das Hinrichtungsinstrument des römischen Regimes, an dem Tausende von Frauen und Männern jüdischer Herkunft und anderer besetzter Länder umgebracht wurden, zum Zeichen des Widerstandes umgedeutet?

Sicher haben Jesus und seine Freundinnen und Freunde auf ihre Art Widerstand geleistet gegenüber dem römischen Imperium[11] – auch wenn sie nicht zu den politisch-militärischen Umstürzlern zu zählen sind. Aber ich denke, der gewichtigere Grund liegt darin, dass wir von der theologischen und liturgischen Tradition her so daran gewöhnt sind, das Kreuz positiv zu deuten, als Zeichen der Erlösung und des Heils, dass es schwer fällt, das Kreuz als Zeichen der Repression und der Gewalt von Herrschenden stehen zu lassen.

Wir können die Tatsache jedoch nicht leugnen, dass das römische Regime neben den Auf- und Widerständigen auch "gewöhnliche Verbrecher" gekreuzigt hat. Ist das Kreuz auch in bezug auf sie Zeichen des Widerstandes? Doch wohl kaum. Dies macht deutlich, dass nicht das Kreuz an sich ein Zeichen des Widerstandes ist, sondern das, woran wir damit erinnern.

Widerständiges Erinnern[12]

Wir können und müssen nach der Realität fragen, die hinter den Kreuzigungen steht: Warum greift eine Besatzungsmacht zu solch brutalen, drastischen und öffentlichen Inszenierungen der Macht? Offenbar, um ihre Machtposition

[11] Einem Imperium gegenüber, das auf Unterdrückung, Ausbeutung, Ausschluss und Sklaverei baut, Leben in Fülle für alle einzufordern, ist Widerstand – damals wie heute!

[12] Opfertheologien und Interpretationen der Kreuzigungen Jesu und anderer Frauen und Männer, die diesen Repressionen Sinn zuschreiben, erinnern m.E. die Opfer (*victims*) nicht, sondern verzwecken sie für irgendeine Heilslehre, für das Wohlergehen anderer, für gesellschaftliche Utopien, für den höheren Gewinn der Aktienbesitzer. Darin liegt keinerlei Widerstand. Aber auch Erinnern ist nicht per se widerständig und befreiend. So gibt es ein nekrophiles Erinnern. Das immer wiederkehrende Nennen der Frauen und Männer, die von den Herrschenden physisch oder psychisch zermalmt worden sind, kann zu Ohnmacht und Resignation führen, statt zu Widerstand – nämlich dann, wenn nur an ihre Ermordung, ihre Kreuzigung erinnert wird und nicht auch an ihre Lebensvision, ihre Gesellschaftsperspektive, ihren Widerstand. In diesem

immer wieder neu zu festigen und allen, die daran zweifeln, mit den Kreuzigungen einzutrichtern: So ergeht es allen, die sich den Vorstellungen der Herrschenden nicht beugen. Wir können folgern, dass dort, wo Menschen gekreuzigt werden, eine Notwendigkeit besteht, dass die Herrschenden ihre Macht gewalttätig demonstrieren und inszenieren müssen. Wo aber die Macht demonstriert werden muss, ist sie bereits in Frage gestellt. Dort ist Widerstand vorhanden.

Allerdings wird deswegen das Kreuz oder die Gaskammer nicht zum Zeichen des Widerstandes! Diese bleiben Zeichen und Ausdruck der Gewalttätigkeit eines Regimes. Nicht das Kreuz, sondern unser Nachfragen und Erinnern ist Zeichen des Widerstandes – und das, was die hingerichteten Menschen getan haben, bevor sie von den Mächtigen gekreuzigt und beseitigt wurden. Das Erinnern dessen, was mit ihrer Hinrichtung zum Schweigen gebracht werden sollte, ist Zeichen des Widerstands. Die Erinnerung an die Gekreuzigten und das zur Rechenschaft ziehen der verantwortlichen Gewalttäter ist Zeichen des Widerstands, aber nicht das Kreuz.[13]

Wenn das Kreuz zum Zeichen des Widerstandes umgedeutet wird, wird die Gewalt der Herrschenden ebenso unsichtbar gemacht wie in der Interpretation des Kreuzes als Konsequenz des Engagements: Das Zeichen der Gewaltausübung der herrschenden Gewalttäter wird nicht mehr als solches benannt und die Gewalt dadurch nicht denunziert, sondern die Gewalttat wird umgedeutet in ein Zeichen des Widerstandes.

Für mich entspringt die Umdeutung des Zeichens der Machtdemonstration der Herrschenden als Zeichen des Widerstandes einer gewissen Verlegenheit: Weil kein anderes Zeichen griffbereit ist, um den Widerstand zu symbolisieren, wird das Kreuz umgedeutet. Ich denke jedoch, dass wir Zeichen des Widerstandes finden müssen, die als solche verständlich sind und nicht erst umgedeutet werden müssen. Zumal gerade mit dieser Umdeutung die Gewaltausübung der Mächtigen wieder verschleiert wird.

Sinn finde ich die Aussage, "Wir kennen nur den Gekreuzigten" nicht nur eine häretische Verkürzung der christlichen Botschaft, sondern auch äußerst gefährlich für unsere konkrete Lebensgestaltung. Denn sie führt in die scheinbare Ausweglosigkeit ("So ist es: wer sich einsetzt, setzt sich aus"), die Depression. Wenn wir nur den Gekreuzigten kennen, nicht auch den Lebenden, der sich für ein Leben in Fülle für alle stark gemacht hat, bleiben wir in Trauer und Resignation stecken.

[13] Ich verstehe auch die auf dem Hunsrück aufgerichteten Kreuze so: Die Protestierenden hielten den Herrschenden vor Augen, was sie mit den Raketen anrichten werden, nämlich das Töten von zig-tausend Menschen.

Die beiden letzten Interpretationen der Kreuzigung Jesu haben sich zwar von der Opfertheologie distanziert. Sie stützen jedoch trotzdem die Zustimmung zum gesellschaftlichen Opferdiskurs. Denn einerseits interpretieren auch sie das Kreuz um und benennen es nicht als das, was es ist, nämlich Gewalt seitens der Herrschenden. Auch sie deuten das Opfer (*victim*) Jesu positiv als konsequentes Handeln, als Treue gegenüber Gott (und den Menschen), als Zeichen des Widerstandes. Damit tragen beide Interpretationen zur Vertuschung der Gewalt der Herrschenden bei, und, weil diese nicht offen gelegt wird, zum Opferwerden vieler Menschen. Andererseits ist auch in diesen theologischen Entwürfen die Botschaft enthalten, dass der konsequente Einsatz für das Leben oder das Leisten von Widerstand gegen lebensverachtende Mächte unvermeidlich ans Kreuz führe.

Es ist m.E. höchste Zeit, aus der Normalität des Opferdiskurses auszubrechen. Und dies nicht nur deshalb, weil er im theologischen Bereich verheerende Gottesbilder und zerstörerische menschliche Verhaltensweisen tradiert, sondern – und dies ist der gewichtigere Grund – weil er im alltäglichen Verhalten zu einer Art kulturellem Unbewussten geworden ist, auf dessen Boden in verschiedenen wirtschaftlichen und politischen Bereichen Opfer als normal oder zumindest als unumgänglich akzeptiert werden. Wir brauchen ein neues Reden vom Kreuz, das den gesellschaftlichen Opferdiskurs weder explizit noch implizit unterstützt.

2. Auf den Weg zu einem neuen Himmel und einer neuen Erde brauchen wir ein neues Reden vom Kreuz

Wenn ich die Umdeutungen der Kreuzigung Jesu kritisiere und für uns als lebensbedrohend, weil Gewalt stützend und Opfer akzeptierend[14] ablehne, werde ich des öfteren mit dem Vorwurf konfrontiert, das Kreuz zu verdrängen und/oder es abschaffen zu wollen. Dies ist aber nicht der Fall. Ich meine allerdings, dass wir grundsätzlich anders von Kreuz, Erlösung und Heilwerden der Welt und der Menschen reden müssen. Wir leben in einer Welt, in der die Herrschenden im globalen Markt die totale Ausbeutung, ja mehr noch den Ausschluss einer zunehmenden Anzahl von Frauen, Kindern und Männern in

[14] Ich bin mir bewusst, dass Menschen in extremen Leid- und Unterdrückungserfahrungen im Kreuz durchaus auch Trost finden können. M.E. spielt in solchen Situationen weniger die Sinngebung für Kreuz und für eigene Leiderfahrungen eine Rolle, als das Wissen darum, dass ein anderer diese Leid bzw. Unterdrückungserfahrungen ebenfalls kennt und teilt. Dieses Wissen um andere, die die eigenen Erfahrungen teilen, ist ein erster Schritt aus der Isolation, in die extreme Schmerzerfahrungen Menschen bringen können.

allen Kontinenten, das heißt, deren Opferung für bessere Rendite als normal und als sinnvoll für alle deklarieren. Wenn wir wirklich die Erde neu gestalten wollen, können wir unsere Theologie doch nicht weiterhin auf einer idealisierenden Umdeutung der Kreuzigung eines Opfers (*victim*) als religiöses Opfer (*sacrifice*), als Befreiung und Heil bringendes Ereignis aufbauen!

Aber das Kreuz bleibt in dem, was es ist – Machtdemonstration von Herrschenden – ein wichtiges Zeichen, das die Opfer verschiedenster Gewaltherrschaften sichtbar machen und ihren Schmerz zum Ausdruck bringen kann. Das Kreuz kann uns zum Widerstand gegenüber jenen, die Opfer produzieren, herausfordern – immer im Wissen darum, dass Herrschende Widerständigen sowohl mit Repression als auch mit Verhandeln und Einlenken gegenübertreten können – je nachdem, wie sie sich entscheiden. Wir werden verschiedene Zeichen suchen müssen, die diesen Widerstand sichtbar machen, ohne lange Umdeutungen und vor allem, ohne die Gewalt zu verschleiern, die Menschen zu Opfern macht. Die Tauglichkeit und Tragfähigkeit solcher Zeichen steht nicht von vornherein fest, sondern wird sich in der Praxis erweisen müssen.

Mir geht es darum, die Realität der Kreuzigungen ernst zu nehmen und das Kreuz als das zu benennen, was es war, nämlich ein öffentliches Hinrichtungsinstrument, das die Macht des Regimes demonstrieren und die Unterworfenen einschüchtern sollte. Wo das Kreuz, die Kreuzigungen nicht in dieser Weise sichtbar gemacht werden, wird – ohne es zu beabsichtigen – an der Vertuschung und Aufrechterhaltung der Gewalt der Mächtigen mitgearbeitet. Im Interesse, den in der Gesellschaft meist unbewussten, jedoch sehr wirksamen Opferdiskurs zu unterbrechen, können und dürfen wir nicht mehr vom Kreuz als Zeichen des Widerstands, als Konsequenz des Engagements für Gerechtigkeit, als Hingabe an göttliche Heilspläne oder als notwendiges Opfer zur Erlösung der Menschen sprechen. Opfer als "Opfer von" (*victims*) zu benennen ist ein erster subversiver, befreiender Schritt, denn die Herrschenden wollen uns weismachen, es handle sich um sinnvolle oder doch notwendige "Opfer für" (*sacrifices*). Darum will ich das Kreuz, an dem ein Opfer (*victim*) der römischen Besatzungsmacht hängt, nicht mehr als erlösend, heilbringend, befreiend interpretieren und besingen.

Der größte Dienst, den wir all den Opfern (*victims*) erweisen können, liegt nicht in einer positiven Deutung ihres Opfers, liegt nicht darin, ihrem Opfersein Sinn zuzusprechen, sondern darin, die Normalität der gängigen Opferdiskurse in Kirche und Gesellschaft zu durchbrechen, uns deren Narkosewirkung zu entziehen und der Gewöhnung an Opfer eine Absage zu erteilen. Solange wir diese Opferdiskurse als normal akzeptieren ("Die Welt ist halt so"), werden einige wenige HeldInnen heroisch dagegen anrennen und als IdealistInnen, die einer Illusion folgen, von andern belächelt, schikaniert, gefoltert oder gekreuzigt werden – je nach der Entscheidung der Herrschenden.

Wir müssen die Realitäten benennen und die Gewalt der Herrschenden nicht umdeuten. Es sind keine Sachzwänge und keine "Logik der Macht", die sie zu befolgen haben. Sie allein sind verantwortlich für die Repressionen und die Ausübung von Gewalt. Es ist im Interesse der Herrschenden, dass wir schon im voraus mit ihren Repressionen rechnen. Sie müssen sich nicht mehr rechtfertigen, weil wir ihre Gewalt ja bereits als normal akzeptiert haben. Diese von Menschen geschaffene "Normalität" lässt sich aber von Menschen verändern, denn sie ist weder in unsern Genen festgeschrieben, noch entspricht sie einem Schöpfungsplan Gottes.

Erst wenn wir die herrschende Realität und den darin enthaltenen Opferdiskurs nicht mehr als normal und unveränderlich akzeptieren, sind Schritte auf Befreiung hin möglich. Die faktische Normalität nicht mehr als normal und naturwüchsig zu akzeptieren, beginnt beim Erinnern der Opfer als Opfer (*victims* als *victims*) und ist eine Form der Transzendenzerfahrung und -hoffnung: Die Erfahrung und Hoffnung, dass es außer der vorgegebenen, als normal deklarierten Realität noch etwas anderes gibt, dass normales menschliches Handeln und Verhalten anders aussieht.

Erlösungs- und Befreiungsprozesse werden nicht durch Kreuzigungen genährt, sondern durch das Engagement von Frauen und Männern, die die Opferung von Menschen durch andere Menschen und von ihnen geschaffene Wirtschafts-, Bildungs-, Politikstrukturen als abnormal und unmenschlich kritisieren. Ihr Engagement, nicht das Kreuz ist Widerstand. Auch unser Erinnern ist Widerstand. Benennen wir die Gewalttäter, erzählen wir von den Menschen, die ihnen zum Opfer (*victim*) gefallen sind, aber hüten wir uns, sie als sinnvolle Opfer (*sacrifice*) zu interpretieren, ihrer Hinrichtung Freiwilligkeit zu unterstellen und sie für ein gutes Ziel zu verzwecken. Dem Opferdiskurs in Theologie, Kirche und Gesellschaft die Normalität zu entziehen, ist ein notwendiger und wichtiger Schritt in Richtung auf Befreiung, Erlösung und Leben in Fülle für alle.

Glaub ihnen nicht,
wenn sie sagen:
Das ist eben so!
Der Mensch ist den Menschen
ein Wolf![15]

[15] Hinter der Aussage Hobbes', "Der Mensch ist dem Menschen ein Wolf", steht ein problematisches Klischee und Feindbild vom Wolf, das wenig mit wirklichen Wölfen zu tun hat.

Die Wölfe unter den Menschen
hören dies gerne.
Es vergrössert ihre Macht.
Weil die andern erstarren
in Ohnmacht.
Weil keine und keiner mehr
sie zur Rechenschaft zieht,
anklagt
für ihr wölfisches Verhalten.

Glaub ihnen nicht,
wenn sie sagen:
Das ist eben so!
Sie haben dich sonst total
in ihrer Gewalt,
sogar dein Wahrnehmen
und dein Denken.

Und sie, die Wölfe?
Sie können ruhig warten,
bis du, wir,
– ermattet durch die Ausweglosigkeit
und 'Normalität',
die wir uns einreden liessen, –
ihnen vor die Füsse fallen.

Deshalb ruf ich Dir zu:
Glaub ihnen nicht,
wenn sie sagen:
Das ist eben so! [RS]

Viele TheologInnen reagieren schockiert auf die Kritik an den verschiedenen theologischen Interpretationen der Kreuzigung Jesu. Sie befürchten, dass dem Christentum das Wesentliche, das eigentlich Christliche abhanden komme, wenn dem Kreuz keine heilbringende und/oder sinnstiftende Funktion mehr zugesprochen wird. Sie sorgen sich um das, was christliche Identität ausmacht.

Ein Blick auf das, was die Frauen, Jesus und die anderen Männer damals zusammengeführt hat – ihr Verlangen nach der "Basileia", dem Reich Gottes, als Alternative zur Herrschaft Roms[16] – könnte auch für uns heute eine tragende

[16] Vgl. dazu auch Schüssler Fiorenza, *Jesus*, 139-151, die die Jesusbewegung als jüdische Emanzipationsbewegung charakterisiert und christliche Identität in diesem Denkrahmen verortet.

Grundlage christlicher Identität (wieder)eröffnen: Die Normalität der *Basileia* Gottes[17] als Vision und als partielle Erfahrung in der Gegenwart macht m.E. christliche Identität aus. Hätten damals die Frauen und Männer nicht bruchstückhaft miteinander erlebt, was Leben in Solidarität und Gerechtigkeit, das heißt, Leben in Fülle ist, wären die Repressalien des römischen Imperiums und der andern Machthaber wahrscheinlich erfolgreich gewesen. Dieselben Erfahrungen gegenwärtiger Solidarität, Gerechtigkeit, Liebe, Verzeihen usw. müssen wir wahrnehmen, wo sie uns geschenkt werden. Wir können sie anderen ermöglichen, damit sie die Vision der *Basileia* Gottes wahrnehmen und für wahr nehmen und leben können.

Natürlich gehört auch dazu, immer wieder darauf hinzuweisen, wo und wem Gottes *Basileia* und ihre Gerechtigkeit verweigert wird. Aber es ergibt sich ein anderes Schwergewicht: Das Kreuz, das scheinbar unweigerliche Verbundensein von Leiden, Gewalt und dem Tod derjenigen, die sich für das Reich Gottes einsetzen, steht nicht mehr als christliches Identifikationszeichen oder als Zeichen der Erlösung und des Heilwerdens im Zentrum. Es müssen andere Zeichen und Symbole dazukommen, um andere als gesellschaftlich verursachte Leidens- und Schmerzenserfahrungen der Menschen sichtbar zu machen, aber auch Zeichen, Symbole, die das Reich Gottes, das Leben für alle usw. sichtbar machen. Ich würde die eingangs zitierte Aussage Augsteins abwandeln und nicht mehr formulieren, "Ohne gekreuzigten Christus ist der christliche Glaube nichts," sondern: "Ohne die Vision vom Reich Gottes und seiner Gerechtigkeit und Liebe – und ohne die immer wieder erfahrbare partielle Realisierung dieser Vision – ist der christliche Glaube nichts."

This article critiques four standard theological interpretations of the crucifixion of Jesus: that Christ was a sacrifice for the salvation of the world; that he laid down his life to redeem humankind; that the crucifixion resulted from his passionate commitment; or that it is a symbol of resistance. Demonstrating the repercussions of these interpretations in secular thought, the author argues that a new way of speaking of

Diese Verortung hätte auch den Vorteil, den Antijudaismus zu überwinden, der allen personenzentrierten Konzeptionen des Christentums inhärent ist.

[17] In biblischen Texten wird das Kommen und Wachsen der *Basileia* Gottes immer mit ganz alltäglichen Erfahrungen und einem menschlichen Verhalten beschrieben, das uns als äußerst selbstverständlich und plausibel erscheint (vgl. Gleichnisse). Nicht irgendwelche Heldentaten zeugen von der Ankunft der *Basileia*, sondern das Tun dessen, was im Moment gerade Not wendend, d.h. notwendig ist.

the cross is necessary "towards a new heaven and a new earth." If the world is to be changed, it is necessary to name the reality of oppression and to fight against it, rather than disguising it in theological meaning or even glorification. Not the cross but the vision of God's kingdom should inform our theology and with it our lives.

Cet article critique quatre interprétations théologiques classiques de la crucifixion de Jésus: le Christ fut un sacrifice pour le salut du monde; il a sacrifié sa vie pour racheter l'humanité; la crucifixion a résulté de son engagement passionné; il est symbole de résistance. L'auteur démontre les répercussions de ces interprétations dans la pensée séculière et affirme la nécessité d'un nouveau discours sur la croix pour s'acheminer «vers un nouveau paradis et une nouvelle planète». Si le monde peut être changé, et pour qu'il le soit, il faut donner un nom à la réalité de l'oppression et la combattre, plutôt que de la masquer derrière une interprétation théologique ou de la glorifier. Ce n'est pas la croix mais la vision du règne de Dieu qui imprègne notre théologie et, avec elle, nos vies.

Regula Strobel, Fribourg/CH, Theologin, ist in der Erwachsenenbildung und in der Forschung tätig.

Andrea Günter

Frauenverachtung, Weltverachtung? Metaphysische Anfragen an den Begriff "Welt" in postmodernen Globalisierungszeiten

Wo bleibt die Welt? Zur Genese der Fragestellung

Seit den Anfängen meiner feministischen Sozialisation habe ich verinnerlicht, dass Frauenverachtung und Weltverachtung unmittelbar zusammengehören. Seitdem weiß ich, dass es sich bei dem Denker, der Frauen- und Weltverachtung miteinander verknüpft hat, um Augustinus handelt.

Auf Augustinus und seinen Begriff der Welt stieß ich wieder bei meiner Auseinandersetzung mit Hannah Arendts "Vita activa". Arendt hat Ende der 20er Jahre des letzten Jahrhunderts ihre Doktorarbeit über den Liebesbegriff bei Augustinus geschrieben. Hierin kritisiert sie, wie die augustinische Vorstellung der christlichen Nächstenliebe die Beziehung der Menschen, die die Welt stiftet, diffamiert und außer Kraft setzt.

Die Auseinandersetzung mit Augustinus kann als Weichenstellung für die späteren Arbeiten Arendts verstanden werden. So sollte die "Vita activa" zunächst den Titel "Amor mundi" bekommen. Der Begriff der Welt und die Liebe zur Welt und zu den Menschen, so, wie sie sind und tätig werden, ist ein wesentlicher inhaltlicher Strang in der "Vita activa". Es geht Arendt immer wieder darum, wie die Welt den Menschen Heimat ist und sein kann. Hierbei übernimmt Arendt von Augustinus den Weltbegriff.[1]

[1] Hannah Arendt, *Der Liebesbegriff bei Augustin. Versuch einer philosophischen Interpretation* (Springer: Berlin 1929); vgl. Andrea Günter, *Die weibliche Hoffnung der Welt: Das Geborensein der Menschen und der freie Sinn der Geschlechterdifferenz* (Chr. Kaiser / Gütersloher Verlagshaus: Gütersloh 2000), v.a. 57-78; dies.: "Die Welt zur Welt bringen. Das Symbolische, Politik und Gebürtigkeit bei Hannah Arendt, den DIOTIMA-Philosophinnen und den Frauen des Mailänder Frauenbuchladens", in: Heike Kahlert / Claudia Lenz (Hg.), *Die Neubestimmung des Politischen. Denkbewegungen im Dialog mit Hannah Arendt* (Helmer: Königstein/Taunus 2001), 167-200.

Arendt und Augustinus verbinden die "Welt" zugleich mit der menschlichen Bedingung der "Gebürtigkeit". Gebürtigkeit heißt für sie, in Form von Beziehungen in das menschliche Beziehungsgefüge einzutreten. An dieser Stelle verbindet sich die Mutter mit dem Begriff der Welt. Das Verhältnis zur Welt korrespondiert mit dem zur Mutter, und umgekehrt. Damit erklärt sich das gemeinsame Schicksal von der "Welt" und der "Frau", genauer gesagt, von der Welt und der Mutter.

Diese Zusammenhänge sind mir immer wieder im Sinn, wenn ich über die Politik in Zeiten der Globalisierung nachdenke. Zumal als Folge der Globalisierung sogleich die These im Raum stand, dass Frauen die neuen alten Verliererinnen sein werden, wenn sie sich nicht schnell genug anpassen. Hierfür sprechen nicht einfach nur Tatsachen wie die Güterverteilung zwischen den Geschlechtern, sondern vor allem symbolische Zusammenhänge. Daher halte ich es für notwendig, dass eine Feministin über den Begriff der Welt und sein – postmodernes – Schicksal nachdenkt.

Ich greife hierzu auf eine Einsicht zurück, die mich sowohl Arendt als auch die feministische Kritik am Androzentrismus gelehrt haben. Von Arendts "Vita activa" habe ich gelernt, dass in Anbetracht der Tatsache, dass die Arbeitsgesellschaft immer weniger Arbeit zu verteilen hat, weniger die Frage ansteht, wie diese neu zu verteilen ist, sondern was Menschsein ist und was Gebürtigkeit bedeutet. Von der Androzentrismuskritik habe ich gelernt, dass ein Teilaspekt, der beansprucht, das Ganze zu sein, dringend auf seinen Platz verwiesen werden muss.[2] Diese Perspektive kann sich auch für die Auseinandersetzung mit der Globalisierung als fruchtbar erweisen: Was repräsentiert die Globalisierung? Die Welt? Oder ist die Welt etwa das, was den Horizont der Globalisierung bildet? Was aber ist dann Globalisierung? Und was ist die Welt?

Erfahrungen mit der Forschungslage: ein Spiegel des öffentlichen Bewusstseins?

Beim Bibliographieren stellte ich fest, dass es unzählige Titel mit dem Stichwort "Welt" gibt. Es handelt sich um Texte über "Weltpolitik", "Weltreligion", "Umwelt" und neuerdings über "Lebenswelt". Die allermeisten Titel folgen

[2] Vgl. Andrea Günter, "Liebe zur Freiheit, Hunger nach Sinn: Weiberwirtschaft, Tausch und die Arbeit am Symbolischen", in: Birge Krondorfer / Corinna Mostböck (Hg.), *Frauen und Ökonomie oder: Geld essen Kritik auf* (Promedia: Wien 2000), 27-38; auch in: Peter Biehl u.a. (Hg.), *Gott und Geld* (Jahrbuch der Religionspädagogik 17; Neukirchener Verlag: Neukirchen-Vluyn 2001), 39-49.

aber dem Schema "Die Welt der Indianer", "... der Delphine", "... der Edelsteine": Der Begriff "Welt" verweist auf ein Ganzes, auffällig häufig auf ein Anderes, Fremdes, Unbekanntes als ein Ganzes, manchmal auch auf das eigene Ganze ("Lebenswelt").

Begrifflich ist zu "Welt" in den letzten Jahrzehnten so gut wie nicht gearbeitet worden. Der letzte Meisterdenker, der mehrfach den Begriff "Welt" in seinen Titeln verwandte, war Heidegger.[3] Ferner kommen auch systematisch theologische Arbeiten aufgrund des ambivalenten christlichen Verhältnisses zur Welt nicht umhin, immer wieder Stellung zum Verhältnis von Christentum und Welt zu beziehen.[4]

Am meisten hat mich bei meinen Nachforschungen jedoch verblüfft, dass von feministischer Seite aus das Verhältnis von "Frauenverachtung" und "Weltverachtung" nicht aufgearbeitet wurde. Die Kritik an der "Frau" als der Anderen hat zwar dazu geführt, dass Wissenschaftlerinnen weitere Phänomene, die des gleichen als das "Andere des Männlichen" galten wie "Natur", "Materie", "Besonderheit", "Schwarzsein", "Jüdischsein" oder "Homosexualität", in Verbindung mit "Weiblichkeit" aufgearbeitet haben. Das Wort "Welt" fällt hier jedoch nicht. Dafür scheint es mehrere Gründe zu geben:

1. Frauenbewegte Frauen haben die Welt als männlich besetzt und geformt erfahren. Der Feminismus hat die Welt in der Folge als männliche theoretisiert. Diese Perspektive hat den Zusammenhang zwischen Frauenverachtung und Weltverachtung verdeckt.
   Was die Mutter betrifft, so wurde sie üblicherweise der Natur zugeordnet. Des gleichen wurde sie nur selten als die "Andere" zum männlich-väterlichen Diskurs in den Blick genommen. Hier spielt Augustinus eine löbliche Ausnahme. Die mütterliche Ordnung ist für ihn der Gegensatz zur väterlichen. Allerdings zählt er die Mutter nicht zur Welt, sondern ihr (richtiges) Tun hat seinen Ursprung in Gott.

[3] In der klassischen Philosophie ist Heidegger die letzte wichtige philosophische Referenz nach Hegel. Außerdem setzt sich die Antikenforschung mit der "Welt" auseinander. Vgl. Gerold Prauss, *Die Welt und wir* (Metzler: Stuttgart 1990); Holger Sonnabend, "Welt", in: *Der blaue Reiter. Journal für Philosophie, Themenheft "Welt-Bilder"* 13 (2001), 82-83.

[4] Johann Auer / Joseph Ratzinger, *Die Welt – Gottes Schöpfung* (Kleine Katholische Dogmatik 3; Pustet: Regensburg 1975); Gerhard Ebeling, *Der Glaube an Gott, den Vollender der Welt* (Dogmatik des christlichen Glaubens 3; Mohr Siebeck: Tübingen 1993); Ernst Jüngel, *Gott als Geheimnis der Welt. Zur Begründung der Theologie des Gekreuzigten im Streit zwischen Theismus und Atheismus* (Mohr-Siebeck: Tübingen 1977; ^{7}2001); Hans Küng, *Projekt Weltethos* (Piper: München 1992; ^{7}2002).

Bei Arendt findet man die ungewöhnliche Aussage, dass die Gebürtigkeit nicht einem natürlichen, sondern einem weltlichen Phänomen entspricht.[5] Für mich heißt dies, die Mutter nicht als Natur, sondern als weltliche Größe zu denken, als erwachsene Frau, die für das Kind zuerst die ganze Welt ist, ihm Welt vermittelt, selbst von der Welt geprägt wurde und auch Welt gestaltet. Die Mutter ist zuerst die Welt und steht später – auch bei Augustinus – zwischen dem Kind und der Welt.

Im Feminismus wurde die Mutter häufig als Figur der Identifikation des Weiblichen im Patriarchat betrachtet. Dies legt allerdings die männliche Tradition selbst nahe. Vielleicht kommt es zu dieser Zuschreibung, weil sie zwischen Kind und Welt steht, und für Frauen aus dieser Perspektive den Übergang zur – vorgefundenen männlichen – Welt markiert.[6] Hier spiegelt sich wohl auch die Tendenz in Frauenbewegung und feministischer Wissenschaft, in Dualismen zu verbleiben. Die Auseinandersetzung mit dem Thema "Welt" erfordert ein differenziertes Denken, das die Gleichzeitigkeit von "männlicher Welt" und "Weltverachtung" analog der "Frauenverachtung", und das heißt, die mehrfache, vielschichtige und ambivalente Positionierung der Frauen in Vergangenheit und Gegenwart in den Blick nehmen will. Der Begriff der Welt erlaubt, einen Zwischenraum zu denken, der Übergänge eröffnet und offen hält. Die Welt ist demnach nicht einfach männlich. Frauen hatten auch schon immer eine fruchtbare Beziehung zur Welt.[7]

2. Phänomene, die die Welt betreffen, werden in Form anderer Fragestellungen verhandelt. Eine zentrale Fragestellung ist beispielsweise "Gesellschaft"

[5] Vgl. Hannah Arendt, *Vita activa oder Vom tätigen Leben* (Piper: München [6]1981), 90; Augustinus, *Bekenntnisse* (dtv: München 1982), 1. Buch; Andrea Günter, *Politische Theorie und sexuelle Differenz. Feministische Praxis und die symbolische Ordnung der Mutter* (Helmer: Königstein/Taunus 1998), 9 u. 189-191.

[6] Eine Ausnahme bildet hier der französisch-italienische Differenz-Ansatz, zu dem ich Denkerinnen wie Cixous, Irigaray und Kristeva zähle. Für den deutschen Feminismus vgl. Inge Stephan / Regula Venske / Sigrid Weigel, *Frauenliteratur ohne Tradition? Neun Autorinnenporträts* (Fischer: Frankfurt 1987), 7-9.

[7] Außerdem scheint sich hier niederzuschlagen, dass die Frauenpolitik zu sehr auf die Spiegelbeziehung zwischen Frauen, auf Anerkennung und Wertschätzung von Frauen und zwischen Frauen gesetzt hat. Die Welt geht dabei verloren, weil es sich lediglich um imaginäre, nicht aber um politische und symbolische Beziehungen handelt. Denn diese meinen immer eine Öffnung für das andere, die die Überschreitung der eigenen Position voraussetzt. Vgl. Andrea Günter, *Die weibliche Seite der Politik. Ordnung der Seele, Gerechtigkeit der Welt* (Helmer: Königstein/Taunus 2001), 80; Libreria delle donne di Milano, *Das Patriarchat ist zu Ende. Es ist passiert – nicht aus Zufall* (Göttert: Rüsselheim 1996), 55-56.

als Repräsentant eines umfassenden Ganzen. Eine andere ist die "Ökologiefrage", in der Welt und Weiblichkeit auf eine bestimmte Art und Weise miteinander verknüpft sind, nämlich als Liebe zur Natur und der ganzen Erde. Hier trifft ein bestimmter Aspekt des Weltbegriffs, nämlich die Welt als "terra", mit einer bestimmten symbolischen Verknüpfung von "Frau" und "Natur" zusammen. Aber es ist auch die "Globalisierung", die ein Ganzes der Erde und auf der Erde behauptet, allerdings einen spezifischen Aspekt dieses Ganzen, nämlich die ökonomisch-kapitalistisch arbeitsteilige Struktur der Welt, so dass auch dieser Weltbegriff eine Einschränkung enthält.[8]

Ein weiteres Beispiel zeigt die Befreiungstheologie: Hier geht es um eine bestimmte Sorge und Tätigkeit für die Welt in Abgrenzung zur christlichen Forderung nach Weltabstinenz, und das heißt in diesem Falle, nach Politikabstinenz. Im Hinblick auf die Befreiungstheologie könnte gefragt werden, inwiefern hier eine "weibliche Position in der Welt" aktiviert wird: Die Option für die Armen ist eigentlich die Politik *der* Armen im Unterschied zur Stellvertreterpolitik. Arme agieren aus der Position des Mangels und der Passivität, die zugleich den Frauen zugeschrieben wird: Weniger zu sein als der Mann, ihn zu ergänzen, niemals aber für das Ganze zu stehen, aber dennoch unauslöschbar Teil des Ganzen zu sein. Zeigt sich hier, dass es sich beim Begriff der Welt um bestimmte Beziehungsformen der Menschen handelt? Und zwar gerade nicht um solche, die ausschließen, wie es die Logik der Macht erzeugt, sondern um solche, die sich vervollständigen, und zwar unabhängig von unserem eigenen Willen?[9]

3. Damit geht es bei der Welt um Verhältnisse, nämlich um die des Einzelnen zum Allgemeinen und des Teils zum Ganzen. Ob und wie das Einzelne und

[8] Vgl. Daniel Bell, *Die kulturellen Widersprüche des Kapitalismus* (Campus: Frankfurt 1991; Neuauflage von: *Die Zukunft der Welt. Kultur und Technologie im Widerstreit* [Fischer: Frankfurt 1976]); Otfried Höffe, "Bausteine für ein ökologisches Weltethos", in: ders., *Moral als Preis der Moderne. Ein Versuch über Wissenschaft, Technik und Umwelt* (Suhrkamp: Frankfurt 1993), 151-171; Carolyn Merchant, *Der Tod der Natur: Ökologie, Frauen und die neuzeitliche Naturwissenschaft* (Beck: München 1994).

[9] Ist diese weibliche Form der Weltpolitik nicht eigentlich jesuanisch? Eine Politik, die die persönliche Rechtfertigung, den Kern der christlichen Kultur, in aller Radikalität zu praktizieren erlaubt? Dann wäre es kein Zufall, dass diese Weise der Politik in den christlichen Kontexten erfunden wurde und aufgegriffen wird. Vgl. José Ignacio González Faus, "Die Welt der reichen Länder und die Welt Lateinamerikas", in: Ignacio Ellacuría / Jon Sobrino (Hg.): *Mysterium Liberationis. Grundbegriffe der Theologie der Befreiung* (Edition Exodus: Luzern 1995); Pedro Trigo, "Schöpfung und materielle Welt", in: ebd., 637-676.

der Teil im Allgemeinen und Ganzen zu finden sind, erweist sich als grundsätzliche Problematik der abendländischen Geistesgeschichte. Slavoi Zizek bearbeitet diese Fragestellung unter dem Titel "Die Nacht der Welt", mit dem er sie zur unbewussten Triebkraft der Philosophie erklärt. Auch hier gibt es ein gemeinsames Schicksal zwischen der Weltproblematik und der Frauenfrage. Luce Irigaray etwa hält fest, dass die Frau in der Tradition zwar immer gedacht wurde, aber immer nur als Abstraktion, nie als konkrete Frau. Auch mit der Frauenfrage stellt sich die Frage nach dem Verhältnis von Abstraktion und Konkretion neu.[10]

4. "Welt" ist von Anfang an einer der zentralen Begriffe der Metaphysik, so bei Aristoteles oder bei Kant. Nachdem nun die Metaphysik zusammen mit der Ontologie von der Postmoderne im letzten Jahrhundert kritisiert und verabschiedet worden ist, ist es kein Zufall, dass kaum mehr zum Begriff "Welt" gearbeitet wurde. Im Vergleich mit der Destruktion von Konzepten wie "Ich" und "Gott" gibt es hier aber keine dermaßen explizite Auseinandersetzung mit dem Begriff "Welt".
Die Kritik am Konzept "Welt" schien mit dieser Diskussion immer implizit zu verlaufen, nämlich in der Kritik an "Identität", "Universalismus" und "Ganzheit". 1991 endlich erscheint ein Buch mit dem sprechenden Titel "Rückblick auf das Ende der Welt". Hier wird das Ende der "Welt" mit den Argumenten konstatiert, mit denen postmoderne Meisterdenker auch die Metaphysik verabschiedet haben. Das Ende der Welt ist keine eigenständige Frage mehr, es ist die logische Konsequenz postmoderner Argumentationen und nur noch wie eine Rechenaufgabe zu behandeln. Die Denker haben ihre Hausaufgaben gemacht, sie sagen es selbst durch ihren Titel, und ihre Texte lesen sich wie Hausaufgaben für jemanden, der die Übungen kennt: langweilige Wiederholungen der selben Argumentationen, Automatisierungen des Denkens, ohne eigenständige Diskussion um den speziellen Begriff "Welt".[11]

[10] Luce Irigaray, *Genealogie der Geschlechter* (Kore: Freiburg/Breisgau 1989), 217; Manon Andreas-Grisebach, "Zwischen Vielheit und Ganzheit", in: Arbeitsgemeinschaft Interdisziplinäre Frauenforschung und -studien (Hg.), *Feministische Erneuerung von Wissenschaft und Kunst* (Frauenforschung und Kunst 2; Centaurus: Pfaffenweiler 1990), 19-25; Slavoj Zizek, *Die Nacht der Welt. Psychoanalyse und Deutscher Idealismus* (Fischer: Frankfurt 1998), z. B. 59-61.

[11] Dietmar Kamper / Christoph Wulf (Hg.), *Rückblick auf das Ende der Welt* (Boer: München 1990).

Ist der Begriff "Welt" deshalb falsch, weil er der Metaphysik angehört oder weil er in dieser dieselbe Funktion erfüllt wie das "Ich" und "Gott"? Dass der Begriff der Welt nicht in dieser metaphysischen Funktion aufgehen kann, darauf verweist die überlieferte begriffliche Unterscheidung von der Welt als "mundus", "saeculum" und "terra". So stellt sich die Welt selbst als Kombination dreier Grundkategorien der Metaphysik heraus, deren Ende bislang keiner erklärt hat. Sie werden im Gegenteil als Alternative der Metaphysik gepriesen: Die Welt erweist sich als eine bestimmte Kombination von Zeit, Ort und Raum.
Für besonders problematisch an diesen Kurzschlüssen halte ich, dass diese Veröffentlichung sich im Kontext der Diskussion um die Globalisierung ansiedelt. Kann es eine politische Antwort auf die Globalisierung sein, dass es Globales nicht gibt, weil wir die Metaphysik und mit dieser die Welt verabschiedet haben? Dies aber legt die Ablehnung der Metaphysik durch die Postmoderne nahe.

5. Zugleich ist die Welt – bei Kant – der Inbegriff der Anschauung. Die Anschauung – sprachliche Verfasstheit der menschlichen Existenz, Bilder, Inszenierungen – wiederum ist der Focus der Postmoderne, so dass man sagen kann, dass die Postmoderne die Weltlichkeit der menschlichen Existenz gerade nicht verabschiedet, sondern ins Zentrum rückt.[12]

Meine persönliche Einschätzung des Verhältnisses von "Welt" und Globalisierung führt mich dazu, dass wir den Begriff Welt unbedingt klären müssen. Ich bin davon überzeugt, dass die Reduzierung der Vorstellung der Welt auf die Politik der Großkonzerne, des Neoliberalismus und der Kultur der neuen Medien – Welt als Anschauung – nur deshalb Sinn macht und machen kann, weil wir keinen angemessenen Begriff der Welt haben.[13] Erst wenn wir einen angemessenen Begriff der Welt gefunden haben oder zumindest in die Diskussion über den Sinn und die Bedingungen dieses Begriffs eingestiegen sind, werden wir einen Rahmen haben, in dem die an Großkonzernen orientierte Globalisierung, die Politik des Neoliberalismus und die neuen Medien als ein Aspekt, und das heißt, nicht als Welt, sondern lediglich als einer der Faktoren deutlich wird, die sie bedingen.

[12] Dies dokumentiert der Themenschwerpunkt "Welt-Bilder" der Zeitschrift *Der blaue Reiter. Journal für Philosophie* 13 (2001).

[13] Vgl. Noam Chomsky, *Profit over people. Neoliberalismus und globale Weltordnung* (Europa: Hamburg / Wien ³2000); Gert Kähler (Hg.), *Dekonstruktion? Dekonstruktivismus? Aufbruch ins Chaos oder neues Bild der Welt?* (Vieweg: Braunschweig 1991).

Dass die Politik der Globalisierung zugleich Parallelen mit der philosophischen Frage aufweist, bestätigt, dass es zugleich auch einen inneren Zusammenhang zwischen Globalisierung und Metaphysik gibt. Denn auch bei der Globalisierung geht es um die Konstituierung eines Ganzen. Eines Ganzen, das sich lediglich als ein bestimmtes Ganzes erweist – etwa alle Internetbenutzer plus alle global agierenden Konzerne –, und bei dem deshalb die anderen, die nicht zu einer solchen Schnittmenge zählen, per definitionem ausgeschlossen sind.

Die Metaphysik und die Welt

Für Aristoteles zählt die Welt zu den Prinzipien, mit deren Hilfe die Menschen ihre Wahrnehmungen ordnen. Um gemeinsames Wissen aus den persönlichen Wahrnehmungen gewinnen zu können, stellen die Menschen Gemeinsamkeiten beim Wahrgenommenen fest. Dabei gibt es grundlegende Größen, die allen von den Menschen wahrgenommenen Dingen zugrunde liegen. Dazu zählen Aristoteles zufolge etwa die Kategorien "Ort" und "Zeit": Alles, was Menschen wahrnehmen, befindet sich zu einer bestimmten Zeit an einem bestimmten Ort. Die Gemeinsamkeit von bestimmten Dingen kann dabei zuweilen in nichts anderem bestehen als darin, dass sie jemand zur gleichen Zeit am gleichen Ort angetroffen und wahrgenommen hat.

Auch die Welt ist Aristoteles zufolge ein Parameter, der eine solche Gemeinsamkeit benennt. Dieser Parameter besteht bei Aristoteles aus einer Kombination mehrerer anderer Parameter. Die Welt besagt die folgende Kombination: von den Menschen Wahrgenommenes an allen Orten und zu allen Zeiten. Der dritte Parameter neben Ort und Zeit ist dabei eine bestimmte Quantität, nämlich "alle". Dieses "alle" ist aber nicht einfach nur als Quantität zu verstehen, sondern zugleich als Qualität. Denn niemand kann an allen Orten und zu allen Zeiten all das wahrnehmen, was es wahrzunehmen gibt. Dieses Alles lässt sich nicht addieren.[14]

Selbst wenn man alle Menschen, die an allen Orten und zu allen Zeiten all das wahrnehmen, was jeweils da und dann ist, zu all den jeweiligen Orten und Zeiten addieren würde, ist eine *Abstraktionsleistung* vonnöten. Denn Menschen lassen sich nicht mit Orten, Orte wiederum nicht mit Zeiten addieren. Ferner

[14] Vgl. Aristoteles: *Metaphysik* (Rowohlt: Reinbek bei Hamburg 1999), 12. Buch; ders.: *Über die Welt* (Reklam: Stuttgart 1991); Immanuel Kant, *Kritik der reinen Vernunft* (Meiner: Hamburg 1998); Josef Schmucker, *Das Weltproblem in Kants Kritik der reinen Vernunft. Kommentar und Strukturanalyse des ersten Buches und des zweiten Hauptstückes des zweiten Buches der transzendentalen Dialektik* (Bouvier: Bonn 1990); Christian Wohlers, *Kants Theorie der Einheit der Welt* (Königshausen uund Neumann: Würzburg 2000).

können Menschen nicht an allen Orten und zu allen Zeiten zugleich sein, weil sie nicht gleichzeitig leben. Ebensowenig werden alle Menschen das selbe wahrnehmen können, weil sie an jeweils unterschiedlichen Orten zu unterschiedlichen Zeiten leben. Außerdem werden auch niemals alle Menschen sich an einem Ort und zu einem Zeitpunkt versammeln können, so dass sie austauschen können, was sie alles erlebt haben.

Dennoch kann an bestimmten Orten und zu bestimmten Zeiten Wahrgenommenes im Hinblick auf seine Gemeinsamkeit mit dem in Beziehung gesetzt werden, was an allen Zeiten und zu allen Orten für Menschen wahrnehmbar ist. "Alles" wird zu der Art und Weise, wie Ort und Zeit bestimmt und miteinander im Denken verbunden werden. Kant nennt diese Qualität "Inbegriff". "Zu allen Zeiten und an allen Orten" wird ein Deutungshorizont der Urteilsfindung, den Hannah Arendt "erweiterte Denkungsart" genannt hat. Als solches ist der Begriff der Welt eine der zentralen Prinzipien des Denkens und der Politik. Er ist das Prinzip des Denkens der Politik.[15]

Das Konzept "Welt" ist folglich eine Kombination aus verschiedenen anderen Parametern, mit denen die Menschen grundlegend Gemeinsamkeiten festhalten, und dabei zugleich eine "Abstraktion", oder anders gesagt, eine Multiplikation dieser Parameter.

Die Parameter "zu allen Zeiten" und "an allen Orten" sind dabei die, die das Konkrete – Zeit und Ort – mit dem Allgemeinen und Abstrakten – alle – verbindet. Das heißt, dass der Begriff "Welt" genau die Schnittstelle zwischen Kontingenz und Essenz, zwischen "Dasssein" – zu einer Zeit an einem Ort sein –, "Sosein" – auf eine bestimmte Art und Weise als in diesem Augenblick sein – und "Wassein" – hier als Inbegriff – benennt. Dass die Welt eine solche abstrakte Kombination ist, die das Abstraktum "alles" zu denken erlaubt, darauf, so kann man sagen, legt die Postmoderne ihr Augenmerk.

Ebenso unausgesprochen wie die postmoderne konturiert auch die feministische Frage die "Welt". Denn in der feministischen Frage wird diskutiert, wie die jeweilige Bestimmung des Verhältnisses von Wassein/"Substanz", Erscheinung und Anschauung in die Konzeptionen von "Sex", "Gender" und Geschlechterdifferenz einfließt. Hier wird ein gemeinsamer Nenner zwischen der Globalisierungs- und den neueren Entwicklungen der feministischen Theorie sichtbar.

Findet sich in der metaphysischen Tradition die Tendenz, das Was – die Ontologie – in den Vordergrund dessen zu stellen, etwas zu bestimmen, dann

[15] Hannah Arendt, *Wahrheit und Lüge in der Politik. Zwei Essays* (Piper: München 1987), 61.

ist im Zuge der Postmoderne die Möglichkeit, etwas zu bestimmen, abhanden gekommen. Die Postmoderne hat darauf aufmerksam gemacht, dass die Ontologie das Sein niemals allein als Sein, sondern immer in Verbindung mit dem Ort – und das heißt auch, mit Positionen – denkt. Der Ort ist jedoch immer mit der Zeit verbunden. Die Zeit wiederum kann durch das Sein am Ort bzw. das Festhalten an der Position wie gefroren sein. In der Folge fordert die Postmoderne ein, die Zeit als Zeit, und das heißt, das Vorher und das Nachher von etwas zu denken.[16]

Dieses Etwas wiederum wäre absolut kontingent und das radikal andere zur Ontologie, wenn es in der Folge lediglich über die Zeit definiert würde, wie es postmodernen Konzepten innewohnt. Als bestimmender und beständiger Faktor bliebe allein die Zeit, das ist die ständige Verschiebung und unendliche Bewegung. Dies gilt aber nur, wenn man ins andere Extrem verfällt, die Zeit absolut setzt und sie über den Ort und das Ding stellt. So muss hier das Absolutsetzen unterschieden werden vom angemessenen Denken der Zeit in Relation zu den Orten, den Dingen und Menschen.

Die zeitgenössische Physik versteht die Zeit als Aspekt des Raums und kombiniert sie mit dem "Ort". Der Raum ist das, was ein Anderes zwischen absoluter Kontingenz und fixem Wassein zu denken erlaubt. Denn der Raum ist kein Ort, wie Irigaray festhält, sondern die Umschließung von Ort, Zeit und den Dingen, die sich in ihm befinden, sowie von der Möglichkeit der Umschließung selbst.[17]

Mit dem Begriff "Welt" wird die Kombinationsmöglichkeit von Zeit, Ort, Dingen und "alle" als Quantität und Qualität sowie von Einzigartigkeit, Allgemeinheit und Abstraktion – in Form der Allheit der menschlichen Anschauung als Schnittstelle und Möglichkeit der Umschließung von allen Orten, allen

[16] Hierfür steht vor allem Heideggers *Sein und Zeit* und die postmoderne Kritik am Subjekt, die dieses als Kombination von Sein – "Vernunft" – und Ort – Position und Ursprung der Handlung – kritisiert und es selbst als bewegt thematisiert. Vgl. Luisa Muraro, "Vorher und Nachher im Leben einer Frau", in: Luce Irigaray (Hg.), *Der Atem der Frauen* (Göttert: Rüsselsheim 1997), 55-67.

[17] Den Hinweis auf die aktuelle Diskussion in der Physik verdanke ich Ulrike Wagener. Bei Irigaray findet sich die gleiche Differenzierung anhand der Begriffe "Raum" und Umschließung wie in der Physik, wobei Irigaray mit diesen Gedanken die traditionelle Deutung der Mutter als Ort kritisiert. Vgl. Luce Irigaray, *Ethik der sexuellen Differenz* (Suhrkamp: Frankfurt/Main 1991), 26-28, 46-70 u. 101-114; Kip S. Thorne, *Gekrümmter Raum und verbogene Zeit. Einsteins Vermächtnis*, (Droemer Knaur: München 1996); Margaret Wertheim, *Die Hose des Pythagoras. Physik, Gott und die Frauen* (Piper: München / Zürich 1998).

Zeiten und all den Menschen begegnenden Dingen – ausgesagt. Somit wird zugleich die Möglichkeit eröffnet, Kontingenz und Wassein miteinander zu verbinden. Die Welt benennt genau diese Schnittstelle und damit diese Möglichkeit.

Auch Arendt markiert die Welt als eine Umschließung, wobei sie dies im Hinblick auf die Menschheit ausformuliert:

> Die Mitmenschen sind nicht (wie bei Heidegger) ein zwar strukturell notwendiges, aber das Selbstsein notwendig störendes Element der Existenz; sondern umgekehrt, nur in dem Zusammen der Menschen in der gemeinsamen Welt kann sich die Existenz überhaupt entwickeln. [...] Innerhalb des ›umgreifenden‹ Seins jedenfalls bewegen sich die Menschen miteinander; und sie jagen nicht dem Phantom des Selbst nach, noch leben sie in dem hybriden Wahn, das Sein überhaupt zu sein.[18]

Die Politik der Globalisierung will auf die Möglichkeit der Umschließung zurückgreifen – die Parameter und Regeln vorgeben, die von nun an global gelten – und behauptet, dies erfüllen zu können, nämlich alle Menschen glücklich zu machen. Globalisierung hieße damit zu beanspruchen, die Welt als menschliche Umschließung von allem menschlichen Weltlichen in Anspruch zu nehmen. Das aber muss Widerstand hervorrufen. Arendts Aussage veranlasst nämlich nachzufragen: Was ist das die Menschen umschließende Sein?

Natalität und Welt bei Hannah Arendt

Hannah Arendts Begriff der Welt präzisiert einen wichtigen Aspekt des vorgestellten metaphysischen Weltbegriffs. Hierzu schließt Arendt an Kant an. Kant definiert "Welt" nämlich als Inbegriff aller Erscheinungen und aller Anschauungen. Damit verweist die Welt auf die Menschen, denn einzig die Menschen bilden Anschauungen aus von dem, was ihnen begegnet, so dass das, dem sie begegnen, durch das Ausbilden von Anschauungen zu Erscheinungen wird.

Die Welt ist Arendt zufolge der gemeinsame Wohnraum der Menschen, in dem ihnen die Dinge erscheinen und in dem sie Anschauungen von diesen Dingen ausbilden. Arendt definiert die Welt damit maßgeblich als Kombination der menschlichen Beziehungen – entsprechend dem "zu allen Zeiten und an allen Orten" – den Dingen, die hier erscheinen, und den menschlichen Möglichkeiten, Anschauungen bzw. Urteile auszubilden.

[18] Hannah Arendt, *Was ist Existenzphilosophie?* (Hain: Frankfurt am Main 1990), 47.

Dabei hält Arendt fest, dass die Menschen Anschauungen in den Beziehungen miteinander ausbilden und dass die Übereinstimmung mit dem Denken anderer die einzige Garantie für die Richtigkeit des Denkens ist.[19] Damit führt sie in ihre Kombination "Welt" ein weiteres Merkmal ein, nämlich die Verschiedenheit der Menschen. Das Alles wird als Möglichkeit aller Menschen zu allen Zeiten und an allen Orten erkennbar. Es ist ein Alles, das immer durch die Kraft der Verschiedenheit – verschieden sein und gleichzeitig sich unterscheiden – gestiftet ist. Als solches ist dieses Alles als eine Form denkbar, nicht aber als ein bestimmter Inhalt.

Die menschliche Verschiedenheit als aktives sich Unterscheiden-Wollen und -Können ist wiederum für Arendt in der Generationsdifferenz begründet.[20] Die Gebürtigkeit verlangt, dass die Welt für die zukünftige Generation offen bleibt, so dass diese die Möglichkeit erhält, Initiative zu ergreifen. Nur dann nämlich ist das Prinzip "alle Menschen zu allen Zeiten und an allen Orten" erfüllt. Denn "alle" in Bezug auf "Menschen" heißt alle Menschen in ihrer Verschiedenheit, wobei die menschliche Seite von allen Orten und allen Zeiten – das Generationengefüge – wiederum diese Verschiedenheit aktiviert. Das menschliche Alles beinhaltet demnach die Kraft des aktiven sich Unterscheidens, die immer wieder für Offenheit sorgen wird, denn sonst, so Arendt, müsste man den Menschen verbieten zu denken. Diese Kraft aber kann Welt genannt werden: Die Welt als Raum der Menschen, in der die Zeit wirkt. Damit wird die Welt als *politisches* Gebilde deutlich.

Wenn man nun die menschliche Kraft des Unterscheidens anheim stellt, ist es nicht einmal realistisch, dass für alle dieselben Regeln gelten können und sollen. Eine Politik, die sich einer solcher Vorstellung verpflichtet, ist falsch und wird scheitern müssen. Das zeigt die Frauenbewegung. Das zeigt die Welt. Denn gerade die christlichen Erfahrungen mit der Welt, die zur Weltverachtung führen, führen vor Augen, dass die Welt nie der Raum ist, in dem die Regeln – die "guten" und moralisch "gerechtfertigten", "göttlichen" Regeln – erfüllt werden. Und die Geschichte der Stellung(en) der Frauen in der Welt demonstriert, wie fatal es war, ihr Leben einem einzigen Maß, nämlich der Beziehung zum Mann zu unterwerfen. Weltverachtung kann als Ergebnis der Ignoranz von Verschiedenheit und Politik verstanden werden.[21]

[19] Arendt, *Wahrheit und Lüge*, 53.

[20] Hier gibt es eine Nähe zwischen Arendts Begriff der Verschiedenheit und Derridas "difference". Vgl. Jacques Derrida, *Die Schrift und die Differenz* (Suhrkamp: Frankfurt [2]1985), 50.

[21] Vgl. Günter, *Die weibliche Hoffnung*, 61-72.

Was die Problematik der Globalisierung betrifft, so erlaubt die Erweiterung und Präzisierung des Arendtschen Weltbegriffs, Anfragen zu stellen. Zeigt sich in der Globalisierung die Welt als Raum der Verschiedenen jenseits des Ein- und Ausschlusses neuer Machtbereiche? Es wird von neuer Nähe auf dem Globus gesprochen, vom Zusammenrücken der Menschen und von der Vereinheitlichung der Verhältnisse. Bleibt die Welt der selbe Raum, in dem sich, wie hier verkündet, das Verhältnis von Ort und Zeit verändert, dann verweist dies jedoch auf eine Gleichzeitigkeit von Annäherung und *Distanzierung*: Einige Menschen werden – unter bestimmten Gesichtspunkten – mehr zusammenrücken, andere aber – unter anderen – eher auseinander. Wer wiederum sind diese? Wohin rücken sie? Und vor allem: Welche sind die Gesichtspunkte, die die neuen Nachbarschaften, und welche sind die, die die Distanzen stiften?

Wenn dies gilt, dann ist der Begriff "Welt" der übergeordnete und orientierende Begriff für das, was Globalisierung heißt. Globalisierung aber ist dann nicht die Welt. Sie ist ihre Reduzierung, der erneute Versuch, die Zeit an Orte und feste Positionen zu binden, und das heißt, die Bewegung der Menschen in ihrer Verschiedenheit zu ignorieren. Gerade dann aber ist es notwendig, dass wir die Welt als Umschließung des menschlichen Tuns verstehen. Als eine Umschließung, in der es Schritte ins Offene gibt.

That hate of women is related to hate of the world is a virulent issue for politics in the era of globalisation, especially since one of the results of globalisation has been to suggest that women would once again be the losers if they were not quick enough to conform. The relationship can be seen not only from hard facts such as the distribution of wealth and possessions between the sexes. It can be seen also from the use of symbolic language and images. The author of this article thus understands it to be necessary to reflect on the concept of the world and its – postmodern – fate.

L'existence d'un rapport étroit entre le mépris de la femme et le mépris du monde a de virulentes répercussions sur la politique à l'époque de la mondialisation. Notamment parce que la mondialisation suscita la thèse que les femmes seraient les vieilles nouvelles perdantes si elles ne s'adaptaient pas assez vite. Certains faits, comme la répartition des richesses entre les sexes, mais aussi l'usage d'un langage et d'images symboliques, semblent confirmer cette thèse. L'auteur pense qu'il est nécessaire de réfléchir sur le concept de monde et son destin – postmoderne –.

Andrea Günter hat sich im Jahr 2000 in Philosophie über "Politische Philosophie und das Denken der Geschlechterdifferenz" habilitiert, beschäftigt sich seit langem mit feministischer Theologie und Postmoderne, arbeitet freischaffend als Autorin, als Dozentin und Gastprofessorin an Hochschulen und in der Fort- und Weiterbildung.

A Feminist-Theological Atlantic? Reflections from European-U.S.-American Hybrids

Introduction – Susanne Scholz

Although oceans are often perceived as dividers, historically they have served as great connectors of peoples, cultures, and religions. In "The Black Atlantic: Modernity and Double Consciousness," Paul Gilroy describes the Atlantic Ocean as the connector of black people from Africa, Europe, and America throughout the modern era.[1] In his view, a full appreciation of modernity presupposes an understanding of this watery connection. The international, transcultural reconceptualization of the Atlantic Ocean changes our views of the political and cultural history of black Americans, of black people in Europe, and of their contributions to the modern world. The reconceptualization moves us beyond "the binary opposition between national and diaspora perspective." The "black Atlantic world" emerges as "a webbed network, between the local and the global."[2] Thus, it is not dualistic divisions between "insiders" and "outsiders" but complex ties between Africa, Europe, and America that have shaped modern consciousness. Understood as a huge cultural and political system, the Atlantic Ocean makes visible the "inescapable hybridity and intermixture of ideas," Gilroy claims.

So how about "A Feminist-Theological Atlantic?" Historically as well as contemporaneously, the Atlantic Ocean has served as a great connector of theological exchange between European and North American scholars, whether feminist or non-feminist. Until the 1970s, many North American theologians traveled across the ocean to study with renowned scholars in mostly German-speaking countries. In fact, American theologians often felt obliged to study in Europe in order to improve their career opportunities in the United States. Particularly in the last decades, American theological and religious scholars have noted, sometimes sourly, the one-sidedness of this travel-exchange and

[1] Paul Gilroy, *The Black Atlantic: Modernity and Double Consciousness* (Harvard University Press: Cambridge, MA 1993).

[2] Ibid., 29.

rightly criticized it as a proof of past and present Eurocentrism in American theological and religious studies.[3]

This situation has, however, changed. The latter part of the twentieth century and the beginning of the twenty-first century have seen much travel in the opposite direction. The end of the so-called Second World War has led to the political, economic, cultural, and scholarly dominance of the United States over Europe. Nowadays, European students and scholars visit North America, mostly the United States, to learn about theological and academic developments. This power shift probably explains why criticism of Eurocentrism flourishes whereas criticism of "U.S.-Americentrism" is strangely absent from contemporary theological discourse.[4]

Whatever the travel direction has been, few publications have examined the impact of "Atlantic crisscrossing" on feminist theological scholars from Europe and North America.[5] A panel organized by the North American Section of the European Society of Women in Theological Research (NA ESWTR) during the annual meeting of the American Academy of Religion (AAR) and the Society of Biblical Studies (SBL) in Nashville, Tennessee, in November 2000 tried to address this situation. Examining hybrid identities among feminist-theological scholars from Europe and North America, the panelists elaborated on the following questions: How do women in theological and religious studies who "move to and fro between nations"[6] relate to the idea of a European-North American Atlantic? How have geographical re-locations from Europe to North America and vice versa influenced our feminist work on theology and religion? Have our multi-located perspectives changed over the

3 For voices critical of the Eurocentric theological tradition in American biblical studies see, e.g., Kwok Pui-lan, "Overlapping Communities and Multicultural Hermeneutics," in: Athalya Brenner / Carole Fontaine (eds), *A Feminist Companion to Reading the Bible: Approaches, Methods and Strategies* (Sheffield Academic Press: Sheffield 1997), 203-215; William H. Myers, "The Hermeneutical Dilemma of the African American Biblical Studies," in: Cain Hope Felder (ed.), *Stony the Road We Trod: African American Biblical Interpretation* (Fortress: Minneapolis 1991), 40-56.

4 For criticism of Eurocentrism in general, see, e.g., Vassilis Lambronpoulos, *The Rise of Eurocentrism: Anatomy of Interpretation* (Princeton University Press: Princeton, NJ 1993); Rajani Kannepalli Kanth, *Breaking with the Enlightenment: The Twilight of History and the Rediscovery of Utopia* (Humanities Press: Atlantic Highlands, NJ 1997).

5 For a recent German publication discussing these issues, see Katharina von Kellenbach / Susanne Scholz (eds), *Zwischen-Räume: Deutsche feministische Theologinnen im Ausland* (Lit: Münster 2000).

6 Gilroy, *Black Atlantic*, 12.

years? Has our hybrid status transformed our relationship to our countries of origin, and how? What is our relationship to the theological and religious discourses in Europe and North America? How do we negotiate the assumptions about both continents in one or the other place? What do we think about the "insider-outsider" dynamics of European feminist theologians/scholars of religious studies in North America? In short, how do our trans-Atlantic perspectives inform our work as feminists, theologians, and researchers of religions? Entitled "A Feminist European-North American Atlantic?", the panel included Teresa Berger (Duke Divinity School, NC), Gabriella Lettini (Union Theological Seminary, NY), Susan Roll (Christ The King Seminary, NY), Karen Torjesen (Claremont Graduate University, CA), and myself (then at The College of Wooster, OH).

All of the panelists are members of ESWTR, which was founded in 1986 as a European umbrella organization with national groups in many European countries.[7] Three years ago, several European women scholars living in the United States decided to organize a "North American Section of ESWTR (NA ESWTR)." Although we also belong to our various national groups in Europe, we sensed that our "trans-continental" lives justified the establishment of a section in North America. The NA ESWTR has welcomed members of European origin living in North America, members of North American origin with European connections, and interested women scholars from around the world. Particularly in light of our hybrid-theological reflections, our membership criteria are more open and provisional than ESWTR recommends. We acknowledge that fluidity and openness have to be an integral part of our membership definition.

Our decision to organize a sub-group of ESWTR was also related to the hesitancy of ESWTR to accept European women theologians as full members when they live in non-European countries, such as the United States. When some of us made such geographical moves, we suddenly found ourselves in the precarious situation of being excluded from the decision-making processes of ESWTR. After lengthy debates and voting procedures, the statutes were finally revised during the international ESWTR-conference in Crete, Greece, in August 1997. European women scholars of theology and religion who

[7] For a historical overview on feminist theology in Europe, see Catharina Halkes, "Towards a History of Feminist Theology in Europe," in: Annette Esser / Luise Schottroff (eds), *Feminist Theology in a European Context* (ESWTR 1; Kok Pharos: Kampen 1993), 11-37.

reside outside Europe are now accepted as full members. Nevertheless, the debate suggested to those of us living in the United States that we had better explore issues related to our "in-between" status in Europe and elsewhere.

A word of caution in regard to our statements about "A Feminist-Theological Atlantic": Our views represent only a fragment of possible positions among women in theological and religious research in Europe and North America. We do not claim to discuss conclusively what it means to live and to work as European women researchers in North America or as North American scholars in Europe. The publication of our panel discussion intends to stimulate further reflection about European-North American hybridity and the experiences, identities, and perspectives of feminist theologians living hybrid lives elsewhere. If our discussion were to resonate beyond the European-North American context and to engage feminist researchers of theology and religion from other oceanic borderlands, our goals would be more than fulfilled. Our contributions are also limited to Christian views. However, we hope for future conversations with feminist scholars from Islam, Hinduism, Buddhism, and other religious traditions.[8]

Geographical and religious hybridities provide complex and deep insights into our world and lives. The following reflections on "A Feminist-Theological Atlantic?" are small steps on the path of grasping the all-encompassing reality that has been called, among many other names, "God," "Goddess," "Allah," "ha-Shem," "chi-energy," or "nirvanah."

Reflections on Shared Space – Teresa Berger

Many of the women gathered at the meeting of the NA ESWTR probably noticed that the title of our "Additional Meeting" was misspelled in the program booklet of the AAR. The NA ESWTR had requested a meeting space for a panel on "A Feminist European-North American Atlantic?" but the booklet informed us that we would discuss a feminist "Atlanta." The misspelling of "Atlantic" to "Atlanta" is, of course, easy to explain. The organizational power base of the American Academy of Religion is in Atlanta, Georgia. In all likelihood, the program booklet was typed there. The location of the production of the booklet clearly proved stronger than the selected title for our

[8] For a beginning of such a discussion among English-speaking feminist scholars of theology and religion, see "Roundtable Discussion: Feminist Theology and Religious Diversity," *Journal for Feminist Studies in Religion* 16/22 (Fall 2000), 73-131.

gathering. In the following I suggest that the change from "Atlantic" to "Atlanta" points to more than the power of geography.

For me as someone with a German passport, the misspelling underlined the need for our panel discussion. The nearest consulate of my country is in Atlanta, Georgia. I contact "Atlanta" when I request a German passport for my child or when I renew my own passport. I wrestle with "Atlanta" when I want to vote in Germany, get one of the new European driving permits, or merely find out whether the *Augsburger Puppenkiste* is available on video in the United States. For almost twenty years now, "Atlanta" has signaled for me a piece of Germany and German bureaucracy in the heart of the southeastern United States.

Postmodern theories of culture help to highlight the theoretical implications of these observations of my intercultural experiences. They stress that – over and against "modern" constructs of culture as single, unified, discreet, and bounded entities – cultures are, in fact, not self-contained units, but permeable, porous, fluid, fragmentary, hybrid, indeterminate, and conflictual. The same applies to cultural identities, whether defined along feminist or geopolitical lines. Those of us who circulate the Atlantic (and beyond) know well that our cultural identities are notoriously slippery and messy. We eat "borscht with chili," as the Chicana poet Gloria Anzaldúa characterized her own cultural hybridity,[9] which means, applied to my own hybridity, that I like to eat Thanksgiving turkey with *Knödel und Rotkraut*. Such experiences and the interpretive frame they generate make me rethink the space I occupy. I am a Catholic feminist theologian dis/located from central Europe to the southeastern United States and remaining here because the Vatican repeatedly vetoed my appointments to European universities.

An example illustrates how postmodern theories of culture have informed my understanding of my Atlantic experiences. During my first years in the United States, the North Atlantic represented a great divide to me. I had left Europe, and was now living in a "strange New World." However, postmodern theories of culture helped me to think and to live with a sense that "oceans connect," as an [ongoing] interdisciplinary research initiative at Duke University has it. Today, I see the North Atlantic as a shared space, not as a great divide. Such a conceptual framework is, however, not new. For many years,

[9] The Chicana poet Gloria Anzaldúa focused attention on the border as a shared space with her much-acclaimed book *Borderlands/La Frontera: The New Mestiza* (Spinsters/Aunt Lute: San Francisco 1987).

anthropologists have defined water masses as connecting features of shared cultural space. We speak of "the Mediterranean world" as well as the "Pacific Rim," the latter being an important concept in particular for the global market. The insight of a shared North Atlantic political space was the basis for the establishment of NATO.

The notion that oceans connect has also been fruitful in the theoretical work of cultural critic Paul Gilroy, as Susanne mentioned in her introduction. Gilroy theorized the "Black Atlantic" as a cultural space initially defined through colonization and now shared by Africans and their descendants from Europe, Africa, and the Americas. In fact, an emergent body of literature highlights the North Atlantic as a shared space for many different cultural formations. Of special interest for feminists are studies on women in the inquisition, women witches, and women in the Western Women's Movement who crisscrossed the North Atlantic.[10] Seeing shared space and not sharp divisions, postmodern theories of cultures privilege multiple and contesting practices of identity, globalization, hybridity, creolization, and borders; they characterize space as decisive sites for the production of meaning.[11] The notion of shared space has profoundly shaped how I understand and live my life between two continents or, rather, around the edges of the North Atlantic.

Theories of culture also transform the task of theology, Christian identity, and feminist theological work. For example, the notion of "borderlands" is crucial for interpreting feminist communities and their rituals. My book, *Dissident Daughters*, maps the global struggle for women's rites. Containing fourteen narratives of feminist communities worldwide, the volume describes the creation and the celebration of women-identified liturgies.[12] Women have claimed new ways of "being church." Most of the included communities have distinctly blurred the boundaries of ecclesial identity. The oxymoronic wording is inten-

[10] Mary E. Giles, *Women in the Inquisition: Spain and the New World* (Johns Hopkins University Press: Baltimore 1999); Elaine G. Breslaw (ed.), *Witches of the Atlantic World: A Historical Reader and Primary Sourcebook* (New York University Press: New York 2000); Leila J. Rupp, *Worlds of Women: The Making of an International Women's Movement* (Princeton University Press: Princeton, NJ 1997).

[11] The work of my colleague Walter D. Mignolo, *Local Histories/Global Designs: Coloniality, Subaltern Knowledges, and Border Thinking* (Princeton Studies in Culture/Power/History; Princeton University Press: Princeton, NJ 2000), made me realize that I tend to focus on the notion of borders as a shared space. In Mignolo's work the notion of borders as the margins of empire is prominent.

[12] Teresa Berger (ed.), *Dissident Daughters: Feminist Liturgies in Global Context* (Westminster John Knox Press: Louisville KY 2001).

tional here. While traditional ecclesiologies find the blurring of ecclesial boundaries deeply problematic, theological reflection attentive to postmodern theories of culture regards Christian identity as hybrid, unstable, composite, and relational to wider cultural materials. "Church" and "denominations" are not fixed categories, but shifting, unstable, flexible bodies, multiply positioned across coordinates such as geography, gender, class, and ethnicity. The women communities in *Dissident Daughters* assume the destabilization of traditional ecclesiological categories.

Theological reflection open to such destabilization presents new ecclesiological possibilities. Traditional ecclesiologies assume that feminist Christian communities exist ultimately "outside" of the church. Several communities in *Dissident Daughters* do not recognize a sharp boundary between traditional Christian worship and Christian movements of feminist spirituality and rituals. Dissident daughters render visible a space described only inadequately as being "in and on the edge of the churches."[13] The description is inadequate because the conjunction "and" seems to suggest two distinct spheres. Yet, many dissident daughters refuse to be defined as "outside the church," *extra ecclesiam*, and thus decline to validate the binary that underlies the description. They have merely left behind the struggle "to fit into" traditional church structures. Thus, women-identified communities defy traditional ecclesiological demarcation, claiming their own space at the very border of traditional ecclesiology. In this "borderland," dissident daughters exist with all the complicated richness that such a space offers.[14] Their rituals are an ecclesial form of border politics – the transgression and the subversion of ecclesial borders and powers.

Kathryn Tanner provides further support for reading ecclesiological issues through the lenses of postmodern theories of culture.[15] Tanner regards ecclesial traditions as a site of struggle over symbolic resources, which are always

[13] Lieve Troch uses this description in her insightful article, "The Feminist Movement in and on the Edge of the Churches in the Netherlands in the Netherlands: From Consciousness-raising to Womenchurch," in: *Journal of Feminist Studies in Religion* 5/2 (1989), 113-128, here 114.

[14] For the theological work the notion of "borderland" can do, see, for example, Maria Pilar Aquino and Roberto S. Goizueta (eds.), *Theology: Expanding the Borders* (The Annual Publication of the College Theology Society 4; Twenty-Third Publications: (Mystic, CN 1998), and, from a European perspective, Hedwig Meyer-Wilmes, *Rebellion on the Borders* (Kok Pharos Publishing House: Kampen 1995).

[15] For a more detailed account, see Kathryn Tanner, *Theories of Culture: A New Agenda for Theology* (Guides to Theological Inquiry Series; Fortress Press: Minneapolis, KY 1997), 128-138.

selective, and never a stable site in the production of meaning. For Tanner, this understanding of tradition suggests that feminist theology is most effective and convincing when it does not distance itself from tradition, but when it claims tradition as a site of struggle over meaning today. Thus, the more feminist theology uses and realigns elements appropriated by patriarchal interests, the greater the feminist claim to theological credibility. Clearly, Tanner does not understand tradition as a fixed and unified block of material that one generation passes on to the next generation. She regards ecclesial tradition as a construct of the present moment struggled over for a diversity of practices and interpretations. What is designated as tradition has, therefore, always been highly selective, rather unstable, and open to redesignation.

Like the notion of borderlands, Tanner's definition of tradition as today's struggle to define meaning helps in understanding the liturgies of feminist communities such as those discussed in *Dissident Daughters*. Women-identified liturgical practices do not represent a decisive break from "The Tradition," but are part and parcel of the continuous construction and reconstruction of liturgy in the life of the church.

Living on the borders of the North Atlantic, I find that borders represent shared space rather than markers of separation. This critical appreciation of the fluidity of one's "identity" is important not only for my life and work, but also for the lives of the women whom I encounter in my theological inquiries. The misspelling "Atlanta" encouraged me to reflect upon the fusion of Germany and the Southern United States, the Atlantic, and Atlanta in my life and how this fusion nourishes my theological work. I am sure that others who inhabit the North Atlantic world struggle with similar issues. Claiming our space as women who circulate the North Atlantic is one way of strengthening and deepening our feminist theological work.

Coming Out as a Hybrid: Pain and Potentiality – Gabriella Lettini

I wonder how many of us needed to travel across continents, from Europe to North America or vice-versa, to experience dis/location. Are we dis/located because we left our context of origin, or did we find it easier to leave that context because we were already feeling dis/located? I have come to admit to myself that dis/location was the starting point of my journey, and that it may be the only location I know. Being "in-between" has always been part of my experience and identity. A few autobiographical strokes will illustrate this point.

I was born in Italy in the late 1960s, in a context which was apparently (but only apparently) highly homogeneous. Although Roman Catholicism was the norm, I grew up in the Waldensian church, a religious minority which had survived centuries of persecutions, discrimination, and marginalization. I was therefore a very visible "other;" yet I was also strongly shaped by the same Roman Catholic culture that was "othering" me. I am the daughter of a woman from Northern Italy and a man from Southern Italy who migrated to the North. One of the many still largely untold stories of my country is the story of deep-seated racism that has shaped relationships between Northern and Southern Italians. Immigrants from the South were subjected to the kind of racist treatment that immigrants of color receive today,[16] and it is uncanny to see the similarity between the language used thirty years ago against Southern Italian immigrants, and the language used today against immigrants from the south of the world.

It took me years to come to terms with my unacknowledged shame at being partly a Southerner. But I also learned that I could not easily re-create a more Southern identity for myself. When traveling and working in Southern Italy, I was constantly identified as a "Northern woman" – an outsider – even when I tried to claim my father's heritage. I was "in-between," part of both Northern and Southern Italy, but also part of a combination that betrayed and transcended both. In addition, I was "in-between" as a working class student studying at prestigious universities. I often felt like a pretender, hiding and silencing "less desirable" aspects of my background and identity. I did it so well that I almost convinced myself! Furthermore, as a woman gaining a strong feminist identity in a patriarchal society and studying theology to become a pastor, I was often construed as an "other" by secular feminists, my sexist church, and larger society. I was more "in-between" these different realities, challenging the barriers constructed between them. Since I arrived in the United States, I have learned to recognize more fully the meaning of my whiteness. Yet, as an Italian woman, I have also realized that whiteness comes in very different shades.

My personal experience has taught me that it is often painful and confusing to accept multiple and fluid identities. When I arrived at Union Theological Seminary in New York City, I felt like coming home, with all the positive and negative connotations that coming home invokes. In the Unites States I have met theologians who address the issues of "otherness" and essentialism in conjunction with the complexities of their identities, such as Renee H. Hill and Elias Farajaje-Jones, who challenge the oppressive forces of racism, sexism,

16 A similar dynamic seems to me to apply to the relationships between Northern and Southern Europeans.

homophobia, and classism.[17] At the same time, theologians who question rigid models of identity construction are seen as a threat. They blur established boundaries that separate "us" from "them," questioning ideologies of the status quo and the oppressive nature of identity constructions.

When I meet other people aware of their "in-between" identities I feel connected to their struggles, and find a broader framework to explore my identity. Meeting such theologians feels to me as if I am coming home. At the same time, for "in-between" people coming home is an ambiguous experience. Thus, my "coming home" to Union Theological Seminary was very provisional: I could not turn these theologians into my community. My "in-between" experience is similar to but also different from that of a Palestinian exile or a lesbian African American woman. It is therefore harder to find one's community of accountability when one recognizes one's status of "in-betweenness." Where do we fit in? What aspects of our multiple identities do we value most?

All members of NA ESWTR probably know about this search for community. What parts of ourselves do we prioritize or silence when we meet in the name of a "Feminist European-North American" reality? What do we leave out at the very moment of creating connections? Further, how does the "European Society of Women in Theological Research (ESWTR)" evaluate the fact that Northern Europeans seem to dominate the Society? How do we prevent particular cultural identities from being assumed as the norm amongst us? How can we ensure that minority voices find space and safety so that we do not forget the particularities of our contexts, stories, and struggles despite our commonalities? Can we really come together before we have acknowledged our differences? And what are the risks of doing that? My work as a theologian has been enormously enriched by being able to articulate such questions.

So far, I have purposely stressed the complex, painful, confusing, and isolating aspects of living "in-between," of being dis/located, for I believe that we must first name and acknowledge these difficulties before we address the enormous potential of coming out as a hybrid, a "marginal being," as someone living at the margin of multiple identities.

[17] For instance: Renée Hill, "Disrupted/Disruptive Movements: Black Theology and Black Power 1969/1999," in: Dwight N. Hopkins (ed.), *Black Faith and Public Talk: Critical Essays on James H. Cone's Black Theology and Black Power* (New York: Maryknoll 1999), 138-149; Elias Farajaje-Jones, "Breaking Silence: Toward an In-the Life Theology," in: James H. Cone / Gayraud S. Wilmore (eds), *Black Theology: A Documentary History*, vol. 2: *1980-1992* (Maryknoll: New York, 1993), 139-159.

A positive and creative symbol that describes us at our best is the image of the cyborg. Probably not by chance, feminist science fiction is full of cyborgs. They are organisms partly human and partly machine. Marge Piercy imagined cyborgs[18] which appropriated modern technology to cross boundaries of gender, race, religion, and sexual orientation. Cyborgs maintain their fully respected individuality and differences. They are a powerful symbol of hope. As boundary crossers, cyborgs know that their identity is based on hybridity. They reject myths of pristine unity and wholeness, which have often led to the homogenization and to the annihilation of difference. They show that in reality everyone lives on the crossroad of multiple, ambiguous, and even contradictory identities. Each of us belongs to numerous communities of accountability. Cyborgs teach us that our identities have never been "natural," but that status quo or a moral majority created them for their benefit. Cyborgs question oppressive politics of otherness because they know that everybody is "other."

Feminist theorist Donna Haraway has used the metaphor of the cyborg in her *Manifesto for Cyborgs*.[19] To her, too, cyborgs represent the permeability and confused edges of boundaries, which are highly creative places. She writes: "A cyborg world might be about lived social and bodily realities in which people are not afraid of permanently partial identities and contradictory standpoints."[20] The recognition of differences can strengthen political struggles and communal work, by liberating them from being centered around the myths of "identity" and "unity" and by showing that they are born out of the recognition of difference. Cyborgs teach women, in particular white women, that a natural matrix or holistic notion of woman does not exist. Thus, Haraway believes, the idea of cyborgs strengthens women's struggles everywhere. By claiming multiple identities cyborgs fight the hegemonic tendencies of Western culture. This is a "theoretical and practical struggle against unity-through-domination or unity-through-incorporation."[21] Such a struggle "not only undermines the justifications for patriarchy, colonialism, humanism, positivism, essentialism, scientism, and other unlamented -isms, but all claims for an organic standpoint."[22]

[18] See Marge Piercy, *He, She and It* (New York: Knopf, 1991).

[19] Donna Haraway, "A Manifesto for Cyborgs: Science, Technology and Social Feminism in the 1980s," in: Linda Nicholson (ed.), *Feminism/Postmodernism* (Routledge: New York 1990), 190-233; originally published in: *Socialist Review* 1985 (80): 65-108.

[20] Ibid., 196.

[21] Ibid., 198.

[22] Ibid.

Some of us understand the idea of multiple identities through our life experiences long before we are able to articulate them. For instance, European women theologians who live "in-between" Europe and North America generally know about the dangers of essentializing women and whiteness because we recognize the difference between a woman in urban Germany and a woman in rural Sicily and know that a normative "European woman" does not exist even though people in the United States seem to think so. We realize that we are white, which gives us many privileges. Yet, the generic definition of "white women," which takes middle class Anglo-Saxon educated American women as the norm, does not apply to most of us. From our experiences of disconnection, some of us recognize the existence of patriarchy and white supremacy as part of the complex web of identities. Our in-between status gives us the potential for understanding the complexities of reality. Yet, we certainly fail. We may be cyborgs, but we may be too blind to recognize it.

For Haraway, cyborgs teach women that we do not need homogenization to be effective. Yet, the fight for social justice from a "cyborg perspective" requires a high sense of responsibility for creating connection, networking, and border crossing. The strength of the "cyborg movement" does not consist in the homogenization of individuals and communities, but in the energy created by the ties of solidarity and the channels of communication among them. Many of us probably know of such communities through our spiritual, academic and political life experiences.

Coming out as a hybrid was a most important step in my spiritual and theological journey. The recognition creates a place of deep solitude and pain, but also one of truth and great potential for growth outside the oppressive matrix of imposed labels and totalizing identities. The process of coming out to one's uncomfortable "otherness" and dis/location has the potential of making one more aware of the complexity of other women's realities, and this prevents us from essentializing, trivializing, appropriating, or silencing "others." Whether our "in-betweenness" as feminists of the North-Atlantic means "good news" will depend greatly on ourselves, on our ability to communicate despite the lack of one language, and on our willingness to work together fully aware of our complexities and the complexities of women everywhere.

Experiencing Exile at Home? – Susan K. Roll

There was a saying among foreigners living in Brussels and Leuven, "Once an ex-pat, always an ex-pat." Expatriates living in Belgium, whether for business or study, or because they had come with a spouse, or because they had somehow drifted in, tended to band together and form enriching friendships across boundaries of race, class, age, and ethnicity. In an odd way, particularly among foreign students and researchers in Leuven, it seemed as if everyone "fitted" precisely because no one "fitted." We embarked on common projects – a multi-cultural English-speaking Catholic parish, a center for women's studies in theology – and managed to negotiate towards a shared vision in spite of inadvertently conflicting cultural presuppositions. We learned to appreciate each others' uniqueness and to modify our stereotypes. And if one stayed long enough to say Goodbye to a number of friends who finished their business and went home, it was surprising how many of them would find their way back in a few years – another assignment, further study, perhaps another relationship. However much they had complained about life in Belgium, or perhaps life *among* the Belgians, many of them proved the axiom, "You can never go home again." 'Home' will be different, and more to the point, *you* will be different.

In my case, perhaps a bit like Gabriella, I had felt like a sort of hybrid from an early age. I had grown up with restlessness at the constraints of living in just one culture, or just one country, or even just one historical period, at a time. In my early teens I already knew that I thrived on the complexity and excitement of crossing boundaries and mixing cultures – and that no one else in my small town did. I was certainly the only high-school kid reading the *Bhagavad-Gita* on the school bus. On my first stay in Europe, a five-month stint as an au pair in Milan soon after I had completed a degree in classical languages, I would walk in awe around third-century columns and cathedral foundations, and fourteenth century castles. I was deeply affected by the realization that these buildings had been inhabited and left behind by real people, not by myths in history books. It was as if I could feel the depth of history, the generations and generations of ancestors, and the cumulative richness of their lives and their cultural heritage.

Twenty years later, in 1995 as I was packing my life into twenty-four boxes to be shipped from Belgium to the United States by air freight, it felt as if a whole depth-dimension dropped out of my life. I had made an entirely sensible decision to return to the States after ten years in Belgium because I had received an offer of a full-time teaching position at the seminary in Buffalo. There were no immediate prospects in Europe, which meant that my type B temporary work permit would expire along with my student visa. I would be returning to my native Western New York, which pleased my family no end. I had been out of the area for some 20 years apart from short holiday visits. I was largely out of touch not only with the local culture but with the situation of the local Catholic church for which I would be preparing theology and ministry students. But I did expect to find the cultural and ecclesial setting more congenial to the presence of women, especially after a Leuven friend reported back that he was sure I was bound to find more acceptance here as a woman theologian. The seminary after all counted some 85% lay students and 15% students in the priestly-formation program. 40% of the student body were women. In Leuven the proportion of women in the English section of Theology had ranged as low as 6% some years.

Yet from the beginning, although I knew that I was *supposed* to fit in, qua language, culture, geography, I did not. Day by day, minute by minute, I had to work consciously at belonging. I would feign interest in Buffalo's local indigenous religion (football!) sit through endless meal conversations amongst my colleagues about the local clergy and parishes (none of whom I knew), then go to my parents and listen to the latest village news. Something inside me was sharply out of joint with my environment, and the rough edges rasped against each other. One day, driving back from the village to the seminary, I suddenly had a strong sense that my body was a large hollow shell, busily bustling about doing its job and responding to others' needs and expectations. At the same time, the real me sat curled up like a little ball inside, just peering out and observing all the activity from a distance.

All of this brought me to a new appreciation of the idea of *exile*, a theme from the Hebrew Bible, a theme common to every people whose homeland has been ravaged and who have been made refugees. But I was not part of a people. I didn't fully belong anywhere. I was more complex than anyone I knew really wanted to hear about. Even though I had several colleagues at the seminary with Leuven doctorates, and several others who had finished in Rome, I had lived abroad by far the longest. In contrast to my colleagues, instead of staying in a largely American residence, which provided a sort of buffer against the local culture, I had settled in among the Flemish, learned the language fairly well, and made a life within the culture on its own terms. Very few of my new friends wanted to hear much about my "other life" on the other side of the Atlantic. Beyond a sentence or two, it made them uncomfortable. They would nod politely and change the subject. I probably seemed snobbish and full of myself.

Exile is a state of unhealed fracture: a perpetual flat note, a sour chord. Exile is a fragmented, perpetually irritated, raw-edged existence. Internal exile is that insidious awareness of disjunction or alienation from dimensions of oneself, within oneself. One might live with a sort of double consciousness or multiple consciousness, a consciousness turned back upon itself, a simultaneous awareness of being both subject and object. Not only a dual but multiple disjunction might occur: one exists in several environments, whether serially or simultaneously, none of which is "home."

For me personally, exile means a juxtaposition of a sense of profound rootedness and organic unity with the continuity of generations, which I experience with every sojourn in Europe, with a paradoxical sense of exile and disconnectedness, which remains with me every moment when I am "home" in the USA. This puzzling yet sharp sense of exile provides a category for articulating the situation of women living under patriarchy, particularly in a church-related professional, vocational, and personal context. As women, Catholic women are perpetual foreigners in the formal structural tradition of the churches, inside-outsiders who are supposed to fit, or pretend to fit. At a certain level of awareness one might really believe that one fits, because no separate identity is allowed to be thought. The entire official version of the Christian tradition, or traditions, has been formulated out of androcentrism, or what I prefer to call "male-normativity:" the assumption that what is male is normatively human. Notwithstanding the multiplicity of cultures and locations, it might not be an overstatement to claim that at some level, all women "fit" because none of us, because of our sex, "fit." Certainly, as I sit five or six days a week in male-identified seminary liturgies which glorify God the Father Almighty, I often think of myself as a guest, a visitor in someone else's culture, observing the goings-on from a perspective somewhat removed, much as I am in Europe.

There are two interrelated aspects of my work and life which are strongly colored by my bi-continental location: the "dueling stereotypes" amongst the various countries and the two continents on the level of theology and church practice, and the question of relative academic freedom. I have been fortunate to be able to attend academic conferences on both sides of the Atlantic with some regularity. I still feel very comfortable as an "inside-outsider" when I return to Europe, and slip easily into the role of a congenial guest, familiar with the household and its habits, so to speak. Yet in the USA, my European connections tend to put people off, or alternatively, to make me seem like a far more internationally renowned scholar than I really am. In the USA, I sense a subtle pressure to restrict my horizons to correspond to the scope of current American concerns and issues. At the same time, as an American I often bring a sort of pragmatic impatience to any highly abstract theological discourse in Europe: I need to see, not just time-consuming talk, but results, whether striking new insights or practical initiatives for the reform of abuses.

As a Roman Catholic feminist scholar and practitioner in the field of liturgy, I find that the ecclesial differences between the two continents and their respective range of variants among cultures produces misunderstandings and often judgmentalism. I greatly appreciate Teresa's presentation on the multiplicity of culture and the permeability of boundaries, and I agree fully with her analysis, particularly as regards new women's liturgies. But I live and work in an ecclesial context in which ever-greater pressure is exerted from the church governing structure to compel conformity to directives in liturgy and belief which presume a normative androcentric hierarchical culture, autocratically fixed boundaries and a static concept of absolute, everlasting truth. North American Roman Catholics, at least in the Northeast USA, tend to comply, however reluctantly, with the latest liturgical and ministerial directives, which progressively restrict the (already limited) scope of participation by lay persons. At the same time, American Roman Catholics criticize European Roman Catholics whose alleged "abuses" of the liturgy are supposed to have precipitated new directives from Rome. In 1997, with the publication of legislation limiting lay involvement in pastoral ministry, sources both in the USA and in Europe told me, "Well it's not due to the Americans, the directives are really aimed at the Dutch and the Swiss." The revised *General Instruction on the Roman Missal* of 2000 is commonly blamed on "the Germans, and/or the Austrians, who just do whatever they want" in liturgy. Yet Roman Catholics in the USA are taking the new directives far more seriously, studying the legislation in detail and organizing instructional sessions with earnest compliance.

After six years in the USA I have continued to do most of my publishing in Europe, as well as serving on the board of several European liturgy journals. It could be just my imagination, but I believe I enjoy more freedom of expression by publishing in Europe, partly because only those who are truly interested and theologically literate will obtain these publications in the USA. Yet another factor is the relative difference in sophistication concerning theological discourse. I can say more, and say it better, in Europe. I am less impelled to weigh my words for their "danger level" – the potential misunderstandings which can develop when new insights and disturbing questions are filtered through a hermeneutic of literalism and loyalty, narrowly understood.

Europe is not a paradise free of misogyny. Yet when I lived so close to the rich root system of European history I could easily maintain a stubborn hope for a future of justice because I was conscious, every day, of how long and complex a journey humanity has covered in less than three millennia. What feminist theologians are doing could hardly have been imagined even a few decades ago, and "taking the long view" can fuel a dynamic and well-grounded hope. Ultimately, I believe the richness and depth dimension inherent in the sense of historicity, as well as the ability to contextualize much of what claims absolute a-historical truth, in the religious life and praxis of Northern Europe could prove not only a rich resource for North American theological discourse. It will also put into perspective current ecclesio-political dominating strategies on both continents. As I tell my students, when I teach them the history of the twentieth century Liturgical Movement, a grassroots evolution originating in Europe which shaped the liturgical reforms of Vatican II, "the more you know of the past, the less you have to fear from the future."

Going West: On the Benefits of a Multi-Locality of Belonging – Susanne Scholz

Going west, crossing the Atlantic and staying on the other side, was never my secret master plan during my years of growing up. Despite uncountable foreign language classes and international study topics throughout my school years, I do not recall thinking: "Wouldn't it be great to live in this or that country?" Instead, I remember quite vividly how horrified I felt when a black-and-white photo in our English textbook showed an overcrowded ship of stern-looking German Jewish immigrants on their way to the United States at the turn of the nineteenth to the twentieth century. "Refugees!" I thought, "what a hardship it must be to find one's way in a new land with another language and unfamiliar customs."

I had heard refugee stories all my life. Both sets of my grandparents had left their homes in Silesia at the end of World War II. I grew up with the stories of my mother's mother who always spoke about her home in *Freiburg in Schlesien*. Like many German women from Silesia, she fled the Russian Army with three little children in 1944-45. She and her husband, my grandfather, had lived in Berlin prior to and during the war. However, in the late 1940s, women and children were evacuated from the city and so my grandmother went back to her parent's town in Silesia. As my grandfather had limped since his youth (as a child he had stepped into a hole from a landmine and the broken foot healed crookedly; his parents did not have the money for good medical care), he was not drafted to the army. During the last years of the war, he was a *Blockwart* in the neighborhood in which my grandparents had made a home. However, I grew up only with my grandmother's stories, not with his. He was a silent and stern man during my childhood and teenage years.

I understood that the war had drastically changed life for my grandparents. For instance, only the unexpected translation help of an American soldier aided my grandmother in surviving the *Flucht* (literally: "escape") after guards of a refugee camp in Czechoslovakia discovered her bread knife. It was considered a weapon and its possession demanded the death penalty. She saw her last hour approaching and placed her three children – one of them my mother – into care with the three women with whom she had fled. But because of the American soldier, she was not shot. The war made my grandmother even more religious than she had already been. As long as I can remember, I understood deeply that the lot of refugees is painful and frightening.

My grandparents established a new home in post-war Bavaria from where my parents moved later to Frankfurt am Main. My sister and I were born there, but still felt as relative newcomers. For instance, I never learned to speak the regional dialect of the state in which I grew up – *Hesse* – because nobody at home spoke *hessisch*, and (interestingly) most of my friends were not "indigenous" *Hessinnen* either. Our visits to my grandparents in Munich and my grandmother's stories reminded me throughout my childhood that our family was originally from somewhere else. As a family we were dispersed in Germany because of the war. Then and later, whenever refugees were mentioned, I remembered the stories of my grandmother.[23] Listening to her painful memories of getting used to a new home, which after all had always remained Germany, I had felt great relief that she and her family had survived the war. To move into a foreign country was never my dream. It never occurred to me that one day I might change countries voluntarily, a process initiated by a scholarship opportunity.

I remember these moments of refugee awareness because they tell me that a multi-locality of belonging has been with me since childhood, for many years unconsciously and in recent years consciously. My appreciation of what it means to belong to different places simultaneously – even if these places look rather similar from my perspective today – made it easy for me to eventually venture out into a "foreign land." I did so because the study of Protestant theology at German universities appeared parochial to me. The professors rarely made multi-local, i.e. international, connections. The study of religion and

[23] According to the "World Refugee Survey 2000," published by the U.S. Committee For Refugees (Immigration and Refugee Services of America, 2000), "more than 35 million people worldwide are uprooted from their homes. More than 14 million people were refugees outside their home countries. Some 21 million others are displaced within their own country – 25 percent more than the year before." See also *www.refugees.org/news/press-release/2000/061300a.htm* (visited 26 March 2001).

Christian theology in Germany in the 1980s emphasized national theological history and tradition. Only research on feminist theologies and the Jewish-Christian dialog embraced eagerly and extensively international conversation partners. Participants of feminist studies and the Jewish-Christian dialog acknowledged the limitations of their perspectives and made their international experiences fruitful for the theological exploration. Many of them affiliated with their religious denominations and with the academy. They were involved in grass-roots educational programs and in serious scholarly research. They usually spoke several languages and had often lived in several countries. They knew about multi-locality in practice and in theory. At the time, I did not understand that my interest in these two areas was related to my inherent appreciation of multi-locality.

When I eventually crossed the Atlantic and found myself staying for far longer than the originally planned year, the strong connections between feminist theological discourse in West-Germany and the political, economic, and cultural influence of the United States on West-Germany became increasingly problematic to me. It has been no accident that many American theological feminist books have been translated into German and become part of the German feminist theological repertoire. Decades of West German orientation toward the United States have made it appear "natural" to West German feminist theologians to be fluent in American feminist theological discourse. The reunification of the German borders in 1990 has not much changed the German orientation towards the United States,[24] and despite some indications of German cultural independence, the Americanization of united Germany continues to be very strong. Politically, and especially economically, Germany continues to follow the lead of the United States, this time under the banner of the European Union.[25] But my geographical re-location from Germany to

[24] For a brief historical description of feminist theology in East Germany prior to 1990, see Christiane Markert-Wizisla, "Feministische Theologie aus der ehemaligen DDR – Tradition und Perspective," in: Annette Esser / Luise Schottroff (eds), *Feministische Theologie im europäischen Kontext* (Yearbook of the European Society of Women in Theological Research 1; Kok Pharos: Kampen 1993), 140-152. For a non-theological view on the influence of the United States on Eastern Germans since 1989, see Andreas Lehmann, *Go West: Ostdeutsche in Amerika* (Schwarzkopf: Berlin 1998). For an opposing view, see Paul Nolte, "Die unamerikanische Nation," in: *Die Zeit* 22 (2002): *www.zeit.de/2002/22/Politik/print_200222_essay.usa.html.*

[25] Publications on the topic abound; see, e.g., Todd Herzog and Sander L. Gilman (eds), *A New Germany in a New Europe?* (Routledge: New York/London 2001); Heide Fehrenbach and Uta G. Poiger (eds), *Transactions, Transgressions, Transformations: American Culture in Western Europe and Japan* (Berghahn Books: New York 2000); Anselm Doering-Manteufel,

the United States has considerably changed my understanding about the pre-eminence of American feminist theologies in Germany.

The influence of such discourse is particularly tricky to determine. The institutional status of feminist researchers in Germany continues to be institutionally and intellectually marginalized.[26] Traditional, i.e. androcentric, study of theology and religion dominates departments and faculties of theology in Germany.[27] Upholding the renowned German history of theological studies, many professors have little interest in feminist studies of theology and religion, considering this area a "fad" and without value for the general theological debate. Many scholars of systematic theology thus continue to focus on the writings of early twentieth century theologians such as Paul Tillich, Karl Barth, or Karl Rahner as if theological discourse had stopped growing in the 1960s. A similar situation applies to biblical studies: many professors of the Bible are not actively involved in the newer developments of the field that have advanced primarily in the English-speaking world, including feminist approaches to the

Wie westlich sind die Deutschen? Amerikanisierung und Westernisierung im 20. Jahrhundert (Vandenhoeck & Ruprecht: Göttingen 1999); Alf Luedtke et al. (eds), *Amerikanisierung: Traum und Alptraum in Deutschland des 20. Jahrhunderts* (Steiner: Stuttgart 1996); Michael G. Hehlshoff et al. (eds), *From Bundesrepublik to Deutschland: German Politics After Unification* (University of Michigan Press: Ann Arbor 1993). For examples from the German newspaper *Die Zeit* see, e.g., Rosemarie Noack, "Amerika in Germany: In deutschen Städten entstehen Urban Entertainment Center – ein Mischung aus Amüsement und Kommerz," *Die Zeit* (5 March 1998), 57-58; Thorsten Stecher, "Rap der neuen Mitte: Der Sprechgesang aus dem schwarzen Ghetto ist deutsch geworden: Die sanfte Vermarktung hat begonnen, der Spass ist noch nicht vorbei: Ein Tauchgang im Hamburger Hip-Hop-Untergrund," *Die Zeit* (7 January 1999), 29-30. See also my essay "Going West: Zur Situation deutscher feministischer Theologinnen," in *Zwischen-Räume: Deutsche feministische Theologinnen im Ausland* (Münster: LIT, 2000), pp. 55-67.

26 The situation appears to be better in other areas of the humanities and the social sciences, see Ulla Bock, "Am Ausgang des Jahrhunderts: Zum Stand der Institutionalisierung von Frauenstudien an deutschen Universitäten," *Feministische Studien* (1998), 103-117.

27 As evidenced by, for instance, the online catalogs of the Humbold University in Berlin (*www2.hu-berlin.de/inside/theologie/inhalt.htm*) or of the University in Hamburg (*www.uni-hamburg.de/theolog/kvv/index.htm*). For the systematic effort to delegitimize feminist theological work in Germany, see the so-called "Tübinger Gutachten," an evaluation of feminist theology by theology professors at the University of Tübingen in 1990; for a critical discussion of this *Gutachten*, see Elisabeth Moltmann-Wendel and Günter Kegel (eds.), *Feministische Theologie im Kreuzfeuer: Der Streit um das 'Tübinger Gutachten'* (Gütersloher Verlagshaus: Gütersloh 1992).

Bible.[28] In other words, many theology departments at German universities are no longer at the forefront of theological and religious studies. Clinging to the undoubtedly eminent tradition of German theology, traditional scholars have successfully undercut their ability to contribute to the international, i.e. English-speaking, world of theological and religious studies.

While traditional scholars continue to engage German history and tradition of theology, West German feminist theologians have followed the orientation of general German society towards the United States, and have become well versed in international feminist theological and religious discussions. Since the end of the 1970s, German feminist theologians have gratefully and eagerly studied the books of American feminist theologians. Although German feminist scholars have developed their own flourishing discourse,[29] theological ideas from American writers continue to shape the debate. For instance, in May 2001, the German organization *Feminismus und Kirche AG* offered a conference on womanist theologies.[30] The integration of American theological

28 An exception is the article by German biblical researcher Helmut Utzschneider, "Text – Reader – Author: Towards a Theory of Exegesis: Some European Viewpoints," in: *The Journal of Hebrew Scriptures* 1 (1996-1997): www.purl.org/jhs. Utzschneider discusses the value of new biblical approaches in contrast to the continuing emphasis on historical criticism among many German researchers of the Bible. However, the author's apologetic stance indicates that such considerations are rare among German-speaking biblical scholars. For an autobiographically oriented discussion by a German feminist biblical scholar, see Luise Schottroff, "Working for Liberation: A Change of Perspective in New Testament Scholarship," in: Fernando F. Segovia / Mary Ann Tolbert (eds), *Reading From This Place: Social Location and Biblical Interpretation in Global Perspective* (Fortress: Minneapolis 1995), 183-198.

29 The establishment of the "European Society of Women in Theological Research (ESWTR)" in 1986 has undoubtedly supported European and also German women theologians. To this day, the German section of the ESWTR is by far the largest of all national groups of the ESWTR. In 2000, the German section had 246 members whereas other countries with strong feminist theological activities, such as the Netherlands, Switzerland, and the U.K. had 54, 62, and 80 members respectively. For further information on the ESWTR, see *www.eswtr.org*. German theological departments continue to produce huge numbers of theologians who become feminist in the process. However, the lack of jobs in the ministry of the German Protestant Churches led to a dramatic reduction in the number of theology students during the 1990s. For more information on the future of theology in Germany, see, e.g., Jürgen Moltmann, "Europäische Kulturpolitik: Werden die Theologischen Fakultäten geopfert?" *Evangelische Theologie* 59, no. 1 (1999): 84-87; Uwe Gerber, "Einige kritische Bemerkungen zum derzeitigen Studium der Theologie," *Theologische Zeitschrift* 47, no. 3 (1991): 275-285; Ulrich Rausch (ed.), *Der Pfarrermangel – und das Ende? Analysen – Modelle – Visionen* (Frankfurt/Main: Knecht, 1994).

30 AG Feminismus und Kirchen e.V.: "Womanistische Theologie – gefährliche Erinnerung für 'uns'? Selbst-Kontextualisierung feministischer Theologie in Deutschland im Blickwechsel

developments is understood to signal openness to international theological ideas and practice. This characteristic of German feminist theologies probably explains something of the popularity of feminist theological studies in Germany, despite the fact that it is now experiencing the effects of the conservative backlash. In other words, student enrollment and enthusiasm for feminist theological work has been decreasing in the 1990s, which is perhaps due to the lack of academic and job opportunities in Christian theology in general and the increase of students of a conservative theological background.

Both the exclusion of German feminist theologians from German universities and their American orientation have tragic consequences. On the one hand, highly motivated and qualified researchers know that they have to be familiar with international scholarship if they want to contribute to it. They read the English literature, attend international conferences, and often take advantage of research or study opportunities in the United States. Seeking to integrate feminist-theological studies, they struggle with a language which is not their own and which originates from a cultural context of which they have little first-hand experience. On the other hand, the German university system is rarely supportive of such research efforts. Instead, traditional German professors of theology actively discourage feminist theologians from immersing themselves in the study of feminist theologies. Often, therefore, German feminist debates do not enjoy the institutional support and remain on the margins of the established theological discourse in Germany.

Will this situation change in the foreseeable future? Although in recent years a few feminist scholars of theology have become professors at prestigious German universities, the general intellectual, cultural, and religious climate does not indicate a "revival" of theological feminist or non-feminist discourse in Germany. The rather secular society of post-Holocaust Germany, both East and West, has not led to a generation of Germans educated and interested in Christian theological matters. Many Germans are engaged in New Age and other alternative spiritual practices and philosophies. Distrusting institutionalized religious life and inherently undereducated in religious and theological discourse, they deal with their religious needs on a personal level. Is this situation just another proof of the continuing Americanization of contemporary Germany?

As a diasporic German feminist theologian located in the United States, I wonder whether the resistance of traditional scholars of theology and the openness

mit womanistischer schwarzer Theologie in den USA," Conference held in Hedwig Drahnsfeld Haus, Bendorft/Rhein, Germany, May 4-6, 2001.

of German feminist theologians to American developments bear witness to the lasting destructive legacy of the Nazi-era and the war. So many people have been silenced and bit their tongues over what they saw and experienced. So many people were killed because they were classified as "other," as Jews, Sinta and Roma, or as gay people. Where is the heart-felt theological mourning? Where is the expression of pain? Where are the tears? The hearts are blocked, and so has been the German theological ability to express "theological truths" about God and our place in the world. I once met a Palestinian woman who said that Germans needed a lot of love after 1945. Perhaps, the integration of a multi-locality of belonging, of people who come from everywhere, of the immigrants and the refugees of our time, into our theological practices and theories is one way of making theological insight again relevant to people living in Germany, Europe, and elsewhere.

Many people have experienced a multi-locality of belonging in Germany before and after 1945 and 1990; my family of origin is one of them. Feminist theologies have much to gain from ruminating about the meaning of our lives on this planet when dis/location and the sour effects of global economic and political structures become everyday experiences for so many people. One does not need to go west in order to make these connections, but, at least for me, going west sharpened my understanding of the connections between the dilemma of identifying as a citizen of my country of origin, the purpose and histories of feminist and traditional theological discourses, and the future of Christian theologies in a world marked by war, destruction, and suffering. Thus, in my view feminist theological discourse, whether here or there, faces enormous responsibilities. We need to build many bridges to cross not only the oceans that separate us, but also to overcome the legal, psychological, and political-economic boundaries of our various locations and mindsets. Whenever we do, we have asserted our right to belong to this world and to the divine.

Epistemological Possibilities of Hybrid Identities – Karen Jo Torjesen

Late in January of 1978, a German letter arrived unexpectedly in my post-office box on Mount Baldy where I was living in a cabin, teaching high school and trying to write a dissertation. The letter, postmarked from Germany, contained an invitation to become a *Wissenschaftliche Assistentin* in *Patristische Theologie* and to teach at the Georg-August-Universitat in Göttingen, Germany.

Three months later, I flew out of my life and landed alone and a stranger in Northern Germany. It was not my first cross-cultural adventure – I had spent several years in Latin America as a child – but it was my first cross-cultural experience as an adult. Now with an adult's self-reflective and analytical eye, I observed the process of moving into another culture at the same time that I was experiencing it. I would become a witness and an interpreter of the process of the creation of a hybrid identity.

As an adult I witnessed the power of language to construct the self. I had arrived in Germany speaking no German; in six months I would be expected to conduct a seminar in the German language. I moved swiftly – albeit awkwardly – into the language and learned painfully the multiple process by which language creates selfhood. Besides having a tutor I worked through eight different textbooks, American and German, learning the very different structure of the German language. Mark Twain commented wryly about his own learning experience that German did not conform to the structures of the human mind. Learning the language would begin the process of creating a German selfhood and it would also force me to think a different way.

The language also set the limits for my German selfhood. When my ability in spoken German corresponded to that of a thirteen-year-old, I became linguistically a thirteen-year-old and the depths and complexities of my mature self were inexpressible. This process of growing up into a language is painful for the adult psyche, for it is experienced as a regression to childhood and a recapitulation of the moments of awkwardness and embarrassment endemic to the process of growing up. On the other hand, learning a language while living in a culture becomes the means for birthing a new selfhood. With the ability to "embody" one's self in a new language comes the exhilaration of being seen, being heard and thereby feeling connected.

Language indeed constructs the self, but it also constructs a culturally specific self. This was a new learning which I experienced as I discovered that language embodies cultural attitudes, values, conventions, as well as its cosmology and larger constructs such as temporality, social order, and modes of being. One learns that you can only say what the language wants you to say. Language shapes you into its own image. The primal experience of that is a loss of selfhood, the American selfhood, before it becomes clear that another selfhood is opened up. The language creates a new and different emotional register expressive of different gestures and postures embodied in expressions like *na ja* or *doch*, which are not translatable into English.

Needless to say, mastery of the language took longer than six months. But by the end of two years, when I returned to the States for a visit, I became acutely aware that I had evolved a German self and that I needed to resurrect my American selfhood that was in storage at the bottom of some psychic closet.

Later, when I went back to Germany, I pondered what seemed at the time to be a strange phenomenon – that I had a German self and an American self. Faced with the reality of having evolved two selves, I came to think of my American self as my authentic self and my German selfhood as a pseudo-self. The problem here was with the conceptual framework that demanded a unitary self and had no place for hybrid identities. But when I examined my German selfhood, she felt to me quite authentic, to be in fact a real me. At some point I decided that both my German selfhood and my American selfhood were authentic selves and I abandoned the concept of unitary selves, simply because it failed to make sense of my experience. This was *before* reading postmodern theory.

I want to play here with the idea of pain as privilege. The first years were difficult, lonely, isolating in a much deeper sense than just the loneliness of the foreigner in a foreign land, because the processes in which I was involved required the deconstruction of an unchallenged, uncontested selfhood that had made me feel safe, protected, and connected. And yet this pain brought with it a peculiar form of privilege. Because of my dual selfhood, my multiplication of selves, and the existence of my German self and my American self, I in effect possess a dual citizenship. I am able to inhabit two different cultural worlds. I have a selfhood that is contiguous with each one. My capacity to know is compounded – to know myself, to know my German-ness and to know my American-ness, to know Germany through my American-ness and more significantly to know America through my German-ness. Herein lies the epistemological privilege of hybrid identities; they open up new ways of knowing. Precisely along the border between my American selfhood and German selfhood a space is opened up that provides unique epistemological possibilities.

By living in Germany as an American, I created my own vortex where German and American cultures collided. The collision itself is what opened up new possibilities of knowing. Where I collided with the otherness of German culture, I discovered and uncovered the otherness of American culture. The jarring experience of difference raised the question, "Why do Germans do x-y-or-z?" That is, how do I account for this anomaly, this otherness on the part of Germans? Why are they so weird? This led to a second question, a self-reflexive one: Why do I find this behavior so anomalous? I am living in Germany; Germans do not find this behavior anomalous. It is anomalous to me by virtue of a different cultural logic, an American one, and not a German one. Underlying the first question is the assumption of the normativity of American culture, a normativity that is so naturalized it is rendered invisible while one is living in

America. In the second question, "Why do I find this German practice so anomalous?," American culture becomes other, against the backdrop of the normativity of German culture. Here is where the learning begins. In moving from an assumed normativity of American culture to a discovery of the particularity of American culture a particular kind of learning takes place. The interior space, opened up along the borders of my German and American selves, creates a new epistemological vantagepoint, one unavailable in any other context. The collision of the tectonic plates of American and German identities shook the foundations of my culture-bound ways of knowing that had remained largely invisible.

Let me provide an example. During the years I was living in West Germany, 90 percent of Germans paid *Kirchensteuer*, a church tax, equivalent to roughly10 percent of their income tax. At the same time, German attendance in the churches was running about 3 to 4 percent. I could make no sense of the disparity between the financial support for the German church and the low attendance at services. Church attendance in America ranged between 30 and 40 percent, but it was unimaginable that even 40 per cent of Americans would commit the equivalent of 10 per cent of their taxes to the churches. The more I grappled with this question, the more clearly I came to see my own assumptions about the nature and function of churches that came from American culture. The outcome of this process was an understanding of the situation of the American churches as idiosyncratic, produced by a particular set of historical and political circumstances, which I came to call the Americanization of Christianity. American churches serve a social function in which the after-service sacrament of coffee and doughnuts is an essential element of the church experience. Yet for Americans the church is located squarely in the private sphere and consequently is not seen as a public bearer of American history and culture. In the end, I understood the relationship between church and society in Germany as more typical and the American relationship as somewhat idiosyncratic – a valuable insight for a church historian. The epistemological possibilities created by this space between my two identities produced insights into American culture that could not have come about in any other way; it opened up insights into the underlying structures and assumptions that remain invisible to most forms of cultural analysis.

There is important work to be done by feminists who enjoy the epistemological privilege of hybrid identities. As feminists, we have been intensively involved in cultural critique, specifically through our forms of gender analysis and our critique of patriarchal social and political structures. Positioned as we are on the boundary between two or more identities, we have the capacity for doing a particular kind of cultural analysis of our own countries. These forms of cultural analysis are vital. We are in a position to make visible for our compatriots the cultural assumptions and cultural structures that are invisible to those of us who inhabit them on a daily basis. We are also well positioned to participate in cross-cultural dialogue by being able to articulate for other cultures the particularities and idiosyncrasies of our own cultures.

Contributors:

Teresa Berger received two doctorates and her "Habilitation" from German universities in 1984, 1989, and 1991 respectively, and is Associate Professor of Ecumenical Theology at the Divinity School of Duke University, NC. She is co-editor of *Liturgie und Frauenfrage* (EOS Verlag: St. Ottilien 1990), author of *Women's Ways of Worship: Gender Analysis and Liturgical History* (Liturgical Press: Collegeville, MN 1999), and editor of *Dissident Daughters: Feminist Liturgies in Global Context* (Westminster John Knox Press: Louisville, KY 2001).

Gabriella Lettini is a graduate of the Waldensian Theological Seminary in Rome, Italy. She holds the degree of Master of Philosophy from Union Theological Seminary in New York City, where she is currently working on a doctoral dissertation in Systematic Theology, focusing on the politics of otherness in feminist and womanist theologies. She is the author of *Omosessualità* (Homosexuality) (Claudiana: Torino 1999).

Susan K. Roll received her Ph.D. from the Faculty of Theology, Catholic University of Louvain (Leuven, Belgium) in 1993, and is currently Associate Professor of Liturgy and Systematic Theology at Christ the King Seminary, Buffalo, New York. She is the author of *Toward the Origins of Christmas* (Kok-Pharos: Kampen 1995), and co-editor of *Women, Ritual and Liturgy / Ritual und Liturgie von Frauen / Femmes, la liturgie et le rituel* (ESWTR Yearbook 9; Peeters: Leuven 2001), and *Re-Visioning Our Sources: Women's Spirituality in European Perspectives* (Kok-Pharos: Kampen 1997).

Susanne Scholz received her Ph.D. from Union Theological Seminary, NY, in 1997, and is Associate Professor of Biblical/Religious Studies at Merrimack College, North Andover, MA. She is the author of *Rape Plots: A Feminist Cultural Study of Genesis 34* (Lang: New York 2000), and co-editor of *Zwischen-Räume: Deutsche feministische Theologinnen im Ausland* (Lit: Münster 2000).

Karen Jo Torjesen received her doctorate in Religion and Church History from Claremont Graduate School in 1982. She taught at the Georg-August-Universität in Göttingen, Germany, from 1978-82, Mary Washington College, from 1982-85, Fuller Theological Seminary 1985-87, and joined the faculty of Claremont Graduate University in 1987 to start a graduate program in Women's Studies in Religion. In 2000, she was appointed Dean of the new School of Religion at Claremont Graduate University. She is the author of *When Women Were Priests* (HarperSanFrancisco: San Francisco, CA 1993).

I. Bibliographie – Bibliography – Bibliographie[1]

Zusammengestellt von Angela Berlis

I.1 Exegese (Erstes Testament, Neues Testament, nicht kanonisierte jüdische und frühchristliche Schriften) und Hermeneutik

Bob Becking / Meindert Kijkstra / Karel Vriezen / Marjo Korpel, **Only One God? Monotheism in Ancient Israel and the Veneration of the Goddess Asherah**, (Biblical Seminar 77), Sheffield Academic Press: Sheffield 2001, 180pp., ISBN 1-84127-199-3, $19.95

*Annette Böckler, **Gott als Vater im Alten Testament. Traditionsgeschichtliche Untersuchungen zur Entstehung und Entwicklung eines Gottesbildes**, Chr. Kaiser / Gütersloher Verlagshaus: Gütersloh 2000, 454 S., ISBN 3-579-02664-X, DM 78,00

Athalya Brenner (ed.), **A Feminist Companion to Exodus to Deuteronomy**, (FCB II, 5), Sheffield Academic Press: Sheffield 2001, 224pp., ISBN 1-84127-079-2, £16.95 / $33.95

Athalya Brenner / Carole R. Fontaine (eds), **The Song of Songs**, (FCB II, 6), Sheffield Academic Press: Sheffield 2000, 216pp., ISBN 1-84127-052-0, £16.95 / $28.50

Athalya Brenner (ed.), **A Feminist Companion to Samuel and Kings**, (FCB II, 7), Sheffield Academic Press: Sheffield 2000, 152pp., ISBN 1-84127-082-2, £16.95 / $33.95

Athalya Brenner (ed.), **A Feminist Companion to the Prophets and Daniel**, (FCB II, 8) Sheffield Academic Press: Sheffield 2002, 320pp., ISBN 1-84127-163-2, £19.99 / $32.95

*Klara Butting, **Prophetinnen gefragt. Die Bedeutung der Prophetinnen im Kanon aus Tora und Prophetie**, Erev-Rav: Wittingen 2001, 230 S., ISBN 3-932810-15-5, € 13,00

[1] Zu Büchern mit * siehe unter “Rezensionen” – Books marked * are reviewed below – Pour les livres avec * voire sous “Critique des livres”.

Gérald Caron et al., **Women Also Journeyed with Him: Feminist Perspectives on the Bible**, Liturgical Press: Collegeville 2000, 179pp., ISBN 0-8146-5892-X, $24.95

Mary Ann Getty-Sullivan, **Women in the New Testament**, The Liturgical Press: Collegeville 2001, 280pp., ISBN 0-8146-2546-0, $7.95

*Irmtraud Fischer, **Rut**, (Herders Theologischer Kommentar zum Alten Testament), Herder Verlag: Freiburg 2001, 277 S., ISBN 3-451-26811-6, € 55,22 / CHF 95,00

*Esther Fuchs, **Sexual Politics in the Biblical Narrative: Reading the Hebrew Bible as a Woman**, (Journal for the Study of the Old Testament Supplement Series 310), Sheffield Academic Press: Sheffield 2000, 244pp., ISBN 1-84127-138-1, £40.00

Judith M. Hadley, **The Cult of Asherah in Ancient Israel and Judah: Evidence for a Hebrew Goddess**, (University of Cambridge Oriental Publications 57), Cambridge University Press: New York 2000, 262pp., ISBN 0-521-66235-4, $64.95

Jill Hammer, **Sisters at Sinai: New Tales of Biblical Women**, The Jewish Publication Society: Philadelphia 2001, 256pp., ISBN 0-8276-0726-1, $24.95

*Claudia Janssen / Luise Schottroff / Beate Wehn (Hg.), **Paulus. Umstrittene Traditionen – lebendige Theologie. Eine feministische Lektüre**, Chr. Kaiser / Gütersloher Verlagshaus: Gütersloh 2001, 208 S., ISBN 3-579-05318-3, DM 39,80 / CHF 37,50

*Anna Kiesow, **Löwinnen von Juda, Frauen als Subjekte politischer Macht in der judäischen Königszeit**, (Theologische Frauenforschung in Europa 4), Lit: Münster 2000, 224 S., ISBN 3-8258-4653-9, DM 39,80

Ingeborg Kruse, **Frauenkonkordanz zur Bibel**, Kreuz Verlag: Stuttgart 2001, 191 S., ISBN 3-7831-1898-0, € 15.29

Amy-Jill Levine (ed.), **A Feminist Companion to Matthew**, (The Feminist Companion to the New Testament and Early Christian Writings 1), Sheffield Academic Press: Sheffield 2001, 248pp., ISBN 1-84127-211-6, £16.95

Amy-Jill Levine (ed.), **A Feminist Companion to Mark**, (The Feminist Companion to the New Testament and Early Christian Writings 2), Sheffield Academic Press: Sheffield 2001, 264pp., ISBN 1-84127-194-2, £16.95

Amy-Jill Levine (ed.), **A Feminist Companion to Luke**, (The Feminist Companion to the New Testament and Early Christian Writings 3), Sheffield Academic Press: Sheffield 2002, 352pp., ISBN 1-84127-174-8, £17.99 / $29.95

Carol Meyers / Toni Craven / Ross S. Kraemer (eds), **Women in Scripture: A Dictionary of Named and Unnamed Women in the Hebrew Bible**, Apocryphal / Deuterocanonical Books, and the New Testament, Houghton Mifflin: New York 2000, 592pp., ISBN 0-395-70936-9, $40.00

Joan L. Mitchell, **Beyond Fear and Silence: A Feminist-Literary Reading of Mark**, Continuum: New York / London 2001, 144pp., ISBN 0-8264-1354-4, £12.99

Erika Mohri, **Maria Magdalena. Frauenbilder in Evangelientexten des 1. bis 3. Jahrhunderts**, N.G. Elwert: Marburg 2000, 393 S., ISBN 3-7708-1148-8, DM 59,90

Jorunn Økland, **Women in their Place: Paul and the Corinthian Discourse of Gender and Sanctuary Space**, 408pp., (unpublished Ph.D., University of Oslo 2000)

Benedikt Otzen, **Tobit and Judith**, (Guides to the Apocrypha and Pseudepigrapha 11), Sheffield Academic Press: Sheffield 2001, 128pp., ISBN 1-84127-246-9, $14.95

Thomas Rohde (Hg.), **Mythos Salome. Vom Markusevangelium bis Djuna Barnes**, Reclam Verlag: Leipzig 2000, 317 S., ISBN 3-379-01720-5, DM 24,00

Norma Rosen, **Biblical Women Unbound: Counter-Tales**, The Jewish Publication Society: Philadelphia 2001, 224pp., ISBN 0-8276-0714-8, $19.95

Silvia Schroer / Thomas Staubli, **Body Symbolism in the Bible**, The Liturgical Press: Collegeville 2001, 256pp., ISBN 0-8146-5954-3, $39.95

Elisabeth Schüssler Fiorenza, **Rhetoric and Ethics. The Politics of Biblical Study**, Augsburg Fortress: Minneapolis 2001, ISBN 0-8006-2795-4, £12.99

Elisabeth Schüssler Fiorenza, **Wisdom Ways: Introducing Feminist Biblical Interpretation**, Orbis: Maryknoll NY 2001, 240pp., ISBN 1-57075-383-0, $20.00

Marit Skjeggestad, **Facts in the Ground? Biblical History in Archaeological Interpretation of the Iron Age Palestine**, (Acta theologica 3), Unipub: Oslo 2001, 279pp.

Ken Stone (ed.), **Queer Commentary and the Hebrew Bible**, (JSOT.S 334), Sheffield Academic Press: Sheffield 2001, 225pp., ISBN 1-84127-237-X, $60.00

*Sonja Angelika Strube **“Wegen dieses Wortes…”. Feministiche und nichtfeministische Exegese im Vergleich am Beispiel der Auslegungen zu Mk 7,24-30**, (Theologische Frauenforschung in Europa 3), Lit: Münster / Hamburg / London 2000, 354 S., ISBN 3-8258-4521-4, DM 49,80

Luzia Sutter Rehmann / Sabine Bieberstein / Ulrike Metternich (Hg.), **Sich dem Leben in die Arme werfen. Biblische und alltägliche Auferstehungserfahrungen**, Gütersloher Verlagshaus: Gütersloh 2002, 200 S., ISBN 3-579-05381-7, ca. € 23,00

Luzia Sutter Rehmann, **Konflikte zwischen ihm und ihr. Sozialgeschichtliche und exegetische Untersuchungen zur Nachfolgeproblematik von Ehepaaren (Mk 10, 1-12par)**, Gütersloher Verlagshaus: Gütersloh 2002, (= Habilitation Basel), ca. 288 S., ISBN 3-579-05380-9, ca. € 23,00

Rannfrid I. Thelle, **Ask God: Divine Consultation in the Literature of the Hebrew Bible**, (Beiträge zur biblischen Exegese und Theologie 30), (Diss. Oslo 1999), P. Lang: Frankfurt/M. 2002, 284pp., ISBN: 3-631-37161-6, $47.95

John L. Thompson, **Writing the Wrongs: Women of the Old Testament Among Biblical Commentators from Philo through the Reformation**, OUP: Oxford 2000, 304pp., ISBN 0-19-513736-1, £40.00

Carey Ellen Walsh, **Exquisite Desire: Religion Erotic, and the Song of Songs**, Augsburg Fortress: Minneapolis 2001, 240pp., ISBN 0-8006-3249-4, $19.00

Satoko Yamaguchi, **Mary and Martha: Women in the World of Jesus**, Orbis: Maryknoll NY 2001, 240pp., ISBN 1-57075-401-2, $24.00

I.2 Kirchen- und Religionsgeschichte

Änne Bäumer-Schleinkofer (Hg.), **Hildegard von Bingen in ihrem Umfeld. Mystik und Visionsformen in Mittelalter und früher Neuzeit. Katholizismus und Protestantismus im Dialog**, Religion-und-Kultur-Verlag: Würzburg 2001, 293 S., ISBN 3-933891-04-3, DM 39,90

Renate von Bardeleben (Hg.), unter Mitarb. von Sabina Matter-Seibel, **Frauen in Kultur und Gesellschaft. Ausgewählte Beiträge der 2. Fachtagung Frauen-/Genderforschung in Rheinland-Pfalz**, Stauffenburg: Tübingen 2000, 599 S., ISBN 3-86057-792-1, DM 98,00

Frances Borzello, **Ihre eigene Welt. Frauen in der Kunstgeschichte**, Gerstenberg: Hildesheim 2000, 224 S., ISBN 3-8067-2872-0, DM 78,00

*Doris Brodbeck, **Hunger nach Gerechtigkeit. Helene von Mülinen (1850-1924) – eine Wegbereiterin der Frauenemanzipation**, Chronos: Zürich 2000, 250 S., ISBN 3-905313-53-7, CH 38,00

Sabine Burkard (Hg.), **Religiöse Frauen des Mittelalters. Mystikerinnen und Prophetinnen**, Gütersloher Verlagshaus: Gütersloh 2002, ca. 176 S., ISBN 3-579-00550-2, € 11,50

Fredric L. Cheyette, **Ermengard of Narbonne and the World of the Troubadours**, Cornell University Press: Ithaca NY 2001, 496pp., ISBN 0-8014-3952-3, $35.00

Jamsheed K. Choksy, **Evil, Good, and Gender: Facets of the Feminine in Zoroastrian Religious History**, P. Lang: New York 2002, 166pp., ISBN 0-8204-5664-0, $49.95 / CHF 74,00

A. Classen, **'Mein Seel fang an zu singen': Religiöse Frauenlieder des 15.-16. Jahrhunderts. Kritische Studien und Textedition**, 395 S., Peeters: Leuven 2002, ISBN 90-429-1098-4, € 65

Sylvie Courtine-Denamy, **Three Women in Dark Times: Edith Stein, Hannah Arendt, Simone Weil**, Cornell University Press: Ithaca NY 2001, 288pp., ISBN 0-8014-8758-7, $17.95

Joy Dixon, **Divine Feminine: Theosophy and Feminism in England**, John Hopkins University Press: Baltimore 2001, 320pp., ISBN 0-8018-6499-2, $49.99

Georgina Dopico Black, **Perfect Wives, Other Women: Adultery and Inquisition in Early Modern Spain**, Duke University Press: Durham 2000, 328pp., ISBN 0-8223-2642-6, $19.95

*Hermann Düringer / Karin Weintz (Hg.), **Leonore Siegele-Wenschkewitz. Persönlichkeit und Wirksamkeit,** (Arnoldshainer Texte 112), Haag + Herchen Verlag: Frankfurt/M. 2000, 371 S., ISBN 3-89846-023-1, DM 64,00

Cynthia Eller, **The Myth of Matriarchal Prehistory: Why an Invented Past Won't Give Women a Future**, Beacon: Boston 2000, 276pp., $16.00

*Hannelore Erhart / Ilse Meseberg-Haubold / Dietgard Meyer (Hg.), **Katharina Staritz (1903-1953). Von der Gestapo verfolgt, von der Kirchenbehörde fallengelassen**. Mit einem Exkurs "Elisabeth Schmitz", Dokumentation Band 1: 1903-1942, Neukirchener Verlag: Neukirchen 1999, 572 S., ISBN 3-7887-1682-7, € 29,90 / CHF 52,50

Sharon Farmer / Barbara H. Rosenwein (eds), **Monks and Nuns, Saints and Outcasts**, Cornell University Press: Ithaca / London 2000, 249pp., ISBN 0-8014-8656-4, £17.99

Doreen Fischer, ***Witwe* als weiblicher Lebensentwurf in deutschen Texten des 13. bis 16. Jahrhunderts**, P. Lang: Frankfurt am Main. 2002, 296 S., ISBN 3-631-38748-2, € 45,50 / $47.95

Ilse E. Friesen, **The Female Crucifix: Images of St. Wilgefortis Since the Middle Ages**, Wilfried Laurier University Press: Waterloo ON 2001, 183pp., ISBN 0-88920-365-2, $45.00

Monica Furlong, **Thérèse of Lisieux**, DLT: London 2001, 160pp., ISBN 0-232-52418-1, £8.95 *(Reprint of Virago: London 1987)*

Britta Gehm, **Die Hexenverfolgung im Hochstift Bamberg und das Eingreifen des Reichshofrates zu ihrer Beendigung**, Olms: Hildesheim 2000, 362 S., ISBN 3-487-11144-6, DM 78,00

Horst Albert Glaser, **Medea oder Frauenehre, Kindsmord und Emanzipation. Zur Geschichte eines Mythos**, P. Lang: Frankfurt/M. etc. 2001, 144 S., ISBN 3-631-37127-6, € 27,80 / $31.95

Margit Göttert, **Macht und Eros. Frauenbeziehungen und weibliche Kultur um 1900. Eine neue Perspektive auf Helene Lange und Gertrud Bäumer**, U. Helmer: Königstein 2000, 256 S., ISBN 3-89741-044-3, DM 48,00

Ann Goldberg, **Sex, Religion, and the Making of Modern Madness: The Eberbach Asylum and German Society, 1815-1849**, OUP: Oxford 2001, 252pp., ISBN 0-19-514052-4, $18.95

Karla Goldman, **Beyond the Synagogue Gallery. Finding a Place for Women in American Judaism**, Harvard University Press: Cambridge MA 2000, 288pp., ISBN 0-674-00705-0, $18.00

Bettina Gruber, **Die Seherin von Prevorst, Romantischer Okkultismus als Religion – Wissenschaft – Literatur**, F. Schöningh: Paderborn 2000, 260 S., ISBN 3-506-73444-X, ca. DM 78,00

Judith Herrin, **Women in Purple: Rulers of Medieval Byzantium**, Princeton University Press: Princeton 2002, 288 pp., ISBN 0-691-09500-0, $29.95

Beate Hofmann, **Gute Mütter – starke Frauen. Geschichte und Arbeitsweise des Bayerischen Mütterdienstes**, Kohlhammer: Stuttgart 2000, 416 S., ISBN 3-17-016190-3, € 22,50

*Constanze Jaiser, **Poetische Zeugnisse. Gedichte aus dem Frauen-Konzentrationslager Ravensbrück 1939-1945**, (Ergebnisse der Frauenforschung 55), J.B. Metzler: Stuttgart / Weimar 2000, 430 S., ISBN 3-476-45253-0, DM 65,00 / CHF 54,50

Anne Jensen, unter Mitarbeit von Livia Neureiter, **Frauen im Frühen Christentum**, (Traditio Christiana, Texte und Kommentare zur patristischen Theologie XI), P. Lang: Bern 2002, 319 S., ISBN: 3-906767-53-1, € 66,00

Anne Jensen, **Femmes des premiers siècles chrétiens**, avec la collaboration de Livia Neureiter, (Traditio Christiana XI), P. Lang: Bern 2002, ISBN: 3-906767-53-1, 319pp., € 66,00

Paula Kane / James Kenneally / Karen M. Kennelly (eds), **Gender Identities in American Catholicism**, Orbis: Maryknoll NY 2001, 348pp., ISBN 1-57075-350-4, $30.00

Ursula King, **Christian Mystics: Their Lives and Legacies throughout the Ages**, Paulist Press: Mahwah NJ 2001, 288pp., ISBN 1-58768-012-2, $20.00

*Anne-Marie Korte (ed.), **Women and Miracle Stories: A Multidisciplinary Exploration**, (Study in the History of Religions 88), Brill: Leiden / Köln / Boston 2001, 350 pp., ISBN 90-04-11681-8, € 87,00 / $101

*Rita Librandi / Adriana Valerio, **I Sermoni di Domenica da Paradiso. Studi e testo critico**, Edizioni del Galluzzo: Firenze 1999, CLXXIX + 170 S., ISBN 88-87027-43-9, € 35

Ann Loades, **Feminist Theology: Voices from the Past**, Blackwell: Boston, MA / Oxford 2001, 240pp., ISBN 0-7456-0869-8, £14.99

Shelly Matthews, **First Converts: Rich Pagan Women and the Rhetoric of Mission in Early Judaism and Christianity**, Stanford University Press: Stanford, CA 2001, 164pp., ISBN 0-804735-92-1, $49.50

Patricia Ranft, **A Woman's Way: The Forgotten History of Women Spiritual Directors**, Palgrave: New York 2000, 254pp., ISBN 0-31221-7129, $39.95

Ulrike Riemer, **Grenzen der Macht. Zur Rolle der römischen Kaiserfrauen**, (Altertumswissenschaftliche Beiträge 3), F.Steiner Verlag: Stuttgart 2000, 174 S., ISBN 3-515-07819-3, DM / CHF 78,00

*Esther Röhr (Hg.), **Ich bin was ich bin. Frauen neben großen Theologen und Religionsphilosophen des 20. Jahrhunderts**, Gütersloher Verlagshaus: Gütersloh 2001, 272 S., ISBN 3-579-00549-9, € 14,90

Beryl Satter, **Each Mind a Kingdom: American Women, Sexual Purity, and the New Thought Movement, 1875-1920**, University of California Press: Berkeley 2001, 394pp., ISBN 0-520-22927-4, £13.95

Lucetta Scaraffia / Gabriella Zarri (eds), **Women and Faith: Catholic Religious Life in Italy from Late Antiquity to the Present**, Harvard University Press: Harvard 1999, 432pp., ISBN 0-674-95478-5, £43.50

Angelika Schaser, **Helene Lange und Gertrud Bäumer. Eine politische Lebensgemeinschaft**, Böhlau: Köln / Wien / Weimar 2000, 416 S., ISBN 3-412-09100-6, DM 68,00

Dennis Schilling / Jianfei Kralle (Hg.), **Die Frau im alten China. Bild und Wirklichkeit. Studien zu den Quellen der Zhou- und Han-Zeit**, F.Steiner Verlag: Stuttgart 2001, 187. S., ISBN 3-515-077751-0, DM / CHF 64,00

Tracy Schier / Cynthia Russett (eds), **Catholic Women's Colleges in America**, John Hopkins University Press: Baltimore 2002, 480pp., ISBN 0-8018-6805-X, $45.00

Kimberly D. Schmidt / Diane Zimmerman Umble / Steven D. Reschly (eds), **Strangers at Home: Amish and Mennonite Women in History**, John Hopkins University Press: Baltimore 2002, 368pp., ISBN 0-8018-6786-X, $39.95

*Gury Schneider-Ludorff, **Magdalene von Tiling. Ordnungstheologie und Geschlechtsbeziehungen. Ein Beitrag zum Gesellschaftsverständnis des Protestantismus in der Weimarer Republik**, Vandenhoeck und Ruprecht: Göttingen 2001, 370 S., ISBN 3-525-55735-3, € 46,00

Ingeborg Schödl, **Zwischen Politik und Kirche – Hildegard Burjan**, Steyler Verlag: Nettetal 2000, 278 S., ISBN 3-8050-0509-1, DM 36,80

Anne Jacobson Schutte, **Aspiring Saints: Pretense of Holiness, Inquistion, and Gender in the Republic of Venice, 1616-1750**, John Hopkins University Press: Baltimore 2001, 360pp., ISBN 0-8018-6548-4, $48.00

Teresa M. Shaw, **The Burden of the Flesh: Fasting and Sexuality in Early Christianity**, Fortress Press: Minneapolis 1998, 320pp., ISBN 0-80062-7652, $27.00

Thomas Späth / Beate Wagner-Hasel (Hg.), **Frauenwelten in der Antike. Geschlechterordnung und weibliche Lebenspraxis**, J.B. Metzler: Stuttgart / Weimar 2000, 494 S., ISBN 3-476-01677-3, DM 78,00

*Christine Stuber, **Eine fröhliche Zeit der Erweckung für viele. Quellenstudien zur Erweckungsbewegung in Bern 1818-1831**, (Basler und Berner Studien zur historischen und systematischen Theologie), P. Lang: Bern 2000 (2., korr. Auflage 2002), 391 S., ISBN 3-906765-03-2, CHF 86,00 / € 55,20

Laura Swan, **The Forgotten Desert Mothers: Sayings, Lives, and Stories of Early Christian Women**, Paulist Press: Mahwah NJ 2001, 224pp., ISBN 0-8091-4016-0224, $13.95

Carol Thysell, **The Pleasure of Discernment: Marguerite de Navarre as Theologian**, OUP: Oxford 2000, 192pp., ISBN 0-19-513845-7, £38.99

Aud Tønnesen, **Et trygt og godt hjem for alle? Kirkelederes kritikk av velferdsstaten etter 1945**, Tapir Akademiske Forlag: Trondheim 2000, 395 S., ISBN 82-519-1611-9 *("A secure and good home for everyone?", Criticism of the welfare state by church leaders after 1945)*

*Claudia Ulbrich, **Shulamit und Margarete. Macht, Geschlecht und Religion in einer ländlichen Gesellschaft des 18. Jahrhunderts**, Böhlau Verlag: Wien / Köln / Weimar 1999, 348 S., ISBN 3-205-98385-8, € 39,80

Val Webb, **Florence Nightingale: The Making of a Radical Theologian**, Chalice Press: St. Louis 2001, ISBN 0-8272-1032-9, $34.99

Hildegard Wustmans, **'und so lag die Welt erhellt in wahrerem Licht, und ich erwachte'. Die Theologie der Sor Juana Inés de la Cruz – eine Sprache des Unerhörten**, P. Lang: Frankfurt am Main 2001, 334 S., ISBN 3-631-37589-1, CHF 72,00 / $47.95

Paul F.M. Zahl, **Five Women of the English Reformation**, Eerdmans: Grand Rapids 2001, 128pp., ISBN 0-8028-3825-1, $18.00

I.3 Systematische Theologie, Ökumene und Interreligiöser Dialog

Rebecca T. Alpert / Sue Levi Elwell / Shirley Idelson (eds), **Lesbian Rabbis: The First Generation**, Rutgers University Press: Piscataway, NJ 2001, 224pp., ISBN 0-8135-2916-6, $24.00

*Marcella Althaus-Reid, **Indecent Theology: Theological Perversions in Sex, Gender and Politics**, Routledge: London / New York 2000, 217pp., ISBN 0-415-23604-5, £14.99

Christiane Ant, **Transsexualität und menschliche Identität. Herausforderung sexualethischer Konzeptionen**, (Studien der Moraltheologie 5), Lit: Münster 2000, ISBN 3-8258-4810-8, DM 24,80

Caroline Arni / Claudia Honegger (Hg.), **Gender. Die Tücken einer Kategorie**, Chronos: Zürich 2001, 122 S., ISBN 3-0340-0505-9, DM 36,00

John P. Bartkowski, **Remaking the Godly Marriage: Gender Negotiation in Evangelical Families**, Rutgers University Press: Piscataway, NJ 2001, 210pp., 0-8135-2919-0, $22.00

Patricia Beattie Jung / Mary E. Hunt / Radhika Balakrishnan (eds), **Good Sex: Feminist Perspectives from the World's Religions**, Rutgers University Press: Piscataway, NJ 2001, 220pp., 0-8135-2884-4, $20.00

Tina Beattie, **Eve's Pilgrimage: A Woman's Quest for the City of God**, Continuum: New York / London 2002, 256pp. ISBN 0-8264-5533-6, £9.99

U. Bechmann / S. Demir / G. Egter, **Frauenkulturen. Christliche und muslimische Frauen in Begegnung und Gespräch**, Klens Verlag: Düsseldorf 2002, 226 S. ISBN 3-87309-165-8, € 15,20

*Sybille Becker / Gesine Kleinschmit / Ilona Nord / Gury Schneider-Ludorff (Hg.), **Das Geschlecht der Zukunft, Frauenemanzipation und Geschlechtervielfalt**, Kohlhammer: Stuttgart 2000, 181 S., ISBN 3-17-026612-3, € 19,00

Ingrid Bennewitz (Hg.), **Lektüren der Differenz, gewidmet Ingvild Birkhan**, P. Lang: Frankfurt am Main / Bern 2001, ca. 227 S., ISBN 3-906767-48-5, CHF 49,00 / $32.95

Kune Biezeveld / Anne-Claire Mulder (eds), **Towards a Different Transcendence: Feminist Findings on Subjectivity, Religion and Values**, P. Lang: Oxford / Frankfurt am Main 2001, 358pp., ISBN 3-906765-66-0, DM 105,00 / $55.95

*Sólveig Anna Bóasdóttir, **Violence, Power, and Justice: A Feminist Contribution to Christian Sexual Ethics**, (= Uppsala Studies in Social Ethics 20), Uppsala Universitiy Press: Uppsala 1998, 202pp., ISBN 91-554-4165-3, 235 SEK

Rosi Braidotti, **Metamorphoses: Towards a Materialist Theory of Becoming**, Polity: Cambridge 2001, 328pp., ISBN 0-745625770, £15.99

Stephanie Brander / Rainer J. Schweizer / Beat Sitter-Liver (Hg.), **Geschlechterdifferenz und Macht. Reflexionen gesellschaftlicher Prozesse**, (SAGW 17), Universitätsverlag: Fribourg 2001, ca. 336 S., ISBN 3-7278-1318-0, DM 59,00

Rita Nakashima Brock / Rebecca Ann Parker, **Proverbs of Ashes: Violence, Redemptive Suffering, and the Search for What Saves Us**, Beacon Press: Boston 2001, 288pp., ISBN 0-80706-7962, $27.50

June Campbell, **Traveller in Space: Gender, Identity and Tibetan Budhism**, Revised Edition, Continuum: New York / London 2002, 256pp., ISBN 0-8264-5719-3, £12.99

Delores C. Carpenter, **A Time for Honor: A Portrait of African American Clergywomen**, Chalice Press: St. Louis 2001, 192pp., ISBN 0-8272-3638-7, $19.99

Elizabeth A. Castelli / Rosamond C. Rodman (eds), **Women, Gender, Religion: A Reader**, Palgrave: Manchester 2001, 352pp., ISBN 0-312-24030-9, $24.95

Catherine Clément / Julia Kristeva, **The Feminine and the Sacred**, Columbia University Press: New York 2001, 224pp., ISBN 0-231115-78-4, $27.50

Elisabeth Conradi / Sabine Plonz (Hg.), **Tätiges Leben. Pluralität und Arbeit im politischen Denken Hannah Arendts**, Verlag des Sozialwissenschaftlichen Instituts der Evangelischen Kirche in Deutschland: Bochum 2000, 185 S., ISBN 3-925895-69-8, DM 27,80

J. Denny Weaver, **The Nonviolent Atonement**, Eerdmans: Grand Rapids MI 2001, 246pp., ISBN 0-802849-08-3, $22.00

Laura E. Donaldson / Kwok Pui-Lan (eds), **Postcolonialism, Feminism and Religious Discourse**, Routledge: New York / London 2001, 288pp., ISBN 0-415928-88-5, £15.99

Jane Duan, **Worlds of Knowing: Global Feminist Epistemologies**, Routledge: London / New York 2001, ISBN 0-415-92740-4, £12.99

Charlene Embrey Burns, **Divine Becoming: Rethinking Jesus and Incarnation**, Augsburg Fortress: Minneapolis 2001, 224pp., ISBN 0-8006-3278-8, $18.00

Rachel Fell McDermott, **Singing to the Goddess: Poems to Kali and Uma from Bengal**, OUP: Oxford 2001, 208pp., ISBN 0-19-513434-6, £17.99

Patricia A. Fox, **God as Communion: John Zizioulas, Elizabeth Johnson, and the Retrieval of the Symbol of the Triune God**, The Liturgical Press: Collegeville 2001, 280pp., ISBN 0-8146-5082-1, $24.95

Susan Frank Parsons (ed.), **Challenging Women's Orthodoxies in the Context of Faith**, Aldershot: Ashgate 2000, 229pp., ISBN 0-754614-20-4, £17.99

Susan Frank Parsons, **The Ethics of Gender**, Blackwell: Boston, MA / Oxford 2002, 216pp., ISBN 0-631-215-17-4, £50,00

Heide Göttner-Abendroth, **Das Matriarchat II, 2. Stammesgesellschaften in Amerika, Indien, Afrika**, Kohlhammer: Stuttgart 2000, 300 S., ISBN 3-17-010568-X, DM 35,80

Kathryn Greene-McCreight, **Feminist Reconstructions of Christian Doctrine: Narrative Analysis and Appraisal**, Oxford University Press: New York 2000, 175pp., ISBN 0-19-512862-1, $29.95

*Mary Grey, **The Outrageous Pursuit of Hope: Prophetic Dreams for the 21st Century**, DLT: London 2000, 116pp., ISBN 0-232-52319-3, £9.95

Mary Grey, **Introducing Feminist Images of God**, (Introductions in Feminist Theology 7), Sheffield Academic Press: Sheffield 2001, 136pp., ISBN 1-84127-160-8, £12.95

*Rita M. Gross / Rosemary Radford Ruether, **Religious Feminism and the Future of the Planet: A Buddhist – Christian Conversation**, Continuum: London / New York 2001, 229pp., ISBN 0-8264-1302-1, $22.95 / £17.99

Andrea Günter / Verena Wodtke-Werner (Hg.), **Frauen, Mystik, Politik in Europa. Beiträge aus Italien, Spanien und Deutschland**, U.Helmer: Königstein/Taunus 2000, 199 S. ISBN 3-89741-043-5, DM 42.00

*Andrea Günter, **Die weibliche Hoffnung der Welt. Die Bedeutung des Geborenseins und der Sinn der Geschlechterdifferenz**, Chr. Kaiser / Gütersloher Verlagshaus: Gütersloh 2000, 128 S., ISBN 3-579-02667-4, DM 38,00 / CHF 36,00

Andrea Günter, **Heilende Zeiträume. Mutter, Sprache, Sinn**, Göttert: Rüsselsheim 2002, 55 S., ISBN 3-922499-60-0

Martin Hailer, **Figur und Thema der Weisheit in feministischen Theologen. Ein kommentierender Forschungsbericht**, P. Lang: Frankfurt/M. etc. 2001, 103 S., ISBN 3-631-37832-7, CHF 36,00 / $23.95

Daphne Hampson, **Christian Contradictions: The Structures of Lutheran and Catholic Thought**, Cambridge University Press: Cambridge 2001, 336pp., ISBN 0-521-45060-8, £40.00

Johannes Heil / Rainer Kampling (Hg.), **Mariologie, Marienfrömmigkeit und Judenfeindschaft**, Schöningh: Paderborn 2001, 271 S., ISBN 3-506-74254-X, DM 78,00

Susanne Heine, **Frauenbilder – Menschenrechte. Theologische Beiträge zur feministischen Anthropologie**, Lutherisches Verlagshaus: Hannover 2000, 159 S., ISBN 3-7859-0795-8, DM 38,00

*Birgit Heller, **Heilige Mutter und Gottesbraut. Frauenemanzipation im modernen Hinduismus**, (Frauenforschung 39), Milena: Wien 1999, 367 S., ISBN 3-85286-074-1, ATS 348,00 / DM 50,00

*Susanne Hennecke, **Der vergessene Schleier. Ein theologisches Gespräch zwischen Luce Irigaray und Karl Barth**, Chr. Kaiser / Gütersloher Verlagshaus: Gütersloh 2001, 298 S., ISBN 3-579-05319-1, DM 78,00

Carter Heyward, **Jesus neu entwerfen. Die Macht der Liebe und der Gerechtigkeit**, Exodus: Luzern 2001, ISBN 3-905577-49-6, DM 49,00 *(dt. Übersetzung von: Saving Jesus from those who are right: Rethinking what it means to be Christian)*

Kerrie Hide, **Gifted Origins to Graced Fulfillment: The Soteriology of Julian of Norwich**, The Liturgical Press: Collegeville 2001, 256pp., ISBN 0-8146-5093-7, $24.95

Kristina Hildebrand, **The Female Reader at the Round Table: Religion and Women in The Contemporary Arthurian Texts**, (= Diss. Uppsala 2001), Uppsala University Press: Uppsala 2001, 175pp., ISBN 91-554-5093-1

Alf Hiltebeitel / Kathleen M. Erndl (eds), **Is the Goddess a Feminist? The Politics of South Asian Goddesses**, Sheffield Academic Press: Sheffield 2001, 180pp., ISBN 1-84127-157-8, £14.95

Anna T. Höglund, **Krig och kön. Feministisk etik och den moraliska bedömningen av militärt våld** (*War and Gender: Feminist Ethics and the Moral Judgement of Military Violence*), (Uppsala Studies in Social Ethics 26), Acta Universatis Upsaliensis: Uppsala 2002, (= Diss. Uppsala 2001), 290pp., ISBN 91-554-4897-6 *(with summary in English)*

Nancy R. Howell, **A Feminist Cosmology: Ecology, Solidarity, and Metaphysics**, Prometheus: Amherst NY 2001, 149pp., ISBN 1-57392-653-1, $45.00

Barbara Hutzl-Ronge, **Feuergöttinnen, Sonnenheilige, Lichtfrauen**, Frauenoffensive: München 2000, 299 S., ISBN 3-88104-324-1, DM 42,00

Luce Irigaray, **Between East and West: From Singularity to Community**, Columbia University Press: New York 2002, 208pp., ISBN 0-231119-34-8, $24.50

Lisa Isherwood (ed.), **The Good News of the Body: Sexual Theology and Feminism**, Sheffield Academic Press: Sheffield 2001, 232pp., ISBN 1-84127-130-6, £14.95

*Anne Jensen / Maximilian Liebmann (Hg.), **Was verändert feministische Theologie? Interdisziplinäres Symposion zur Frauenforschung (Graz, Dezember 1999)**, (Theologische Frauenforschung in Europa 2), Lit: Münster 2000, 224 S., ISBN 3-8258-4616-4, DM 39,80

*Manuela Kalsky, **Christaphanien. Die Re-Vision der Christologie aus der Sicht von Frauen in unterschiedlichen Kulturen**, Chr. Kaiser / Gütersloher Verlagshaus: Gütersloh 2000, 368 S., ISBN 3-579-05317-5, DM 54,00

Katharina von Kellenbach / Bjoern Krondorfer / Norbert Reck (Hg.), **Von Gott reden im Land der Täter. Theologische Stimmen der dritten Generation seit der Shoah**, Wissenschaftlich Buchgesellschaft: Darmstadt 2001, 303 S., ISBN 3-534-15770-2, DM 49,90

*Katharina von Kellenbach / Susanne Scholz (Hg.), **Zwischen-Räume. Deutsche feministische Theologinnen im Ausland**, (Theologische Frauenforschung in Europa 1), Lit: Münster 2000, 163 S., ISBN 3-8258-4289-4, € 25,45

Alvin F. Kimel Jr., **This Is My Name Forever: The Trinity & Gender Language for God**, InterVarsity Press: Downers Grove 2001, ISBN 0-8308-1506, $15.99

Elmar Klinger, **Christologie im Feminismus. Eine Herausforderung der Tradition**, Pustet: Regensburg 2001, ca. 303 S., ISBN 3-7917-1742-1, DM 48,00

James Kottoor (ed.), **Woman why are you Weeping? A discussion on Women's Ordination in the Roman Catholic Church in the context of WOW 2001 Dublin**, Media House Indian Edition: New Delhi 2002, 224pp., $5 *(distributed via: Media House, 375-A, pocket 2, Mayur Vihar, Phase 1, New Delhi, India, jkottoor@vsnl.com)*

Marita Krauss / Holger Sonnabend (Hg.), **Frauen und Migration**, F.Steiner Verlag: Stuttgart 2001, 190 S., ISBN 3-515-07815-0, DM / CHF 74,00

Latina Feminist Group, **Telling to Live: Latina Feminist *Testimonios***, Duke University Press: Durham 2002, 400pp., ISBN 0-8223-2765-1, $19.95

K.K. Lim, **Het spoor van de vrouw in het ambt. Een historische studie naar de openstelling van het ambt voor de vrouw in de Evangelisch-Lutherse Kerk van het Koninkrijk der Nederlanden, de Nederlandse Hervormde Kerk en de Gereformeerde Kerken in Nederland** (*On the trail of women in office. A historical study of the opening of the ordained ministry to woman in three Dutch Protestant Churches*), Kok: Kampen 2001, 320 S., ISBN 90-435-0441-6, € 22,64

Karen McCarthy Brown, **Mama Lola: A Vodou Priestess in Brooklyn**, University of California Press: Berkeley 2001, 447pp., ISBN 0-520-22475-2, £13.95

Sallie McFague, **Life Abundant: Rethinking Theology and Economy for a Planet in Peril**, Augsburg Fortress: Minneapolis 2000, 251pp., $18.00

Loraine MacKenzie Shepherd, **Feminist Theologies for a Postmodern Church: Diversity, Community and Scripture**, P. Lang: New York 2002, 264pp., ISBN 0-8204-5572-5, $29.95 / CHF 49,00

Rebekah L. Miles, **The Bonds of Freedom: Feminist Theology and Christian Realism**, OUP: Oxford 2001, 256pp., ISBN 0-19-514416-3, £37.50

*Anne Claire Mulder, Divine Flesh, **Embodied Word: Incarnation as a hermeneutical key to a feminist theologian's reading of Luce Irigarays work**, Eigenverlag: Amsterdam 2000, 389pp., ISBN 90-9013830-7, NLG 50,00

Carol Ochs, **Our Lives as Torah: Finding God in Our Stories**, Jossey-Bass: San Francisco 2001, 224pp., ISBN 0-7879-4473-4, $24.95

Mercy Amba Oduyoye, **Introducing African Women's Theology**, (Introductions in Feminist Theology 6), Sheffield Academic Press: Sheffield 2001, 150pp., ISBN 1-84127-143-8, £12.95

*Eva Pelkner, **Gott, Gene, Gebärmütter. Anthropologie und Frauenbild in der evangelischen Ethik zur Fortpflanzungsmedizin**, Chr. Kaiser / Gütersloher Verlagshaus: Gütersloh 2001, 286 S., ISBN 3-579-02657-7, DM 68,00

Kwok Pui-Lan, **Introducing Asian women's Theology**, Sheffield Academic Press: Sheffield 2000, 136pp., ISBN 1-84127-066-0, £12.95

Rosemary Radford Ruether, **Christianity and the Making of the Modern Family**, SCM Press: London, ca. 304pp., ISBN 0334-02822-1, £15.95

John C. Raines, **The Justice Men Owe Women: Positive Resources from World Religions**, Augsburg Fortress: Minneapolis 2001, 128pp., ISBN 0-8006-3281-8, $13.00

Ida Raming, **Priesteramt der Frau – Geschenk Gottes für eine erneuerte Kirche**, (Theologische Frauenforschung in Europa 7), Lit: Münster / Hamburg 2002, 304 S., ISBN 3-8258-5579-1, DM 39,80

Anne-Sofie Roald, **Women in Islam: The Western Experience**, Routledge: New York / London 1999, 360pp., ISBN 0-415248-96-5, £15.99

Jone Salomonsen, **Enchanted Feminism: The Reclaiming Witches of San Francisco**, Routledge: London / New York 2001, 318pp., ISBN 0-415-22393-8, £12.99

Barbara Schiffer, **Fließende Identität. Körper und Geschlechter im Wandel. Symbole von Krankheit und Heilung, feministisch-theologisch gedeutet im Kontext postmoderner Körper- und Geschlechterkonstruktionen**, P. Lang: Frankfurt am Main 2001, 245 S., ISBN 3-631-38155-7, € 37,80 / $39.95

Arvind Sharma, **Through Her Eyes: Women's Perspectives on World Religions**, Westview: Boulder CO 2002, 256pp., ISBN 0-8133-6906-1, $24.00

Eva Skærbæk, **Who cares: Ethical Interaction and Sexual Difference**, (Acta Theologica 2), Unipub: Oslo 2001, 276pp.

Gezina Margharieta Speelman, **Keeping Faith: Muslim-Christian Couples and Inter-religious Dialogue,** Meinema: Zoetermeer 2001, 332 pp., ISBN 90-21170-27-2, € 31,40

Lucy Tatman, **Knowledge that Matters: A Feminist Theological Paradigm and Epistemology**, The Pilgrim Press: Cleveland 2001, ISBN 0-8298-1448-5, $18.00

Kathryn Tanner, **Jesus, Humanity and the Trinity: A Brief Systematic Theology**, Fortress: Minneapolis 2001, 144pp., ISBN 0-80066-3293-1, $15.00

Emilie M. Townes, **Breaking the Fine Rain of Death: African American Health Issues and a Womanist Ethic of Care**, Continuum: New York / London 2001, 224pp., ISBN 0-8264-1368-4, $19.95

Cheryl Townsend Gilkes, **If It Wasn't For The Women: Black Women's Experience and Womanist Culture in Church and Community**, Orbis: Maryknoll, NY 2001, 260pp., ISBN 1-57075-343-1, $24.00

Masathoshi Ueki, **Gender Equality in Buddhism**, P. Lang: New York 2001, 215 S., ISBN 0-8204-5133-9, $35.95

*Karin Ulrich-Eschemann, **Vom Geborenwerden des Menschen. Theologische und philosophische Erkundungen**, Lit: Münster / Hamburg / London 2000, 263 S., ISBN 3-8258-5098-6, DM 39,80

*Marianne Wallach-Faller, **Die Frau im Tallit. Judentum feministisch gelesen**, hg. von Doris Brodbeck und Yvonne Domhardt, Chronos-Verlag: Zürich 2000, 272 S., ISBN 3-905313-65-0, CHF 34,00

*Sharon D. Welch, **A Feminist Ethic of Risk**, Revised Edition, Augsburg Fortress Press: Minneapolis 2000, 206 S., ISBN 0-8006-3185-4, £11.99

N. Lynne Westfield, **Dear Sisters: A Womanist Practice of Hospitality**, The Pilgrim Press: Cleveland 2001, 134pp. ISBN 0-8298-1449-3, $17.00

*Patricia A. Williams, **Doing without Adam and Eve: Sociobiology and Original Sin**, Augsburg Fortress: Minneapolis 2001, 201pp., ISBN 0-8006-3285-0, $18.00

John Wijngaards, **The Ordination of Women in the Catholic Church: Unmasking a Cuckoo's Egg Tradition**, DLT: London 2001, 224pp., ISBN 0-232-52420-3, £10.95

Yvonne Yazbeck Haddad / John L. Esposito (eds), **Daughters of Abraham: Feminist Thought in Judaism, Christianity, and Islam**, University Press of Florida: Gainesville 2001, 208pp., ISBN 0-8130-2103-0, $55.00

Phyllis Zagano, **Holy Saturday: An Argument for the Restoration of the Female Diaconate in the Catholic Church**, Crossroad: New York 2000, 192pp., ISBN 0-8245-1832-2, $16.95

I.4 Praktische Theologie, Spiritualität, Liturgiewissenschaft, Religionspädagogik, Homiletik

*Kristina Augst, **Religion in der Lebenswelt junger Frauen aus sozialen Unterschichten**, Kohlhammer: Stuttgart / Berlin / Köln 2000, 331 S., ISBN 3-17-016297-7, DM 71,00

Liz Barr / Andrew Barr, **Jobs for the Boys? Women who Became Priests**, Hodder & Stoughton: London / Sydney / Auckland 2001, 262pp., ISBN 0-340-78534-9, £7.99

*Teresa Berger (ed.), **Dissident Daughters: Feminist Liturgies in Global Context**, Westminster John Knox: Louisville / London 2001, 249pp., ISBN 0-664-22379-6, US $24.95

Lyn Brakeman, **Aufbegehren. Frauen in der Bibel und der Wert negativer Gefühle**, Echter: Würzburg 2001, 109 S., ISBN 3-429-02333-5, DM 19,80

Ninna Edgardh Beckman, **Feminism och liturgi – en ecklesiologisk studie** (*Feminism and Liturgy: An ecclesiological study*), Verbum Förlag AB: Stockholm 2001, (= Diss. Uppsala), 532pp., ISBN 91-526-2706-3 *(with Summary in English)*

Christie Cozad Neuger, **Counseling Women: A Narrative, Pastoral Approach**, Augsburg Fortress: Minneapolis 2001, 280pp., ISBN 0-8006-3422-5, $18.00

Freda Dröes / Kitty Mul / Jasja Nottelman / Marian Papavoine (red.), **Met passie en verbeelding. IWFT-Vrouwennetwerk Theologie 25 jaar. Een terugblik met handreikingen voor de toekomst** (*With Passion and Imagination. Twenty-five years of IWFT Women's Network. A retrospective with promptings for the future*), Narratio: Gorinchem 2001, 128pp., ISBN 90-5263-228-6

Bettina Eltrop / Anneliese Hecht / Hedwig Lamberty-Zielinsky / Gabriele Theuer (Hg.), **FrauenTrauer**, (FrauenBibelArbeit 8), Klens Verlag / Katholisches Bibelwerk: Düsseldorf / Stuttgart 2002, ca. 90 S., ISBN 3-87309-197-6, € 8,40

Andreas Feige / Bernhard Dressler / Wolfgang Lukatis / Albrecht Schöll, **'Religion' bei ReligionslehrerInnen**, Lit: Münster 2001, 608 S., ISBN 3-8258-5006-4, DM 68,80

Edith Franke / Gisela Matthiae / Regina Sommer (Hg.), **Frauen Leben Religion. Ein Handbuch empirischer Forschungsmethoden**, Kohlhammer: Stuttgart 2001, 240 S., ISBN 3-17-016969-6, DM 49,00

Susan K. Hedahl, **Listening Ministry: Rethinking Pastoral Leadership**, Augsburg Fortress: Minneapolis 2001, 128pp., ISBN 0-8006-3174-9, $14.00

Mary Catherine Hilkert, **Speaking with Authority: Catherine of Siena and the Voices of Women Today**, Paulist Press: Mahwah NJ 2001, 184pp., ISBN 0-8091-4031-4, $9.95

*Birgit Hoyer, **Gottesmütter. Lebensbilder kinderloser Frauen als fruchtbare Dialogräume für Pastoral und Pastoraltheologie**, (Tübinger Perspektiven zur Pastoraltheologie und Religionspädagogik 2), Lit: Münster 1999, 344 S., ISBN 3-8258-4329-7, DM 49,80

*Isolde Karle, **Der Pfarrberuf als Profession. Eine Berufstheorie im Kontext der modernen Gesellschaft**, (Praktische Theologie und Kultur 3), Chr.Kaiser / Gütersloher Verlagshaus: Gütersloh 2001, 352 S., ISBN 3-579-03483-9, DM 58,00

Siegfried Keil / Michael Haspel (Hg.), **Gleichgeschlechtliche Lebensgemeinschaften in sozialethischer Perspektive. Beiträge zur rechtlichen Regelung pluraler Lebensformen**, Neukirchener: Neukirchen-Vluyn 2000, ca. 250 S., ISBN 3-7887-1787-4, € 24,90

Gudrun-Axeli Knapp / Angelika Wetterer, **Soziale Verortung der Geschlechter. Gesellschaftstheorie und feministische Kritik**, (Forum Frauenforschung 13), Westfälisches Dampfboot: Münster 2001, ISBN 3-89691-213-5, DM 45,00

Anneliese Knippenkötter / Marie-Luise Langwald (Hg.), **Hoffnung schenkt Kraft. Frauengottesdienste**, Bd. 10, Klens Verlag / Schwabenverlag: Düsseldorf / Ostfildern 2001, 80 S., ISBN 3-7966-1015-3, € 7,80

Anneliese Knippenkötter / Marie-Luise Langwald, unter Mitarbeit von Isolde Niehüser und Christel Voß-Goldstein (Hg.), **Wege zum Licht. Frauengottesdienste**, Bd. 11 Weihnachtsfestkreis, Klens Verlag / Schwabenverlag: Düsseldorf / Ostfildern 2001, 80 S., ISBN 3-7966-1030-7, € 7,80

Anneliese Knippenkötter / Marie-Luise Langwald (Hg.), **Biblische Frauen, Frauengottesdienste**, Bd. 12, Klens Verlag / Schwabenverlag: Düsseldorf / Ostfildern 2001, ca. 90 S., ISBN 3-87309-195-X, € 7,80

Andrea Lehner-Hartmann, **Wider das Schweigen und Vergessen. Gewalt in Familien. Sozialwissenschaftliche Erkenntnisse und praktisch-theologische Reflexionen**, Tyrolia: Innsbruck 2002, ca. 300 S., ISBN 3-7022-2429-7, € 23,90

Ingrid Lukatis / Regina Sommer / Christof Wolf (Hg.), **Religion und Geschlechterverhältnis**, (Veröffentlichungen der Sektion "Religionssoziologie" der Deutschen Gesellschaft für Soziologie 4), Leske + Budrich: Opladen 2000, 300 S., ISBN 3-8100-2546-1, DM 64,00

Karen A. McClintock, **Sexual Shame: An Urgent Call to Healing**, Augsburg Fortress: Minneapolis 2001, 176pp., ISBN 0-8006-3238-9, $16.00

*Dorothea McEwan / Pat Pinsent / Ianthe Pratt / Veronica Seddon (eds), **Making Liturgy: Creating Rituals for Life**, Canterbury Press: Norwich 2001, 189pp., ISBN 1-85311-440-5, £7.99

Ilona Nord, **Individualität, Geschlechterverhältnis und Liebe. Partnerschaft und ihre Lebensformen in der pluralen Gesellschaft**, (Öffentliche Theologie 16), Gütersloher Verlagshaus: Gütersloh 2001, ca. 368 S., ISBN 3-579-05316-7, ca. DM 88,00

Carol M. Norén, **In Times of Crisis and Sorrow: A Minister's Manual Resource Guide**, Jossey-Bass: San Francisco 2001, 324 pp., ISBN 0-7879-5420-9

Sabine Pemsel-Maier (Hg.), **Zwischen Alltag und Ausnahme. Seelsorgerinnen – Geschichte, Theologie und gegenwärtige Praxis**, Schwabenverlag: Ostfildern 2001, 188 S., ISBN 3-7966-1036-6, € 15,50

Helga Riebe / Sigrid Düringer / Herta Leistner (Hg.), **Perspektiven für Frauen in Organisationen. Neue Organisations- und Managementkonzepte kritisch hinterfragt**, Votum: Münster 2000, 151 S., ISBN 3-933158-42-7, DM 29,80

Susan K. Roll / Annette Esser / Brigitte Enzner-Probst, with Charlotte Methuen & Angela Berlis, Women, **Ritual and Liturgy – Ritual und Liturgie von Frauen – Femmes, la liturgie et le rituel**, (ESWTR Yearbook 9), Peeters: Leuven 2001, 313pp., ISBN 90-429-1025-9, € 23,00

*Sylvia Rothschild / Sybil Sheridan (eds), **Taking up the Timbrel: The Challenge of Creating Ritual for Jewish Women Today**, SCM Press: London 2000, 211pp., ISBN 0-334-02806-X, £12.95

Sandra M. Schneiders, **Selling All: Commitment, Consecrated Celibacy, and Community in Catholic Religious Life**, Paulist Press: Mahwah NJ 2001, 512pp., ISBN 0-8091-3973-1, $24.95

*Gury Schneider-Ludorff / Leonore Siegele-Wenschkewitz (Hg.), **Frauenarmut als Herausforderung**, (Arnoldshainer Texte 113), Haag + Herchen Verlag: Frankfurt am Main 2000, 121 S., ISBN 3-89846-039-8, DM 34,80

*Susanne Schniering (Hg.), **Ich trage Dich in meinem Herzen. Der Gedenkplatz für nicht beerdigte Kinder in Ohlsdorf**, Hanna Strack Verlag: Pinnow 2001, 120 S., ISBN 3-929813-53-X, € 10,10

Barbara Schoppelreich / Kathrin Althans / Inken Mädler (Hg.), **Inmitten von Lust und Last. Frauenalltag und Religiosität**, Matthias-Grünewald-Verlag: Mainz, 136 S., ISBN 3-7867-8334-9, DM 19,80 / ATS 145 / CHF 19,80

Claudia Seeger (Hg.), **FrauenFürbitten. Ich schütte mein Herz aus vor dir**, 120 S., ISBN 3-87309-194-1, € 10,50

Jeanne Stevenson-Moessner (ed.), **In Her Own Time: Women and Developmental Issues in Pastoral Care**, Augsburg Fortress: Minneapolis 2001, 387pp., ISBN 0-8006-3137-4, $21.00

*Helen Thorne, **Journey to Priesthood: An In-depth study of the First Women Priests in the Church of England**, (CCSRG Monograph Series 5), University of Bristol: Bristol 2000, 213pp., ISBN 0-86292-499-5, £15.00

Brigitte Vielhaus u.a., **FrauenAlter. Neue Wege in der Arbeit mit älteren Frauen**, Klens-Verlag: Düsseldorf 2002, 226 S., ISBN 3-87309-192-5, € 12,70

Ulrike Wagner-Rau, **Segensraum: Kasualpraxis in der modernen Gesellschaft**, Kohlhammer: Stuttgart 2000, 240 S., ISBN 3-17-016430-9, DM 49,80

Janet H. Wootton, **Introducing a Practical Feminist Theology of Worship**, (Introductions in Feminist Theology 5), Sheffield Academic Press: Sheffield 2000, 152pp., ISBN 1-84127-160-8, £12.95

II. Rezensionen – Book Reviews – Critique des Livres

II.1 Exegese (Erstes Testament, Neues Testament, nicht kanonisierte jüdische und frühchristliche Schriften) und Hermeneutik

Annette Böckler, *Gott als Vater im Alten Testament. Traditionsgeschichtliche Untersuchungen zur Entstehung und Entwicklung eines Gottesbildes*, Chr. Kaiser / Gütersloher Verlagshaus: Gütersloh 2000, 454 Seiten, ISBN 3-579-02664-X, DM 78,00

Durch den Wandel der Geschlechterrollen sind traditionelle Gottesbilder wie das des Vaters problematisch geworden. Eine eingehende Untersuchung zu Gott (JHWH) als Vater im Alten Testament gibt es bislang nicht. Böcklers Dissertation möchte diese Forschungslücke schließen. Nach einer Einführung zum Bild Gottes als Vater in Judentum, Christentum und Islam folgt im ersten Teil ein Durchgang durch die Forschung zum Thema. Im zweiten Teil diskutiert die Verfasserin alttestamentliche Stellen mit Personennamen, die das Element "Vater" (*'ab*) enthalten, im dritten Teil behandelt sie diejenigen Texte, die von Gott als Vater sprechen. Abschließend wertet sie ihre These aus; das Buch endet mit Registern sowie einem Glossar.
Schon als Bezeichnung für einen Menschen ist das hebräische Wort "Vater" mehrdeutig (48): Je nach Kontext steht "Vater" für den Familienvater, Vorfahr/Ahn oder Stammvater eines Landes. Daneben bezeichnet das Wort natürliche oder statusbedingte Autoritätspersonen wie politische oder religiöse Oberhäupter, Lehrer und Propheten. In poetischer Sprache steht "Vater" für Schöpfer oder Erzeuger, Wohltäter oder Fürsorger.

Auf dem dritten Teil (175-387) liegt mit der Untersuchung der Einzelverse der Schwerpunkt der Arbeit. Die Verfasserin beginnt beim jeweiligen Textzusammenhang, analysiert dann unter historisch-kritischer Perspektive exegetische Einzelfragen, um schließlich zur Bedeutung des Vaterbildes im Text Stellung zu nehmen. Die wichtigsten Ergebnisse: Als Vater des davidischen Königs erscheint JHWH in 2 Sam 7,14; Ps 89,27f; 1 Chr 17,13a; 22,10a; 28,6b. Von Israel als Sohn JHWHs ist in Hos 11,1.3a; Ex 4,22f die Rede; umgekehrt wird JHWH in Jer 31,9b; Jes 63,16; 64,7; Dtn 32,6; Jer 2,27a; 3,4; 3,19; Mal 1,6; 2,10 und Ps 103,13 als Vater Israels bezeichnet. Als Mann mit

Sohn wird JHWH in Dtn 1,31a; 8,5; Mal 3,17b tituliert, und die eigenständige Vorstellung JHWHs als väterlicher Rechtsbeistand der Waisen entwirft Ps 68,6a. Das Ergebnis der Untersuchungen ist eine zeitliche Anordnung der Texte und das Nachzeichnen einer traditionsgeschichtlichen Linie: Erstmals wird die Vorstellung JHWHs als Vater in 2 Sam 7,14 verwendet und auf König David bezogen. JHWH sagt hier seine bleibende Treue dem König gegenüber zu. Diese Vorstellung wird später durch die Personifikation des Volkes in der Gestalt Davids (Ps 89,27-33) bzw. Salomos (1 Chr 17,13a; 22,10; 28,6b) auf das gesamte Volk übertragen, wobei der Gehorsam des Volkes Vorbedingung der göttlichen Treue wird. Diesen Aspekt behalten auch die späteren Texten bei, die das Verhältnis von Vater zu Sohn explizit auf das Volk Israel und seine Beziehung zu JHWH übertragen. Als alttestamentlicher Abschluss des Motivs ist Ps 103,13 anzusehen; hier wird ein einzelner Mensch als Sohn (Kind) JHWHs angesprochen.

Böcklers Arbeit besticht an vielen Stellen durch die gründliche Aufarbeitung der Forschungsgeschichte, durch die exegetische Detailarbeit und durch instruktive Exkurse, vor allem zu altorientalischen Paralleltexten oder zur rabbinischen Auslegung. Insbesondere im Bereich der Hermeneutik bleiben jedoch viele Fragen offen. Das Ausgangsproblem – die Beheimatung der Vorstellung JHWHs als Vater in einem patriarchalen Entstehungskontext – wird am Schluss nicht behandelt. Es fehlt jegliche Kritik am Gewaltaspekt der Vorstellung (schon im "Ursprungstext" 2 Sam 7,14 züchtigt JHWH den ungehorsamen "Sohn"). Leider reflektiert die Autorin zudem die Besonderheiten der alttestamentlichen Gottesmetaphorik nicht. Auch wenn Böckler feministische Exegese kaum rezipiert, können feministische Exegetinnen trotzdem aus diesem Werk Gewinn ziehen, wenn sie die detaillierten Untersuchungen mit kritischem Blick auswerten.

Gerlinde Baumann (Marburg / Deutschland)

Klara Butting, *Prophetinnen gefragt. Die Bedeutung der Prophetinnen im Kanon aus Tora und Prophetie*, (Erev-Rav-Hefte. Biblisch feministische Texte 3), Erev-Rav: Wittingen 2001, 232 Seiten, ISBN 3-932810-15-5, € 13,00

Mit ihrem Buch *Prophetinnen gefragt*, das als Habilitationsschrift an der Evangelisch-Theologischen Fakultät in Bochum angenommen worden ist, lässt Klara Butting die Prophetinnen der Hebräischen Bibel aus dem exegetischen Schattendasein heraustreten, das sie in der ersttestamentlichen Forschung aufgrund deren Konzentration auf die Schriftprophetie führten. Mit ihrer These, "daß die Prophetinnen (...) Sinn und Bedeutung der kanonischen Konzeption 'Tora und Prophet/innen' paradigmatisch in Erscheinung treten lassen" (9), geht sie methodisch den Weg kanonischer Bibelauslegung weiter, den sie bereits in ihrem Buch "Die Buchstaben werden sich noch wundern" (1994) beschritten hat. Die Dreiteilung des Tenach wird als Interpretationszusammenhang verstanden, der die Prophet/innen an die Seite der Tora treten lässt und Prophetie als "geschichtsbezogene Aktualisierung der Tora" (13) versteht.

Der in Kapitel A sehr knapp skizzierte Konflikt zwischen Nehemia und Noadja (Neh 6,14) als RepräsentantInnen von Tora und Prophetie eröffnet den im *ersten Teil* zentralen Fragehorizont nach dem Verhältnis von Tora und Prophetie. Den sich hier einstellenden Verdacht, die Tora, deren Endkomposition in eben diese Zeit der persischen Fremdherrschaft fällt, sei un – wenn nicht gar antiprophetisch und ihre Kanonisierung sei mit einer Absorption innerisraelitischer Opposition (Prophetie) einhergegangen, findet Butting gerade nicht bestätigt, wenn sie in Kapitel B der Mirjamfigur als Repräsentantin der Prophetie im Pentateuch (neben Mose und Aaron als Repräsentanten von Tora und Priestertum) nachgeht. So zeuge Ex 15,20-21 nicht von einer Verdrängung, sondern Wiedereinschreibung Mirjams in die Exodustradition und Num 12 dokumentiere neben ihrer Marginalisierung (alleinige Bestrafung mit Aussatz) auch ihre Bedeutung als Führungspersönlichkeit für die Gemeinschaft (das Volk wartet, bis sie geheilt ist). Num 20,1-13 erweise in ihrem Tod, der augenblicklich Wassermangel auslöst und die Verfehlungen Moses und Aarons einleitet, die Unverzichtbarkeit der Prophetie. Dem Verhältnis von Tora und Prophetie geht auch das Kapitel C nach und wendet sich u.a. der Bedeutung Moses gemäß Dtn 34,10-12 zu. Eine Vorrangstellung der Tora vor den ProphetInnen lässt sich daraus nicht ableiten, vielmehr steht neben dem Beharren auf der Einzigkeit Moses die Überzeugung, Gott offenbare sein Wort durch die ProphetInnen in der Geschichte immer wieder (92). Dass Prophetie jedoch nicht Nachfolge Mirjams, sondern Moses ist, gerät dadurch sehr in den Hintergrund.

Die Bezogenheit von Tora und Prophetie weist Butting auch im Kanonteil Vordere ProphetInnen (Jos bis 2 Kön) nach, der von zwei Frauen, Debora und Hulda, gerahmt wird und dem sich der *zweite Teil* des Buches widmet. Kapitel D interpretiert das Lied Deboras (Ri 5) nicht nur als Ausdruck von Frauenkultur, sondern als Paradigma prophetischer Interpretation von Geschichte mit ihrem herrschaftskritischen Potential, als "Einspruch gegen Gesellschaftsstrukturen, die Gleichgültigkeit und Brutalität begünstigen und die Lebensmöglichkeiten von Frauen beeinträchtigen" (121). Betonte laut dem ersten Teil die Tora die Gültigkeit der Prophetie, so bekräftigt laut Kapitel E die Prophetie durch Hulda (2 Kön 22-23) die "Autorität der Tora" (144), wenn sie König Joschija das im wiedergefundenen Buch angekündigte Unheil bestätigt. Kapitel F interpretiert die Rahmung mit den zwei Prophetinnen als Indiz, dass auch das deuteronomistische Geschichtswerk an der Notwendigkeit prophetischer Aktualisierung der Tora festhalte (176). Der zusammenfassende *dritte Teil* erweist die Prophetinnen nicht als Einzelpersönlichkeiten, sie stehen vielmehr für Butting in der Tora wie in den ProphetInnenbüchern paradigmatisch und programmatisch dafür ein, "dass der kanonisierte Text einen Gott bezeugt, dessen Weisungen durch neues Erzählen und neue Verwirklichungen entdeckt werden" (194).

Die Stärke des Buches liegt in seinem kanonisch entworfenen Gesamtbild, weniger in der Auslegung der jeweiligen Einzeltexte um die Prophetinnen. Sie treten angesichts der zentralen Frage nach dem Verhältnis von Tora und Prophetie sogar stark in den Hintergrund. Konsequent feministisch befreiungstheologisch orientiert, erweist Butting Prophetie als herrschaftskritische Tradition, in der Frauen aktiv waren. Das ist möglich, weil sie sich auf den ersten prophetischen Kanonteil beschränkt. Ihr Buch markiert den Beginn einer erhöhten feministischen Aufmerksamkeit für die Prophetinnen, weitere werden folgen (Irmtraud Fischer zu den Prophetinnen im Hebräischen Kanon, Ursula Rapp zur Prophetin Mirjam). Dass die Auseinandersetzung mit den Prophetinnen in kanonischer Perspektive ergiebig ist, zeigt Klara Buttings Studie. Im Detail wird noch so manches ergänzt werden können. Wir dürfen gespannt sein, was feministische Exegese in diesem Bereich noch alles zutage fördern wird.

Claudia Rakel (Bonn / Deutschland)

Irmtraud Fischer, *Rut*, (Herders Theologischer Kommentar zum Alten Testament), Herder Verlag: Freiburg / Wien 2001, 277 pages, ISBN 3-451-26811-6, € 55,22 / CHF 95,00

Irmtraud Fischer presents the story of Ruth as a very topical story, which confronts us, its readers, with to-day's social and political issues, including questions of solidarity between women and women's relations. According to Fischer, it can be a learning process for women not to orient themselves only towards men when looking for security, commitment and support. We are often are better off trying to place more trust in women's friendship and to build on its strength. Other issues which are raised by Ruth include: the relationships between generations – younger generations cannot shed responsibility for older generations; poverty – the face of poverty in our world is still primarily a women's face; and the role of woman's body in the struggle for survival – the book of Ruth cannot be used as a legitimation of bartering with women, but must be explained in accordance with its intention to favour the position of women. A further issue is the position of refugees. In an era in which only "political" refugees are accepted, the book Ruth shows especially that the "economic refugee", who flees in search of bread, should in no way be disqualified. With these insights Fischer connects the story of Ruth with our present time.

In her introduction, which takes up almost half the book, Fischer focuses in detail on the literary structure of the four chapters of the book Ruth (the context; schemes of time and place, the actors, the meaning of their names, their interactions, etc.), questions of literary criticism, the origin and the place of the book in the Hebrew and Greek Bible and its interpretation in church, art and culture. Fischer is very precise, also in her exegesis (pp. 116-262). Every text unit in each chapter is analysed according to central (theological) themes, and every verse is explained. The exegesis is enriched by story and dialogue schemes, by use of Midrasji'm (rabbinic commentary), historical and geographical notations, maps and drawings. A complete German translation of the Hebrew text is included at the end of the book.

Looking at the most exciting and crucial scene of the Ruth story, the erotic encounter between Ruth and Boaz in the night on the threshing floor, Fischer draws a parallel between the "coming" (בוא) of Boaz to the floor and his "lying down" (שכב) there with the "coming" of Ruth and her "lying down" at his feet. The act of a woman or women approaching a man who is lying down is one that is found also in the story of the daughters of Lot (Gen. 19). Like the daughters of Lot, Ruth also comes in the night. Like Lot, Boaz had been drinking heavily. Both cases evoke the encounter as bringing about the birth of new life, a child, and as moving women from an outside position into a new, socially integrated, position. Fischer notes that the action of the daughters of Lot is traditionally explained as a vital act born out of the will to live. This may be the same in the case of Ruth's act although, according Fischer, an additional motivation can be identified, namely her concern for herself and her mother-in-law. By drawing a parallel between these powerful acts by women, however, Fischer misses a opportunity to focus on the deeper, metaphorical meaning of these "incestuous" acts and their impact on women and girls readers now.

Fisher's book is a very usable, well-ordered and well-illustrated commentary that invites the (professional) reader to enjoy and consider her insights on the events in the book of Ruth.

Barbara Leijnse (Arnhem / The Netherlands)

Esther Fuchs, *Sexual Politics in the Biblical Narrative: Reading the Hebrew Bible as a Woman*, (Journal for the Study of the Old Testament Supplement Series 310), Sheffield Academic Press: Sheffield 2000, 244 pages, 1-84127-138-1, £40.00

Fuchs's fascinating book states that its purpose is "to expose the links between the politics of male domination and the representation of women in the Hebrew Bible" (11). Fuchs succeeds admirably in fulfilling this aim. Employing the techniques of literary analysis in successive, and differently focused, close readings of the text, she shows readers the thorough-going and persistent operation of patriarchal modes of thought, self-perception, self-interest and attitudes in a wide range of key narratives about women in the Hebrew Bible. Fuchs lays the "blame" for this one-sided construction of the biblical characters and their lives in the biblical world firmly on the male narrators of the texts, producing point after inescapable point of insightful exegesis from the variety of layers and levels within which texts may be read. Following a powerful introduction that sets the tenor and scope of her work, Chapter 2 on the "Objective Fallacy of Contemporary Biblical Criticism" makes plain how male attitudes are portrayed as "the attitudes" of all "right-thinking" people, both in the Hebrew Bible and in much of the secondary literature. She finds that the reader is constructed as a compliant learner who will not raise "awkward" questions about the gaps in stories about women, for example, Dinah and Bathsheba. Fuchs notes further that feminist attempts to fill those gaps are often described as "illegitimate".

Chapters 3, 4 and 5 deal successively with stories that portray women as would-be mothers, whether barren wives (Sarah and Rachel) seeking a (preferably) male child, or fertile women manipulating appropriate males into impregnating them within the law (Ruth and Tamar); or as virgins who become betrothed after an encounter at a well (Rebekah and Zipporah); or as people who exist as men's possessions, chattels or sexual facilities, apportioned to appropriate males under biblical law. For each story, Fuchs highlights how male interests predominate and male concerns are brought to voice through the situation and narratives revolving around the women. These men never have problems in conceiving (according to the narrators) or with temptation to adultery; such problems are laid at the door of women. Men can always rely on YHWH to support them in their need; God will help make their wives pregnant as a sign of favour to the men – not to the women.

Chapters 6 and 7 provide the same type of productive and detailed analysis about key stories referring to women as daughters, sisters and also as rape victims – although, in the Hebrew Bible, it is always males who are the "true" victims of the rapes, and it is they who exact revenge.

The main strength of Fuchs's work is its provision of chapters and sections that can be read equally as units in their own right or as part of a compelling book that provides a full range of current scholarship. Both scholars and methodologies are presented to the reader along with thought-provoking insights into how these narratives construct and confirm the ideals of the androcentric society that produced them.

Heather A. McKay (Ormskirk / England)

Claudia Janssen / Luise Schottroff / Beate Wehn (Hg.), *Paulus. Umstrittene Traditionen – lebendige Theologie. Eine feministische Lektüre*, Chr. Kaiser / Gütersloher Verlagshaus: Gütersloh 2001, 208 Seiten, ISBN 3-579-05318-3, DM 39,80 / CHF 37,50

Dieses Buch zur paulinischen Theologie enthält Aufsätze, die in Englisch bereits in der Zeitschrift *Journal for the Study of the New Testament* 79 (2000) veröffentlicht wurden. Die deutsche Fassung ist aus mehreren Gründen sehr empfehlenswert und hilfreich für das Studium der paulinischen Theologie: Zum einen sind die Aufsätze übersichtlich in fünf Themenbereiche gegliedert. Nach einem ersten hermeneutischen Teil, der mit "'Unrettbar frauenfeindlich'?" (*Luzia Sutter Rehmann*; *Marlene Crüsemann*) überschrieben ist, werden Themenfelder wie Rechtfertigung und Gesetz (*Luise Schottroff*; *Luzia Sutter Rehmann*), Auferstehung und Geschöpflichkeit (*Claudia Janssen*; *Klara Butting*), "...nicht Sklave noch Freier, nicht mehr männlich und weiblich" (*Sabine Bieberstein*; *Brigitte Kahl*), sowie Anpassung und Widerstand (*Annette Merz*; *Angela Standhartinger*; *Beate Wehn*) in jeweils mehreren Aufsätzen diskutiert. Dabei werden sowohl in den einzelnen Beiträgen, als auch im Vorwort und im ersten Aufsatz von *Luzia Sutter-Rehmann* dargestellt, welche unterschiedlichen hermeneutischen Arbeitsweisen bei der Bearbeitung der Texte jeweils angewandt wurden. Gemeinsam ist ihnen, "daß sie den gesellschaftlichen Kontext der paulinischen Schriften berücksichtigen und sie im Zusammenhang der praktischen Gemeinderealität ihrer Zeit zu begreifen suchen" (10). Darüber hinaus wenden die Autorinnen die Methodenbandbreite feministischer Exegese an. Eine große Rolle spielt dabei die Wirkungsgeschichte. Die "sorgfältige Trennung von feministisch-kritischer Wirkungsgeschichte und Textanalyse" (11) fördert einen beinahe unbekannten Textcorpus der paulinischen Schriften zu Tage, den es zu entdecken gilt. Auch die kritische Auseinandersetzung mit der eigenen Kulturgeschichte wird zur Voraussetzung. Dabei entsteht ein Paulus, der mit jüdischen Gemeinden, Frauen und Männern in heftigem Diskurs stand.

Explizit antifeministische Texte wie das Schweigegebot 1Kor 14,35f. bleiben ein Problem. *Marlene Crüsemann* macht auf die antijudaistische Wirkungsgeschichte aufmerksam, die in diesem Gebot jüdische Praxis vermutet, und plädiert anschließend eindrücklich für eine Anmerkung in den Übersetzungen zu dieser Stelle, die "auf die unterschiedliche Plazierung in den Handschriften, sowie auf die strittige Frage einer Interpolation" (37) hinweisen.

Aus dem Untertitel mag der Eindruck entstehen, dass sich die Autorinnen in ihren Untersuchungen lediglich auf *feministische Theologie* richten. Das neue Paradigma der Paulus-Forschung wird in diesem Buch jedoch nicht ausschließlich auf das jüdisch-christliche Verhältnis und die feministische Perspektive bezogen. Auch befreiungstheologische Ansätze sind integriert, wie etwa im Artikel über Rechtfertigung von *Luise Schottroff*. Für die Paulusdeutung ist die befreiungstheologische Konzeption der "strukturellen Sünde" (45) außerordentlich fruchtbar. Gesellschaftliche Strukturen, die ein Schuldigwerden zwingend zur Folge haben, werden aufgedeckt. Die alleinige Annahme der individuellen Sündenvergebung christlicher Rechtfertigungsbotschaft engt die paulinische Botschaft ein. Diese Tradition wurde zu oft als Instrument zur Rechtfertigung der TäterInnen missbraucht.

Dass auf der Suche nach einem neuen Paulusbild auch die Grenzen des christlichen Kanons überschritten werden müssen, steht außer Frage. Um die Geschichte des frühen Christentums rekonstruieren und die Kämpfe der Frauen für Ehefreiheit und ihre Anerkennung durch Männer in christlichen Gemeinden nachvollziehen zu können, wird apokryphe Literatur wie die Theklaakten herangezogen (*Beate Wehn*). Sie setzen sich mit der frauenfeindlichen Verwendung und Wirkungsgeschichte paulinischer und nachpaulinischer Traditionen im 2. Jahrhundert auseinander. Hier zeigt sich, welche "Diskrepanz zwischen der propagierten und nicht eingelösten Gleichstellung von Frauen und Männern in Christus" (196) besteht.

An diesen wenigen Beispielen wird deutlich, wie nötig ein Prozess der Neugestaltung christlichen Lebens und christlicher Theologie ist, die sich in vielfältiger Weise auf Paulus beruft. Das Aufbrechen der scheinbar festgeschriebenen Deutungsmuster des paulinischen Werks ist in diesem Buch gelungen. Zudem macht die methodische Transparenz das Lesen sowohl für EinsteigerInnen in die paulinische Theologie, als auch für SpezialistInnen fruchtbar. Durch die am Ende jedes Artikels angegebene weiterführende Literatur kann dieses Paulusbuch als Arbeitsbuch und Anregung zur weiteren Lektüre benutzt werden.

Nach dem Studium der einzelnen Beiträge ist eines gewiss: Das Buch verdient dank der Leistung der Autorinnen den Untertitel "*lebendige Theologie*" zu Recht!

Elke Tönges (Bochum / Deutschland)

Anna Kiesow, *Löwinnen von Juda. Frauen als Subjekte politischer Macht in der judäischen Königszeit*, (Theologische Frauenforschung in Europa 4), Lit Verlag: Münster 2000, 224 Seiten, ISBN 3-8258-4653-9, DM 39,80

In ihrer 1997 an der Berliner Humboldt-Universität als Dissertation eingereichten Arbeit verfolgt Anna Kiesow das Ziel, ein Stück altisraelitischer Frauengeschichte zu rekonstruieren. Neben den biblischen Texten zieht die Autorin weitere schriftliche Quellen, v.a. Siegelfunde und anderes epigraphisches Material heran. In einem einleitenden Teil nähert sie sich den Begriffen "Geschlecht" und "Macht", um anschließend den historischen Aussagewert der unterschiedlichen Quellen zu diskutieren. In Bezug auf die biblischen Texte als historische Quellen nimmt sie eine Kompromissposition zwischen minimalistischen und maximalistischen Ansätzen, "eine skeptische, nicht aber erkenntnispessimistische Haltung" (25) ein. Im Verlauf der Untersuchung hält die Autorin diese Skepsis durch; eine konkrete Bewertung der einzelnen Quellen und daraus resultierende Schlüsse für die Rekonstruktion der Königszeit gibt sie aber häufig nicht.

Nach dem hermeneutischen ersten Teil wendet sich Kiesow den "Frauen im antiken Israel/Juda" zu; hier zeigt sich der sozialgeschichtliche Ansatz der Autorin besonders deutlich. Zwei Exkurse, einer zu Frauen in Elefantine und einer zu Frauensiegeln, geben Einblick in außerbiblisches Quellenmaterial; sie hätten ausführlicher und systematischer sein können. Im weiteren Verlauf stützt sich Anna Kiesow hauptsächlich auf biblische Texte. Sie konzentriert sich auf die Frauen am Jerusalemer Hof, insbesondere auf den Begriff der *Gebirah* und auf die Königsmütter. Die methodische Entscheidung, den Begriff *Gebirah* getrennt von den Belegstellen der Königsmütter zu untersuchen, zeigt, dass vor einer zu schnellen Ineinssetzung dieser beiden Rollen und vor einer Interpretation des Begriffs *Gebirah* als Amtstitel Vorsicht geboten ist. *Gebirah* wird "meist als relationaler Begriff zur Bezeichnung eines Herrschaftsverhältnisses verwandt. (...) Die These, *Gebirah* sei (auch) Amts-, also Funktionsbezeichnung für die judäischen Königsmütter gewesen, scheint folglich wenig einleuchtend" (133), zumal nur zwei der insgesamt 18 judäischen Königsmütter mit diesem Begriff bezeichnet werden. Dieser Befund sagt noch nichts über die Macht der Königsmütter aus. Neben der literarischen Präsenz in der die judäischen Könige einführenden Formel in den Königsbüchern gibt es weitere Nachrichten, die politisches Handeln von Königsmüttern darstellen: Batsebas Aktivität im Kontext der Thronbesteigung ihres Sohnes Salomo oder Isebels und Ataljas Nutzung des königlichen Siegels mögen hier als Beispiele genügen.

Die systematisierte Analyse der "Königsmütter-Stellen" und die exakte semantische Analyse des Begriffs *Gebirah* gehören zu den Hauptverdiensten der Arbeit. Anna Kiesow bleibt gegen voreilige historische Schlüsse durchgängig skeptisch – das macht die Lektüre des Buchs anregend und quellennah, an manchen Stellen aber auch unbefriedigend, zumal die Zusammenfassung der gesamten Arbeit reichlich kurz geraten ist. Beeindruckend bleibt der Einblick in die Vielfalt der dargestellten Frauenrollen der vorexilischen Zeit Israels und Judas und die Reflexion der Handlungskompetenzen einzelner Frauen im Umfeld der königlichen Macht.

Ilse Müllner (Münster / Deutschland)

Sonja Angelika Strube, *"Wegen dieses Wortes..". Feministische und nicht-feministische Exegese im Vergleich am Beispiel der Auslegungen zu Mk 7,24-30*, (Theologische Frauenforschung in Europa 3), Lit Verlag: Münster / Hamburg / London 2000, 354 pages, ISBN 3-8258-4521-4, DM 49,80

"Wegen dieses Wortes..." is the published version of Strube's doctoral dissertation. As the subtitle suggests, feminist and non-feminist works on Mark's story of the Syro-Phoenician woman are compared with the aim of showing the specific profile of feminist biblical exegesis.

After the introduction, Strube presents her own reading of Mark 7:24-30. The main part of the study is organised around problems dealt with in exegetical works on this text. Strube covers the whole range from text criticism and text-oriented readings to historical questions. In each chapter, the problem is introduced, views in non-feminist and feminist works are presented and compared, and their implicit presuppositions and implications are discussed. There are also two thematic sections, one on anti-Judaism in interpretations and one on different kinds of interpretations, such as the paranetic, the christological and the salvation historical (*heilsgeschichtlich*). Strube applies a wide definition to this designation, applying it to all interpretations in which Mk 7:24-30 is read as a text about the mission of Christ and his followers to the Gentiles, and thus as a text in which views about Jews and other non-Christians become evident.

In her conclusions, Strube points to both the diversity of feminist exegesis and its common traits. Emphasising that the feminist exegetes she discusses have related to non-feminists while the opposite is not the case, Strube calls for change in the attitudes of non-feminist scholars. However, she makes no secret of the fact that feminist exegesis is not an addition to the discipline but a new paradigm which makes it necessary for non-feminist scholars to learn new ways of thinking.

Strube's work is clearly contextual, oriented towards the German exegetical scene. This context is obvious in her choice of material and statement of aims. She includes works written in German or influential in the German debate. The latter are primarily North-American feminist exegetical writings, many of them translated into German. Strube states explicitly her desire to counter misunderstandings concerning feminist exegesis; therefore, she starts with particular works. In this way, Strube builds a view of feminist exegesis based on what is actually being done, rather than on any one particular influential feminist hermeneutical programme or an abstract definition.

Its contextual character does not make this work irrelevant outside Germany, although the description of the place of feminist exegesis in the discipline might have been somewhat different in another context. I think all European exegetes influenced by traditional German exegesis and North-American feminist theology will find the material relevant. The book is written not only for feminist exegetes, but for everyone interested in hermeneutical and methodological issues and, of course, for those working with Mark 7:24-30. Teachers of New Testament who need examples of how a text can be interpreted differently from different perspectives, especially from feminist perspectives, may find the work useful.

Strube's work is stamped by a wish to be taken seriously as a voice in the internal exegetical debate. It is one effort, amongst many, to find room for feminists in the guild of exegesis, without allowing them to lose their subversive potential. I hope that this wish will be fulfilled and that this work may contribute to the common feminist effort.

Hanna Stenström (Uppsala / Sweden)

II.2. Kirchen- und Religionsgeschichte

Doris Brodbeck, *Hunger nach Gerechtigkeit. Helene von Mülinen (1850-1924) – eine Wegbereiterin der Frauenemanzipation*, Chronos Verlag: Zürich 2000, 250 Seiten, ISBN 3-905313-53-7, CH 38,00

Eine reguläre universitäre Theologinnenausbildung und eine bezahlte Berufstätigkeit blieben der geistig hochbegabten Helene von Mülinen (1850-1924) aufgrund ihres Frauseins und ihrer großbürgerlichen Herkunft im ausgehenden 19. Jahrhundert verwehrt. Nur als Hörerin durfte sie an der Evangelisch-Theologischen Fakultät Bern Vorlesungen besuchen. Aber "die Sehnsucht nach dem Geistleben konnte man nicht ausrotten, und zu einem nützlichen Küchenkraut konnte man mich nicht machen", bekannte sie später in einem Brief (40).

Die intellektuelle Biographie dieser bedeutenden Exponentin der frühen Schweizer Frauenbewegung und ihre frauenemanzipatorischen Anliegen vor dem Hintergrund philosophischer und theologischer Systeme bilden das zentrale Thema der vorliegenden Publikation von Doris Brodbeck.

Brodbeck hat ihre Untersuchung, mit der sie Helene von Mülinens Denken und Wirken erstmals der feministischen Theologie und Kirchengeschichtsschreibung zugänglich macht, in sieben Abschnitte gegliedert. Die ersten drei behandeln den persönlichen Lebensweg und die intellektuellen Beweggründe Helene von Mülinens (I), ihre Bedeutung für die Anfänge einer Frauenbewegung in einem sozialreformerischen Umfeld (II) sowie ihre rechtlichen Forderungen zu Gesetzeswerkentwürfen als damals erste Präsidentin des Bundes Schweizerischer Frauenvereine (III). Die Teile IV und V analysieren die philosophischen und theologischen Überzeugungen, auf denen das juristische und soziale Engagement der Wegbereiterin der Frauenemanzipation aufbauen. In ihren "Schlussbetrachtungen" (VI) formuliert Brodbeck aus dem Denken und Handeln Helene von Mülinens Anstöße für die Gegenwart und vergleicht sie mit heutigen feministischen Ansätzen. Die Autorin stützt sich in ihrer Arbeit auf umfangreiches Quellenmaterial, hauptsächlich aus Schweizer Archiven, und Sekundärliteratur (VII).

Aufschlussreich für das seelische Fühlen und geistige Denken Helene von Mülinens sind die erstmals sorgsam ausgewerteten Briefe an Susanna Schlatter (1860-1907), die Ehefrau Theodor Schlatters. Die biographisch-bibliographische Skizzierung wichtiger Personen im Umkreis der Schweizer Frauenbewegung runden die akribische Untersuchung ab. Ihr inneres Aufbäumen gegen die intellektuelle und geistige Unterdrückung von Frauen und gegen das einengende Gesellschaftskorsett stürzten Helene von Mülinen in schwere persönliche und gesundheitliche Krisen. Um das vierzigste Lebensjahr gewann sie aus der Erkenntnis, dass sie "befähigt und daher berechtigt sei, etwas Anderes zu thun als 'flicken und stricken'"(179), neue Lebenskraft, die sie im Engagement für sozial Benachteiligte aufgehen ließ.

Einfluss auf ihre sozialpolitische Tätigkeit und ihren Kampf um eine freiere Stellung der Frau übte die drei Jahrzehnte währende Lebensgefährtinnenschaft mit Emma Pieczýnska-Reichenbach (1854-1927) aus. Von 1900-1904 fungierte Helene von Mülinen als erste Präsidentin des Bundes Schweizerischer Frauenvereine (BSF), der mehrere Petitionen zu Eherecht, Strafrecht und Mutterschaftsversicherung verabschiedete und bereits früh das politische und kirchliche Frauenstimmrecht einforderte.

Helene von Mülinen reflektierte die Frauenbewegung theologisch als "Gottes Werk", mit dem "den Frauen neue Handlungsmöglichkeiten eröffnet wurden" (188). Die Kirche forderte sie nicht nur dringend auf, den Frauen zu helfen, sondern erwartete von ihr "neue Schritte zur Partizipation der Frau" (192). Mit Recht qualifiziert Brodbeck Helene von Mülinen "gewissermassen als frühe feministische Theologin oder auch als Befreiungstheologin" (200), die am eigenen Leib unter der standes- und geschlechtsbedingten Zurücksetzung der Frauen litt und Frauenemanzipation und Theologie verband.

Kleine Ungenauigkeiten – wie etwa divergierende Angaben des Sterbetages von Mülinens (206; 208) – sowie das Fehlen eines Personenregisters schmälern die Bedeutung der vorliegenden Untersuchung für die Frauengeschichtsschreibung und für die feministische Theologie nicht.

Michaela Kronthaler (Graz / Österreich)

Hermann Düringer / Karin Weintz (Hg.), *Leonore Siegele-Wenschkewitz. Persönlichkeit und Wirksamkeit*, (Arnoldshainer Texte 112), Haag + Herchen Verlag: Frankfurt am Main 2000, 371 Seiten, ISBN 3-89846-023-1, DM 64,00

Der Abschied leitet dieses Buch ein. Die im Trauergottesdienst für Leonore Siegele-Wenschkewitz gehaltenen Ansprachen spiegeln die vielen Facetten ihres Lebens und Arbeitens, die im folgenden ihre eigenen Texte aus den Jahren 1992-1999 dokumentieren. Facettenreich wie die Themen sind auch die Gattungen der Texte: Vorträge, wissenschaftliche Aufsätze, Andachten, Ansprachen usw.

Herausragend ist der Vortrag, den Leonore Siegele-Wenschkewitz 1999 anlässlich der Entgegennahme des Edith-Stein-Preises in Göttingen gehalten hat, der letzte längere Text, den sie abschließen konnte. In diesem "Plädoyer für ein angemessenes Gedenken an Edith Stein" greifen ihre drei wissenschaftlichen Schwerpunkte – die kirchliche Zeitgeschichte, das Verhältnis zwischen jüdischen und christlichen Menschen und die feministische Theologie – am deutlichsten ineinander. Jenseits des Aufeinanderprallens jüdischer und katholischer Erinnerungsmale stellt Leonore Siegele-Wenschkewitz sich die Frage: Wie erforschen Kirche und Theologie ihren Umgang mit verfolgten jüdischen Menschen sowie mit ihren getauften Mitgliedern jüdischer Abkunft während der NS-Zeit, und wie wird dabei von der Verantwortung der Amtskirche gesprochen (93f.)? Immer wieder stellt sie die Frage nach den Handlungsspielräumen kirchlicher Amtsträger, auch der Mitschwestern Edith Steins, die sie nicht schützen konnten oder wollten. Differenziert geht sie Edith Steins Beiträgen zu einer Verständigung zwischen jüdischen und christlichen Menschen und Glaubensweisen nach und plädiert auch hier für eine differenzierte Erinnerung, die Edith Steins Verständigungsbemühungen und ihren Einsatz für die Verbreitung jüdischen Selbstverständnisses würdigt, ohne dabei ihre theologischen Deutungsmuster (etwa den Absolutheitsanspruch des Christentums) zu übernehmen (103). Diese sind der Autorin vielmehr Anlass, der Judenmission eine deutliche Absage zu erteilen und dazu aufzufordern, die Eigenständigkeit jüdischen Glaubens und Lebens zu respektieren.

Differenzierte Wahrnehmung und Beurteilung ihrer Forschungsobjekte kennzeichnen auch die folgenden Beiträge über die Stuttgarter Schulderklärung sowie über die Schriften Gerhard Kittels und Walter Grundmanns, in denen beide nach 1945 auf ihre Haltung im und zum Nationalsozialismus zurückblicken. In beiden Aufsätzen führt Leonore Siegele-Wenschkewitz zudem ihre Verhältnisbestimmung von Ethik und Geschichtsschreibung vor (vgl. ihren Beitrag "Ist Ethik eine Kategorie der Historiographie?" in: EvTh 51 [1991], 155-168).

Die Kirchenpolitikerin und Akademiedirektorin tritt in den Überlegungen zur Neuorientierung der Evangelischen Akademie Arnoldshain in den Vordergrund. Ihre Gedanken trugen wesentlich dazu bei, die Arbeit der Akademie auch in finanziell kritischen Zeiten zu sichern – ein Ziel, das Leonore Siegele-Wenschkewitz in ihren letzten Lebensjahren mit Priorität verfolgte.

Drei Beiträge wenden sich dezidiert der feministischen Theologie zu: die ungekürzte Fassung des Interviews, das gekürzt bereits in dem Buch "Wie wir wurden, was wir sind" (Gütersloh 1998) erschien. Es bringt verschiedene theologisch begründete Auseinandersetzungen zur Sprache: den Streit um ihre Forschung zur Geschichte der Tübinger Fakultät während der NS-Zeit, das Aufeinanderprallen von akademischem Stil und Frauenerfahrung zu Beginn ihrer Arnoldshainer Tätigkeit, die Antijudaismusdebatte in der feministischen Theologie, Vorhaben und Rückschläge bei der Institutionalisierung feministischer Theologie. Letztere ist auch Thema der beiden anderen Beiträge zur feministischen Theologie: ein Diskussionsbeitrag auf der EKD-Synode 1996 sowie der Wiederabdruck eines bereits in der Festschrift für H. Erhart (*Querdenken*, Pfaffenweiler 1992) erschienenen Berichtes darüber.

Ulrich Siegele zeigt in einem ausführlichen Lebenslauf den inneren und biographischen Zusammenhang ihrer Arbeitsschwerpunkte und Veröffentlichungen auf. Ein umfangreiches Verzeichnis der von ihr geleiteten Tagungen und Schriften schließen den Band ab.

Ein authentisches Zeugnis eines engagierten Lebens und Zeichen einer reichen geistigen Hinterlassenschaft!

Britta Jüngst (Münster / Deutschland)

Hannelore Erhart / Ilse Meseberg-Haubold / Dietgard Meyer (Hg.), *Katharina Staritz (1903-1953). Von der Gestapo verfolgt, von der Kirchenbehörde fallengelassen. Mit einem Exkurs "Elisabeth Schmitz"*, Dokumentation Band 1: 1903-1942, Neukirchener Verlag: Neukirchen 1999, 572 Seiten, ISBN 3-7887-1682-7, € 29,90 / CHF 52,50

Noch vor einem Jahrzehnt waren sie und ihr Lebensschicksal relativ unbekannt. Eine 1990 von Gerlind Schwöbel erschienene Biographie, eine Wanderausstellung über das Konzentrationslager Ravensbrück und die 1999 erschienene, vorliegende Dokumentation sind Signale dafür, dass das Interesse an der evangelischen Theologin Katharina Staritz wächst. Denn ihr Lebensschicksal ist nicht nur ein Beispiel für die Geschichte evangelischer Theologinnen im 20. Jahrhundert, sondern auch für die Geschichte des Widerstands aus religiöser Motivation im Dritten Reich.

Katharina Staritz, geboren 1903 in Breslau, studierte dort ab 1922 zunächst Philologie, ab 1926 in Breslau und in Marburg Theologie. In Marburg promovierte sie 1928 als erste Frau an der Theologischen Fakultät. Ihr Interesse galt der Anfangszeit des Christentums und der Frage, was das eigentlich Christliche im Verhältnis zum Judentum und anderen Religionen in der Spätantike ausmacht. Ihr wichtigster theologischer Lehrer war Hans von Soden, mit dem sie in regem Briefverkehr stand. Er lehnte es 1938 ab, sie zu habilitieren, wodurch ihr der Weg an die Universität verschlossen war. Ab 1938 wandte sie sich orientalistischen und Islam-Studien zu. Seit 1932 arbeitete sie in Breslau in verschiedenen kirchlichen Sonderbereichen, am 6. November 1938 wurde sie (aufgrund des seit 1927 geltenden Vikarinnengesetzes) in der Kirche St. Maria Magdalena (heute alt-katholische Kathedralkirche) als Vikarin eingesegnet bzw. – wie sie selbst immer sagte – ordiniert.

Drei Tage später brannten in Deutschland die Synagogen. Katharina Staritz übernahm die Leitung der Breslauer Hilfsstelle für "nicht-arische" Christen in Verbindung mit dem "Büro Pfarrer Grüber" in Berlin. Auf die "Stern-Verordnung" vom 5. September 1941, die allen, die Jude bzw. Jüdin im Sinn der Nürnberger Gesetze waren, das Tragen eines Sterns vorschrieb, wandte sie sich in einem Rundschreiben an die Breslauer Pfarrer, in dem sie es als Christenpflicht bezeichnete, sich den solchermaßen gekennzeichneten Gemeindegliedern gegenüber solidarisch zu verhalten. Dieses Rundschreiben hatte für Katharina Staritz weitreichende Konsequenzen: Sie wurde suspendiert und die schlesische Kirchenleitung distanzierte sich von ihr. In der von Joseph Goebbels veranlassten und von SS-Organen weitergeführten Propaganda-Aktion gegen "Judenfreunde" im Winter 1941/42 wurde sie als "Frau Knöterich" Ziel der Hetzkampagne. Im März 1942 erfolgte ihre Verhaftung. Bis zu ihrer Freilassung im Mai 1943 verblieb sie die meiste Zeit im Frauenkonzentrationslager Ravensbrück. Nach dem Krieg arbeitete sie bis zu ihrem Tod 1953 in Frankfurt am Main.

Die Dokumentation, die mit der Verhaftung Katharina Staritz' endet (ein zweiter Band ist in Vorbereitung), leistet folgendes: die drei Herausgeberinnen haben Briefe und andere wichtige Dokumente zusammengestellt und damit einem größeren Lesepublikum zugänglich gemacht. Hannelore Erhart und Ilse Meseberg-Haubold haben die Dokumente verschiedenen Lebensabschnitten der Katharina Staritz zugeordnet und für jeden Abschnitt eine längere Einleitung verfasst, die den Leser, die Leserin ins Thema einführt, historische Hintergründe erläutert, die Aussagen von Zeitzeuginnen, u.a. der Schwester Charlotte Staritz (1909-1993) berücksichtigt, Ansätze zur Auswertung des dokumentierten Materials bietet und dabei die Möglichkeit zu weiterer Forschung bewusst offen hält. Dietgard Meyer hat in gleicher Weise eine Einleitung zur Berliner Studienrätin Elisabeth Schmitz (1893-1977) verfasst; diese ist die Autorin der Denkschrift "Zur Lage der deutschen Nichtarier" (1935/36), die bisher Marga Meusel (1897-1953), der Leiterin des Evangelischen Bezirkswohlfahrtsamts in Berlin zugeschrieben wurde. Elisabeth Schmitz erkannte hellsichtig die Konsequenzen der Rassentheorie und setzte sich deshalb nicht nur für die evangelischen, sondern für *alle* verfolgten Juden ein. Ihr Protest ging weit über andere Aufschreie hinaus, fand aber kaum Gehör. Nach dem November-Pogrom 1938 ließ sie sich in den Ruhestand versetzen; sie wollte nicht länger "Beamtin einer Regierung (...) sein, die Synagogen anstecken lässt" (266).

Katharina Staritz und Elisabeth Schmitz kannten einander nicht; was sie verbindet, ist ihr Mut und ihre Scharfsichtigkeit, ihre Hilfsbereitschaft verfolgten Juden gegenüber. Was an beider Geschichte ebenfalls deutlich wird, ist die Verflechtung von persönlicher Biographie und kirchenpolitischen Entscheidungen sowie die Frage nach der (Ohn-)Macht von Frauen im Widerstand, die kein (ordentliches Pfarr-)Amt oder eine kirchliche Position im Rücken hatten. Das Buch ist ein Beitrag zur Aufarbeitung des Widerstands von Frauen und besticht durch Aufmachung und Inhalt. Im April 2002 wurde es in Jena mit dem "Hanna-Jursch-Preis" der EKD ausgezeichnet.

Angela Berlis (Arnheim / Niederlande)

Constanze Jaiser, *Poetische Zeugnisse. Gedichte aus dem Frauen-Konzentrationslager Ravensbrück 1939-1945*, (Ergebnisse der Frauenforschung 55), J.B. Metzler: Stuttgart / Weimar 2000, 430 Seiten, ISBN 3-476-45253-0, DM 65,00 / CHF 54,50

Frauengeschichte, speziell die des Dritten Reichs, ist noch immer ein Randthema, das oft von Mythen und politisch-ideologischen Projektionen beherrscht und wenig mit historischen Fakten untermauert ist. Es ist Constanze Jaisers Verdienst, über 1200 Gedichte, die von zumeist christlichen Frauen aus 15 Nationen im Konzentrationslager Ravensbrück verfasst wurden, gesammelt, übersetzt und erstmals veröffentlicht zu haben. Zusammen mit den 137 Einzelbiographien der Autorinnen bietet das Buch ein bewegendes Zeugnis des Überlebenswillens und -kampfes von Frauen unter den Extrembedingungen eines KZs. Als Literaturwissenschaftlerin und Theologin untersucht Jaiser die Gedichte nach Form, Inhalt und Funktion. Dabei entwickelt sie eine Theorie zum Verständnis dieser Texte, deren Wert ja weniger in ihrer ästhetischen und lyrischen Qualität, als vielmehr in ihrer Bedeutung als Zeugnis liegt. Indem sie

Zeugnis ablegen, widersetzen sich diese Frauen dem übermächtigen Versuch der Nazis, sie seelisch und körperlich auszulöschen.

Mit dem Rekurs auf die biblische Tradition des/r ZeugIn und der Zeugenschaft begründet Jaiser den Anspruch der Gedichte, mehr zu sein als historische Dokumente: sie wollen nicht nur beschreiben, sondern eine Botschaft vermitteln, die die Verpflichtung zur Zeugenschaft an die Hörerinnen weitergibt. Die Fülle der Gedichte allein zeigt bereits, wie wichtig den Autorinnen der Appell gegen das Vergessen, gegen ihr Verschwinden in der Maschinerie des Massenmords ist. Mit ihrer Poesie halten sie an ihrer Menschlichkeit, am Sinn und Wert menschlichen Lebens fest und fordern Außenstehende und Nachgeborene auf, ihre Botschaft aufzunehmen. Während in der Bibel die Existenz und Treue Gottes durch Krisen hindurch bezeugt wird und LeserInnen in die Heilsgeschichte einbezogen werden, konfrontieren die Gedichte aus Ravensbrück mit dem Zeugnis vollständiger Vernichtung. Sich den theologischen Dimensionen dieses Zeugnisses zu stellen, ist eine Aufgabe, der sich noch immer viel zu wenige TheologInnen stellen.

Da die meisten Häftlinge Ravensbrücks christlich sozialisiert waren, benutzten viele von ihnen religiöse Symbole, um ihre Erfahrungen auszudrücken: In einzelnen Kapiteln arbeitet Jaiser besonders die Motive des Exils, des Himmels, der Hölle und des Kreuzes heraus. Dabei stellt sie wichtige Verschiebungen fest. So wird das Kreuz weniger als spirituelles Heilsereignis, sondern als Identifikationsmöglichkeit mit dem leidenden Jesus gedeutet. Der ursprüngliche historische Kontext des Kreuzes als Folter- und Hinrichtungswerkzeug tritt in den Vordergrund. Im folgenden zitiere ich das Gedicht einer französischen Überlebenden, das diese 1950 niedergeschrieben hat:

Es war Karfreitag, die neunte Stunde am Tag,
Da hörte sein Leiden auf, und er, Jesus, starb.
Die Frauen, mein Gott, sie leiden noch immer,
sie hungern und frieren noch immer,
allein und in Tränen.

Die Frauen, mein Gott, vor dir auf den Knien,
betrachten Jesus zur Rechten,
im Glanz neben dir.

Was Jesus einst rief, sie rufen's noch heute:
Warum nur mein Gott, hast Du mich verlassen?
Das ist es, mein Gott, das will ich dir heute sagen. (149)

Auch in anderen Gedichten identifizieren sich die Frauen mit dem Leiden Jesu, können aber die Auferstehung nur bedingt nachvollziehen. Denn die Erlösung, sprich die ersehnte Befreiung aus dem KZ, lässt allzu lange auf sich warten. Gottes Allmacht ist in Frage gestellt. Die traditionelle Heilsgewissheit, die im Kreuz symbolisiert wird, wird zugunsten einer miterlittenen Passion umgedeutet, deren Ausgang ungewiss bleibt. Damit verbunden ist Jaisers Feststellung, dass viele Gedichte in der Tradition biblischer Klagelieder und Protestgebete stehen, während die in der Kirche vorherrschenden Lob- und Dankgebete in den Hintergrund treten.

Das vorliegende Buch ist nicht nur eine unschätzbare Quelle bislang unerschlossener Texte von Frauen, sondern wagt auch erste Schritte zum rechten Umgang mit diesen Texten. Weder Aneignung noch Gleichgültigkeit, sondern behutsame Aufnahme des Zeugnisses dieser Frauen, deren außergewöhnliche Situation stets mitbedacht werden muss, ist Kriterium einer angemessenen theologischen Auseinandersetzung mit dieser Vergangenheit. Es ist zu hoffen, dass viele TheologInnen dieses Buch lesen und seine Herausforderung annehmen.

Katharina von Kellenbach (St. Mary's City / USA)

Anne-Marie Korte (ed.), *Women and Miracle Stories: A Multidisciplinary Exploration*, (Studies in the History of Religions 88), Brill: Leiden / Köln / Boston 2001, 350 Seiten, ISBN 90-04-11681-8, NLG 191,72 / $101

Ohne Frage sind Wunder "modern" und haben in Zeiten vermehrter Sinnsuche und Hinwendung zu spirituellen Erfahrungen Hochkonjunktur. Im wissenschaftlichen Bereich zeugen zahlreiche Veröffentlichungen der letzten zehn Jahre von der Entstehung einer neuen Mirakelforschung. Wenn auch für eine Richtung der feministischen Theologie, die stark auf die sexuelle Differenz der Geschlechter setzt und von dieser Grundlinie aus gerade den Frauen einen engeren Bezug zur Sphäre des Magischen, Über-Sinnlichen zuschreibt, nun eine Verbindung zwischen Frau und Wunder auf der Hand liegt, sollten Leser und Leserinnen diesen Ansatz im vorliegenden Sammelband jedoch nicht erwarten, sonst werden sie sich schnell enttäuscht sehen. Das Buch ist eine grundsolide und facettenreiche Veröffentlichung im Bereich der Vernetzung von universitärer Forschung und Anliegen von Frauen. Dem Gesamtthema widmen sich zehn subtile Einzeluntersuchungen von Forschern und Forscherinnen der verschiedenen Fachdisziplinen, eingeleitet durch eine profunde Einführung ins Thema und abgerundet durch einen zusammenfassenden Epilog.

Das Buch gibt einen breiten Einblick in den Themenkomplex, einen zum Teil verblüffenden und zum Nachdenken anregenden. Neben sehr bekannten Texten wie den Theklaakten oder der Biographie der Christina von St. Trond sind ungewöhnliche, reizvolle zu finden wie ein lateinisches Gebet während der Geburtswehen, das an Gen. 3,16 anschließt. Unerwartete Beiträge wie der zu Ingeborg Bachmann oder zur *Genizah* (dem Aufbewahrungsort nicht mehr gebrauchter Handschriften) von Kairo gesellen sich bereichernd zu Beiträgen, denen sicher eine Schlüsselfunktion bei der Untersuchung von Frauen und Wundern zuerkannt werden wird, wie der Beitrag zur gallischen Königin Radegunde oder der zu Friederike Hauffe. Der Blick über den jüdisch-christlichen Kontext hinaus mit einer Untersuchung über hinduistische Wundervorstellungen oder auch durch die Beschäftigung mit der Postmoderne wirkt befreiend. Alle Beiträge sind methodisch sauber und in ansprechendem Stil geschrieben. Nachvollziehbar stellen die Forscher und Forscherinnen ihre Hypothesen vor und geben Einsicht in eine nicht immer einfach zu erschließende Materie. Das Niveau aller Beiträge ist beachtlich, so dass hier keine Namen im einzelnen genannt werden sollen, um niemanden zu kurz kommen zu lassen.

Die Ehrlichkeit der Herausgeberin Anne-Marie Korte, das Buch nicht als interdisziplinär, sondern als multidisziplinär zu bezeichnen, sollte Schule machen, legt den Finger aber an einen wunden Punkt: Die so vielfältigen Themen und Gesichtspunkte können sicher die zu Recht angesprochene Vielfältigkeit des Wunders widerspiegeln und unterstreichen, doch bleibt der größere systematische Zusammenhalt ein wenig auf der Strecke. Teilweise wäre auch ein kritischerer Umgang bei der ins Religiöse gewendeten Leidensannahme durch Frauen wünschenswert gewesen. Denn verhindert nicht gerade diese religiöse Legitimierung des Leidens auch jeden strukturellen Widerstand, der sehr wohl auch zu leisten wäre, dann nämlich, wenn das Leiden menschengemachtem Unrecht entspringt? Doch trotz all dieser Anmerkungen überwiegt der Respekt vor der gelungenen Leistung. Das Thema wird in seiner Vielschichtigkeit und Komplexität den Lesern und Leserinnen in erhellenden Nuancen nahegebracht.

Als Fazit lerne ich aus dem Buch, dass Wunder eine dem Religiösen wie spezifisch dem Christlichen innewohnende Komponente sind, die die Klammer ausdrücken zwischen Gott und Mensch, zwischen Körper und Geist. In dem Augenblick, in dem Frauen in diese Sphäre eintreten, erhält der Begriff Wunder einen neuen Klang und die Frauen werden durch das Wunder verändert.

So wird und muss aus der Not eine Tugend gemacht werden: Dem eigentlichen Geschehen, der “Realität” des Wunders, können wir nicht nahe kommen, nur seiner Spiegelung durch den je konkreten Menschen und der Bewertung hierüber von anderen Menschen. Dieser dreifache Bruch sollte immer methodisch sichtbar bleiben. Wunder sind also nicht nur "subjektiv", sie hängen von den die Gemeinschaft bestimmenden Vorstellungen ab, erhalten erst in Abstimmung mit dem Kollektiv ihre Bewertung als "Wunder". So könnten Studien zu "Negativ-Wundern", also zu Erfahrungen von Frauen, deren religiöses Erleben von der Kirche ausgegrenzt wurde, noch stärker diesen sozialen Bewertungsprozess deutlich machen, der verständlich werden ließe, warum es ja schon im Mittelalter so manche "Betrügerin" in Sachen Wunder gegeben hat – wobei wir nur von den enttarnten noch Kenntnis haben. Die Mirakelforschung hat mit der Zuspitzung auf die weibliche Sichtweise sicher eine Bereicherung erfahren, die es in Zukunft durch weitere methodische und inhaltliche Abklärungen zu untermauern gilt.

Daniela Müller (Utrecht / Niederlande – Emmerich / Deutschland)

Rita Librandi / Adriana Valerio, *I Sermoni di Domenica da Paradiso. Studi e testo critico*, Edizioni del Galluzzo: Firenze 1999, CLXXIX + 170 Seiten, ISBN 88-87027-43-9, € 35

Vor allem die wörtliche Auslegung des Satzes *mulier taceat in ecclesia* in 1 Kor 14,34 war lange Zeit Begründung genug, Frauen das Wort im öffentlichen Raum der Kirche zu verweigern. Wie wir wissen, gab es in der Geschichte dennoch immer wieder große Frauengestalten, etwa Hildegard von Bingen, Katharina von Siena oder Teresa von Avila, die ihr machtvolles Wort in der Kirche aussprachen und deren Rede als prophetisch galt. Aber auch sie mussten sich gegen das Verbot durchsetzen, mussten Erklärungen und Begründungen liefern und nach Legitimation ihrer prophetischen Gabe suchen. Meist waren es mystische Erlebnisse, Visionen, Auditionen, Offenbarungen und Ekstasen, auf die sich die Frauen beriefen und so ihrem Wort göttliche Provenienz und Autorität verliehen. Auch die Bibel bot immer einen reichen Fundus dafür, dass Gott nicht nur durch die Gelehrten, sondern gerade auch durch die Ungebildeten, Unwissenden und durch die Frauen spricht.

Domenica Narducci da Paradiso (1473-1553) muss sich ebenfalls mit dem paulinischen Verbot auseinandersetzen. Dabei verfolgt sie einen sehr eigenständigen spirituellen Weg. Nach ersten religiösen Erfahrungen wird sie zunächst dominikanische Terziarin und Anhängerin Savonarolas, dann Gründerin des Klosters Santa Croce in Florenz. Domenica da Paradiso hält ihre *Sermoni* anfangs für ihre Mitschwestern, mit zunehmendem Bekanntheitsgrad kommt aber bald ein größerer Kreis an Priestern und Laien aus der florentinischen Umgebung, um sie zu hören. Zu der oben genannten Bibelstelle findet sie eine andere, eigenwillige Interpretation, die ihrer Tätigkeit nicht nur nicht widerspricht, sondern sie selbst als Predigerin bestätigt. Paulus erscheint ihr eines Nachts persönlich in einer Vision und erklärt ihr, dass er mit seiner Aussage den Frauen keinesfalls grundsätzlich habe verbieten wollen, in der Kirche das Wort zu ergreifen. Wie hätte er dies wagen können, da Frauen ja Geschöpfe Gottes seien und Gott sich ihrer nach eigenem Gutdünken als Werkzeug bedienen könne. „Gott hat sich auch des Werkes der Frau bedient, um Mensch zu werden; da der Geist Gottes weht, wo er will, muss sowohl der Frau als auch dem Mann die Türe aufgemacht und ihnen Platz gemacht werden“ (158). Indem er fragt, wie er dem Heiligen Geist hätte Widerstand leisten können, fährt Paulus fort: „Ich war weit davon entfernt, ein solches Verbot für irgend jemanden auszusprechen, im Gegenteil, ich sagte, dass niemand schweigen dürfe, sondern alle ohne Angst über das reden sollten, was Gott ihnen eingegeben hat“ (158). So wird Domenica da Paradiso durch ihre Vision von 1507 (im Anhang des Buches abgedruckt) in ihrer Berufung bestätigt.

Diese Vision und die Predigten von Domenica da Paradiso wurden von ihrem treuen spirituellen Begleiter Francesco Onesti da Castiglione und einigen Mitschwestern niedergeschrieben. Denn Domenica ist, wie sie sich auch selbst bezeichnet, *analfabeta* und *illetterata*, sie beklagt in ihren Visionen und Predigten ihre Unzulänglichkeit und Unfähigkeit zu lesen und zu schreiben. Es ist heute schwer, den tatsächlichen Grad ihrer Bildung zu beurteilen, auch wenn einige Hinweise dafür sprechen, dass sie zumindest ein Minimum an Bildung hatte. Auf jeden Fall grenzt es an ein Wunder, dass zumindest ein Teil der Predigten von Domenica da Paradiso aufgezeichnet wurde und bis in unsere Zeit erhalten blieb. Jetzt liegen die von 1515 bis 1534 gesammelten *Sermoni* und die oben beschriebene Vision in einer modernen, textkritischen Ausgabe von Rita Librandi und Adriana Valerio vor. In einer ausführlichen Einführung stellt Adriana Valerio den spirituellen und theologischen Werdegang von Domenica Narducci da Paradiso im soziokulturellen und historischen Kontext im Florenz des 16. Jahrhunderts dar. Rita Librandi führt danach aus philologischer Sicht in die Texte ein. Die *Sermoni* und die Einführungen dazu sind ein herausragender theologiegeschichtlicher Beitrag zur Frauenforschung und liefern zugleich neuen Diskussions- und Argumentationsstoff zur Frage der Laienpredigt in der römisch-katholischen Kirche.

Valeria Ferrari Schiefer (Ludiano / Schweiz – Bobingen / Deutschland)

Esther Röhr (éd.), *Ich bin was ich bin. Frauen neben großen Theologen und Philosophen des 20. Jahrhunderts*, (Gütersloher Taschenbücher 549), Gütersloher Verlagshaus: Gütersloh 2001, 272 pages, ISBN 3-579-00549-9, € 14,90

Une édition de poche du receuil de biographies *Je suis ce que je suis. Des femmes aux côtés de grands théologiens et philosophes du XXe siècle*, publié en 1997 et réédité en 1998, vient de paraître en Allemagne. Quatre portraits en furent retirés: ceux de Clara Ragaz, de Nelly Barth, de Renate Köbler et de Doreen Potter. Le recueil est dédié aux femmes qui vécurent «aux côtés» de Dietrich Bonhoeffer, de Paul Tillich, de leurs amis et de leurs détracteurs.

Marlies Flesch-Thebesius décrit ses années d'apprentissage obligatoire à Béthel dans l'agriculture et l'économie domestique et présente Julia von Bodelschwingh, une artiste exceptionnelle, admirable aussi dans son rôle d'épouse de prêtre. Sieglinde Denzel et Susanne Naumann font le portrait de Paula Buber qui, baptisée catholique, se convertit à la religion de son compagnon de vie, un sioniste autrichien, dont elle fut la collaboratrice dévouée. Elle connut le succès en tant qu'écrivain sous le pseudonyme masculin de Georg Munk, et coucha ses expériences durant le national-socialisme dans un roman réaliste intitulé *Muckensturm*. Les mêmes auteures rapportent la vie de Hélène Schweitzer, qui tenta à Lambaréné (Afrique) de réaliser aux côtés de son mari Albert, pour qui elle était, aux dires de celui-ci, une épouse, mais plus encore une «amie», son idéal d'humanité. Après la naissance de sa fille, Hélène Schweitzer, extrêmement douée mais de santé très fragile, ne se rendit plus que très rarement à l'hôpital de Lambaréné sur l'Ogooué. Tandis que son mari parvient à la célébrité, elle se retire de plus en plus et vit dans son ombre.

Hedwig Jahnow, chercheuse spécialiste de l'Ancien Testament, est présentée par Tina von Hülsebus. Voulant devenir enseignante, elle fit des études universitaires à Berlin, où elle rencontra Adolf von Harnack et Hermann Gunkel. Sa première grande publication, *La femme dans l'Ancien Testament*, parut en 1914. Elle écrivit en outre un commentaire sur le *Cantique des Cantiques* et une monographie sur le chant funèbre hébraïque. Hedwig Jahnow se considérait comme féministe de la première génération. Elle fut contrainte d'arrêter de travailler par la force des lois racistes de Nuremberg, bien que son père, déjà, se fût converti au chistianisme. Elle mourut en 1944 à Theresienstadt.

Sabine Böttcher décrit Greti Wever. La jeune femme, d'un naturel gai, et peu conventionnelle, qui disait «organiser sa vie comme elle l'entendait» (133), rencontra à Berlin, juste après son mariage avec Paul Tillich, «Dox» Wegener, un ami de Paul, qui deviendra le père de ses deux fils. À la séparation de

Tillich, succède celle de Wegener. Plus de trente ans après leur séparation, Paul Tillich dit à sa première femme: «C'est toi qui as fait de moi ce que je suis devenu» (134).

Anne Marie Heiler, que portraiture Antje Gaedt, rencontre pendant ses études Friedrich Heiler, l'épouse et devient son assistante. Mère de trois enfants, elle assure seule la publication du recueil de textes *Le Mysticisme des femmes au Moyen Âge allemand.* Après la guerre, elle se présente aux élections du premier parlement fédéral (Bundestag). Tandis qu'au sein de l'Union chrétienne démocrate (CDU), elle encourage les femmes à lutter pour l'égalité des droits, les hommes du parti, presque tous membres de l'Église catholique romaine, soutiennent à fond le pouvoir de décision patriarcal dans le mariage. Elle est co-fondatrice de l'Association Indépendante des Femmes du Réseau des Femmes de Marburg.

Hannah Werner, portraiturée par Esther Röhr, voulait devenir peintre. Les idéaux de la jeune fille de 17 ans, depuis toujours méfiante à l'égard des rôles traditionnels attribués à la femme, s'écroulent complètement au début de la Première Guerre mondiale. À ses yeux, le monde était devenu un «monde masculin». Après une courte liaison matrimoniale avec son collègue Werner Gottschow et la perte de leur enfant, Hannah épouse Paul Tillich. Hannah et Paul partent en exil aux États-Unis. Après la mort de son mari, Hannah Tillich publie des recueils de poèmes, des nouvelles et des écrits autobiographiques.

Maria von Wedemeyer est décrite par Renate Wind comme une femme de tête, éprise de liberté, pleinement consciente de son état et de sa mission. Sa relation et ses fiançailles avec Dietrich Bonhoeffer sont attestés dans sa correspondance. La relation fut soumise, dès le début, à une forte pression. La grande différence d'âge entre eux incita la mère de Maria à demander un an de réflexion avant le mariage. Leur avenir est compromis à la suite de l'arrestation de Bonhoeffer. À la fin de la guerre, Maria commence les études de mathématiques dont elle avait toujours rêvé et va s'installer avec son mari Paul-Werner Schniewind aux États-Unis, où elle ne s'adapte pas plus qu'ailleurs à un cadre de vie imposé.

Je suis ce que je suis, est une lecture agréable et intéressante. Je recommande ce recueil de portraits de femmes à quiconque aime les biographies de femmes ou s'intéresse à l'histoire contemporaine.

Livia Neureiter (Graz / Autriche)

Traduction de l'allemand par Annick Yaiche

Gury Schneider-Ludorff, *Magdalene von Tiling. Ordnungstheologie und Geschlechtsbeziehungen. Ein Beitrag zum Gesellschaftsverständnis des Protestantismus in der Weimarer Republik*, (= Arbeiten zur Kirchlichen Zeitgeschichte, Reihe B, 35), Vandenhoeck und Ruprecht: Göttingen 2001, 370 Seiten, ISBN 3-525-55735-3, € 46,00

Diese Monographie ist eine der ersten geschlechtersensibilisierten Darstellungen, die sich einer nationalprotestantischen, lutherischen Lehrerin, Theologin und Politikerin widmet, das heißt, nicht unter feministischem Postulat eine fortschrittliche oder im weitesten Sinne progressive Persönlichkeit untersucht. Mit Magdalene von Tiling (1874-1974) wird der Focus vor allem auf die 1920er und -30er Jahre der Weimarer Republik und des beginnenden Nationalsozialismus gerichtet. Während Kapitel 1 zunächst kurz die Biographie der als Tochter eines Pfarrers geborenen, konfessionell lutherisch geprägten Baltendeutschen nachzeichnet, widmen sich die Kapitel 2 und 3 vor allem den theologischen Betätigungen Magdalene von Tilings. Das letzte Kapitel zeigt ihr partielles Arrangement mit dem nationalsozialistischen Staat, aber auch ihre Distanzierung von dessen Zielen.

Hatte Magdalene von Tiling zunächst als Lehrerin an einem Oberlyzeum unterrichtet, so wurde sie bald zur Leiterin der Schule. Sie war Mitglied des Gesamtvorstandes der Konferenz von Religionslehrerinnen und von 1919 bis 1939 im Vorstand des Verbandes Evangelischer Religionslehrerinnen. Nach dem Eintritt in die Deutschnationale Volkspartei (DNVP) wurde sie 1921 Abgeordnete im Preußischen Landtag und blieb bis 1930 hauptberuflich Politikerin. 1923 wurde sie erste Vorsitzende des Arbeitsausschusses der Vereinigung Evangelischer Frauenverbände. Seit 1930 gehörte sie dem Reichstag an, verlor jedoch in der NS-Zeit ihre Ämter und wurde ab 1934 Studienrätin in Berlin.

Strebte Magdalene von Tiling in den Jahren 1918 bis 1925 eine "Politisierung" der Frauenbewegung an, so verband sich damit die Forderung an die evangelischen Frauen, das "mütterliche Prinzip" in das öffentliche Bewusstsein zu bringen und zur Wiederherstellung einer Gesellschaft beizutragen, die sie in den verbindlichen Ordnungen bedroht sah. Das moderne Luthertum sollte als ethische Aufgabe die Berufs- und Kulturarbeit erkennen, an der sich die evangelischen Frauen maßgeblich beteiligen sollten. Der Zusammenarbeit mit dem zehn Jahre jüngeren Theologen Friedrich Gogarten wird minutiös nachgegangen (insgesamt vier Mal erwähnt, vgl. 13, 131, 133, 136). Überzeugend kann Gury Schneider-Ludorff nachzeichnen, wie beide voneinander profitiert haben (vgl. 137). In der Theologie der Geschlechterbeziehungen entwickelte

Magdalene von Tiling als Hauptfunktionen der Geschlechter nach christlichem Ideal Führung bzw. Mütterlichkeit. 1931 gründete sie den Arbeitsbund für wissenschaftliche Pädagogik auf reformatorischer Grundlage (178 steht in der Überschrift fälschlich 1930, vgl. aber 190). Auch wenn die Machtergreifung von Magdalene von Tiling zunächst begrüßt wurde, trat sie doch nie in die NSDAP ein und schrieb 1934: "Nicht Staat, Volk, Rasse, Blut sind das Letzte, sondern der Herr ist der erste und der Letzte..." (283).

Gury Schneider-Ludorff würdigt Magdalene von Tiling im Kontext ihrer Zeit und beschreibt präzise ihre Theologie der Geschlechterbeziehungen, die eine Integration der Frauen in die "Volksgemeinschaft" beabsichtigte. Dabei werden nebenbei die Handlungsspielräume einer gebildeten protestantischen Frau, die noch im 19. Jahrhundert geboren wurde, sichtbar. Auch wenn die Staatsauffassung Magdalene von Tilings zu Recht als antimodernistisch, antiliberal und antidemokratisch charakterisiert wird (vgl. 250), zeigt die Darstellung doch auch die erstaunliche Fortschrittlichkeit dieser konservativen Altlutheranerin in Bezug auf die Geschlechterbeziehungen. Unbedingt zuzustimmen ist Schneider-Ludorff in der Annahme, dass die Frauenverbände und ihre Publikationen vor allem für den weiblichen Protestantismus orientierungs- und handlungsleitend waren und deshalb in der Kirchengeschichtsschreibung ihren Platz zu beanspruchen hätten. Ihre Arbeit leistet einen wichtigen Vorstoß in diese Richtung.

Ute Gause (Siegen / Deutschland)

Christine Stuber, *Eine fröhliche Zeit der Erweckung für viele. Quellenstudien zur Erweckungsbewegung in Bern 1818-1831,* (Basler und Berner Studien zur historischen und systematischen Theologie), Peter Lang Verlag: Bern 2000 (2., korr. Auflage 2002), 391 Seiten, ISBN 3-906765-03-2, CHF 86,00 / € 55,20

Fröhlicher Aufbruch unter Frauen? Die Untersuchung zu den Anfängen der Erweckungsbewegung in Bern, mit der Christine Stuber in Bern promovierte, beweist einen aufmerksamen Blick für die Leistungen von Frauen in dieser Aufbruchsbewegung. Zwar wählt die Autorin keinen ausdrücklich feministischen oder geschlechtertheoretischen Ansatz, ist aber selbst bei den Ehefrauen und Töchtern der erweckten Männer um präzisierende Angaben bemüht. Frauen erscheinen auch als Leiterinnen und Gründerinnen von innovativen und effizienten (Missions-)Hilfsvereinen und als geachtete Krankenseelsorgerinnen (darunter auch die Gründerin des Berner Diakonissenhauses, Sophie von Wurstemberger), ferner als Spenderinnen und als Gastgeberinnen für

Versammlungen. So war neben privaten Wohnzimmern von Frauen auch die Ochsenscheuer der "blinden Eisi" (Elisabeth Kohler) ein beliebter Versammlungsort. Besonders stark treten Frauen (Mägde wie auch Patrizierinnen) in der separatistischen Bewegung der "Eglise de Dieu" hervor. Sie werden wie die Männer an ihren Bürgerort ausgewiesen oder als Berner Patrizierinnen gar unter Vormundschaft (!) gestellt. Durch die ergriffene Schilderung von Predigern erfährt man ferner – mit namentlicher Nennung – von der Bekehrung einer Kindsmörderin auf dem Schafott oder einer geheilten Kranken. Schließlich bieten Texte von Frauen reiches Quellenmaterial: die autobiographischen Berichte der Sophie von Wurstemberger und der Pfarrfrau König-Küpfer sowie Briefe Julie Heblers an die Familie Blumhardt (Basler Mission) und die Briefe Esther Burckhardt-Socins in Basel an Julie von Graffenried; dies gilt auch für die Darstellung von Antoine Gallands Theologie die Predigtmitschriften von R. Furer-Küpfer.

Während Frauen bei der Schilderung der sozialen Gestalt der Bewegung viel Raum einnehmen, bezieht sich die (knappere) theologische Darstellung nur auf die (männlichen) Erweckungsprediger. Besonders interessant für die aktuelle feministische Theologie erscheint die "Betrachtung des Leidens Jesu" (253-258), die – der Buchtitel deutet es bereits an – eine "fröhliche" war. So schreibt die Pfarrfrau König-Küpfer im Rückblick um 1870: "Bei vielen Seelen war die Erweckung eine schnelle und fröhliche, sie gelangten bald zu Ruhe und Frieden, währenddem andere grosse Mühe hatten sich zurechtzufinden und gleichsam tief graben mussten bis das Kleinod ihr Eigenthum wurde" (326). Ein solches, doch auch schmerzliches In-sich-gehen der Frauen ihres Missionshilfsvereins beschreibt Julie Hebler 1820 in einem Brief an Frau Blumhardt: "Mehrere, die sich früher für erwekt hielten, gieng auf einmal bey H[errn] Galland geist- und lebenvollen Vorträgen wie neues Licht auf, sie bekamen einen tiefern Blik in ihr Verderben und klagten mir voller Angst ihre Noth" (83). Im theologischen Teil fehlt jedoch ein Brückenschlag zu solchen, sonst reichlich genannten Glaubenserfahrungen von Frauen. Dennoch ist das Buch (mit Register!) aus Frauenperspektive interessant zu lesen.

Doris Brodbeck (Zürich / Schweiz)

Claudia Ulbrich, *Shulamit und Margarete. Macht, Geschlecht und Religion in einer ländlichen Gesellschaft des 18. Jahrhunderts,* (Aschkenas. Zeitschrift für Geschichte und Kultur der Juden, Beiheft 4), Böhlau Verlag: Wien / Köln / Weimar 1999, 348 Seiten, ISBN 3-205-98385-8, € 39,80

Um das Leben mit Grenzen geht es in Ulbrichs Untersuchung: Grenzen zwischen der jüdischen und der christlichen Bevölkerung eines kleinen Dorfes, Grenzen zwischen Frauen und Männern, Grenzen zwischen verschiedenen Ständen und nicht zuletzt zwischen Norm und Realität. Der Mikrokosmos, in dem diese Grenzen ausgelotet werden, ist Steinbiedersdorf (heute: Pontpierre) in Lothringen, gelegen im deutsch-französischen Grenzgebiet. Es geht um ein gemischtreligiöses Dorf, der Landesherr war protestantisch, die Mehrheit der Bevölkerung katholisch, eine relativ bedeutende Minderheit von 18% jüdisch. Aufgrund einer ausgezeichneten Quellenlage ist eine detaillierte Beschreibung der dörflichen Lebenswelt möglich, die durch Ulbrichs anthropologischen Ansatz geradezu paradigmatischen Charakter gewinnt.

Ausgangspunkt der Studie sind "biographische Rekonstruktionen" der Lebenswelten christlicher und jüdischer Frauen, von der Meiersfrau und der katholischen Pfarrhaushälterin bis zur wohlhabenden jüdischen Witwe und ihrer Magd. Genauere Konturen erhalten die Biographien durch ihre präzise Verortung im weiteren sozioökonomischen, politisch-administrativen und kulturellen Rahmen der Dorfgesellschaft, auf den Ulbrich jeweils ausführlich eingeht, so dass der Blick auch über die Grenzen des Dorfes hinaus gelenkt wird. Deutlich wird dabei, welch große Vielfalt an Handlungsmöglichkeiten die Frauen ungeachtet gegenläufiger normativer Vorgaben wahrnahmen und wie differenziert die Frage nach den "Grenzen" – zwischen den Geschlechtern, den Ständen, den Religionen – zu beantworten ist.

Ulbrich versteht Religion als kulturelles Phänomen, das für das Verhalten und die Selbst- und Weltdeutung der Menschen konstitutiv ist. Die Institutionen Kirche und Synagoge sind dabei Fixpunkte, die für alle Dorfbewohner eine zentrale Rolle spielen, deren normierende Funktion aber nicht überschätzt werden darf. Das religiöse Leben der katholischen Dorfbevölkerung realisierte sich in einer großen Variationsbreite: Neben offiziellen kirchlichen Veranstaltungen (Gottesdiensten, Prozessionen) waren vor allem die verschiedenen Formen der Volksfrömmigkeit und des Brauchtums, besonders im Zusammenhang mit Eheanbahnung, Schwangerschaft und Geburt, von Bedeutung. Die praktizierte Religion sprengte dabei häufig die Grenzen, die durch die kirchliche Obrigkeit gesetzt wurden. Auf andere Weise bieten die Verhältnisse in der jüdischen

Gemeinde Beispiele für Grenzüberschreitungen: Der Vorsteher der Synagoge und seine Frau gehörten zu den Honoratioren des Dorfes, ihr großes Haus war gleichermaßen soziales wie religiöses Zentrum der Gemeinde und insofern ein "öffentlicher" Ort, was vor dem Hintergrund, dass der Talmud das "Haus" als den spezifisch weiblichen Lebensbereich schlechthin idealisiert und die jüdischen Frauen engen religiösen Normen unterworfen waren, besonders bemerkenswert ist. Das Verhältnis zwischen katholischer und jüdischer Bevölkerung war in Steinbiedersdorf nicht anders als sonst in Mitteleuropa von Ungleichheiten und Animositäten geprägt. Ulbrich stellt allerdings heraus, dass die Menschen in Steinbiedersdorf zwar nicht konfliktfrei, aber konfliktfähig waren und damit in der Lage, mit den Normen und Institutionen, in und mit denen sie lebten, souverän umzugehen, sie je nach Bedarf zu stabilisieren oder zu verändern. Diese Konfliktfähigkeit bestimmte auch die christlich-jüdische Koexistenz. Die jüdische Bevölkerung lebte nicht im Ghetto, sondern in enger räumlicher Nachbarschaft zur christlichen, was einerseits die Differenzen um so deutlicher machen musste, andererseits zu einem vergleichsweise unbefangenen nachbarlichen Umgang miteinander beitrug. Bei aller Ungleichheit gab es daher vielfältige positive Beziehungen: geschäftliche Verbindungen, pragmatische Nachbarschaftshilfe, bis hin zur Gastfreundschaft und Tischgemeinschaft.

Dass die Einsicht in dieses eigentlich naheliegende konfliktfähige Miteinander von jüdischen und christlichen Männern und Frauen und die dabei gegebenen Grenzüberschreitungen zu den wichtigen Erkenntnissen gehört, die Ulbrichs Studie vermittelt, verweist über den Einzelfall hinaus auf die Voraussetzungen einer Historiographie des jüdisch-christlichen Verhältnisses überhaupt. "Shulamit und Margarete", die beiden Frauennamen aus Paul Celans "Todesfuge", stehen nicht nur für verschiedene Kulturen, sondern auch dafür, dass das Wissen um den Holocaust immer unseren Blick auf die jüdisch-christliche Geschichte mitbestimmt, auch den Blick auf ein kleines lothringisches Dorf im 18. Jahrhundert.

Anne Conrad (Hamburg-Köln / Deutschland)

II.3 Systematische Theologie, Ökumene und Interreligiöser Dialog

Marcella Althaus-Reid, *Indecent Theology: Theological Perversions in Sex, Gender and Politics,* Routledge: London / New York 2000, 217 Seiten, ISBN 0-415-23604-5, £14.99

Marcella Althaus-Reids *Indecent Theology* beginnt auf den Straßen von Buenos Aires – dort, wo Zitronenverkäuferinnen ihre Früchte verkaufen; dort, wo sich der Geruch der Zitronen mit dem Geruch der Frauen vermischt, die in materieller Armut leben und keine Unterwäsche tragen; dort, wo postmoderne Einsichten erlangt werden, ohne dass je Lyotard gelesen worden wäre; dort, wo die Nähe von Sexualität und Ökonomie ganz offensichtlich wird; dort, wo soziale, göttliche und ökonomische Interaktionen und deren moralische Bewertung neu und anders geordnet werden.

Das Bild der Zitronenverkäuferinnen zieht sich als lebendige Metapher wie ein roter Faden durch die theologischen Reflexionen der argentinischen Theologin, die ihre Arbeit sowohl als Weiterführung als auch als Unterbrechung und Zerrüttung klassischer Befreiungstheologie versteht. Gleichzeitig illustriert das Bild der Zitronenverkäuferinnen den zentralen Appell der Autorin an ihre Kolleginnen: Feministische Theologinnen, so Althaus-Reid, mögen ihre Unterwäsche ausziehen und ihre theoretischen, theologischen und ökonomischen Analysen mit dem Geruch ihrer Sexualität vermischen! So werde eine Theologie entstehen, die den Reichtum armer Frauen ohne Unterwäsche nicht länger ignoriert, die eigene sexuelle und politische Praxis radikal ernst nimmt und die herrschende moralische Ordnung samt heterosexueller Wirklichkeitskonstruktion zu dekonstruieren vermag.

Mit spürbarer Leidenschaft widmet sich Marcella Althaus-Reid auch selbst diesem Projekt. Ihre *Indecent Theology*, ihre "unanständige Theologie", die sie an der Schnittstelle von "queer"-Denken und Befreiungstheologie ansiedelt und unter Bezugnahme auf postkoloniale, marxistische, feministische und systematisch-theologische Arbeiten weiter entwickelt, ist eine radikale Theologie des Begehrens, die ihren Ausgangspunkt in scheinbar unanständigem sexuellen und politischen Handeln sucht.

Nach einem kritischen Überblick über Erkenntnisse und Defizite bisheriger (feministisch-)befreiungstheologischer Arbeiten wird am Beispiel von Maria und der Entwicklung einer "unanständigen Mariologie" die Methode des "indecenting" vorgestellt und schließlich u.a. anhand von Vorstellungen eines bisexuellen Christus die Verbindung zwischen Lust und Auferstehung aufgezeigt. "Sexualitäts-Geschichten" aus dem Alltag von Armen widerlegen die scheinbare Bedeutungslosigkeit bzw. Nachrangigkeit von Sexualität für Menschen der sogenannten Dritten Welt und machen deren politische und theologische Sprengkraft deutlich. Abschließend werden ökonomische Globalisierungsprozesse aus der Perspektive einer sexuellen, unanständigen Theologie in den Blick genommen.

Dabei ist es nicht immer einfach, dem Gedankengang der Autorin zu folgen. Die Vielzahl an Geschichten, Bildern, Theorien, der ungewohnte Blick und die – für mich – bisher kaum gedachten, möglichen theologischen Schlüsse provozieren zum Nachdenken. Viele Passagen musste ich mehrfach lesen, um sie zu verstehen.

Die wirkliche Herausforderung jedoch liegt wie so oft in der Antwort auf die Frage nach der Umsetzung, die im Buch selbst unbeantwortet bleibt. Theologie treiben ohne Unterwäsche – wie würde das aussehen, wie kann das gehen und was könnte das konkret bedeuten für unsere Arbeit an Schreibtischen, Rednerinnenpulten, in Universitäten, Pfarr- und Gemeindeämtern und an vielen anderen Orten?

Michaela Moser (Wien / Österreich)

Sybille Becker / Gesine Kleinschmit / Ilona Nord / Gury Schneider-Ludorff (Hg.), *Das Geschlecht der Zukunft. Frauenemanzipation und Geschlechtervielfalt*, Kohlhammer: Stuttgart 2000, 182 Seiten, ISBN 3-17-016612-3, € 19,00

Die Generation der nach 1960 geborenen Töchter mischt sich konstruktiv ein in die feministische Debatte – nicht mit einer Verabschiedung des Feminismus, sondern mit lohnenswerten Beiträgen für ein zukunftsgerichtetes Gespräch. Zusammen mit Frauen aus der ersten und zweiten Generation der neuen Frauenbewegung stellen sich junge Wissenschaftlerinnen mit einem Beitrag ihres Denkens und Forschens der Frage nach der Zukunftsfähigkeit feministischen Engagements. Der Sammelband *Das Geschlecht der Zukunft* dokumentiert zum größten Teil Beiträge, die für die neunte Ringvorlesung an der Frankfurter Johann Wolfgang Goethe-Universität mit dem Titel "(Post-)Feminismus? Zwischen Frauenbewegung und Geschlechterkonstruktion" im Sommer 1998 entstanden. Die Themen bewegen sich quer durch die geisteswissenschaftlichen Fächer. Was sie verbindet, ist das gemeinsame Interesse, in der "Postmoderne" und unter den Bedingungen der Dekonstruktion des Subjektes und der Kategorie "Frau" feministisch zu denken. Deutlich wird bei allen Beiträgen der selbstkritische Impetus, mit dem das feministische Erbe gemustert wird, und eine Offenheit, Theorieentwicklungen aus anderen Bereichen zu prüfen und Ambivalenzen nicht um jeden Preis aufzulösen. Die Herausgeberinnen beanspruchen nicht, eine umfassende Antwort zu haben, sondern präsentieren neun allesamt lesenswerte und gehaltvolle Einzelbeiträge.

Den Anfang machen die Soziologin *Ute Gerhardt* und die Philosophin *Cornelia Klinger* mit einem kritisch-analytischen Blick auf "alte", aber gegenwärtig durchaus noch wirkkräftige Wirklichkeiten. *Gerhardts* Resümee bleibt verhalten: der unbestreitbare Wandel und das Erreichen von Etappenzielen wie dem

Zugang von Frauen zu Wissenschaft und Bildung habe noch nicht zur Beseitigung der strukturellen und sozialen Frauendiskriminierung in Kernbereichen und in den Zentren der Macht geführt. Der Geschlechterkonflikt habe sich durch das gewachsene Selbstbewusstsein und die neuen Lebensentwürfe der "Töchter" ohne entsprechend äquivalenter Entwicklung auf Seiten der Söhne eher verschärft. *Klingers* luzide Darstellung der Bedeutung der bürgerlichen Geschlechterordnung für die Herausbildung der Moderne schließt ähnlich skeptisch. Der Bereich des Subjektiven, dem Weiblichkeit in negativer wie in positiver Einschätzung zugeordnet werde, diene in seiner wachsenden Bedeutung für die Einzelnen faktisch zur Kompensation der Modernisierungsdefizite der modernen Gesellschaft (48f.).

Der Pädagogin *Annemarie Prengel* gelingt mittels perspektivitätstheoretischer Überlegungen ein sehr konstruktiver Blick auf "Interpretationen der Geschlechterverhältnisse" (139). Sie zeigt auf, wie die Kategorien "natürlich", "sozialisiert" und "konstruiert" aufeinander bezogen werden könnten, ohne sie in ihrer jeweiligen Geltung aufzulösen. *Prengel* schlägt vor, evolutionsbiologische Perspektiven, die von feministischer Seite bisher kaum ernsthaft zur Kenntnis genommen wurden, verstärkt wahrzunehmen.

Neue Wirklichkeiten, auch in alten und ältesten Texten, scheinen in den folgenden Beiträgen durch: In *Lena Lindhoffs* aufschlussreicher Analyse von Ingeborg Bachmanns und Gertrude Steins Konzept von Autorschaft, die *Lindhoff* zu einem Plädoyer für die feministische Besetzung des Konzepts der Androgynie führt; in *Ulrike Bails* spannender rezeptionsästhetischer Auslegung von Psalm 55 als literarischer Repräsentation von Vergewaltigung, die dem Schweigen der Gewalt eine weibliche Gegensprache abgewinnt.

Neue Wirklichkeiten wollen auch die anderen Autorinnen aufzeigen: die Theologin *Gesine Kleinschmit* mit ihrem theologisch dringend notwendigen und spannenden Versuch, den Sündenbegriff nach Foucault und Butler "poststrukturell" feministisch weiterzudiskutieren und die Politikwissenschaftlerin Antje Schrupp mit dem Vorschlag, ausgehend von *Lisa Muraros* Ansatz des "weiblichen Subjektivismus" politisches Handeln nach dem Ende des autonomen politischen Subjekts zu denken.

Die Philosophin *Andrea Günter* wendet sich gegen die Gleichsetzung der Rede vom Ende des Patriarchats mit dem Postfeminismus. Durchaus Feminismus-kritisch plädiert sie dafür, dass frauenbewegte Politik aus "Liebe der Frauen zur Freiheit" (154), jedoch nicht als Entgegensetzung zum Patriarchat erfolgen müsse. Es gehe um eine Praxis, die dem Konflikt nicht ausweiche, sondern Autorität übernehme und auf beziehungsstiftende Vermittlung in Differenzen und Konflikten setze.

Den Abschluss macht die Theologin *Helga Kuhlmann* mit einem anregenden Beitrag zur Auferstehungsverheißung, in dem sie – über die bisherige feministische kritische Behandlung der Rede von der Auferstehung der Toten hinausgehend – die paulinische Rede von der Auferstehung der Toten in 1 Kor 15 als "ver-rückte" Verheißung (161) für Frauen und Männer entdeckt.

Elisabeth Hartlieb (Marburg / Deutschland)

Sólveig Anna Bóasdóttir, *Violence, Power, and Justice: A Feminist Contribution to Christian Sexual Ethics*, (Uppsala Studies in Social Ethics 20), Uppsala Universitiy Press: Uppsala 1998, 202 Seiten, ISBN 91-554-4165-3, 235 SEK

Mit ihrer Dissertation "Gewalt, Macht und Gerechtigkeit. Ein feministischer Beitrag zur christlichen Sexualethik" legt Bóasdóttir einen sozialethischen Entwurf aus feministischer Perspektive zur Thematik "Gewalt gegen Frauen" vor.

In ihrer Analyse von männlicher Gewalt in Beziehungen verbindet die Autorin feministische Theorien zur Funktion männlicher Gewalt in patriarchalen Gesellschaften mit Theorien zu Macht und zur sozialen Konstruktion von Sexualität sowie Theorien über die Institution der Ehe. Dies führt die Autorin zu einer Kritik der Ehe als Institution, die nicht sicher für Frauen ist, da sie die patriarchalen Machtstrukturen zwischen den Geschlechtern reproduziert und bestätigt. Für eine angemessene christliche Sexualethik entwickelt Bóasdóttir vier Kriterien: die Berücksichtigung von Erfahrungen und deren Historizität und Kontextualität, die Förderung der Gleichheit der Geschlechter, die kritische Sichtung biblischer und christlicher Traditionen sowie die Integration von Kenntnissen aus feministisch orientierten Sozialwissenschaften. Diese Kriterien sind Grundlage ihrer Untersuchung der ethischen Entwürfe von Helmut Thielecke, James Nelson und Bernhard Häring, insbesondere deren Verständnis von Ehe, Sexualität und der menschlichen Natur. Der Hauptpunkt der Kritik der Autorin ist, dass der zumeist optimistische Blick auf menschliches Sein und menschliche Sexualität die fehlende Reflexion des Problems männlicher Gewalt gegenüber Frauen zum Teil erklärt.

Unter der Überschrift "Toward Justice in Intimate Relationships" (175) stellt Bóasdóttir im letzten Kapitel ihren eigenen Ansatz vor, in dem der Begriff "Gerechtigkeit" im Mittelpunkt steht: Ihr Ausgangspunkt ist eine Analyse der Gewalterfahrungen von Frauen, die sie nicht als absolute und zu verallgemeinernde, sondern als unterschiedliche und konkrete Erfahrungen in den Blick nimmt. Männliche Gewalt gegen Frauen in Beziehungen benennt sie als ein

Problem der (Un-)Gerechtigkeit. "Ich verstehe Gerechtigkeit eher als einen 'neuen Anfang' und eine Vision denn als perfekte Gerechtigkeit im Sinne einer Befreiung von Zwang und Unterdrückung" (182). Visionen von Gerechtigkeit als ein Akt des Widerstandes, des Kampfes und des Protestes gegen Ungerechtigkeit sind ihrer Meinung nach eingebunden in ihren historischen und sozialen Kontext. Männliche Gewalt ist aus feministischer Perspektive in ihrer Verknüpfung mit Macht und Sexualität zu erfassen: "Meine Schlussfolgerung ist, dass es sich bei männlicher Gewalt gegen Frauen nicht um zufällige individuelle moralische Vergehen handelt, sondern um soziale Praxis in patriarchalen Gesellschaften" (193).

Bóasdóttir entwickelt somit ausgehend von Erfahrungen der Ungerechtigkeit in Beziehungen eine kritische Theorie männlicher Macht, der sozialen Konstruktion von Sexualität und von männlicher Gewalt. Ein derartiger Ansatz erweist sich als notwendig, wenn christliche Sexualethik fähig sein will, einen moralischen Schutz für Frauen zu bieten.

Insgesamt stellt die Autorin in ihrer Dissertation einen eigenen sexualethischen Ansatz vor, den sie stringent in der Auseinandersetzung mit feministischen Theorien und ethischen Modellen entwickelt. Durch die Einführung des Begriffs "Gerechtigkeit" in die Thematik der Gewalt gegen Frauen gelingt Bóasdóttir eine sozialethische Analyse, welche die gesellschaftlichen Machtstrukturen berücksichtigt, die männliche Gewalt möglich machen. Besonders lesenswert ist ihre Analyse der Verknüpfungen von Gewalt, patriarchaler Macht und sozialer Konstruktion von Sexualität. Es ist eine Arbeit, die für die Forschung zu den theologischen Aspekten der "Gewalt gegen Frauen" neue Impulse bringt!

Stephanie Lüders (Dortmund / Deutschland)

Mary C. Grey, *The outrageous Pursuit of Hope. Prophetic Dreams for the Twenty-first Century* (= L'outrageante quête de l'espérance. Rêves prophétiques pour le XXIe siècle) Darton, Longman and Todd: Londres 2000, 116 pages, ISBN 0-232-52319-3, £9.95

En une centaine de pages, Mary Grey nous présente les sources immensément riches d'une théologie d'avenir, nous encourageant avec ferveur, en ce nouveau millénaire qui ravive plus que jamais le motif de l'apocalypse, à une nouvelle rencontre avec l'espérance, la prophétie et la spiritualité. Mary Grey n'eût sans doute pas cru, à la publication de son livre, que son motif fût d'une actualité aussi imminente, que la violence et la menace pour l'humanité, hommes, femmes et enfants, seraient plus que jamais dans l'air du temps, après les événements du 11 septembre.

Elle introduit son sujet par une présentation de la vision prophétique d'Isaïe. Alors, pourquoi ce choix? Pourquoi le prophète juif Isaïe? Isaïe vivait à une époque où le désastre menaçait, où le danger était sans cesse imminent. Quand Israël fut condamné à vivre en captivité, après la destruction du temple, une des missions prophétiques d'Isaïe fut de garder l'espoir vivant dans l'ombre de l'oppression. Isaïe transmet une spiritualité de l'espérance enracinée dans l'histoire, une spiritualité qui, combattant la culture de l'assimilation, donne un sens et une signification à la vie de l'homme. Il met le doigt sur une attitude de résistance intérieure, et fait comprendre que la mémoire du passé, tant des jours de liberté que des jours d'oppression, peut être une «mémoire dangereuse», comme l'appelle Mary Grey. Elle cite les notions de colère et de compassion développées par Isaïe, comme sources de cette attitude. Isaïe parle de colère pieuse et d'amour, de sein maternel compatissant, en usant de représentations symboliques bienveillantes à l'égard des femmes, mais aussi sexistes. Mary Grey découvre dans le livre d'Isaïe les semences d'une contre-culture féminine, le germe d'un imaginaire féminin, les métaphores d'une culture maternelle et florissante, d'une culture centrée sur la naissance, la croissance et la créativité. Une spiritualité de l'espérance se doit d'intégrer ce symbolisme de l'enfantement dans la vie de tous les jours, c'est à la fois une nécessité et un défi à notre ministère et à notre diaconat. Mais à mon avis le livre ne répond pas à la question du comment parvenir à cette intégration. Non plus qu'à celle de l'insensibilité d'Isaïe, comme l'affirme Grey, face à un contexte social vulnérable pour les femmes. Je me demande, par ailleurs, si nous pouvons ignorer les semences de l'espérance, dont tout le livre d'Isaïe est profondément pénétré, même s'il était vrai qu'Isaïe est insensible à la situation des femmes. Et si nous pouvons, à l'inverse, construire sur cette semence, sur cette croissance, une imagerie procréatrice à transmettre aux femmes? Mary Grey soulève cependant une question importante: comment ouvrir une brèche dans la culture européenne au niveau de l'imagination? Grey prétend que les gens ne recherchent pas la justice, mais une vie qui les satisfasse, une vie de nature plus introspective. Cela ne fait-il pas protester l'Esprit saint à cor et à cri au nom des disparus, réduits au silence?

Le discours d'Isaïe sur l'enfantement est transformé en langage du Saint-Esprit à la recherche des fissures de la culture pour y ensemencer de nouvelles possibilités. Mary Grey voit aussi cette brèche dans une perspective politique cosmopolite: le monde tel que nous le voyons est formé de communautés s'entravant mutuellement au lieu d'entrer en relation. Restaurer des liens brisés est une tâche complexe et ne peut réussir que si la douleur remémorée est un deuil commun exprimé par toute la communauté à travers certains rituels, et que s'il est partagé par un groupe solidaire dans la responsabilité. Cette image de communautés liées par des rapports contredit celle de l'illustration en couverture montrant une jeune femme assise une lyre à la main, les yeux bandés sur un globe, qui symbolise bien un monde dénué d'espérance.

The Outrageous Pursuit of Hope est un ouvrage dense, inspirant et idéaliste. Il comporte des idées nouvelles et anciennes, qu'il serait bon de mettre en pratique, et que toute personne ayant mission de direction spirituelle pourrait fort bien mettre à profit.

Barbara Leijnse (Arnhem / Pays-Bas)

Rita M. Gross / Rosemary Radford Ruether, *Religious Feminism and the Future of the Planet. A Buddhist – Christian Conversation*, Continuum: London / New York 2001, 229 pages, ISBN 0-8264-1302-1, $ 22.95

This book considers feminist and ecological aspects of interreligious dialogue. The authors are open-minded enough to show how essential one's life-story is to a feminist inter-religious dialogue. Both give personal accounts of their religious life-stories. Gross was raised as a strict Lutheran in a farming area in the Mid West of the U.S.A.. Her study of Latin opened the way to further education and led her into an academic and religious odyssey which took her through feminist consciousness, philosophy, conversion to Judaism, studies in Sanskrit and pioneering studies in women and religions, to end in practising Vajrayana Buddhism. She regards meditation and the dharma as sources that have helped her survive the difficulties she has faced. As Buddhist, she offers a feminist critique of Buddhist patriarchy.

Ruether stresses the religiously plural and intercultural perspective of her North-American family background. Defending pluralism in Catholicism, she was active in the Civil Rights and Peace Movements. The prophetic mode of spirituality shaped her liberation theology and led her to Black and Latin American liberation theologies, anti-Semitism and ecology. Via involvement in Middle East issues she moved on to Christian-Muslim dialogue, and then further to a dialogue with Buddhists. Also quite an odyssey! I found this feminist approach of telling religious life-stories a key to understanding the rest of the book.

The book is based on friendly conversations between Gross and Ruether that took place at a weekend workshop in 1999. They have extended their papers, but the flavour of oral conversations is still present in the book, and makes it easy to read. One may choose from the different parts: "What Is Most Problematic about My Tradition?", "What Is Most Liberating about My Tradition?" "What Is Most Inspiring for Me about the Other Tradition?" or the final outlook, "Religious Feminism and the Future of the Planet" (the title of the book). However, the relaxed tone between the authors does not lead them to avoid difficult questions.

Difficult questions are addressed head on. Inter-religious dialogue is "threatening to many adherents of Semitic monotheistic religions: that have connected the oneness of the (male patriarchal) God with an exclusivist view of religious truth" (5). In Asia, however, it is common for people to adopt plural religious identities, depending on context. The question of feminism in religion adds to the difficulties, but since the world has always been religiously diverse with tensions and hostility between religions, it is all more important engage in dialogue. One of the great moral issues of our time is to find viable ways of accepting and appreciating religious diversity. Gross recommends comparative studies as well as dialogue. Both Ruether and Gross stand firm against religiously based discrimination against women. Gross stresses empathy as an important critical tool in order not to create more tension between different religious communities.

Both authors struggle to differentiate culture, gender and religion. Gross pinpoints the relative lack of female gurus, which to her is the major deficiency in Buddhism. In the essay "Oppressive Aspects of Christianity" Ruether critiques a patriarchal reading of Christian symbols in an excellent historical overview of Christian doctrinal development. Gross comments that Buddhist feminists do not need to deal with "fall and redemption, sin and grace or the need for vicarious divine atonement because of the deity's displeasure with human beings…At this point I also sense the greatest difference between Christian and Buddhist thought" (104). To me Gross seems less eager than Ruether to seek common ground. In search of an ethic for an ecological sustainability, Gross discusses "views and practices that are deeply transformative when personally internalised." Her feminist anger has been transformed through Buddhist meditation. Ruether is more optimistic. She hopes that the world's religions may have a key role in the process of sustaining the planet if they are able to reach a new sense of mutual respect and solidarity with another.

Feminist voices in inter-religious dialogue are rare, so this book is valuable. Some basic knowledge of Buddhism is helpful, but not a prerequisite to enjoy the book.

Lise Tostrup Setek (Oslo / Norway)

Andrea Günter, *Die weibliche Hoffnung der Welt. Die Bedeutung des Geborenseins und der Sinn der Geschlechterdifferenz*, Chr. Kaiser / Gütersloher Verlagshaus: Gütersloh 2000, 128 Seiten, ISBN 3-579-02667-4, DM 38,00 / CHF 36,00

Dieses schmale Buch hat es in sich. Die dichte Gedankenfolge der Philosophin Andrea Günter ist eine anspruchsvolle Lektüre und wirkt durch Originalität zu anhaltender Beschäftigung mit ihren Denkwegen. In sechs selbständigen und zugleich inhaltlich eng verbundenen Kapiteln zeigt sie eindrucksvoll die Essenz einer befreiten weiblichen Existenz und die daraus entspringende neue Interpretation aller ihrer Bezüge zur Welt. Sie entfaltet ein Verständnis von Weiblichkeit als geschichtsmächtiger Größe jenseits patriarchaler und konventioneller Konzepte, das Weltgestaltung durch das Sprechen und Handeln von Frauen als eine Hoffnung erweckende Realität glaubhaft macht.

Ihr Ansatz ruht auf drei Säulen: Da ist zunächst Hannah Arendts grundlegender Gedanke der Gebürtigkeit, womit die Einzigartigkeit und zugleich die Pluralität der Menschen gegeben ist sowie das stets sich ereignende Wunder eines Neuanfangs in der Geschichte durch menschliches Handeln. Dazu kommt Andrea Günters an Luisa Muraro anknüpfendes Verständnis von der Ordnung des Geborenseins durch eine Frau und damit des mütterlichen Prinzips, der weiblichen Genealogie, welches die Autorin bereits in früheren Arbeiten entfaltet hat. Hier beginnt sie, es biblisch-theologisch zu verankern. Die Bibel war bei den Denkerinnen von Mailand und Verona, abgesehen von der Bedeutung der Ruth-Geschichte, bisher keine wesentliche Bezugsgröße. Die Schöpfungserzählungen, die Bedeutung der biblischen Genealogien und des Zusammenlebens in Generationen, die selbstständig handelnden "Gottesstreiterinnen" (Irmgard Fischer) der Schrift und weitere jüdisch-christliche Denkfiguren (Walter Benjamin, Augustin) bilden nun den dritten Teil des Günterschen Fundaments.

Aus den dicht geschriebenen Kapiteln mit ihren zahlreichen erhellenden Einzelheiten kann hier nur weniges angedeutet werden. Wesentlich ist das Verständnis der eigenen Existenz als Töchter – und Söhne – einer Mutter, nicht die eigene Generativität. Ein auch feministisch weiter verbreiteter Mutterhass ist eine Falle des Patriarchats. Doch ist die Konflikthaftigkeit der Beziehung zur eigenen Mutter ein wichtiges Element ihrer Lebendigkeit. Die Differenzierung der eigenen Geschlechtlichkeit wird zuerst hier erfahren, nicht in der Paarbeziehung, bedeutet also, Tochter oder Sohn zu sein. Genau dieses Austragen von Konflikten, das Hadern, wird von Günter (mit Letizia Tomassone) als Kernpunkt einer eigenständigen Beziehung von Frauen zu Gott beschrieben. Daher ist das beliebte Bild von Gott als Mutter kritisch zu sehen, wenn es nichts anderes bedeutet als Fürsorge, Beschwichtigung und Geborgenheit. Die Gotteskämpfe von Frauen in der Bibel (es gibt mehr davon, als Günter meint) und in der Gegenwart sind Quelle der Autorität von Frauen. Dabei ist die allen gemeinsame Töchterlichkeit das aktive Element. Tochter zu sein bedeutet: eigener Wille, Entscheidungsfreudigkeit gegenüber Eltern und Ehemännern, Aktivität zur Veränderung der Umstände und Zeitläufte, eigene Beziehungen zu anderen Frauen, zu Gott, zur Frage, ob sie selbst Mutter werden will. Somit scheinen viele Wunder der Neuanfänge in der/einer Geschichte seit biblischen Zeiten von eigenwilligen Töchtern bewirkt zu werden.

Insgesamt ist Andrea Günters Buch ein fesselndes Zeugnis jener bevorzugten Art des Forschens, das Hannah Arendt "Denken ohne Geländer" genannt hat. Der letzte Abschnitt über die Sprache und Autorität von Frauen sollte wegen seiner Ermunterung zum freien, selbstverantworteten Wort eine Pflichtlektüre für alle Predigerinnen sein: Denn es ist "eine Wohltat für die Mitwelt, wenn eine Frau von sich selbst ausgehend spricht" (121), "die den Horizont der weiblichen Freiheit und der leidenschaftlichen Beziehung der Frauen mit Gott spürbar werden läßt" (122).

Marlene Crüsemann (Bielefeld / Deutschland)

Birgit Heller, *Heilige Mutter und Gottesbraut. Frauenemanzipation im modernen Hinduismus*, (Frauenforschung 39), Milena Verlag: Wien 1999, 367 pages, ISBN 3-85286-074-1, ATS 348,00 / DM 50,00

In this study of two modern Hindu movements, Heller explores several questions: How do women relate to their own tradition? What status do Hindu women have in modern Hindu movements? What images of women are transmitted and what self-esteem do women have? Do modern Hindu women have a critical attitude towards their own tradition? How do they relate to their androcentric inheritance? What potential for change could Hinduism deliver for women? Beginning from these questions, Heller describes the *Rāmakrsna* and the *Viśva Dharma* movements within modern Hinduism. Both recognise women as official members and allow them leadership roles.

Before considering these movements, Heller discusses traditional *Brahmanic*-Hindu conceptions of femininity, and their predominantly negative view of women. Women are seen as not autonomous; all their roles are conceived in relation to men; traditionally women have been excluded from religious education and religious rituals. Heller also sketches some of the characteristics of the Indian women's movement. There are many organisations with different ideologies, strategies and goals, but almost no communication or cooperation between them.

Heller then moves on to explore the origins of the *Rāmakrsna* movement, describing the life and teachings of its nineteenth-century founder *Rāmakrsna* before tracing the development of the movement, strongly influenced by *Vivekānanda*, *Rāmakrsna*'s first disciple, and sketching some of the movement's characteristics, organisation and membership. Moving on to the women's history of the movement, Heller considers *Sāradā Devi*, the wife of the founder, who was seen as the ideal or Holy mother, and by the end of her life had many disciples. A further important factor in establishing a women's branch in the movement was the large number of *Vivekānanda*'s female students in the West, some of whom accompanied him to India and remained there. However, although the plans date from much earlier, it was only in 1954 that the *Srí Sāradā Math*, the order for women, was established. In a second part Heller describes the *Rāmakrsna* movement's attitude to women and considers the ideal-typical roles expected of women and the self-esteem of women of the *Srí Sāradā Math*.

Heller's description of the *Viśva Dharma* movement is structured in the same way. She examines the life of its founder, *Basava*, who lived in the twelfth century, sketches the characteristics of the movement, its revival in the twentieth century and its organisation and membership. She then describes the women's history of the movement, portraying significant women at the time of its foundation and through its history, and the role of *Māte Mahādēvi*, its present leader, who established an āśrama for women. Again she discusses the attitude to women held by the founders of the movement, the ideal-typical roles expected of women and the self-esteem of women within the *Viśva Dharma* movement.

Heller draws on the questions thrown up by the first part of her study to reflect systematically on the two Hindu women's organisations. She describes similarities and differences in the conception of femininity of traditional Brahmanic-Hinduism and the two modern Hindu movements and asks whether there has been any change in the status of women, and whether this is the same for both movements. Finally, Heller discusses the movements in the light of feminist religious studies, considering the legitimacy of women's emancipation by male authorities and raising questions about the equality of the sexes, sexuality and spirituality and God and gender.

Heller has written a thoroughgoing study, in which she presents and analyses new material, and which makes an interesting contribution to the field of Hindu women's studies.

Christa Anbeek (Utrecht / The Netherlands)

Susanne Hennecke, *Der vergessene Schleier. Ein theologisches Gespräch zwischen Luce Irigaray und Karl Barth*, Chr. Kaiser / Gütersloher Verlagshaus: Gütersloh 2001, 298 Seiten, ISBN 3-579-05319-1, DM 78,00

Anne Claire Mulder, *Divine Flesh, Embodied Word: Incarnation as a hermeneutical key to a feminist theologian's reading of Luce Irigaray's work*, Eigenverlag: Amsterdam 2000, 389 Seiten, ISBN 90-9013830-7, NLG 50,00

Die französische Philosophin Luce Irigaray macht in ihren Texten nicht nur einen Durchgang durch die philosophischen und psychoanalytischen, sondern auch durch die theologischen Traditionen des Abendlandes, um diese zu ihrem Beitrag zur Geschlechterdifferenz zu befragen. Ihr kritischer Rekurs auf jüdisch-christliche und religionsphilosophische Aspekte ist bislang kaum beachtet. Die beiden in den Niederlanden arbeitenden Theologinnen Susanne Hennecke und Anne Claire Mulder haben die Rezeption abendländischer Theologumena durch Irigaray aufgearbeitet und ihre Bedeutung für die feministische Theologie herausgestellt.

Für *Anne Claire Mulder* ist "Inkarnation" der theologische Schlüsselbegriff, der die christliche Beziehung zwischen Gott und den Menschen benennt. Durch ihn werden Mensch- und Gottsein, Immanenz und Transzendenz, Materie und Geist, Körper und Wort, Ich und der Andere sowie – und diese Seite arbeitet Mulder anhand der Texte Irigarays heraus – Frauen und das Göttliche ebenso wie das Mütterliche und Transzendenz miteinander verbunden. Mulder betont die politische Seite des Ansatzes von Irigaray, in dem es wesentlich darum geht, den Muttermord der patriarchalen Gottes-Kultur in Form einer immanenten Transzendenz zu überwinden. Dazu vollzieht Mulder anhand der psychoanalytischen Kulturtheorie (Freud/Lacan) die Dimension des Muttermordes nach und untersucht dessen Auswirkungen im Prolog des Johannes-Evangeliums, im Glaubensbekenntnis, im Dogma von Chalcedon und in der Eucharistiefeier. Denn auch bei der Psychoanalyse handelt es sich um eine Erzählung über die Wechselbeziehungen von Wort und Fleisch, so dass die unterschiedlichen Qualitäten, aber auch die Störungen dieser Beziehung ausdifferenziert und das Göttliche anhand von Irigarays Rekonstruktion für Frauen und das Weibliche geöffnet werden können. Die Bedeutung Gottes für die Frauen wird dabei als politische Funktion (Objektivierung), als transzendenter Horizont der weiblichen Differenz, das heißt, als Beziehung zur göttlichen Andersheit sichtbar, die weibliches Werden als eigenständigen Prozess ansieht: Gott wird als Inkarnation im Menschlichen durch das Weibliche fassbar; zugleich transzendieren sich die Menschen in Form des Göttlichen als Weibliches.

Mulder schließt mit ihrer Arbeit nicht nur eine Lücke in der feministischen Theologie im Hinblick auf die fehlende Rezeption der französischen Differenzdiskussion, sondern auch in der Irigaray-Rezeption im Hinblick auf die christlich-religiöse Dimension der abendländischen patriarchalen Kultur. Inkonsequent erscheint mir jedoch, dass Mulder das Erarbeitete als säkulare und post-theistische Konzeption des Göttlichen bezeichnet. Damit schreibt sie den Dualismus zwischen Immanenz und Transzendenz fort. Denn die Transzendenz des Menschlichen im Göttlichen stellt sich demnach als das Säkulare und Post-Theistische, und das Theistische wiederum als die Inkarnation Gottes im Menschlichen heraus. Vor dem Hintergrund der metaphysischen Tradition – Gott als erste Ursache – leuchtet dies ein. Als Problem der christlichen Tradition erwiese sich demnach nicht der Dualismus zwischen Wort und Fleisch, sondern die Fokussierung auf die Bewegung vom göttlichen Wort zum menschlichen Fleisch bei gleichzeitiger Diskreditierung der Bewegung vom Fleisch zum Wort. Diese Problematisierung stimmt mit wesentlichen Aspekten von Irigarays Kritik und Mulders Analyse überein. Solange dieser Dualismus aber dennoch in Form von "theistisch" – "post-theistisch" reproduziert wird, bleibt die Tür für die Inkarnation des Menschlichen im Göttlichen geschlossen. Zugleich wird der Kreislauf zwischen Wort und Fleisch unterbrochen, vielleicht sogar für Jesus Christus, aber jedenfalls für Frauen. Die Moderne, aber auch der mystische Diskurs scheint diese andere Seite der Inkarnation einzuklagen.

Susanne Hennecke vergleicht in ihrer Doktorarbeit Irigarays Entwürfe mit der Theologie Karl Barths. Anhand der Aspekte "Engel", "Rose", "Dichter",

"Prophet", "Raum" und "Schleier" klärt sie die innere Struktur und Argumentation des Beitrags "Der Glaube selbst", in dem Irigaray das christliche Glaubensbekenntnis sowie die Geschichte der blutflüssigen Frau als weibliche christologische Alternative und als Hoffnungsgeschichte des Bundes Gottes mit den Frauen durcharbeitet. Ferner stellt Hennecke Irigarays Kritik an der für Frauen unzumutbaren Interpretation der Geschlechterdifferenz in der christlichen Tradition vor, durch die die Philosophin zur Anklägerin eines Glaubens wird, der dem weiblichen Geschlecht keinen eigenen christologischen Raum bietet. Barths Theologie wiederum soll diese Tradition verteidigen können, denn bei ihm finden sich Anknüpfungspunkte, um die Rekonstruktion Irigarays als Richtigstellung der christlichen Tradition anzuerkennen. Zudem liefert Barth Kriterien für das Urteil darüber, ob dem Religiösen in Irigarays Text der Status einer Projektion oder einer "wahren Religion" zuzusprechen ist, was die Autorin nach einer ausführlichen Darstellung der Kriterien Barths bejaht.

Henneckes Interpretation und Vergleich haben mich immer wieder fasziniert und überzeugt. Seltsam bleibt jedoch der Schluss: Das Nachvollziehen des differenzierten und diffizilen Einschreibens der sexuellen Differenz in die christliche Theologie im Sinne der Suche nach einem Glauben, der Frauen einen christologischen Raum und die Zeit einer weiblichen Offenbarung bietet, wie Irigaray es auf beeindruckende Weise vornimmt, endet mit dem Credo Henneckes an "Gott den Vater, Jesus Christus und den Heiligen Geist" (293). So bleibt am Ende doch wieder die männliche Trinität Dreh- und Angelpunkt der christlichen Glaubensaussage. Da hilft es auch nicht, zwischendurch die Männlichkeit Jesu für unwichtig zu erklären, wenn die blutflüssige Frau am Ende wieder hinter dem Schleier, den sie lüften sollte, verschwindet, allen Engeln und Rosen, Dichtern und Propheten sowie Bekenntnissen zur Wichtigkeit der Verbindung von theologischem Inhalt und darstellender Form zum Trotz. Vielleicht liegt dieser männliche Schluss aber nahe, weil auch die von Irigaray eingeführten Vermittlungsinstanzen der Engel, Dichter und Propheten in der abendländischen Tradition männlich konnotiert sind, was weder Irigaray noch Hennecke aufzufallen scheint. Auf diesem Umweg scheint es dem Männlichen wieder zu gelingen, die weibliche Offenbarung in Form der männlichen Vermittlung zu vermännlichen, was den Raum für weibliche Offenbarung abermals verschließt. Ohne Änderung der Form des Credos aber, und das heißt, ohne ausdrückliche Referenz auf ein weibliches Christologumenon im Credo wird dem nicht abzuhelfen sein.

Andrea Günter (Freiburg / Deutschland)

Manuela Kalsky, *Christaphanien. Die Re-Vision der Christologie aus der Sicht von Frauen in unterschiedlichen Kulturen*, Chr. Kaiser / Gütersloher Verlagshaus: Gütersloh 2000, 368 Seiten, ISBN 3-579-05317-5, DM 54,00

Um es gleich vorwegzunehmen: Die Dissertation von Manuela Kalsky ist ein Meilenstein auf dem Weg zu einer feministischen Christologie. Die Autorin – deutsche evangelisch-lutherische Theologin, die seit vielen Jahren in den Niederlanden lebt und arbeitet – legt nicht nur eine umfassende Studie zur feministischen Re-Vision der Christologie in unterschiedlichen Kontexten vor, was für sich genommen schon bemerkenswert ist. Sie leistet mit ihrer Suche nach einer Neubestimmung christlicher Identitätsverortung, die die "Logik des Kontrastes" (Kap. IV) durchbricht, auch einen fundamentalen Beitrag zu einer feministischen Christologie, die nicht nur den Antijudaismus christlicher Theologie überwinden kann, sondern auch Raum schafft für die "Anerkennung der Anderen" (313-316) und die Pluralität ihrer kontextuell unterschiedlichen Heilserfahrungen.

Am Beginn ihrer Studie stand das Interesse an den Differenzen zwischen Frauen und der damit verbundenen Vielfalt unterschiedlicher Unheils- und Heilsvorstellungen von Frauen in der weltweiten Ökumene. Dies hat die Autorin zu einer vertieften Auseinandersetzung mit den christologischen Modellen von Frauen in unterschiedlichen Kulturen geführt, geleitet von der Frage, wie die daraus resultierenden Unterschiede für eine feministisch-ökumenische Re-Vision der Christologie "heilsam" zu nutzen wären. Das vorliegende Buch – Resultat dieser Auseinandersetzung – ist in vier Kapitel gegliedert: Das erste Kapitel gibt einen Überblick über die Suche nach dem historischen Jesus in den letzten zwei Jahrhunderten, und reicht somit von der Leben-Jesu-Forschung im 19. Jahrhundert bis zur Frage nach dem historischen Jesus aus befreiungstheologischer Sicht.

Das zweite Kapitel widmet sich der Christologie aus feministischer Sicht. Nach einem Rückblick auf die Entwicklung der feministisch-christologischen Diskussion in Nordamerika und Europa geht die Autorin am Beispiel des Antijudaismusvorwurfs auf die drohende Reproduktion der epistemologischen Logik des Kontrastes als Erbe der Väter in feministischen Christologien ein. Anschließend stellt sie die christologischen Entwürfe von Rosemary Radford Ruether und Carter Heyward vor.

Im dritten Kapitel stehen christologische Modelle afrikanischer (Mercy Amba Oduyoye), asiatischer (Virginia Fabella, Chung Hyun Kyung) und afrikanisch-amerikanischer Theologinnen (Jacquelyn Grant, Kelly Brown Douglas, Delores Williams) im Mittelpunkt.

Im vierten Kapitel werden zuerst kurz gemeinsame Tendenzen in den behandelten kontextuellen christologischen Ansätzen aufgezeigt, bevor die Frage nach der "heilsamen" Nutzung der Differenzen anhand dreier Themenkomplexe näher untersucht wird. Es sind dies: Erstens, die Suche nach einer Bestimmung christlicher Identität, welche die Kontrast-Logik christlicher Identitätsbestimmung zugunsten einer beziehungshaften, inter-subjektiven Identitätsfindung unter Berücksichtigung der Differenzen aufgibt; zweitens, die Suche nach messianischen Vorstellungen und Geschichten von Frauen, in denen sich das Christusgeschehen in kontextuellen Christaphanien re-lokalisiert; drittens, die Anerkennung des Andersseins der Anderen, die damit verbundene Pluralität an Heilsvorstellungen, die eine auf Einheit fixierte Christologie unmöglich macht, sowie eine auf Begegnung hin angelegte "interaktive Universalität" (326-329).

Manuela Kalskys Reflexionen zu den drei Themenkomplexen basieren auf der Einsicht, dass eine feministische Re-Vision der Christologie, die nicht weiter in den Spuren der Väter christliche Identität in Jesus Christus und damit meistens in "Abgrenzung" zu legitimieren sucht, aufs Engste mit einer Re-Vision ihrer erkenntnistheoretischen Voraussetzungen verbunden sein muss. Damit eröffnet sie neue Perspektiven einer feministischen Christologie, die über eine befreiende Re-Interpretation Jesu Christi aus der Sicht von Frauen hinausgeht und eine andere Art der christlichen Identitätsbestimmung zur Diskussion stellt.

Doris Strahm (Basel / Schweiz)

Katharina von Kellenbach / Susanne Scholz (eds), *Zwischen-Räume. Deutsche feministische Theologinnen im Ausland* (Theologische Frauenforschung in Europa 1), Lit Verlag: Münster 2000, 163 pages, ISBN 3-8258-4289-4, DM 39,80

Anne Jensen / Maximilian Liebmann (eds), *Was verändert feministische Theologie? Interdisziplinäres Symposion zur Frauenforschung (Graz, Dezember 1999)* (Theologische Frauenforschung in Europa 2), Lit Verlag: Münster 2000, 224 pages, ISBN 3-8258-4616-4, DM 39,80

Each of these volumes, the first of a new monograph series in Feminist Theology edited by Hedwig Meyer-Wilmes and Marie-Theres Wacker, offers a collection of essays. The former, *Zwischen-Räume*, brings together reflections on the experience of German women theologians living and working outside Germany. The latter documents a colloquium organised by Anne Jensen in Graz in December 1999.

As a British theologian living and working in Germany I turned with interest to *Zwischen-Räume*. The twelve essays are organised in four sections which move from a discussion of the specific and profound problems associated with being a German abroad to a more general reflection on the experience of foreignness. The book opens with a section focusing on the effect of encounters with Judaism on the author's understanding of her (German) identity; part two reflects on the experience of being a German feminist theologian elsewhere. The third part discusses aspects of multi-linguism, and the fourth considers the re-orientation that results from the encounter with other cultures.

The role of history in determining identity is perhaps more apparent to Germans abroad than to members of any other nation, and the editors suggest that "for German theologians abroad, the holocaust is always present and a strong influence on their theological work" (7). This would seem to be particularly true of those working in the USA: Tanja Oldenhage's description of how the encounter with Judaism led her to new interpretations of a familiar text, Katharina von Kellenbach's courageous impulse to uncover both her own family history of involvement in National Socialist massacres in Russia and the story of "Fräulein Rabbiner Regina Jonas", and Charlotte Elisheva Fonrobert's fascinating account of her journey from the German Protestant Church to Judaism are all rooted in their experience of moving to the USA. These essays raise difficult questions about the relationship of the individual to the collective guilt attributed to German history of the mid-twentieth century. They also point to a further question, also touched upon by Ulrike Wiethaus's thoughtful discussion of the way her life history has been shaped by the absences she has encountered (125): to what extent do citizens of other countries use the "guilt of Germany" to avoid engaging with the guilt intrinsic to their own history (as witnessed, for instance, by the lack of knowledge in Britain of the widespread devastation caused by the blanket bombing of the Germany towards the end of the Second World War, or by some American reactions to the events of 11 September 2001)? But these accounts also left me pondering with some sadness the apparent inability of German (perhaps especially Protestant) theology to value the richness of its tradition at the same time as recognising that tradition's poverties and failures.

The pain of being forced into "Going West" (Susanne Scholz, 55) or living as a "resident alien" (Elisabeth Schüssler Fiorenza, 69) in order to find acceptance as a feminist theologian is witnessed to by their respective articles, which perhaps also illuminate the way in which this pain can lead emigrants to caricature the land they have left (at least, the situation in the Germany to which

I have emigrated seems to me not as hopeless as the Germany that is painted here). This illustrates the way in which one determining factor in the emigrant's view of her birth-country may be the manner of her leaving it: in her autobigraphical sketch of her – apparently fulfilling – "wanderings through [the] theological space" of France, India and England, Ursula King comments that this road resulted from her choices; unlike some of the others contributors, she was not "forced into exile" (88). Reflecting on her encounters with various degrees of strangeness as she journeyed from Europe to the USA and on to the Philippines, Renate Papke-Rose also highlights the liberating privilege of being able to choose (140).

The discovery of the permeability of boundaries is an experience common to all who move between cultures. This is an important theme for Elisabeth Gössmann, whose long years of commuting between Japan and Germany have left her sometimes unsure whether a particular tradition is Christian or Buddhist in origin (118). In a fascinating article, Ute Seibert-Cuadra points to the way language acquires new textures and depths after years spent living bilingually, so that boundaries ("*Grenzen – límites – fronteras*", 104) are redefined and "home" becomes a place where she is a visitor (102). Teresa Berger reflects that to live bi- or multi-lingually actually means to live bi- or multi-theologically, a recognition which brings new depth to the understanding that all theology is contextual. Finally, Ursula Riedel-Pfäfflin comments on the process homecoming: for her, travelling ended in the re-discovery of a theological homeland in Germany.

This is an intriguing collection of essays not only which tells interesting stories but offers insights into the challenges and frustrations of living as a foreigner. However, overall I was disappointed by the lack of theological reflection on the authors' experiences of what might be seen as some of the central themes of Christian (or perhaps religious) experience: the exile experience with its challenge of being "in the world but not of the world" (for instance, as a tax-paying member of society who is unable to vote).

Was verändert die feministische Theologie?, the second volume of the series, opens with an introductory essay in which Annette Kuhn draws on Christine de Pisan's *The City of Women* in order to address the question "What is changed when we consider the question of the sex of women?" This is succeeded by three pairs of papers considering equality and difference (Herta Nagl-Docekal and Josef Wohlmuth), Christology (Hedwig Meyer Wilmes and Hermann Häring) and practical theology (Helga Kohler-Spiegel and Michael Raske). As Hedwig Meyer-Wilmes points out in her concluding comments

(185-186), the radically differing assumptions and experiences, particularly about and of the Roman Catholic Church, but also about and of theology, which underlie these pairs of contributions is very noticeable but not explicitly discussed. A second part documents the changing situation of women pastors in the German Protestant Chuches (Maria Jepsen) and the problems of the political realisation of the aims of feminism in the universities (Irmtraud Fischer) and in the church (Ingeborg Schrettle). Also included are a record of the closing panel-discussion, pictures (by Ute Leimgruber) and texts from an exhibition which accompanied the colloquium, and a bibliography of (German) feminist theology. The collection offers snap-shots of the situation of feminist theology and some of what it has achieved, but suggests that those achievements are in many ways peripheral. It offers little reflection on the continuing exclusion of feminist theology from much of the German mainstream.

And that exclusion, of course, is the reason why most of the authors of *Zwischen-Räume* are no longer in Germany.

Charlotte Methuen (Essen / Germany)

Eva Pelkner, *Gott, Gene, Gebärmütter. Anthropologie und Frauenbild in der evangelischen Ethik zur Fortpflanzungsmedizin*, Chr. Kaiser / Gütersloher Verlagshaus: Gütersloh 2001, 286 Seiten, ISBN 3-579-02657-7, DM 68,00

Eva Pelkner hat mit ihrer Dissertation eine für die aktuelle Debatte um Präimplantationsdiagnostik (PID) und Embryonenforschung hochbrisante Untersuchung vorgelegt. Im Zentrum des Buches stehen die feministisch-kritische Revision der Beiträge evangelischer Ethiker aus den 80er Jahren im Bereich der Fortpflanzungsmedizin unter besonderer Berücksichtigung der In-Vitro-Fertilisation (IVF) und die Darstellung aktueller Ansätze zu einer feministischen Bioethik.

Zunächst fragt Eva Pelkner nach den Ursprüngen des Begriffes Bioethik. Es zeigt sich, dass die Theologie auf diesem Gebiet eine Vorreiterinnenrolle hatte. Als dann in den 70er Jahren verstärkt Anwendungsfragen in den Blick rückten, zog sich die Theologie allerdings aus diesem Bereich zurück. Es etablierte sich in dieser Zeit eine Bioethik, die primär in Kommissionen und Ausschüssen entwickelt wird und vor allem zur rechtlichen und ethischen Absicherung der Anwendungsvorhaben beiträgt (97). Auf eine solche Ethik will sich Eva Pelkner nicht einlassen. Sie hinterfragt die Prämissen und Folgerungen der theologischen Überlegungen zur IVF aus feministischer Perspektive.

Dabei verfolgt sie zum einen die Frage, wie Frauen und ihr Erleben in den Untersuchungen wahrgenommen werden, zum anderen nimmt sie in den Blick, inwieweit sich androzentrische Ausschlussverfahren in der Anlage der Arbeiten ausmachen lassen. Fazit ihrer Untersuchungen ist, dass Frauen weder Teil haben an bioethischer Urteilsfindung noch ihre konkreten Erfahrungen wahrgenommen werden in einem Bereich, in dem sie die primär durch die angewendete Technik Betroffenen sind. In den theologischen Ethiken lassen sich dabei drei Schlüsselbegriffe ausmachen, die für die Urteilsfindung maßgeblich sind: Nächstenliebe, Menschenwürde und Verantwortung.

Unter dem Aspekt der Nächstenliebe werde IVF grundsätzlich bejaht, weil damit das vermeintliche Leiden Kinderwunsch geheilt werden könne. Der Begriff der Menschenwürde tauche in den Untersuchungen vor allem im Blick auf den Embryo auf. Unter diesem Aspekt werden Fragen um den Lebensbeginn verhandelt. Die Frage nach der Menschenwürde von Frauen, die sich den IVF-Behandlungen unterziehen, werde nicht gestellt. Von Verantwortung sei schließlich in doppelter Weise die Rede: Der Begriff signalisiere einerseits Problembewusstsein, während andererseits die konkrete Verantwortung den Frauen übertragen werde. Die den neuen Gen- und Fortpflanzungstechnologien innewohnende Gefahr der zunehmenden eugenischen Auslese werde weitgehend verharmlost, während zugleich Frauen kritisiert würden, die sich zu Schwangerschaftsabbrüchen entscheiden.

Entscheidungsfreiheit in Fragen von Schwangerschaft und Geburt, die keine reine "Consumer's Choice" ist, ist eine zentrale Frage der feministischen Bioethiken, die Eva Pelkner im dritten Teil ihrer Arbeit vorstellt. Zentral sind hier die Arbeiten der US-amerikanischen Theologin Margaret A. Farley und der kanadischen Philosophin Susan Sherwin. In diesen Entwürfen wird der für die Frauenbewegung so wichtige Begriff "Autonomie" in Beziehung gesetzt zum feministisch-ethischen Begriff der "Relationalität". Bei Margaret Farley ist dieser Beziehungsbegriff in dreifacher Weise bestimmt: gegenüber Mitmenschen, dem verleiblichten Selbst und der Natur und (Welt-)Gesellschaft.

Eva Pelkner hat eine systematisch aufgebaute, kenntnisreiche und in ihren Vorannahmen und Konsequenzen klare Arbeit verfasst. Die Kritik an den androzentrischen Ausblendungen theologisch-ethischer Entwürfe wird überzeugend veranschaulicht und es werden äußerst hilfreiche Ansatzpunkte für eine feminisch-theologische Standortbestimmung in den Diskussionen um Gen- und Reproduktionstechnologie vorgestellt. Die Arbeit fordert dazu heraus, sich deutlicher in die aktuelle Diskussion einzumischen – aus guten feministischen wie theologischen Gründen. Dabei muss meines Erachtens allerdings noch stärker in den Blick genommen werden, warum ein unerfüllter Kinderwunsch für so viele Frauen Anlass ist, sich anhaltenden, schmerzhaften und zum Teil sehr aussichtslosen Behandlungen zu unterziehen – zumal diese Behandlungen eine verbrauchende Embryonenforschung erst möglich machen.

Rose Wecker (Oberhausen / Deutschland)

Karin Ulrich-Eschemann, *Vom Geborenwerden des Menschen. Theologische und philosophische Erkundungen*, (Studien zur systematischen Theologie und Ethik 27), Lit Verlag: Münster / Hamburg / London 2000, 263 Seiten, ISBN 3-8258-5098-6, DM 39,80

In ihrer Studie untersucht Karin Ulrich-Eschemann, inwieweit die Geburt des Kindes Jesu mit unserer eigenen Geburt gedanklich zu verbinden ist und welche Bedeutung das Werden dieses Kindes für das Verständnis unseres Werdens und unserer Geburt als Neuanfang hat.

Am Anfang des Buches steht eine Interpretation des Begriffs Geburtlichkeit (Natalität) bei Hannah Arendt. Menschen werden als Neuankömmlinge und Anfänger in die bestehende Welt hineingeboren. Aufgrund ihrer Geburt *haben* Menschen nicht nur einen Anfang, sondern *sind* selbst Anfang und Anfänger; durch ihr Sprechen und Handeln ergreifen sie Initiativen und beweisen damit ihre Freiheit. Freiheit ist für Arendt eine politische Kategorie. Handeln bedeutet für sie, etwas Neues anzufangen und zusammen mit anderen Menschen in der Öffentlichkeit politisch aktiv zu werden. Philosophisch gesprochen ist Handeln die Antwort des Menschen auf das Geborenwerden.

Ulrich-Eschemann fährt danach mit einer phänomenologischen Erkundung des Werdens und der Geburt von Menschen fort. Dabei definiert sie Menschen als werdende und nicht als fertige Lebewesen und die Beziehung zwischen der werdenden Mutter und ihrem werdenden Kind als "Miteinander-Personsein". Sie spricht vom "in-der-Mutter-Sein", vom "Mit-sein" von Kind und Mutter und identifiziert das werdende Kind von Anfang an als eine "werdende Person". Für die Autorin ist das Geborenwerden nicht nur, wie bei Hannah Arendt, in einer politischen Theorie von Bedeutung, sondern es wird zum zentralen Thema der Anthropologie.

An dieser Stelle wird Ulrich-Eschemanns Argumentation im eigentlichen Sinn theologisch. Sie definiert Menschen als Geschöpfe und Kinder als Gabe Gottes. Das Geborenwerden ist das Paradigma für das Handeln Gottes mit den Menschen schlechthin; Mütter kooperieren dabei im schöpferischen Tun mit

Gott. Im Folgenden geht die Autorin auf die Geburt der Menschen nach der Geburt Jesu ein und nimmt diese als Beispiel für den Neuanfang der Geschichte Gottes mit uns. Die Geschichte des Werdens Jesu ist aufs engste mit dem Mutterwerden Marias verknüpft. Der Autorin zufolge geschieht hier eine Kooperation Gottes mit Maria. Sie greift die Theologie Martin Luthers und der Kirchenväter auf, auf die Luther sich bezieht.

Am Ende verdeutlicht Ulrich-Eschemann ihre eigene christlich-theologische Perspektive. Im Mittelpunkt steht nicht mehr – wie bei Arendt – das initiierende Handeln der Menschen, sondern das schöpferische Handeln Gottes, "das sich über die Menschen ergießt, und gegen das sich die Menschen kaum wehren können" (232, Anm. 24). Der Mensch wird Arendt zufolge nicht "frei" geboren, sondern als "ein zu Befreiender" (214). Die *vita activa* Arendts scheint eine *vita passiva* zu werden, und die eschatologische Dimension gewinnt die Oberhand: Das Neue geschieht nicht mit der Geburt, sondern das wirklich Neue fängt mit der noch ausstehenden Vollendung, dem ewigen Leben an.

Das interessante und originelle Buch bekommt durch diesen Perspektivwechsel von der Geburt zur Auferstehung ein etwas vorhersagbares und traditionelles christlich-theologisches Ende. Auf neue feministisch-theologische und philosophische Erkenntnisse greift die Autorin dabei nicht zurück. Indem sie in ihrer Argumentation vom Anfang des Lebens (Geburt) sogleich zu deren Ende (Tod und eschatologische Verheißung) springt, scheint sie das Leben *selbst* (in der Welt, mit anderen Menschen) zu überspringen. Dadurch wird übersehen, was Hannah Arendt mit ihrer Wortschöpfung "Geburtlichkeit" oder "Natalität" eigentlich beabsichtigt: das Geschenk der Geburt in den Mittelpunkt des Lebens und des Denkens zu stellen. Dies heißt jedoch, das Leben und die Welt ernst zu nehmen und sich zu bemühen, die Welt für künftige Generationen zu erhalten und zu erneuern. Kurzum: Das Gesicht *diesem* Leben zuzuwenden. Der eigene Tod (und die Erwartung der Auferstehung) sind "später" dran.

Marijke Verhoeven (Tilburg / Niederlande)

Marianne Wallach-Faller, *Die Frau im Tallit. Judentum feministisch gelesen*, herausgegeben von Doris Brodbeck und Yvonne Domhardt, mit einem Vorwort von Eveline Goodman-Thau und Marie-Theres Wacker, Chronos-Verlag: Zürich 2000, 272 Seiten, ISBN 3-905313-65-0, CHF 34,00

Marianne Wallach-Faller kannte die ganze Bandbreite zeitgenössischen Judentums: Aus konservativ jüdischem Hause stammend und in der sogenannten

"Einheitsgemeinde" aufgewachsen, hat sie diese später – zusammen mit ihrem Ehemann – verlassen, um in der Jüdischen Liberalen Gemeinde von Zürich, "Or Chadasch", ein vollwertiges, liturgisch aktives Mitglied sein zu können.

Den "feministischen Impuls" erhielt sie bereits früh durch eine schmerzliche persönliche Erfahrung: Jahrelang hatte sie in der Synagoge stets beim Großvater gesessen – unten, dort, wo das liturgische Leben spielt, wo männliche Gemeindemitglieder den Gottesdienst halten, Gebete sprechen und aus der Tora vorlesen – eingehüllt in seinen Gebetsmantel (Tallit), geborgen, integriert und zugehörig. Doch mit Erreichen ihres zwölften Lebensjahres habe der geliebte Großvater sie abrupt "hinausgeworfen", "verstoßen", nämlich: hochgeschickt auf die Frauen-Galerie. So ihre eigenen Worte, noch Jahre später.

Dieses traumatische Erlebnis – sie hat es der Rezensentin einmal selbst erzählt – erscheint im Rückblick richtungsweisend für das jüdisch-feministische Wirken von Marianne Wallach-Faller: Voller Liebe und Fürsorge für ihre jüdische Tradition, in der sie tief verwurzelt war, aber nicht bereit, im Interesse irgendwelcher Konventionen auf ihr eigenes vollwertiges Jüdin-Sein zu verzichten. So wurde Marianne zur Grenzgängerin, zur Vermittlerin zwischen unterschiedlichen Welten: Dem konservativen Judentum gegenüber verteidigte sie das feministische Anliegen, den Nicht-Jüdinnen erklärte sie jüdische Bräuche, Traditionen, Liturgien und Auslegungen mit schier unerschöpflicher Geduld.

Ihre Vorträge und liturgischen Angebote auf zahlreichen christlich-jüdischen Begegnungsveranstaltungen sind im ersten Kapitel des vorliegenden, posthum edierten Sammelbandes dokumentiert. Immer wieder gegenseitigen "liebevollen Respekt" (44) für die Religion der Anderen einfordernd, scheute sie sich nicht, die zahlreichen interreligiösen "Fettnäpfchen und Tabus" (43) in Bereichen wie Sabbat, Speisevorschriften und Themenwahl beim Namen zu nennen.

Zahlreiche Vorträge "über biblische Themen aus Frauensicht" (113) und "biblische Frauengestalten" (163) zeigen, wie tief die studierte Germanistin sich eingearbeitet hatte in die aktuelle Fachdiskussion jüdischer Theologinnen. Dabei wurde ihr Judith Plaskows Entwurf (*Und wieder stehen wir am Sinai*, Luzern 1992) einer biblischen Relecture aus Frauensicht zum Leitfaden: In ihren Auslegungen versuchte sie, zentrale Kategorien jüdischen Denkens – Tora, Gott, Israel – aus weiblicher Sicht neu zu definieren und an unterschiedlichen Texten durchzudeklinieren.

Für das Reden von Gott finden sich in der biblischen wie mystischen Tradition auch weibliche Bilder, die jedoch in die fest- und alltägliche Gebetssprache bislang nicht aufgenommen wurden. Einen Hauptakzent ihres Forschens und Wirkens legte Marianne Wallach daher auf neue Formen der *Liturgie*: inklusive Sprache, Vermeidung einseitig männlicher Gottesattribute, Einführung weiblicher oder geschlechtsneutraler Bilder aus dem Bereich der Natur. Ein eigens zusammengestellter Reader mit neuen liturgischen Texten, inspiriert von Marcia Falk (*The Book of Blessings*, San Francisco 1996), wurde zum Gebetbuch ihrer Gottesdienste. Diese führte sie sowohl innerjüdisch als auch interreligiös durch: In Zürich gründete sie die "Vereinigung jüdisch-feministischer Theologinnen und an Theologie interessierter Frauen" sowie eine Rosh-Chodesh-Gruppe (Liturgiekreis für jüdische Frauen), auf christlich-jüdischen Begegnungstagungen hielt sie Freitag-Abend-Gottesdienste, bei denen sie es verstand, auch Nichtjüdinnen sorgsam durch die Liturgie zu führen und in die feierliche Sabbatstimmung mit hinein zu nehmen.

Diese konkreten und für die gegenseitige religiöse Verständigung äußerst hilfreichen Begegnungen mit Marianne Wallach-Faller werden allen, die sie kennen lernen durften, lebhaft und dankbar in Erinnerung bleiben. Gut, dass nun auch ihr schriftlicher Nachlass in diesem (übrigens sorgfältig edierten und typografisch ansprechenden) Band zugänglich ist!

Bettina Kratz-Ritter (Göttingen / Deutschland)

Sharon D. Welch, *A Feminist Ethic of Risk*, Revised Edition, Augsburg Fortress Press: Minneapolis 2000, 206 S., ISBN 0-8006-3185-4, £11.99

Sharon D. Welch hat ihre in den achtziger Jahren unter dem Eindruck des Wettrüstens verfasste "Feministische Ethik des Risikos" aktualisiert. Jetzt bildet die nachsowjetische Ära mit ihren enttäuschten Friedenshoffnungen und neuerlichen Aufrüstungsbestrebungen der USA angesichts lokaler Konflikte – Ex-Jugoslawien, Somalia, Ruanda u.a. – den Kontext ihrer Überlegungen.

Welchs zentrale These heißt: Auch ein "guter Wille" führt zu mehr Krieg und Zerstörung, solange die Konzepte vom gutem Handeln, die der patriarchalischen euro-amerikanischen ethischen Tradition zugrunde liegen, nicht revidiert sind. Das entscheidende Dogma ("Master Belief") im Zentrum dieser Tradition besagt, dass "Handeln" bedeutet, eine Situation unter Kontrolle zu bekommen und vorausberechenbare Resultate zu erzielen. Im lernbegierigen Dialog mit der literarischen Tradition der afroamerikanisch-womanistischen Gemeinschaft entfaltet Welch demgegenüber ein Verständnis von theologisch-spiritueller Ethik, das die prinzipielle Unberechenbarkeit der Ergebnisse des Handelns voraussetzt. Ziel ihrer Überlegungen ist es, ihrer eigenen von Resignation und Zynismus bedrohten weißen Mittelklasse ein Verständnis von moralischem Handeln nahe zu bringen, das auch jenseits revolutionärer Aufbruchsstimmungen zum kontinuierlichen Einsatz für ein besseres Leben befähigt.

Fünf afroamerikanische Romane (Paule Marshall, *The Chosen Place, The Timeless People*; Toni Morrison, *The Bluest Eye*; Mildred Taylor, *Roll of Thunder, Hear My Cry*; Mildred Taylor, *Let The Circle Be Unbroken*; Toni Cade Bambara, *The Salt-Eaters*) bilden das Analysematerial, anhand dessen Welch im zweiten Hauptteil des Buches die Unterschiede zwischen der Mainstream-"Ethik der Kontrolle" und der in Unterdrückung entstandenen "Ethik des Risikos" erläutert: Aufgrund einer Reihe oft uneingestandener Privilegien – Rechte, Besitz – erliegt die Ethik in aufklärerisch-kantischer Tradition der Täuschung, Menschen könnten allein, z.B. als professionelle Aktivisten handeln. Demgegenüber behauptet die Ethik der Unterdrückten die Unabdingbarkeit von Gemeinschaft. Während die Ethik des Risikos sich eingebettet sieht in Geschichte und Geschichten, begreift konventionelle Ethik Handeln tendenziell als geschichtslose Technik. Das weiße Mittelstandsethos verfällt in Resignation, wenn sich kein sichtbarer Erfolg einstellt, während die schwarze Gemeinschaft im Vertrauen auf generationenübergreifenden Widerstand handelt und Reife nicht als rationale Urteilsfähigkeit, sondern als tägliche Bejahung des Am-Lebens-Seins begreift.

Im letzten Teil des Buches bringt Welch die Ergebnisse ihrer Analyse mit aktuellen (feministisch-)theologischen und ethischen Debatten ins Gespräch. Von der Widerstandskultur in womanistischer Tradition aus gesehen erweisen sich kommunitaristische Ansätze als ebenso reduktionistisch wie Habermas' Theorie des kommunikativen Handelns, postmoderne Fragmentierungen oder herkömmliche theologische Denkfiguren wie die Rede von der Allmacht Gottes oder vom eschatologische Vorbehalt. Zum Schluss entfaltet Welch eine Theologie der "beloved community", die gegen Ungerechtigkeit dauerhaft Widerstand leistet, menschliche Kontingenz aber akzeptiert und aushält.

Dass die nicht unproblematische Methode, literarische Texte direkt mit theoretischen Konzepten zu konfrontieren, die Gefahr der romantisierenden Überfrachtung einer kulturellen Tradition in sich birgt, sieht Welch selbst (45). Dieser Gefahr hätte sie möglicherweise konstruktiv begegnen können, hätte sie sich selbst nicht nur als "Angehörige der weißen Mittelklasse" – ein Selbstkonzept, die nach der intensiven Arendt-Rezeption und den Debatten um Affidamento leicht antiquiert wirkt –, sondern als unverwechselbare Person zur Sprache gebracht.

Ina Praetorius (Krinau / Schweiz)

Patricia A. Williams, *Doing without Adam and Eve: Sociobiology and Original Sin*, Augsburg Fortress Press: Minneapolis 2001, 201 pages, ISBN 0-8006-3285-0, $18.00

In this contribution to the Fortress Press series "Theology and the Sciences", Patricia Williams, philosopher of biology, explores the doctrines of the Fall and of original sin, offering a new perspective on the eternal philosophical and theological question of human nature and a valuable contribution to an area in need of re-interpretation. Williams recognises that it is necessary to take account of science's knowledge of our evolved nature and our innate dispositions. She applies three philosophical tests of truth to science, doctrine and scripture before seeking solutions which unite Christianity with science, as she believes is necessary for Christianity. Such solutions are only possible, she suggests, if Christianity consents to doing without Adam and Eve (201).

Williams offers a negative argument – "The Demise of Adam and Eve" – and a positive – "The Unification of Science and Christianity." The first part (chapters 1-6), considers biblical narratives, especially Genesis 2 and 3, together with three doctrines of original sin. Williams shows how Christianity derived an idea of human nature not found in the biblical texts. The narrative of Adam and Eve neither portrays true historical figures, nor is it a myth about the human condition: rather, it represents the social situation of peasants and the biological circumstances of all biological organisms (chapter 6). Williams sees Christianity's misunderstandings as in part a reaction to the catastrophic death of Jesus. The second part (chapters 7-11), discusses the theory of evolution and socio-biology's understanding of our evolved nature and presents Williams's understanding (chapter 9). We are not depraved, but flexible and free, capable of love, but also of nepotism and genocide, and we thus need guidance through ethics and role-models. Williams offers a new solution to the problem of evil by arguing that evil cannot be banished without also banishing the good that is equally a mark of our humanity (or possibly of any other species with the same capacities). Finally, she argues that doctrines of atonement have wrongly emphasized sacrifice over God's longing for unity (at-one-ment) with us, a longing shown in the life and words of Jesus.

In a book ranging over such diverse fields it is inevitable that some aspects need elaboration. Williams's treatment of the relationship between Christianity and the socio-biological theory of altruism, although recognising the demand for totally self-sacrificial behaviour to be problematic (especially for women, I would add), still shows an over-dependence on the agape-tradition of Anders Nygren. I would also welcome a more thorough discussion of her vision of the transformation of human nature, necessary because of our evolved disposition to confuse good and evil, which would enable us to overcome egocentricity and show agape (197). What is the relation between reason, symbol, reciprocity, altruism and love in this transformation, and how does this relate to religion?

Williams's book documents an interesting and challenging quest for a unification of disciplines including cosmology, evolution, Biblical scholarship and theology. She is searching for truth in an area which is weighed down with hierarchical, sexist, determinist arguments. The result is liberating but ambiguous. We are not entirely bad, but we are not very good either.

Eva-Lotta Grantén (Lund / Sweden)

II.4 Praktische Theologie, Spiritualität, Liturgiewissenschaft, Religionspädagogik, Homiletik

Kristina Augst, *Religion in der Lebenswelt junger Frauen aus sozialen Unterschichten*, Kohlhammer: Stuttgart / Berlin / Köln 2000, 331 Seiten, ISBN 3-17-016297-7, DM 71,00

Kristina Augsts Untersuchung versteht sich als eine Arbeit aus feministisch-theologischer Perspektive. Sie will keine Ergänzung zu traditionellen Ansätzen sein, sondern "Kritik" und "Neuentwurf" zugleich (15). Mit der Konzentration auf junge Frauen aus sozialen Unterschichten trägt Augst jedoch gleichzeitig auch zur Kritik am deutschsprachigen feministisch-theologischen Diskurs bei, der noch sehr stark auf Mittelschichtfrauen fixiert ist. Ferner versucht die Autorin im theoretischen Teil, die Lebensbedingungen ostdeutscher Frauen eigens zu reflektieren; in den empirischen Auswertungsteil ging allerdings nur ein Interview ein.

Die Untersuchung gliedert sich in drei Hauptteile: einen theoretischen Eingangsteil ("Der soziale Kontext und das Religionsverständnis der Arbeit", 21-97), einen empirischen Mittelteil ("Methodik und die Auswertung der Interviews", 99-234) sowie die Diskussion der Ergebnisse ("Ergebnisse und Ausblick", 237-303). Der empirischen Untersuchung liegen zwanzig Leitfaden-Interviews zugrunde (vgl. den Leitfaden im Anhang, 330f.). Von ihnen sind sieben im empirischen Teil ausgewertet. Dieser Teil bleibt gut leserlich und bringt in seinem Auswertungsstil die interviewten Frauen nicht nur wissenschaftlich objektiviert, sondern auch emotional nahe. Augst ging es aus ihrer Wahrnehmungsperspektive darum, nicht einseitig die Interviewten an akademisch-theologischen Maßstäben zu messen, sondern eher umgekehrt die Theologie auf ihre Erschließungskraft für heutige Alltagswelten und dort gelebte Religiosität zu befragen. Die Autorin gelangt dabei zu dem Ergebnis, dass der herrschende praktisch-theologische Diskurs von der untersuchten Lebenswelt so weit entfernt ist, dass sich der eigene Ertrag kaum mit ihm verbinden lässt. Sie stellt bei den Frauen zwei Leitmotive der Lebensdeutung fest: "Das Leben meistern/'struggle for life'" (262-264) sowie "Das Leben als Problem" (264-266). "Das Leben zu meistern bedeutet, gutes Essen und Kleidung zu besitzen, die Tiere verpflegen zu können und genug Geld zur Verfügung zu haben, um lebensnotwendige Dinge zu bezahlen" (263). Die Ebene der "Sinnfrage" hat für die Befragten keine Bedeutung: "Die Befragten verneinen einen speziellen Sinn ihres Lebens" (275). "Das Leben an sich muß bewältigt werden, es geht kaum um weitere Ziele oder Ansprüche. Daher gibt es auch keinen 'höheren' oder 'tieferen' Sinn. (...) Sinn assoziieren die Befragten offensichtlich nicht mit 'einfach nur leben'" (276). Theologie muss beachten, dass Kategorien wie Bildungsabschluss, Einkommen und Beruf, Geschlecht und Volkszugehörigkeit nach wie vor großen Einfluss auf die Verortung in und auf die Wahrnehmung von sozialer Wirklichkeit haben. Mit dem theologischen Übersehen bzw. der Abwertung der materiellen Lebensbasis vernachlässigen Theologie und Kirche zugleich Menschen, die solche Probleme täglich meistern müssen. Augst knüpft zur theologischen Einordnung ihrer Arbeitsergebnisse an die womanistische Theologie an (vgl. 299f.). Dort steht nicht das Exodus-Motiv der Befreiung zu Neuem im Vordergrund, sondern die Hagar-Erzählung und Jeremias Brief an die Exilanten. Christliche Religion hilft hier, das Leben in feindlicher Umgebung oder in abhängiger Position zu meistern. Dabei führt auch ein Religionsverständnis (wie z.B. das Henning Luthers) nicht weiter, das Religion einseitig als Destabilisierung des Alltags versteht, sondern ebenso muss Theologie das Alltagsstabilisierende für solche Menschen benennen können (vgl. 295). Ferner verweist Augst auf die theologische Blindheit für die emotionale Dimension von Religiosität – wodurch sich z.B. die gegenwärtige Popkultur besser als funktionales Äquivalent eignet als ein verkopft inszeniertes Christentum.

Alles in allem hat die Autorin ein gut lesbares Buch vorgelegt, das den feministisch-theologischen Diskurs bereichert und auf wichtige Defizite im akademisch-theologischen Bereich aufmerksam macht, die für eine theologische Wende hin zu Biographie- und Alltagsthemen bearbeitet werden müssen.

Sabine Bobert-Stützel (Berlin / Deutschland)

Teresa Berger (ed.), *Dissident Daughters: Feminist Liturgies in Global Context*, Westminster John Knox: Louisville / London 2001, 249 pages, ISBN 0-664-22379-6, US $24.95

Dorothea McEwan / Pat Pinsent / Ianthe Pratt / Veronica Seddon (eds), *Making Liturgy: Creating Rituals for Life*, Canterbury Press: Norwich 2001, 189 pages, ISBN 1-85311-440-5, £7.99

Each of these two new books on women's liturgy illustrates, in its own way, both the coming-of-age of women as agents, that is, as doers of liturgy, and the inherently contextual nature of women's ritual gatherings. They also demonstrate that the growth and flourishing of women's liturgical traditions, new and old, cannot be stereotyped as merely a North American, or even a North Atlantic phenomenon.

Teresa Berger has amassed reports and reflections from women's groups themselves, spanning a considerable geographic and cultural range: from the North Atlantic to South America, from Korea and the Philippines to Australia and South Africa. European contributors include Denise J. J. Dijk (the Netherlands), Herta Leistner (Germany), Veronica Seddon (U.K.), Auđur Eir Vilhálmsdóttir (Iceland), and Ninna Edgardh Beckman (Sweden). Each of the fourteen groups provides a description of its own context and history as a ritualizing group of women, as well as a model liturgy with an "order of service" and indications of the texts, music and ritual actions used.

As Teresa Berger indicates in her introduction, there is considerable cross-influence and borrowing from the women's ritual resources of different cultures, yet for the most part these groups consciously choose to express their own local identities in their liturgies. Berger, a liturgical historian whose previously published works include monographs on women in the twentieth-century Liturgical Movement (*Liturgie und Frauenseele*, Kohlhammer: Stuttgart, 1993) and the Women's Liturgical Movement in historical context (*Women's Ways of Worship,* Liturgical Press: Collegeville, 1999, reviewed in the ESWTR *Yearbook* 9 [2001], 303-304) shows the tension between the malestream liturgical "tradition" and the new insights arising not only from feminist theory and analysis but from theory of cultures. At the same time that some religious denominations and institutions are striving to tighten their legal authority over liturgy and belief in such a way as to keep women (and the laity in general) marginalized, theorists of culture point to the fluidity of boundaries and the instability of categories such as "woman" across racial, class and ethnic lines.

Yet Berger concludes her book with Kathryn Tanner's call for women-identified women to "remain traditional," that is, not to lose the credibility and leverage gained by re-visioning the tradition from within. Needless to say this is easier said than done, particularly when one's personal feminist vision greatly outstrips that of one's colleagues and work climate, faith community, or family and friends.

Making Liturgy provides both a wealth of models of women's liturgies celebrated in Britain by a variety of local groups, and a very helpful "how-to" manual. The introductory chapters on themes including large-group and small-group planning, symbols, language, music, street liturgy provide abundant practical and organizational tips which will help to give beginning planners the sense of self-confidence necessary to assume effective liturgical agency. Among the models of liturgy found here, the well-thought-out Seder incorporates women's names and women's history brilliantly. Two suggestions: printing the name of each author next to her contributed chapter would have been helpful for identification particularly when the first-person singular is used (although the names do appear in the table of contents). And the omission of a Christmas liturgy, although explained as due to the practical reality that women prefer to be with their families at Christmas-time (52), leaves a lacuna in feminist liturgical visioning of the overall tradition. Surely a time during the twelve days of Christmas could be found for women to gather to reinterpret the Christmas story, traditionally a celebration of the infant boy-king, from a women-centred perspective.

Susan K. Roll (Buffalo, New York / USA)

Birgit Hoyer, *Gottesmütter. Lebensbilder kinderloser Frauen als fruchtbare Dialogräume für Pastoral und Pastoraltheologie*, (Tübinger Perspektiven zur Pastoraltheologie und Religionspädagogik 2), Lit Verlag: Münster 1999, 344 Seiten, ISBN 3-8258-4329-7, DM 49,80

Ist Kinderlosigkeit gewollt, fällt sie leicht unter den Verdacht des Egoismus. Ist sie ungewollt, wird erwartet, dass sie durch Reproduktionsmedizin gelöst wird. Leiden an Kinderlosigkeit hat weder kirchlich noch gesellschaftlich einen rechten Ort. Notwendig sind Hilfen, die (auch) jenseits der – zu 85-90% fehlschlagenden – medizinischen Behandlungen liegen und einen Dialograum für die konkreten Erfahrungen der Betroffenen öffnen. Birgit Hoyer tut dies in ihrer Dissertation, in der 27 kinderlose Frauen zu Wort kommen. Im ersten

Kapitel skizziert sie die zentralen Begriffe Mütterlichkeit, Fruchtbarkeit und Kinderlosigkeit. Dabei ist es ihr Anliegen aufzuzeigen, dass auch eine Frau, die keine Kinder gebiert, fruchtbar sein, und auch ein Leben ohne Kinder im eigenen Haushalt mütterlich sein kann. Gemeint ist damit eine lebenspendende, lebensförderliche, lebenpflegende Haltung. Hoyer stellt sich die Frage, wie Religion und Lebenserfahrung dieser Haltung förderlich sein können. Das zweite Kapitel steckt den methodischen Rahmen ab: Die Interviews versteht sie als heilende pastorale Gespräche, als "Ermöglichung eines Blickes auf Ungesehenes" (58). Im dritten Kapitel werden die befragten Frauen vorgestellt; sichtbar werden unterschiedliche Lebenswege und eine bunte Vielfalt an Umgangsweisen mit Kinderlosigkeit. Die Aussagen der Frauen bringt die Autorin im vierten Kapitel in Überlegungen zu Facetten der Kinderlosigkeit ein. Sie nennt Zahlen und kritisiert eine verengte bevölkerungspolitische Sicht, stellt die Frage nach der "Natürlichkeit" des Kinderwunsches, hinterfragt Weiblichkeit und tastet mögliche Zusammenhänge zwischen weiblicher Sexualität und Kinderwunsch ab. Weiter wird Kinderlosigkeit als Anfrage an Paarbeziehungen dargestellt, "Altern" und "Arbeiten" werden als wesentliche Faktoren benannt und die Probleme medizinischer Sichtweisen und Behandlungen diskutiert.

Das letzte Kapitel skizziert eine "Pastoral-Theologie der Mütterlichkeit" (286), die sich Göttinnentraditionen ebenso verbunden weiß wie mütterlichen Darstellungen des biblischen Gottes, die Beziehungen pflegt, Leben gibt, Gastfreundschaft und Geborgenheit gewährt. Eine solche Theologie, so die Autorin, eröffnet Frauen Raum und Zeit für ihre je eigenen Wege und Wandlungen und begleitet diese, unter anderem auch mit Ritualen. Ausführlich werden in diesem Teil nochmals Aussagen der befragten Frauen herangezogen, die ihr Gottesbild und ihr Verhältnis zur Kirche beleuchten. Das Buch schließt mit Thesen, die für ein Ernstnehmen kinderloser Frauen in ihrer Verschiedenheit und für eine damit verbundene lebensvolle Theologie und Pastoral plädieren.

Birgit Hoyers Arbeit hinterlässt bei mir einen zwiespältigen Eindruck: Als kinderlose Pastoraltheologin bin ich froh, dass das Thema aufgegriffen wird. Auch teile ich das Anliegen der Autorin, kinderlosen Frauen Gehör und ihrem menschlichen wie spirituellen Wachstum Raum zu verschaffen. Doch für eine wissenschaftliche Auseinandersetzung ist mir dies zu wenig. Klarheit und Stringenz, etwa im Aufbau lassen oft zu wünschen übrig. Außerdem werden Begriffe nicht geklärt: Nicht nur der verwendete Religions- oder der Naturbegriff oder die Weiblichkeitskonstruktion, auch der für die Arbeit zentrale Begriff der Mütterlichkeit. Er wird zwar vielfach umschrieben, eine sorgfältige Dekonstruktion des Begriffs fehlt jedoch, ebenso eine Diskussion der

Zusammenhänge und Abgrenzung zu Mutterschaft und ihrer gesellschaftlichen Institutionalisierung. Dass mit dem Begriff der sozialen oder öffentlichen Mütterlichkeit traditionelle Geschlechterklischees perpetuiert wurden und werden, kommt überhaupt nicht in den Blick.

So geht das Konzept des Dialogs nicht auf, vieles wird einfach ohne Analyse nebeneinander gestellt. So werden etwa die vorkommenden Gottesbilder lediglich aufgelistet, eine Reflexion der Bedeutung von Religiosität für den Umgang mit dem Kinderwunsch bleibt jedoch aus. Es bleibt zu hoffen, dass Kinderlosigkeit endlich ein Thema feministisch-theologischer Forschung wird.

Veronika Prüller-Jagenteufel (Wien / Österreich)

Isolde Karle, *Der Pfarrberuf als Profession. Eine Berufstheorie im Kontext der modernen Gesellschaft,* (Praktische Theologie und Kultur 3), Chr.Kaiser / Gütersloher Verlagshaus: Gütersloh 2001, 352 Seiten, ISBN 3-579-03483-9, DM 58,00

In diesem Buch löst ich Isolde Karle dezidiert von der Subjekt-Orientierung der Pastoraltheologie und beschreibt das Verhältnis von Kirchengemeinde und AmtsträgerIn im Rahmen der Ausdifferenzierung von Funktionssystemen (mit Niklas Luhmann) und das theologische Amt näherhin als Profession (im Anschluss an Robert Stichweh, Kapitel I). Die klassischen Professionen Medizin, Jura und Theologie sind hier durch die Erziehungswissenschaft ergänzt. Ein professionsbestimmtes System zeichnet sich durch die Monopolstellung einer Berufsgruppe für die "Leistungsrolle" aus. Die Kommunikation in diesen Systemen ist durch persönliche Begegnung (Interaktion), durch die Vermittlung einer "kulturell relevanten Sachthematik" (41), im ganzen durch Bearbeitung existenzieller Situationen gekennzeichnet. In zwei großen Kapiteln (II und IV) entfaltet Karle die Grundpfeiler des Modells: Interaktion und Sachgemäßheit, unter Rückgriff auf theologische Tradition (Paulus, Luther, Schleiermacher) und ein breites soziologisches Repertoire. Kapitel III versucht, den kirchlichen Anspruch des "allgemeinen Priestertums" mit der hier intendierten "Leistungsrolle"/Sonderposition des Pfarramts zu vermitteln. Kapitel V führt ergänzende Überlegungen aus.

Isolde Karle hat mit ihrer Habilitationsschrift ein interessantes und ambitioniertes Buch geschrieben. Der Entwurf ist klar konzipiert, und Karle verfügt über enorme Darstellungskraft und überragende Eloquenz. Der größere Zusammenhang der Professionstheorie wirkt auf die Debatte um Rechte und Pflichten des Pfarramts bereichernd und entlastend. Dass der Professionsansatz ein gewissermaßen idealtypisches Modell ist und nicht in jedem Falle und für alle Professionen greift, könnte deutlicher gesagt werden. Karle verharrt gelegentlich etwas eng am eigenen System, das sie sehr zielsicher, aber teilweise unter Verlust historischer Komplexität, aus der theologischen Tradition ergänzt. So zwingt der präzise Denkrahmen einige Ergebnisse herbei, die in einem anderen Zusammenhang vielleicht offener diskutiert werden könnten.

Erstens: Karle geht konsequent auf einen delegativen Amtsbegriff zu (Kapitel III). Sie greift dabei, jenseits der komplexen Forschungsdebatte, mit reichlichen Zitaten auf Luther selbst zurück, dessen noch ständisch bestimmte Theorie des "Berufs" als Vorbild des Professionssystems interpretiert wird. Damit wird die spannungsvolle Vorstellung vom "allgemeinen Priestertum" mit raschem Griff in ein System integriert, das für derlei Unruhe eigentlich keinen Platz hat.

Zweitens: Gleichermaßen sympathisch, heilsam provozierend wie gelegentlich ärgerlich ist Karles Tendenz, die Deskription der Pfarramtswirklichkeit anhand der Professionstheorie unterschwellig ins Normative zu wandeln. Manchen Seitenhieb auf unbefangen "subjektive" und darin herzlich unprofessionelle KollegInnen kann ich gut verstehen; weniger plausibel ist mir Karles Forcierung der klassischen Tugenden des ländlichen Gemeindepfarramtes (Präsenz, Residenz, tendenziell durchgehende persönliche Ansprechbarkeit, 72-82 und öfter). Für keine andere der Professionen würde man heute ein derart enges Raster an Verbindlichkeiten aufstellen.

Drittens: Ihre Überlegungen zum "weiblichen Pfarramt" entwickelt Karle überzeugend und differenziert unter dekonstruktivistischem Vorzeichen (Kapitel V,5). Diese Differenziertheit fehlt mir, wenn Karle schließlich mittels des Professionsbegriffs die Geschlechterfrage weitgehend relativiert (303-310). Es wäre zumindest zu fragen, wieweit sich der professionsethische Codex an männlichen Normalbiographien entwickelt hat, demnach als gesellschaftliche Konstruktion auch seinerseits der Überprüfung bedarf.

Christine Globig (Wuppertal / Deutschland)

Sylvia Rothschild / Sybil Sheridan (eds), *Taking up the Timbrel: The Challenge of Creating Ritual for Jewish Women Today*, SCM Press: London 2000, 211 Seiten, ISBN 0-334-02806-X, £12.95

Bereits 1994 hat Sybil Sheridan bei SCM einen Sammelband zur Situation rabbinisch ausgebildeter Jüdinnen herausgegeben (*Hear our Voice: Women in the British Rabbinate*). Dahinter steht ein mehr oder minder fester Kreis jüngerer, am (liberalen) Leo-Baeck-College in London ausgebildeter oder tätiger Jüdinnen. Durch Teilnahme einiger dieser Frauen am Berliner Projekt Bet Debora wird der Impuls des Reformjudentums, ursprünglich von Deutschland ausgegangen, dorthin zurückgetragen. Der vorliegende Sammelband enthält 26 Beiträge von insgesamt 15 im liberalen Kontext tätigen Rabbinerinnen zu frauengerechter Liturgie.

Den vielfältigen Entwürfen neuer religiöser Rituale für Frauen sind grundsätzliche Reflexionen voran gestellt: "Grenzen des Gebets erweitern", "betende Frauen in der Bibel" und hier besonders die Gestalt der inbrünstig betenden Hanna als Vorbild und Inbegriff betender Frauen. Die Jahrhunderte lang als selbstverständlich geltende Voraussetzung, dass die jüdische Frau in der Regel eine verheiratete Frau und Mutter war, ihr Wirkungskreis das Haus und ihre Religiosität institutionell repräsentiert durch den Ehemann in der Synagoge, ist schon lange nicht mehr gegeben. Doch ernsthafte Ansätze, die reale Lebenssituation moderner Jüdinnen theologisch zu reflektieren und liturgisch umzusetzen, kamen erst mit der zweiten Frauenbewegung und der Ordinierung von Rabbinerinnen. Der bangen Frage, ob Frauen ohne Kinder als Jüdinnen überhaupt existieren (1), wird die Freude über "our new-found courage in creating liturgy" (3) entgegengesetzt.

In vier Großkapiteln sind diverse Entwürfe zu folgenden Themenblöcken zusammengestellt: Rituale für Zuhause, Fruchtbarkeit / Unfruchtbarkeit, in Beziehungen, in Krankheit und Heilung. Ein Folgeband mit Liturgien und Ritualen zu weiteren Themen (Menopause, Pensionierung, Großmuttersein, Krankheit, Tod) wird bereits in der Einleitung angekündigt (5).

Steil ist die These *Sybil Sheridans*, dass gerade das Einhalten der drei Frauen-Gebote *Challa*, *Nidda*, *Hadlaka* (Teighebe, Mikwe, Sabbatlichter) in den Jahrhunderten nach dem Untergang des Tempels eine trotzig-selbstbewusste Verhöhnung des männlich-rabbinischen Prinzips dargestellt habe (27).

Wenn *Tikvah Sarah*, Dozentin am Leo-Baeck-College, eigene, sehr persönliche Texte präsentiert, die sie beim Anlegen von Gebetsmantel und Gebetsriemen spricht, so nimmt sie dabei ausdrücklichen Bezug auf die alten *Techinnes*: jiddische, voraufklärerische Frauengebete, die sämtliche und auch sehr intime Aspekte des (damals noch überwiegend) häuslich-familialen Wirkungsbereichs von Jüdinnen abdeckten. Was beide verbinde, sei die Möglichkeit, "to speak in our own language and resonate with the beat of our own lives" (33).

Der Sammelband ist sehr heterogen: So enthält er etwa auch den Erfahrungsbericht einer mit Krebsdiagnose konfrontierten Rabbinerin, die lernt, innerhalb des Gemeindedienstes mit ihren Kräften zu haushalten (*Amanda Golby*), sowie Überlegungen der Rabbinerin *Miri Lawrence* zur religiösen Unterweisung eines – ihres eigenen – autistischen Kindes.

Doch das Hauptanliegen ist, "the exclusion of the experience of Jewish women from the conceptual framework and rituals of rabbinic Judaism" (99) grundsätzlich zu überwinden, was nicht weniger heißt, als die Praxis jüdischen Glaubenslebens völlig neu zu konstituieren durch die Etablierung eigener, auf frauenspezifische Aspekte zugeschnittener Texte und Rituale. Dabei tut sich ein bunter Fächer von Themen und Anlässen auf, der offen und jederzeit erweiterbar ist und hier kaum erschöpfend dargestellt werden kann, etwa: Kinderlosigkeit, Ritual für ein verlorenes Baby / für eine Schwangerschaftsunterbrechung, Zeremonien für schwule und lesbische Lebensbündnisse, ein Gebet in Depression, eine religiöse Antwort auf Totaloperation.

Exemplarisch sei daher das Menarche-Ritual näher betrachtet, ein bisher nicht vorhandenes "welcome into womanhood" (61). Das Fehlen eines weiblichen Pendants zum Initiationsritus der Beschneidung wird als schmerzliche Lücke empfunden. Von daher kommt dem wichtigen Übergang – vom Mädchen zur gebärfähigen Frau – große Bedeutung zu. Er wird nun mit einem neu kreierten Ritual in Anlehnung an die *Hawdala*-Zeremonie gestaltet: Ende des Sabbat – Beginn einer neuen Arbeitswoche. Mit symbolisch aufgeladenen Zutaten wie Wein, geflochtener Kerze und duftenden Gewürzen, über die Segen gesprochen, die mit allen Sinnen wahrgenommen und genossen werden. Der Passageritus blickt mit Dank zurück auf eine behütete Kindheit, begleitet von wohlmeinenden, am Ritual beteiligten (weiblichen) Bezugspersonen, und mit Vorfreude auf das Leben als bewusste jüdische Frau. "Blessed are You, Eternal One, sovereign of the universe, who has made me a woman."

Bettina Kratz-Ritter (Göttingen / Deutschland)

Gury Schneider-Ludorff / Leonore Siegele-Wenschkewitz (Hg.), *Frauenarmut als Herausforderung,* (Arnoldshainer Texte 113), Haag + Herchen Verlag: Frankfurt am Main 2000, 121 Seiten, ISBN 3-89846-039-8, DM 34,80

Das Thema Armut in der Bundesrepublik Deutschland rückt, nicht zuletzt durch den 2001 erstmals erschienenen offiziellen Armuts- und Reichtumsbericht der Bundesregierung, inzwischen immer mehr in die Aufmerksamkeit der

Öffentlichkeit. Doch obwohl regelmäßig darauf hingewiesen wird, dass die Armut weiblich sei, ist diese grundlegende Dimension der Armut noch nicht aufgearbeitet. So ist die vorliegende Publikation von Gury Schneider-Ludorff und der inzwischen verstorbenen Leonore Siegele-Wenschkewitz eine der wenigen Publikationen zum Thema Frauenarmut. Der Band dokumentiert eine Tagung, die 1996 an der Evangelischen Akademie Arnoldshain stattgefunden hat. Die Beiträge stammen von Referentinnen aus Politik, Wissenschaft, Wirtschaft, Publizistik und Kirche.

Ruth Köppen zeichnet die Entwicklung der Frauenarmut in der Bundesrepublik von 1945 bis 1988 nach. Sie macht deutlich, wie die Gesetzesreformen die Lage der Frauen zwar verbesserten, doch gleichzeitig neue subtile Benachteiligungen einbauten. Die Armut der Frauen wird hauptsächlich durch die Ernährerabhängigkeit der Frauen sowie die "Nichtin-wertsetzung" (28) weiblicher Arbeit produziert. *Gisela Notz* nimmt den Reichtum in den Blick, der unter Männern weiter vererbt wird, sowie die hierarchisch zunehmende Männerdominanz in Wirtschaft, Wissenschaft und Politik. Frauenarmut hängt – bei inzwischen etwa gleichen Schulabschlüssen von Mädchen und Jungen – mit der unterschiedlichen Erwerbsbiographie zusammen. Frauen bekommen nicht so leicht einen Ausbildungsplatz, sie sind in den unteren Lohngruppen beschäftigt, viele sind teilzeitbeschäftigt, sie verdienen oft, obwohl in den gleichen Positionen, weniger als Männer. Betroffen sind besonders Frauen mit Kindern, vor allem allein Erziehende, sowie Migrantinnen, die bei dem Scheitern ihrer Ehe leicht abgeschoben werden können. Das soziale Renten- und Sicherungssystem ist an der Norm der männlichen Erwerbsbiographie orientiert und geht an der Lebensrealität der Frauen vorbei. *Mechtild Jansen* geht ideologiekritisch auf den Diskurs über die Frauenarmut in der politischen Öffentlichkeit ein. Dieser hat sich auch in der Frauenbewegung von der Patriarchats- und Herrschaftskritik wegbewegt. Frauenpolitikerinnen werden zu Sozialpolitikerinnen gemacht und damit auf die karitative Seite der Gesellschaft gestellt. Das alte Ziel der Selbstbestimmung ist verschwunden, geblickt wird allenfalls auf die soziale Sicherung der Frauen. Die Erfolge der Frauenbewegung werden von neuen Rissen begleitet; die patriarchale Herrschaft hat sich gewandelt, um verlängert zu werden. Sie ist subtiler geworden und geht auf die anonymen Strukturen der Gesellschaft als Ganzer über. Doch die Achse der verschärften Oben-Unten-Spaltung ist unverändert die Geschlechterspaltung. In einem zweiten Beitrag plädiert *Jansen* für eine Umverteilung von Arbeit, Arbeitszeit und Geld und zeigt dafür Strategien auf. *Sylvia Wilz* geht konkret auf das statistische Material zur Frauenarmut am Beispiel der Stadt Frankfurt am Main ein.

Die Auswertung des Materials müsse die strukturellen Probleme im Auge behalten. Dies zeigt sie auf an der Verlagerung der Diskussion von der Frauenarmut auf die Kinderarmut. Indem die Kinderarmut in den Vordergrund gerückt wird, wird das strukturelle Problem der Frauen, Erwerbstätigkeit und Kinderbetreuung vereinbaren zu müssen, privatisiert oder als Familien- und Kinderproblem etikettiert und so von den geschlechtsspezifischen Asymmetrien abgelenkt. *Dörte Folkers* und *Siegrid Häfner* zeigen sozialpolitische Perspektiven zur Veränderung der strukturellen Frauenarmut auf. Sie fordern Veränderungen im Sozialrecht, das bislang vorrangig an die Erwerbsarbeit anknüpft, und ein "Teilen statt Spalten" (93). Der Band wird gerahmt von einer einleitenden Predigt von *Leonore Siegele-Wenschkewitz* über die biblische Reichtumskritik und die Dokumentation der abschließenden Podiumsdiskussion der Tagung.

Der Band ist ein wichtiger Beitrag, um die Armutssituation von Frauen gezielt in den Blick zu nehmen. Zwar sind einzelne Argumente und Beispiele durch die sich dauernd verändernde Gesetzeslage bereits überholt. Die Lektüre bietet aber einen guten Einstieg in das Thema und schult die Wahrnehmung, mit der die aktuellen Statistiken, Diskussionen und Publikationen über Armut kritisch gelesen werden können, die die Frauenarmut oftmals verschweigen, individualisieren oder verschleiern; zudem fordert sie zum sozialpolitischen Engagement heraus.

Stephanie Klein (Mainz / Deutschland)

Susanne Schniering (Hg.), *Ich trage Dich in meinem Herzen. Der Gedenkplatz für nicht beerdigte Kinder in Ohlsdorf*, Hanna Strack Verlag: Pinnow 2001, 120 Seiten, ISBN 3-929813-53-X, E 10,10

Susanne Schniering hat mit der Herausgabe dieses Buches eine schon lange fällige Hilfe und Unterstützung für Betroffene und SeelsorgerInnen geschaffen. Mit ihrem Grußwort führt Bischöfin Margot Käßmann zum Thema hin. Sorgsam zeichnet dann Susanne Schniering die Auseinandersetzung mit der Trauer um ihre beiden in der Schwangerschaft verlorenen Kinder nach, berichtet vom langsamen Wachsen der Idee eines Gedenkplatzes für nicht beerdigte Kinder, vom Finden einer Skulptur und eines Ortes, von der Einweihungsfeier und von den Begegnungen mit Menschen, denen ähnliches widerfahren ist. Wortbeiträge, Liedtexte, Gedichte und Selbstzeugnisse von der Einweihungsfeier bilden einen Hauptteil des Buches und werden jeweils auf der linken Seite durch Fotos unterstützt. Dem folgt im zweiten großen Abschnitt eine persönliche und seelsorglich anregende Auseinandersetzung mit Tod und Trauer in unserer Kultur, insbesondere mit dem Tod innerhalb der Schwangerschaft und der Trauer von Müttern und Vätern, die kein sichtbares Zeichen ihrer Elternschaft haben. Geschlechtsspezifisch unterschiedliche Erfahrungen mit dem Tod am Beginn des Lebens werden angesprochen: größere Betroffenheit und Nahbeziehung der Mutter zum Kind, die Erfahrung des Todes im eigenen Leib, verschiedener Umgang mit Trauern. Angesprochen wird auch die Trauer um Leben, das durch einen Schwangerschaftsabbruch "freiwillig" beendet wurde. Es folgen Anregungen für die rituelle Gestaltung einer Gedenkfeier: Themenwahl, symbolisches Gehen eines Weges, Wortbeiträge von Betroffenen und von SeelsorgerInnen, musikalische Gestaltung, symbolische Erinnerungs- oder Abschiedsgesten, gemeinsames Essen. Ein Beitrag von Hanna Strack behandelt Fehlgeburten in biblischen Texten. Quellennachweise, Kurzbiografien der Beitragenden, Literaturhinweise und die Kontaktadresse der Herausgeberin sind angefügt.

Mit dem Gedenkplatz für nicht beerdigte Kinder auf dem Friedhof von Ohlsdorf bei Hamburg ist etwas Sinnvolles und Notwendiges entstanden. Die bisher individualisierte Trauer um Kinder, die in der Schwangerschaft durch Fehl- und Totgeburten oder durch Schwangerschaftsabbruch verloren wurden, hat nunmehr einen konkreten Ort gefunden. Mit dieser Dokumentation macht die Herausgeberin die Erfahrungen vieler Betroffener öffentlich und spricht in ihren Beiträgen Grenzsituationen an, für deren Reflexion häufig kein Platz ist. Dabei fließt ihre eigene intensive Beschäftigung mit dem Thema fruchtbar ein. So vermag diese Veröffentlichung es, Mut zu machen, dem eigenen Trauerprozess, besonders der Trauer des eigenen Körpers, "in dem ein Tod geschehen ist" (87), zu vertrauen.

Ein sehr achtsames Buch, das Frauen mit ähnlichen Erfahrungen aus der Einsamkeit herausführen kann, Anregungen für Trauerriten gibt und hoffentlich als Vorbild dient für die Errichtung weiterer Gedenkplätze für die Kleinsten an anderen Orten.

Gertraud Ladner (Innsbruck / Österreich)

Helen Thorne, *Journey to Priesthood: An In-depth study of the First Women Priests in the Church of England*, (CCSRG Monograph Series 5), University of Bristol: Bristol 2000, 213 pages, ISBN 0-86292-499-5, £15.00

Journey to Priesthood records Helen Thorne's research into the effects of the long journey to the ordination of women in the Church of England. Seven years after the Act of the General Synod of the Church of England and five years after the first ordination of women priests in England, at Bristol Cathedral, Thorne studied the impact of women's ordination both on the Church as a whole and on the female priests of the first years. Her underlying question, which, she writes, crystallized during her research, is whether the ordination of women has enabled the Church of England to embrace the qualities offered by these women, as exemplified by the Movement for the Ordination of Women (MOW), or whether it has rather stifled them by incorporating women without granting them any scope to initiate change.

As a first step Thorne reviews the struggle before the Act of the General Synod was passed in November 1992, giving a thorough historical overview, and discussing the successes and dead ends encountered by the supporters of the ordination of women. Although she is describing the process as it was experienced within the Church of England, Thorne's reflections on the feminist movement in general and on its impact in creating a new vision of the priesthood of women offer a reflection on church structures generally. A further focus is the theory of gender differences and therefore on the different contributions of women and men to ministry and in the wider Church.

In the second part Thorne offers a detailed consideration of her research methodology. Her approach combines the advantages of the positivist and the interpretative traditions while taking into account her own experiences and development during the research. This results in a circular methodological approach which allows the data and experience collected initially to influence her further research during the study. Thorne's subject group was the women ordained priest in 1993, who had generally completed their training before the passing of the Act of Synod. The use of questionnaires guaranteed a broad representative basis; Thorne then challenged and verified the hypotheses she derived from the resulting data by in-depth interviews with ordained women.

In a third part Thorne presents a detailed analysis of the data collected. She investigates the different "language games" in the life of a female priest, showing that the social role of women still clashes with their profession as ministers in our patriarchal world. Both theological orientation and sociological views, and, therefore, the attitudes towards change within the Church, vary widely amongst the subjects of Thorne's research. At the same time it emerges that a tendency towards a more collective leadership style and an emphasis on the necessity of empowerment for all members of the Church is common to most.

The description of the status quo is followed by suggestions for the future of the feminist movement within the Church of England. The Church's internal structures can and will be changed when attitudes towards women change. Keeping up the anger against patriarchy, critical internal involvement and maintaining connection and exchange between women in the Church are all vital if such a change of attitude is to be brought about.

Thorne provides a detailed analysis of the practical implications of the ordination of women on a thorough and informed theological and sociological basis. While it is densely written, her book enables the reader to come to a differentiated understanding and encourages further involvement in the feminist movement in the Church.

Anne Kröger (Göttingen / Germany)

EUROPEAN SOCIETY OF WOMEN IN THEOLOGICAL RESEARCH

EUROPÄISCHE GESELLSCHAFT FÜR THEOLOGISCHE FORSCHUNG VON FRAUEN

L'ASSOCIATION EUROPÉENNE DES FEMMES POUR LA RECHERCHE THÉOLOGIQUE

President – Präsidentin – Président:
Prof. Dr. Irmtrand Fischer, University of Bonn, Germany

Vice-President – Vize-Präsidentin – Vice-Président:
Associate Professor Dr. Else Marie Wiberg Pedersen, University of Aarhus, Denmark

Secretary – Sekretärin- Secrétaire:
PD Dr. Luzia Sutter-Rehmann, Basel, Switzerland

Vice-Secretary – Vize-Sekretärin – Vice-Serétaire:
Dr. Judith Hartenstein, University of Marburg, Germany

Treasurer – Schatzmeisterin – Trésorière:
Drs. Freda Dröes, Amsterdam, The Netherlands

Vice-Treasurer – Vize-Schatzmeisterin – Vice-Trésorière
Dr. Sabine Bieberstein, Bamberg, Germany

Elżbietha Adamiak, Poznan, Poland
Dr. Charlotte Methuen, University of Bochum, Germany

Contact for the ESWTR's Bulletin:
Dr. Luzia Sutter-Rehmann,
Bäumlihofstr. 198, CH-4058 Basel

Yearbook of the European Society of Women in Theological research

1 **Luise Schottroff, Annette Esser**, *Feministische Theologie im europäischen Kontext - Feminist Theology in a European Context - Théologie féministe dans un contexte européen*, 1993, 255 p., ISBN: 90-390-0047-6
21 EURO

2 **Mary Grey, Elisabeth Green**, *Ecofeminism and Theology - Ökofeminismus und Theologie - Ecoféminisme et Théologie*, 1994, 145 p., ISBN: 90-390-0204-5
23 EURO

3 **Angela Berlis, Julie Hopkins, Hedwig Meyer-Wilmes, Caroline Vander Stichele**, *Women Churches: Networking and Reflection in the European Context - Frauenkirchen: Vernetzung und Reflexion im europäischen Kontext - Eglises de femmes: réseaux et réflections dans le contexte européen*, 1995, 215 p., ISBN: 90-390-0213-4
23 EURO

4 **Ulrike Wagener, Andrea Günter**, *What Does it Mean Today to Be a Feminist Theologian? - Was bedeutet es Heute, feministische Theologin zu sein? - Etre théologienne féministe aujourd'hui: Qu'est-ce que cela veut dire?*, 1996, 192 p., ISBN: 90-390-0262-2
23 EURO

5 **Elisabeth Hartlieb, Charlotte Methuen**, *Sources and Resources of Feminist Theologies*, 1997, 286 p., ISBN: 90-390-0215-0
23 EURO

6 **Hedwig Meyer-Wilmes, Lieve Troch, Riet Bons-Storm**, *Feminist Pespectives in Pastoral Theology - Feministische Perspektive in Pastoraltheologie - Des perspectives féministes en théologie pastorale*, 1998, 161 p., ISBN: 90-429-0675-8
23 EURO

7 **Charlotte Methuen**, *Time - Utopia - Eschatology. Zeit - Utopie - Eschatologie. Temps - Utopie - Eschatologie*, 1999, 177 p., ISBN: 90-429-0775-4
23 EURO

8 **Angela Berlis, Charlotte Methuen**, *Feminist Perspectives on History and Religion - Feministische Zugänge zu Geschichte und Religion - Approches féministes de l'histoire et de la religion*, 2000, 318 p., ISBN: 90-429-0903-X
23 EURO

9 **Susan K. Roll, Annette Esser, Brigitte Enzner-Probst, Charlotte Methuen, Angela Berlis**, *Women, Ritual and Liturgy - Ritual und Liturgie von Frauen - Femmes, la liturgie et le rituel,* 2001, 312 p., ISBN: 90-429-1028-9 23 EURO

All ESWTR-Yearbooks can be ordered from Peeters Publishers,
Bondgenotenlaan 153, B-3000 Leuven
Fax: +32 16 22 85 00; e-mail: order@peeters.be

PRINTED ON PERMANENT PAPER • IMPRIME SUR PAPIER PERMANENT • GEDRUKT OP DUURZAAM PAPIER - ISO 9706
N.V. PEETERS S.A., WAROTSTRAAT 50, B-3020 HERENT